WITHDRAWN FROM
TSC LIBRARY

D1599063

THE NEW DEAL AND BEYOND

Social Welfare in the
South since 1930

EDITED BY ELNA C. GREEN

The University of Georgia Press
Athens and London

© 2003 by the University of Georgia Press
Athens, Georgia 30602
All rights reserved

Designed by Jennifer Smith
Set in Minion by Bookcomp, Inc.
Printed and bound by Maple-Vail
The paper in this book meets the guidelines for
permanence and durability of the Committee on Production
Guidelines for Book Longevity of the Council on Library
Resources.

Printed in the United States of America
07 06 05 04 03 C 5 4 3 2 1
07 06 05 04 03 P 5 4 3 2 1

Library of Congress Cataloging-in-Publication Data
The New Deal and beyond : social welfare in the South
since 1930 / edited by Elna C. Green.
p. cm.
Includes bibliographical references and index.
ISBN 0-8203-2481-7 (hardcover : alk. paper)
— ISBN 0-8203-2482-5 (pbk. : alk. paper)
1. Public welfare—Southern States—History—20th century.
2. Social service—Southern States—History—20th century.
3. Southern States—Social policy—History—20th century.
I. Green, Elna C.
HV98.S9 N48 2003
361.975'09'04—dc21   2002011034

British Library Cataloging-in-Publication Data available

Contents

Introduction

ELNA C. GREEN

The amount of literature on the history of the twentieth-century South is voluminous, and the amount on social welfare since 1930 is rapidly growing so. With few exceptions, however, those two fields seldom meet in one monograph. Although the field of social welfare history has been highly productive in recent years, relatively little of it has paid attention to the South. A recent handful of monographs is just beginning the task of exploring the South's social welfare history.[1] In the first volume of this series, *Before the New Deal: Social Welfare in the South, 1830–1930,* I suggested that the time had come to give definition to the South's emerging social welfare history. The current volume returns to this task by focusing on the years since the Great Depression, an era when the development of a federal welfare state changed the nature of public provision in the South and simultaneously complicated historical analyses of welfare.

Social welfare scholarship has grown increasingly sophisticated in recent years, developing multiple models of interpretation, some of which draw inspiration from the disciplines of sociology and political science. Hence, historians, historical sociologists, and public-policy analysts have fiercely debated theories of welfare and state formation, the politics of social policy, and the role of race, gender, and class in the development of public policy. Often explicitly comparing the United States to other industrial democracies that developed different systems of public provision, scholars of the twentieth-century welfare state have generally looked at the question from the top down—that is, national trends, national policies, and national programs have dominated the discussion. When it comes to understanding twentieth-century public policy and state formation, state or local case studies have seemed less fruitful as methodology.[2]

This volume argues implicitly that local, state, and regional studies nevertheless can occupy an important place in social welfare history. Particularly when it comes to examining the actual operation of welfare policies (as opposed to the underlying ideological and political constructions), local or state studies can be a useful approach. The considerable amount of state and/or local discretion included in many federal welfare programs means that outcomes could vary according to locality. Local conditions and local initiatives frequently dictated the terms under which federal programs operated. State or local analyses therefore often work well when testing how public policies functioned "on the ground."[3]

Moreover, regional studies of all sorts recently have seen a renaissance, spurred in part by the rise of environmental history and by studies of globalization. Regionalism as a concept has generated new academic enthusiasm, and that new vitality indicates that scholars see in "regionalism" a continuing opportunity for the analysis of both micro- and macrosystems. The more standardized and globalized our contemporary society has become, the more important past regional distinctions seem.[4] Social welfare scholarship, then, may similarly profit from a regional approach to public policy.

One of the central and perennial questions of southern regional history has been that of southern exceptionalism. As applied to social welfare history, this encourages scholars to ask just how different social welfare policy has been in the South. Has the South's public and private welfare system ever been uniquely "southern?" And, if such is the case, when did it cease to be so regionally distinctive? A related set of questions includes how the South (or southerners) has affected social welfare in the nation as a whole and how the South's policies, politicians, and practitioners have influenced the evolution of social welfare outside the region. This volume will continue to address these questions, covering the period since 1930, and will provide an overview of the current state of the literature and make original contributions to the furthering of this historiography.

Much like the first volume, this book is intended to highlight the work currently under way in southern social welfare history as well as to draw attention to the many possibilities for future research in the field. The volume makes no claim to comprehensive coverage—either topical or chronological—of the period since 1930. Numerous important social welfare topics are not included here: for example, none of the chapters treats the critical Social Security Act.

The absence of such coverage should not imply that the Social Security Act was unimportant to southern social welfare history or that Social Security has been thoroughly exhausted as a research topic. Rather, the absence of a chapter on Social Security in the South suggests that little work is currently in progress on this issue and points to a place where productive scholarship might be waiting.[5]

The Current State of the Field

In the first volume of this series, I noted that the literature on the South's social welfare history for the years between 1830 and 1930 was spotty, with much work yet to be done. If anything, the historiography for the period since 1930 is even less well developed than that on the previous century. As will become clear here, historians of social welfare have concentrated on two broad eras, the New Deal and the Great Society, and have devoted far less attention to developments in welfare policies in the 1940s–50s or since 1970. This volume accurately reflects that trend but hopes to stimulate scholarship that will ultimately address these shortcomings.

The first volume in this series emphasized the regional differences in social policy. The nineteenth-century South followed the broadest outlines of national trends in welfare provision, but the region's welfare practices diverged from national norms in several important ways. For example, southern states joined in the national enthusiasm for institutionalization, examined by David Rothman, and built asylums for the blind, the orphaned, and the insane.[6] Tennessee, much like other southern states, established a state-funded Hospital for the Insane in 1832 and schools for the deaf, dumb, and blind in 1846.[7] But local and/or state government control over welfare institutions assured that regional mores regarding race, class, and gender would be obliged. Even when the law did not specify racial segregation or racial exclusivity in social-service provision, local authorities often practiced segregation or exclusion.

Progressive-era reforms in social policy helped to push the South closer to the national "standard" in welfare practices, as southern progressives eagerly adopted practices that seemed to offer the region solutions to New South poverty. Mothers' aid, professional social work, state asylums for the "dependent classes," public-health campaigns, and a host of other early-twentieth-century innovations helped to bring a generation of southerners ever closer to a national model of social welfare practice. Still, on the eve of the New Deal, the

South continued to lag behind the rest of the country in both the quantity and the quality of welfare provision, leaving untold numbers of southerners living in desperate poverty. Many localities remained without public-welfare departments of any kind: for example, only seventeen of Florida's sixty-seven counties had public-welfare programs in 1931.[8] Funding for programs such as mothers' aid was never as generous as in other states. In Virginia, the state legislature approved but did not fund a mothers' aid program in 1918. With localities forced to provide their own funding, only the city of Richmond and Wise County took advantage of the enabling legislation.[9] Although larger cities such as New Orleans and Charleston hosted dozens of private charitable organizations and public-welfare agencies, vast stretches of the rural South were void of any alternative to the county almshouse, an institution that rightfully shamed the rare visitor who darkened its door.

The establishment of a federal welfare state thus seemed particularly innovative in the South, a region previously underserved by public and private welfare institutions. While residents of other states, already accustomed to the benefits of unemployment insurance, old-age pensions, and worker's compensation, might not have seen the New Deal as a dramatic shift in welfare practices, many southerners saw it differently. (By 1935, for example, only five states had failed to provide funds for unemployment relief, with four of the five in the South.)[10] For rural southerners in particular, the arrival of New Deal–mandated county welfare offices represented a fundamental break with the past.

Most of the scholarship on the New Deal in the South has focused on one of three areas: economics (particularly agriculture), politics, or the civil rights movement.[11] Historians have yet to evaluate the influence of the New Deal on social welfare policy and philosophy in the South. This seems like a tremendous oversight, as the New Deal agencies compelled southern states to create statewide welfare programs for the first time. Under pressure from such agencies as the Federal Emergency Relief Administration, the states had to hire professional staff, establish systematic reporting procedures, and learn how to calculate family budgets. When the New Deal came to a close, those state welfare bureaucracies continued to exist, a lasting legacy of New Deal–era reform.[12]

By establishing national policies and programs and then coercing the states to participate, the New Deal helped to bring the South ever more closely into the mainstream of national welfare practice.[13] Ironically, however, the federalization of welfare seemed to result in the nationalization of racism in welfare. Rather than compelling southern states to abandon race as a criteria of relief, southern politicians instead wrote regional racial mores into federal welfare policy. The one-party South, doggedly reelecting incumbent Democrats to Congress, benefited from Washington's seniority system. Leading southern politicians, by virtue of their positions heading powerful congressional committees, could shape federal welfare legislation into regionally acceptable forms.[14]

The federal government's impact on state and local social welfare policies in the South serves as the starting point for this volume, with part 1 focusing on the effects of the New Deal. Georgina Hickey examines the complex relationships between New Dealers, relief clients, and political activists at the local level. By hiring women, work programs such as the WPA generated intense debates about gender and public policy. How should government treat "deserving" poor women? "Work relief," after all, meant taking a job: should the federal government be encouraging women to go to work? What jobs were appropriate for women? Should the federal government offer job training that might raise women's skill levels? These and other policy questions emerge from New Deal social welfare programs.

Other New Deal programs that have been previously examined for their impact on politics and civil rights can also be mined for information on social welfare policy. The Farm Security Administration, as Brenda J. Taylor explains, included programs for the "rehabilitation" of farm wives. Hiring public-health nurses and home economists to educate rural women about sanitation, food conservation, family budgeting, and scientific medical care, the FSA created a large network of professional women who acted as de facto social workers. While trained as nurses and home economists, their supervisory activities paralleled those of social workers. According to one recent study, home demonstration agents for the federal farm programs came to see themselves as rural social workers.[15] And, like social workers, they could find themselves crossing over the line into areas the FSA never intended, such as advocacy of birth control. FSA programs' effects on their own workers were arguably as striking as those felt by program recipients.

In a very different vein, Jeffrey S. Cole's work on transients suggests that the depression crisis and governmental responses to it helped to further the division of labor among government welfare agencies. Local governments had long preferred to care for their own poor while resisting provisions for "outsiders." By stepping in to care for transients, the federal government effectively reinforced this long-standing tradition. Rather than challenging the traditional view of outsiders and their eligibility for relief, New Deal policy invigorated it. The buttressing of a hierarchy of eligibility had long-term consequences, especially in a region prone to view government activism through the lens of states' rights.

Ann Short Chirhart suggests, however, that local and state political concerns could greatly impede federal efforts to influence social policy. A determined and powerful southern politician such as Eugene Talmadge could in fact do a great deal to inhibit the implementation of federal programs and to limit the effectiveness of those in place. The federal government might have the power of the purse backing up its policy goals, but American political federalism handed state and local politicians a useful defensive weapon against federal incursions. Local and state governments could mitigate the impact of the federal welfare state.[16]

How to assess those federal incursions lies at the heart of Ted Olson's chapter on the Blue Ridge Parkway. While social welfare historians have often applauded the development of a federal welfare system, they also have been quick to critique the specifics of the various programs. Olson examines the cultural clash that occurred when the Blue Ridge Parkway exposed a previously isolated population to the outside world. Progressive social welfare policy assumed that these "cultures of poverty" were themselves part of the problem. While the New Deal might challenge traditional gender roles, race relations, and class formulations in a positive fashion, it is also clear that the New Deal could be blind to the value of rural and traditional cultures.

Part 2 of this volume turns to the years after the New Deal. Examining the U.S. health-care system on the eve of Medicare, Jill Quadagno and Steve Macdonald suggest that civil rights and social welfare were more intertwined than is often thought to be the case. The civil rights victory over segregation in education in 1954 gave activists a tool with which to challenge Jim Crow in other public facilities. Federal Medicare money, available only to integrated facilities, ultimately ended racial segregation in hospitals in the South.

Medicare was part of the War on Poverty, a multifaceted, much-misunderstood descendant of the New Deal. The War on Poverty had far bolder goals than did the New Deal: President Lyndon B. Johnson's programs were intended to eradicate poverty, not merely to ameliorate it. Such an ambitious agenda grew out of a very different economy: where the New Deal tried to minimize suffering during a devastating depression, the strong post–World War II economy encouraged policy makers to dream of the complete elimination of poverty. However, as several scholars have made clear, the War on Poverty foundered on the rocks of racism, and southern politicians played an important role in this failure.[17]

Lee Alston and Joseph Ferrie's *Southern Paternalism and the American Welfare State* considers southerners' role in the development of the 1960s welfare state. Alston and Ferrie ask why southern politicians largely dropped their traditional opposition to the federal welfare state and allowed Johnson's proposals to make their way through Congress. Their answer, planter paternalism and the mechanization of cotton production, complicates the story of southern welfare history. Freed by technology from their traditional need for a large, unskilled, dependent labor force, cotton planters lost the major reason for opposing the expanding welfare state.[18] Indeed, according to Alston and Ferrie, cynical planters saw federal antipoverty programs as a benefit. Concentrated in urban communities, federal funds and programs would likely result in black outmigration from the South. Such a demographic shift would reduce the tax burdens on the South's rural elites while draining off potentially dangerous black voters. Under these new circumstances, southern members of Congress helped to pass Great Society antipoverty programs after crafting them to minimize their impact on the South.[19]

Like Alston and Ferrie, Robert R. Korstad and James L. Leloudis engage directly the question of how the South influenced national welfare policies. Their study of the North Carolina Fund argues that this experimental program served as a model for the Great Society that followed it and that the lessons learned in North Carolina shaped federal policy makers' thinking. The young Volunteers who served as foot soldiers in the Fund's state-level war on poverty were profoundly changed by their experiences. As New Dealers had discovered a generation earlier, the reformers and activists were often among the most affected by their activities.

Kent B. Germany also finds unanticipated consequences to Great Society welfare policies. In New Orleans, a city with a large black population and a white civic leadership, the War on Poverty's insistence on local input translated into a shift in political power. To the white liberals crafting welfare programs, creating a "stable community" meant assuring that all citizens felt tied to it. Assuming that civic alienation could be remedied by adjusting the individual's personality traits, white middle-class reformers concentrated on changing the "culture" of poverty. But the process of turning the poor into "community partners" also afforded them many of the tools of political power, including a political consciousness that would inform the emerging black power movement of the late 1960s.

In Mobile, another Gulf South city with a large African American population, the War on Poverty also produced unanticipated consequences, as

Susan Youngblood Ashmore's chapter explains. Coinciding with the Catholic Church's Vatican II reforms, the War on Poverty opened an opportunity for the local diocese to gain federal funding for racially integrated educational programs. Although George Wallace seldom hesitated to use his power to interfere with such federal intrusions, the governor permitted Mobile's Catholic-based Head Start program to proceed. Wallace's perception of the power of the Catholic Church in Mobile, accurate or not, restrained his usual combativeness. This tiny wedge then served as the platform from which new organizations and activism could spring.

Finally, Marsha S. Rose's chapter on Sallie Bingham and the Kentucky Foundation for Women draws attention to private philanthropy and regional mores. In the 1970s, the women's funding movement began as an outgrowth of the women's movement. Private foundations devoted to assisting women and girls, the women's funds were a small national movement with few southern examples. Kentucky's Sallie Bingham, a wealthy heiress and feminist activist, drew on her regional identity for her philanthropic ideology. Bingham's feminism derived in part from her experiences as a woman writer struggling to be heard, and her feminism in turn shaped her philanthropic initiatives.

The Future of the Field

The large gaps between these chapters highlight several potential areas for further research. Chronologically, a vast lacuna stands between the New Deal era and the Great Society. The impact of World War II on southern poverty and social provision has yet to be analyzed. How did wartime spending priorities affect welfare budgets? Did the war offer private charities opportunities to reposition themselves after the dislocation and upheaval of the depression and New Deal? In the postwar period, how did the GI Bill and other veterans' programs affect social welfare policy? Did the Cold War and anticommunism work to undermine federal welfare programs? How did the antiradicalism of the 1950s affect the "suitable homes" criteria under which Aid to Dependent Children was administered?[20]

Topical gaps are numerous as well. Much more attention is needed on private charitable efforts. The Salvation Army in the South, the welfare activities of the Urban League in the South, and the Community Chest/United Way charitable federations are all awaiting their scholars. Catholic charities, Jewish benevolent associations, and Protestant missions all helped to shape social welfare policy, yet scholars know very little about such late-twentieth-century activities. Similarly, there is a great deal yet unknown about black self-help organizations, both secular and religious, during the late twentieth century. Private institutions for the dependent, such as orphanages and homes for the elderly, have received far less coverage in the twentieth century than in the nineteenth.

There is still much room for analysis of public-welfare policy as well. Numerous local and state agencies (boards of public welfare, reformatories, public hospitals and clinics, and schools of social work, among others) helped to shape public policy and have yet to receive scholarly assessment. While New Deal agencies, Great Society programs, and 1990s welfare "reform" have received varying degrees of coverage, our knowledge of federal welfare and the South remains limited. Although scholars have begun analyzing welfare reform,[21] case studies for the South have yet to appear.

Southern social workers both during and after the New Deal have yet to receive scholarly treatment. As mediators between the state and relief recipients, social workers lived daily with the problems and possibilities of southern social welfare programs. Analyses of the lives, training, careers, and views on welfare of social workers such as Gay Shepperson could greatly enhance the understanding of the forces that shaped social welfare in the South. Moreover, the scholarly tendency to separate public welfare and private charity remains unabated despite numerous calls for an integration of the two arenas. Such an approach would likely work best in local- or state-level studies, although regional studies could remain viable.

Given the current state of the field, there is at present no synthetic or comprehensive treatment of southern social welfare history. The time is not yet ripe for such a work. Much remains to be done first, and we hope this anthology will help to stimulate new scholarship in this potentially fruitful field. We also hope that future scholarship will work to link southern social welfare history more directly to the broader literature on the welfare state. Focusing on the South's role in shaping national policy sometimes makes it even clearer that the welfare state, much like the state itself, is fundamentally amoral. Neither intrinsically good nor intrinsically evil, the welfare state can flow into many potential shapes. Responding amoeba-like to the pressures of various power brokers, the welfare state can buttress or undermine racism. Depending on who holds the keys to the bureaucracy, the welfare state can discourage mothers from working or put upward pressure on women's wages. Changing directions in response to shifting political winds, the welfare state can be either an asset or an impediment to organized labor. For the purposes of southern history, this suggests that the amorphous welfare state can be used to reinforce regional distinctions or to challenge them, depending on what interest group(s) set policies at the time.

Thus, the New Deal–era welfare state, crafted by Democratic-controlled Congresses in which southern conservatives still held power, permitted the South's regional aberrations to remain mostly unchecked. Agricultural and domestic workers were excluded from coverage, permitting southern planters to run their operations in much the same fashion as had been the case for decades. The Great Society–era welfare state, influenced by a different set of political pressure groups, was less accommodating of the South's traditional concerns.

This volume, together with its predecessor, offers a blueprint for the history of social welfare in the South. In a field with so much yet to be done, historians are limited only by their imaginations.

Notes

1. For example, Barbara Bellows, *Benevolence among Slaveholders: Assisting the Poor in Charleston, 1670–1860* (Baton Rouge: Louisiana State University Press, 1993); Steven Noll, *Feeble-Minded in Our Midst: Institutions for the Mentally Retarded in the South, 1900–1940* (Chapel Hill: University of North Carolina Press, 1995); Peter McCandless, *Moonlight, Magnolias, and Madness: Insanity in South Carolina from the Colonial Period to the Progressive Era* (Chapel Hill: University of North Carolina Press, 1996); Gilles Vandal, "Nineteenth Century Municipal Responses to the Problem of Poverty: New Orleans' Free Lodgers, 1850–1880," *Journal of Urban History* 19 (November 1992): 30–59; and Daniel Levine, "A Single Standard of Civilization: Black Private Social Welfare Institutions in the South, 1880s–1920s," *Georgia Historical Quarterly* 81 (spring 1997): 52–77.

2. For example: Mimi Abramovitz, *Regulating the Lives of Women: Social Welfare Policy from Colonial Times to the Present* (Boston: South End Press, 1988); Michael B. Katz, *The Undeserving Poor: From the War on Poverty to the War on Welfare* (New York: Pantheon, 1989); Stanley Wenocur, *From Charity to Enterprise: The Development of American Social Work in a Market Economy* (Urbana: University of Illinois Press, 1989); Edward Berkowitz, *America's Welfare State: From Roosevelt to Reagan* (Baltimore: Johns Hopkins University Press, 1991); Linda Gordon, *Pitied but Not Entitled: Single Mothers and the History of Welfare* (New York: Free Press, 1994); Charles Noble, *Welfare as We Knew It: A Political History of the American Welfare State* (Ithaca: Cornell University Press, 1997); Suzanne Mettler, *Dividing Citizens: Gender and Federalism in New Deal Public Policy* (Ithaca: Cornell University Press, 1998).

3. Magaly Queralt, Ann Dryden Witte, and Harriet Griesinger, "Changing Policies, Changing Impacts: Employment and Earnings of Child-Care Subsidy Recipients in the Era of Welfare Reform," *Social Service Review* 74, no. 4 (2000): 588–619 (a case study from Miami); Marian J. Morton, "Institutionalizing Inequalities: Black Children and Child Welfare in Cleveland, 1859–1998," *Journal of Social History* 34, no. 1 (2000): 141–62; Michael O'Keefe, "Social Services: Minnesota as Innovator," *Daedalus* 129, no. 3 (2000): 247–67; Lisa Levenstein, "From Innocent Children to Unwanted Migrants and Unwed Moms: Two Chapters in the Public Discourse on Welfare in the United States, 1960–1961," *Journal of Women's History* 11, no. 4 (2000): 10–33 (case study from Newburgh, New York); Ellen Reese, "The Politics of Motherhood: The Restriction of Poor Mothers' Welfare Rights in the United States, 1949–1960," *Social Politics* 8, no. 1 (2001): 65–112 (compares Georgia and California).

4. Raymond A. Mohl, ed., *Searching for the Sunbelt: Historical Perspectives on a Region* (Athens: University of Georgia Press, 1993); Edward L. Ayers, Patricia Nelson Limerick, Stephen Nissenbaum, and Peter S. Onuf, *All over the Map: Rethinking American Regions* (Baltimore: Johns Hopkins University Press, 1996); Patricia Nelson Limerick, *Something in the Soil: Legacies and Reckonings in the New West* (New York: W. W. Norton, 2000); William G. Robbins, ed., *The Great Northwest: The Search for Regional Identity* (Corvallis, Oreg.: Oregon State University Press, 2001); Joseph A. Conforti, *Imagining New England: Explorations of Regional Identity from the Pilgrims to the Mid–Twentieth Century* (Chapel Hill: University of North Carolina Press, 2001); Robert D. Johnston, "Beyond 'The West': Regionalism, Liberalism, and the Evasion of Politics in the New Western History," *Rethinking History* 2, no. 2 (1998): 239–77; James C. Cobb, "An Epitaph for the North: Reflections on the Politics of Regional and National Identity at the Millennium," *Journal of Southern History* 66, no. 1 (2000): 3–24; John Alexander Williams, "Appalachian History: Regional History in the Post-Modern Zone," *Appalachian Journal* 28, no. 2 (2001): 168–87; and Jennifer Lee Collins-Friedrichs, "Constructing Community: Nineteenth–Early-Twentieth-Century Women's Regionalist Writing" (Ph.D. diss., Claremont Graduate School, 2000).

5. The Social Security Act received considerable attention from social welfare scholars during the 1980s and 1990s; some of this literature paid attention to the South. See, for example, Roy Lubove, *The Struggle for Social Security, 1900–1935* (Pittsburgh: University of Pittsburgh Press, 1986); Ann Shola Orloff, *The Politics of Pensions: A Comparative Analysis of Britain, Canada, and the United States, 1880–1940* (Madison: University of Wisconsin Press, 1993); Mettler, *Dividing Citizens;* Gareth Davies and Martha Derthick, "Race and Social Welfare Policy: The Social Security Act of 1935," *Political Science Quarterly* 112, no. 2 (1997): 217–35.

6. David J. Rothman, *The Discovery of the Asylum: Social Order and Disorder in the New Republic* (Boston: Little, Brown, 1971).

7. *The History of Public Welfare in Tennessee, 1796–1963* (Nashville: Tennessee Department of Public Welfare, 1963), 1.

8. Charlton W. Tebeau, *A History of Florida* (1971; Coral Gables, Fla.: University of Miami Press, 1980), 398.

9. Arthur Wilson James, *Virginia's Social Awakening: The Contribution of Dr. Mastin and the Board of Charities and Corrections* (Richmond: Garrett and Massie, 1939), 50–52. By contrast, North Carolina enacted a mothers' aid law in 1923, and by 1926, seventy-one counties were participating in the program (Roy M. Brown, *Public Poor Relief in North Carolina* [Chapel Hill: University of North Carolina Press, 1928], 145).

10. Anne E. Geddes, *Trends in Relief Expenditures, 1910–1935* (Washington, D.C.: U.S. Government Printing Office, 1937), 5. The five states were Georgia, North Carolina, South Carolina, Vermont, and Virginia.

11. For example, Harvard Sitkoff, *A New Deal for Blacks: The Emergence of Civil Rights as a National Issue* (New York: Oxford University Press, 1978); Douglas L. Smith, *The New Deal in the Urban South* (Baton Rouge: Louisiana State University Press, 1988); Roger Biles, *The South and the New Deal* (Lexington: University Press of Kentucky, 1994); Patricia Sullivan, *Days of Hope: Race and Democracy in the New Deal Era* (Chapel Hill: University of North Carolina Press, 1996); and James C. Cobb, " 'Somebody Done Nailed Us on the Cross': Federal Farm and Welfare Policy and the Civil Rights Movement in the Mississippi Delta," *Journal of American History* 77, no. 3 (1990): 912–36.

12. One of the few books to consider the impact of the New Deal on the South's public-welfare provision is Edward LaMonte, *Politics and Welfare in Birmingham, 1900–1975* (Tuscaloosa: University of Alabama Press, 1995).

13. Several state studies have demonstrated how much pressure Washington had to exert on some southern states to get them to cooperate with the New Deal agenda. See esp. Ronald L. Heinemann, *Depression and New Deal in Virginia: The Enduring Dominion* (Charlottesville: University Press of Virginia, 1983); Roger Biles, *Memphis in the Great Depression* (Knoxville: University of Tennessee Press, 1986); Douglas Carl Abrams, *Conservative Constraints: North Carolina and the New Deal* (Jackson: University Press of Mississippi, 1992); Jerry Bruce Thomas, *An Appalachian New Deal: West Virginia in the Great Depression* (Lexington: University Press of Kentucky, 1998).

14. See Jill Quadagno, *The Transformation of Old Age Security* (Chicago: University of Chicago Press, 1988); and Lee J. Alston and Joseph P. Ferrie, *Southern Paternalism and the American Welfare State: Economics, Politics, and Institutions in the South, 1865–1965* (Cambridge: Cambridge University Press, 1999).

15. Melissa Walker, *All We Knew Was to Farm: Rural Women in the Upcountry South, 1919–1941* (Baltimore: Johns Hopkins University Press, 2000), 98.

16. This is a recurrent theme in studies of the New Deal in the South. See, for example,

Anthony J. Badger, *Prosperity Road: The New Deal, Tobacco, and North Carolina* (Chapel Hill: University of North Carolina Press, 1980); Heinemann, *Depression and New Deal*; and Abrams, *Conservative Constraints.*

17. For example, Katz, *Undeserving Poor*; Michael B. Katz, ed., *The "Underclass" Debate: Views from History* (Princeton: Princeton University Press, 1993); and Jill Quadagno, *The Color of Welfare: How Racism Undermined the War on Poverty* (New York: Oxford University Press, 1994). This is one area of American history where historians have taken seriously the role of racism in shaping society. For a critique of scholarship that ignores the centrality of racism in U.S. history, see Nell Irvin Painter, "The Shoah and Southern History," in *Jumpin' Jim Crow: Southern Politics from Civil War to Civil Rights*, ed. Jane Dailey, Glenda Elizabeth Gilmore, and Bryant Simon (Princeton: Princeton University Press, 2000), 309.

18. For a similar line of reasoning, see Jill Quadagno, "From Old-Age Assistance to Supplemental Security Income: The Political Economy of Relief in the South, 1935–1972," in *The Politics of Social Policy in the United States*, ed. Margaret Weir, Ann Shola Orloff, and Theda Skocpol (Princeton: Princeton University Press, 1988).

19. For example, one economic opportunity program that would have facilitated the purchase of tracts of land for resale to tenants and sharecroppers was eliminated at the behest of southern congressmen (Alston and Ferrie, *Southern Paternalism*, 140–41).

20. Scholars have seen the impact of the Cold War and anticommunism on a wide range of social issues: Elaine Tyler May, *Homeward Bound: American Families in the Cold War Era* (New York: Basic Books, 1988); Lary May, *Culture and Politics in the Age of Cold War* (Chicago: University of Chicago Press, 1989); Margot A. Henriksen, *Dr. Strangelove's America: Society and Culture in the Atomic Age* (Berkeley: University of California Press, 1997); Joel Foreman, *The Other Fifties: Interrogating Midcentury American Icons* (Urbana: University of Illinois Press, 1997); Richard M. Fried, *The Russians Are Coming! The Russians Are Coming! Pageantry and Patriotism in Cold-War America* (New York: Oxford University Press, 1998); and John D'Emilio, "The Homosexual Menace: The Politics of Sexuality in Cold War America," in *Passion and Power: Sexuality in History*, ed. Kathy Peiss and Christina Simmons (Philadelphia: Temple University Press, 1989). It would in fact be surprising to find that the Cold War had no impact on social welfare policy.

21. For example, Katz, *Undeserving Poor*; Joel F. Handler, *The Poverty of Welfare Reform* (New Haven: Yale University Press, 1995); Joseph Dillon Davey, *The New Social Contract: America's Journey from Welfare State to Police State* (Westport, Conn.: Praeger, 1995); Gwendolyn Mink, *Welfare's End* (Ithaca: Cornell University Press, 1998); and Randy Albelda and Ann Withorn, eds., *Reforming Welfare, Redefining Poverty* (Thousand Oaks, Calif.: Sage, 2001).

PART 1

The New Deal . . .

"The Lowest Form of Work Relief"

*Authority, Gender, and the State in
Atlanta's WPA Sewing Rooms*

GEORGINA HICKEY

In the summer of 1935, Estelle Stevenson became a part of the New Deal. The election of Franklin Delano Roosevelt and the New Deal invigorated the flagging spirits of Stevenson and other white middle-class club women from the Atlanta area. In the early 1930s, they created the Georgia Woman's Democratic Club, a partisan version of the League of Women Voters. The GWDC dedicated itself to "an acceptance of [our] responsibility as citizens, and as Democrats" and pledged to uphold "the cardinal principles of democracy—of liberty and justice, of human and individual rights, condemning the predatory special interests, and those whose political philosophy does not beat in unison with the heart throbs of struggling humanity."[1] As president of this organization, Estelle Stevenson wrote numerous passionate letters, sparsely praising and vociferously complaining to New Dealers at every level during the latter half of the Great Depression. Stevenson's efforts to alter conditions in local sewing rooms, the major form of work relief for women under the New Deal, forced administrators and politicians to articulate their positions on the function and purpose of welfare as well as their views on women as workers and mothers.

What makes Stevenson's actions appealing to study is that she focused so intensely on what the Works Progress Administration (WPA) and New Deal could and should be. Stevenson believed that women aided by a newly involved and caring federal government would be housewives and domestic workers once the depression lifted. She believed that government had a responsibility to treat its workers as individuals and to uplift those under its care. Drawing on her history of service to community, party, and nation, Stevenson

challenged wpa administrators and elected Democratic officials to stop thinking of New Deal programs in terms of "emergency" relief and to reconceptu-
alize government's role in society and in individuals' lives. Her story reveals
inherent contradictions between key components of the emerging federal welfare program. Stevenson's sundry challenges to the New Deal power structure
illuminate the slippery and controversial nature of liberalism, welfare, and bureaucratic agendas. The most ardent supporters of the emerging welfare state
sometimes could also be its harshest critics.

Estelle Stevenson had belonged to a number of Atlanta-area women's clubs
and served as president of her local League of Women Voters in the 1920s
and early 1930s. Her elevation to avid New Dealer and loyal Democrat in 1935
flowed almost seamlessly from these experiences. The Democratic National
Committee's "Reporter Plan" served as the vehicle for this progression.[2] The
plan, first introduced in January 1934 by Molly Dewson, head of the party's
Women's Division, targeted Progressive club women such as Stevenson in the
hopes that they would "discover that at heart they have been Democrats all
along."[3] Dewson intended to draw this vital constituency firmly into the party
by giving them a purpose, a mission that would feel much like the club work
they had been doing for years but would also bind them to the Roosevelt ticket
in the 1936 election. Reporters signed up at the county level to study local New
Deal programs and committed to sharing their knowledge with local civic organizations while defending federal programs against conservative criticism.

Defense of the New Deal in Georgia was certainly needed. Dewson, her
successors, and other party leaders had good reason to worry about keeping
the party together between national elections, especially in the South. Storms
were brewing in Georgia from the moment of Roosevelt's election. The most
vocal New Deal critic in the state, conservative Democratic Governor Eugene
Talmadge, resented the introduction of federal officials and their substantial
resources into state politics. He twice stymied attempts to establish New Deal
programs in the state, forcing federal officials to administer directly programs
that all other states were allowed to oversee on their own.[4] Other political
attacks emerged from the legislature as the statehouse took up the patronage issue early in 1935. House Democrats called the New Deal a "new era of
carpetbag days," complaining that administrative, professional, and white-
collar jobs were going to non-Georgians.[5] With the 1936 elections looming,
federal officials launched investigations to counter these allegations, while the
Democratic National Committee set about shoring up party loyalty among
the state's middle classes, women, old-time Progressives, urbanites, and other
liberal elements.

Stevenson and the twenty-eight official reporters in the Atlanta area plunged into the New Deal with great enthusiasm. As president of the GWDC, Stevenson tracked reporters' work in the city and around the state and served as the liaison between them and the national committee. Of all the economic and relief programs Stevenson's group studied, the WPA's District 5 sewing rooms (those located in and around the city of Atlanta) garnered the most attention.[6] Across the country, sewing bedding and simple clothing for distribution to the indigent provided the bulk of work relief for women during the Great Depression. In 1935, workrooms in Georgia's fifth district employed more than a thousand women, and while most of the sewing went to whites, three of the five local WPA projects provided work to both black and white women.[7] The "cruel inefficiency" GWDC reporters found in the greater Atlanta sewing projects, as well as a significant decrease in women employed there in the spring of 1936, started Stevenson, as the president of the organization, on a four-year campaign to change the methods and ideals guiding government aid to destitute women and the poor in general.[8]

Administrators of the federal work relief offered to women through the WPA had few precedents on which to draw. Before the 1930s, Atlanta's social welfare network aided women, primarily mothers, through means-tested direct relief to women in their role as caretakers of the family.[9] The city's social workers knew that many of Atlanta's poorest women—those with dependents and without a male breadwinner—relied on work outside the home but only grudgingly supported paid work by women, preferring that they remain in the home caring for their families. New Deal work relief for women, then, represented a dramatic shift in early-twentieth-century patterns of social welfare. A number of factors led to this shift, not the least of which was the collapse of the American economy at the end of the 1920s. As the effects of the Great Depression worsened in the early 1930s and private, local, and state agencies exhausted their resources, the federal government finally stepped into the world of social welfare and changed the playing field on which those deemed in need would be aided.

The transition away from the standards of Progressive-era assistance to the poor was not a smooth one. Having little experience with welfare of any kind, early New Deal agencies funneled federal money to public organizations on the state and local levels. Georgia, like other southern states with limited infrastructure, rushed to create agencies to receive this money.[10] The president's chief relief officer, Harry Hopkins, disliked this system, however, and longed for a more permanent structure that would provide jobs to those left unemployed by the ravages of the depression.[11] Roosevelt, who also believed that direct relief undermined individualism, endorsed such a plan first under the short-lived Civil Works Administration (CWA) of 1933–34 and later by using emergency relief money to create the WPA, with Hopkins at the helm. With this move in 1935, the federal government returned "unemployables" to the states for assistance and embraced for itself the job of putting America's unemployed to useful work.[12]

As potential recipients of relief from the federal government, women survived these shifts mainly through the dogged efforts of prominent feminists within the New Deal. Eleanor Roosevelt initially convinced Hopkins to create a special division within the Federal Emergency Relief Administration (FERA) to provide aid for the country's destitute women. When the CWA was established in the fall of 1933 in anticipation of the worst winter of the depression, the First Lady called together public and private officials to advise Hopkins on how to construct work-relief projects to aid unemployed women.[13] Ellen Woodward, head of the women's divisions of the FERA, CWA, and WPA, promised that "women are going to get a square deal" under federal relief and fought faithfully, if not always with great success, for an expansion of projects available to women and for better pay.[14] At its peak, the WPA employed more than 450,000 women nationwide, though female workers never held more than 17.5 percent of the program's relief jobs.[15]

The changes in federal policy brought by these New Deal programs, combined with the depression's substantial impact on Atlanta, challenged established relationships in the local power structure and brought new players onto the city's political scene. Traditional sources of authority within the community and especially in social welfare circles now had to compete with government administrators.[16] Older systems of local patronage, city boosters, and Progressive reform networks that might have coexisted in uneasy harmony in earlier decades now faced a changing political landscape with the insertion of federal dollars. At least some of the parameters of the emerging order can be found in the debate between local club women and the administration of the centerpiece of New Deal welfare, the WPA.

At the heart of Stevenson's and the GWDC's criticisms of New Deal work relief for women lay the question of who should be responsible for carrying out these programs and what principles should guide their actions. These questions focused not so much on President Roosevelt or other elected officials as on state and local administrations and public versus private interests. The GWDC wanted non-Georgians working in the state to be replaced by native authorities who would act in Georgia's best interest, but the organization also suggested that the federal administration ought to take more control over local projects. The club women were at once both frustrated over the decentralized, almost informal nature of the WPA and enamored of the possibilities for implementing traditional Progressive welfare ideals on a grander scale.

The organization of the WPA bore the imprint of its leader, Harry Hopkins. As a veteran of Progressive-era campaigns for work relief and mothers' pensions, Hopkins had developed an extensive network of contacts among social workers and a leadership style in which he put these experienced acquaintances to work, giving them wide latitude to do their jobs as they saw fit.[17] Hopkins valued creativity and encouraged experimentation among his staff, and he had a well-established reputation for thinking big and spending freely to put America back to work.

One of the colleagues Hopkins pressed into service in the early days of the New Deal was Gay Bolling Shepperson, a native of Virginia and a seasoned social worker. Shepperson took charge of relief in Georgia in 1933, her career paralleling on the state level that of Hopkins as she headed up Georgia's FERA, CWA, and WPA programs. Like Hopkins, she had a reputation for honesty and integrity but garnered more than her fair share of criticism, particularly from Georgia's conservative rural Democrats. Her leadership philosophy also mirrored that of her boss, and she once remarked that no "administrator of any business can be any better than his staff."[18] The staff Shepperson assembled to administer relief in Georgia drew on her social welfare contacts from time spent working in Virginia, New York, and Washington, D.C. Among these was Jane Van De Vrede, a nurse, former Red Cross worker, and Atlanta resident since World War I who became the head of women's relief in the state and as such oversaw Georgia's sewing projects.

By contrast, Stevenson and her cohort of Progressives used their formal relationship to the Democratic Party as well as their status as middle-class, white club women to justify the "constructive recommendations" they offered New Dealers such as Hopkins, Shepperson, and Van De Vrede on administering relief programs.[19] "Can't you see," Stevenson asked, "that if organized Democratic Women say a thing is all right when it is not . . . , they become a part of the cruel injustice which exists?"[20] In this case, Stevenson drew her authority from her role in the Democratic Party, which had, after all, invited her to study New Deal programs under the Reporter Plan. In writing to the president (and she only used this tactic in letters to Roosevelt and other elected officials), Stevenson lodged her complaints as a "tax-payer" and a "voter" distressed by the "waste" and "inefficiency" of the local sewing rooms.[21] "We—the ordinary voters," Stevenson explained to the president, "believe that your splendid programs would benefit individuals in need of help if they were carried out with efficiency, honesty and vision."[22]

When addressing administrators, especially on the state level, the GWDC relied more heavily on the legacy of its members' volunteer work in the Atlanta area, their local connections, and traditional local hierarchies to justify their challenges to WPA policies and personnel. Stevenson in particular demonstrated a deep familiarity with the language and practices of local welfare, and she used this experience to challenge the qualifications of those running the state's WPA projects. Stevenson referred to relief recipients in the Progressive-era language of "clients," for example, and challenged administrators' determination of the "deserving" poor, a holdover from nineteenth-century relief practices.[23] Local destitute women sought out Stevenson and other club members to act as go-betweens in dealings with relief administrators, further reinforcing the club women's sense of entitlement in the application of federal power. Stevenson apparently saw no need to choose one voice over another. Her combination of identities can be read as a testament both to the lingering power of the Progressive movement, at least on the local level, and to a still emerging definition of citizenship for women that rested in part on their monetary contributions to and political participation in the maintenance of the state.

According to Stevenson, the GWDC had a number of problems with the Atlanta's WPA administration that went beyond officials' hometowns. The club women viewed state administrators as "order-taker[s]" with "no initiative" and "few experiences to base any judgement upon."[24] Using its local connections, the GWDC looked into the background of supervisors in the various sewing rooms and discovered that many of the women on the "administrative pay-roll" did not need the jobs because they had working husbands. The club women argued that truly destitute women in the area might be found to fill those positions or that women like themselves might take on some administrative duties as volunteers. Local supervisors, in the eyes of the GWDC reporters, also showed little respect for the poor women at work in the sewing rooms. Work assignments rarely reflected workers' skills, and the jobs did not encourage the workers to improve themselves. Stevenson and the GWDC claimed that administrators had dragged morale among relief workers down to an extreme low "because these unfortunate women have suffered the tortures of the damned before they can get certified for work, they are intimidated, threatened with loss of the job, and if any dare exhibit any courage or independence of thought, a way is found to bring them into line."[25]

Intriguingly absent from the GWDC's list of complaints about the sewing rooms was the racial integration of three local projects. Historians have mistakenly characterized Stevenson and the GWDC as objecting to New Deal programs' color-blind policies, which put blacks and whites together in government workrooms.[26] Stevenson expressed sporadic but heartfelt sympathy for unemployed African American women, who generally received dreary tasks that required no imagination. She rarely referred to race, but when she did, she specifically noted that her criticisms applied to the treatment of women of both races, making it difficult to read her pleas for aid to women as code for aiding white women alone. "Can you picture a crowded room," Stevenson once asked the head of the women's division of the Democratic Party, "day after day, running into weeks, months and years and many of the women, (both white and colored) ignorant, from homes of extreme poverty, doing the same thing over and over with no variation?"[27]

Motivated by a desire to continue their role as a "force for good in a community" and to serve the national Democratic Party, not by racism or the antiurban provincialism of Governor Talmadge and others in the state, Stevenson and the GWDC started their crusade to oust administrators and improve conditions in local sewing rooms.[28] GWDC members visited the projects in the Atlanta area during the spring of 1936 and shared their observations and suggestions with project and district supervisors. Genuinely surprised that their advice had no impact on local WPA officials, the GWDC had moved up the administrative ladder to Van De Vrede, to Shepperson, to regional director Blanche M. Ralston, to national women's division director Woodward, to Hopkins, and then to the attorney general, congressmen and senators, President Roosevelt, and finally Eleanor Roosevelt. The purposely bottomweighted administration of the WPA, however, meant that even when those on the national level took some interest in the charges raised by the GWDC, the case always passed back down the ladder to the state level. In a moment of frustration over this process, Stevenson wrote to the WPA director of finance (to whom Hopkins had handed a file of her complaints), "if all you can do is to take it up with the very persons who have demonstrated their inefficiency, you can hardly expect them to do much about it. Sometimes we wonder where the blame really lies."[29]

When the GWDC realized it could make little headway in changing local sewing room conditions even with appeals to state administrators, the club women aimed their increasing frustration in that direction as well. Accusations that regional and national investigators "simply cover up the mistakes made and protect the wrong-doers" flowed across Stevenson's missives in sprawling script.[30] She challenged Shepperson's ability even to "appreciate the values of the President's great program to preserve . . . human values" and referred to letters from WPA officials as "the most inane replies."[31] Frustrated by the circular evasions of her criticisms, Stevenson took to writing her own notes on responses sent to her by state administrators and then sending them on to the national level.[32] Her inability to get local and state administrators removed pushed Stevenson to change her tone with Hopkins and even President Roosevelt by the summer of 1937. Fed up with the entire WPA administration and FDR's apparent unwillingness to intervene, Stevenson accused the president of looking at the WPA "through the eyes of a politician" and forgetting the "unfortunate individuals who loved and trusted" him.[33]

Stevenson and the GWDC raised several serious and potentially explosive issues. The earliest of these came when the reporters in Stevenson's organization discovered that, while WPA officials and the Democratic Party had been using the Atlanta-area sewing rooms in their pro–New Deal propaganda, the "splendid" training programs being touted had never actually been implemented.[34] The problem for the GWDC was not the training program being discussed—the organization wholeheartedly endorsed teaching women household skills—but that these classes had never been held in the District 5 sewing projects. "Our 'Reporters,' " Stevenson wrote directly to Ralston when the regional director continued to proclaim the success of Georgia's training programs, "are extending our investigations over the state and are not able to find one sewing room where they are giving the type of program you describe."[35] In addition to bringing the initial error and its continuing propagation to the attention of WPA and party officials, the GWDC passed a resolution calling for an implementation of an hour per day of instruction for women relief workers, in accordance with WPA guidelines. The organization wanted women to learn to tend gardens, raise cows and chickens, launder, care for babies and invalids, and study current events.[36]

Many of Stevenson's early criticisms about the false publicity campaign and the lack of training for women on work relief focused on Alice Owens, the district supervisor of women's work for the Atlanta area under both the FERA and the WPA. Owens admitted to the regional director during a brief investigation that she had fallen behind in placing women in projects and was not offering training in the sewing rooms. She defended her actions, however, referring to the directives from the state office on training as mere "suggestions" that she felt justified to ignore and arguing that instruction programs offered under the FERA had already reached most of the women on work relief in the area.[37] Ralston, who had been singing the praises of instructional programs to the Democratic Party, expressed "some concern" with Owens's work and attitude, conceding that she "seemed absolutely unconcerned and indifferent to the fact that she was responsible for any failure or any shortcomings in the discharge of her duties."[38] Nevertheless, Shepperson chose not to bring in anyone to help Owens complete the transition between programs. At least during the sewing rooms' first year of operation, district-level administrators determined activities with very little interference or guidance from their already overworked superiors.

The shift from relief programs under the FERA to the new WPA in late 1935 and early 1936 caused numerous administrative difficulties. Contemporary observers admitted that the "administration of relief has never been the routine matter, the simple observance of provisions and regulations, the huge but smoothly working affair that it was once hoped it would be."[39] New federal guidelines, pay structures, and work projects ran officials on all levels ragged. Correspondence between state and national leaders suggested that there were "difficulties" in women's projects, especially the large, urban sewing rooms, but the resources to create smaller projects simply did not exist.[40] Staff shortages even forced some administrators to pull double duty. Van De Vrede, the director of women's work for Georgia, for example, also served as supervisor for work projects in District 4 in the mountains of northwest Georgia. Shepperson and her staff worked in new and, given the conservative politicians who predominated in the state, often hostile territory. Considering these conditions and the demanding workload, it is not surprising that Shepperson would be reluctant to remove or even reprimand a proven local administrator such as Owens.

Stymied by the bureaucratic structure she encountered, Stevenson recounted how the GWDC "took this matter up,—in all kindness—first with the local, then district and state, then [Hopkins], and then the President," only to have the women's director of the WPA send the issue back to the state office. Stevenson asked in obvious frustration, "Does the state have authority over the Regional Director?" Stevenson demanded that Hopkins fire "those who are responsible for the failure to carry out a program they say is being used, and let the Regional director think was being used," but no immediate action was taken.[41] Stevenson finally as much as admitted defeat, writing, "I, who for months have thought that the condition would be improved when it was known,—am beginning to think they do not care,—for I have seen that this Club's protest reached Senators and Congressmen,—agency forces from local to federal . . . with the result that everything is shunted into Mr. Hopkins' office where Mrs. Woodward sends it to Miss Shepperson in Georgia and there it ends. Surely a vicious circle."[42]

The controversy Stevenson and the GWDC caused over the training program publicity had little impact on the Democratic Party's descriptions of the "wonderful work" being done in the state's sewing rooms or public perceptions of women's work relief in the months leading up to FDR's 1936 reelection. The GWDC received a fleeting moment in the spotlight when the Atlanta daily newspapers picked up the story in September, but even this created little public reaction.[43] The ramifications of the organization's efforts were largely internal. The relationship between the Atlanta-area club women and the national Democratic Party leadership soured. Mrs. J. A. Rollison, president of the Georgia Affiliated Democratic Women Clubs, the rival of Stevenson's GWDC, became the unquestioned voice of the party for women in the state.[44] Rollison and the party chose to overlook Stevenson's accusations that training programs were not being offered to sewing room workers, even after internal investigations had confirmed the charges' accuracy. Rollison's profile of Georgia's programs for women published in *The Democratic Digest* in July 1937, for example, claimed that the "simple course of home-making instruction given in the sewing rooms . . . has tended to improve conditions in these groups and has resulted in increased pride of accomplishment in production."[45] After a year of agitation, Stevenson found herself frozen out of national party channels on which she had based much of her activism and divested of her power to speak for Georgia club women.

The GWDC and Stevenson had little to show for all their zealous crusading in 1936 and early 1937. The Democratic Party and publicity machines for the New Deal continued to tout women's work relief as a form of rehabilitation for the working-class housewife temporarily fallen on hard times. The club and its president did force an investigation of local sewing projects that eventually led to a shift in the administration on the local level, but WPA officials ignored the GWDC's advice on whom to hire for these positions. Commenting on what she sarcastically referred to as this "wonderful advance," Stevenson concluded that "inefficient persons have been left in authority [and] deserving persons have not been promoted" because the new administrators, like the earlier directors, were also "new people" to the state.[46] Despite their inability to affect the administration of New Deal sewing rooms, Stevenson and the GWDC continued their efforts. The energy that Stevenson poured into her protests and the continuing frustrations she would experience in her attempts to shape federal welfare policy do not represent the isolated rants of an individual or even the play of petty politics but rather point to the often competing ideologies being played out during the creation of a welfare state in the midst of efforts to recover a capitalist economy.

The controversies stemming from the nonexistent training programs in Georgia's sewing rooms and the hiring of administrators not only reveal contentious issues surrounding patronage and authority but also point to the assumptions based on gender and class that Americans applied to work relief in the 1930s. WPA programs for women, in particular, troubled many in that they represented the unresolved and newly surfacing tensions among desires for work relief rather than the dole, retaining women in the domestic sphere, and shoring up capitalism under the weight of a collapsed economy. Many of the contradictions these ideas created were never resolved in the welfare system established by the New Deal because of a prioritization that favored welfare work for men as family breadwinners, direct assistance for mothers, and work relief for women only when the gendered wage economy dictated.

The GWDC, with Stevenson at its helm, represented one common perspective on these issues. The organization approached the "unfortunate" women in need of relief during the Great Depression as mothers (or at least potential mothers) first and workers second, much as advocates of protective labor legislation had done a generation earlier. The organization's early advocacy for training programs to teach women to care for livestock, kitchen gardens, babies, and the elderly supported the belief that women's role in society fell primarily in the domestic sphere. Ideally, women aided by the WPA would return to the role of housewife, but finding a "good home and a small salary" as a domestic worker was an acceptable substitute for women who needed to generate wages.[47] These club women, in the tradition of women's voluntary work, wanted more than simple work or relief payments for women. They wanted a program of "intelligent rehabilitation" created to uplift destitute women before sending them back to the home sphere.[48]

Stevenson and her organization saw the "sewing room women" not merely as individuals with economic need but as teachable women in need of better skills. When local WPA programs failed to give women promised instruction, Stevenson suggested that the women be reimbursed for what "they have lost" by being relieved of work to spend two months in training programs.[49] The GWDC became concerned when WPA supervisors acted more like employ-ers than social workers. When some materials went missing from the large downtown Atlanta sewing room, workers were searched. "Imagine," Steven-son protested, "an American citizen having to submit to being 'patted' all over her person to see if a sheet, for instance, was concealed under her thin summer clothing!"[50] Officials did not find the material, but to prevent future problems, they permanently removed the sewing machine drawers where items might be hidden. Stevenson howled in protest at the further and, in her mind, undue humiliation this action brought on the women in the sewing room. Stevenson and the GWDC never gave any significant consideration to labor and the pro-duction of goods: they were interested only in using government relief money to "intelligently rehabilitate the very poor."[51] In their minds, then, the money paid out by the WPA was more a form of direct relief than wages for work per-formed. This distinction derived from their understanding of women's con-nection to the domestic realm.

Among New Deal administrators, perspectives similar to Stevenson's were not uncommon, though they never triumphed over other concerns held by government officials and therefore never became guiding principles in en-acting work relief for women. Georgia's director of the FERA, CWA, and WPA women's divisions, Van De Vrede, for example, applauded workroom educa-tional programs designed to improve women's skills in "all manners of home-making" because she believed that most women on relief "cannot and should not be absorbed in[to] the industrial system."[52] While Hopkins, head of the WPA, had publicly committed himself to providing women consideration equal to that given men, his own views on the matter undercut the possibility that this could happen. A wholehearted proponent of work relief, Hopkins's endorsement of and design for these programs always gave primacy to their therapeutic effects for men. "Without work," Hopkins argued, "men actually go to pieces. They lose the respect of their wives, sons and daughters because they lose respect for themselves."[53] As his most recent biographer admits, Hopkins ultimately believed that "waged work for mothers threatened the well-being of children" and that "women looking for work to support their families were competing with men on relief who were also seeking work."[54] Historian Linda Gordon goes further, asserting that one reason women did not fare better under the New Deal was "Hopkins's personal disinterest in providing work to women" stemming from his acceptance of "the argument that they were not accustomed to real jobs and/or were accustomed to low wages and poor working conditions."[55] In the end, Hopkins's views of the relationship between gender and work undercut the efforts of women such as Stevenson despite their similar understandings of women's role in society.

For all those who may have placed women's domestic associations in front of their identities as workers, at least some within the New Deal felt otherwise. Shepperson, Georgia's WPA administrator, criticized the GWDC's recommendations for training women in domestic skills as "not practical from a work basis for wages."[56] She suggested that these activities be relegated to educational and vocational programs, clearly defining the domain of the WPA as wage work, even for women. Owens, the district supervisor who refused to hold training programs in her sewing rooms, ran her projects as if they were a shop floor, justifying her position by reporting to her superiors that "many of the women were frankly fed up" with the domestic instruction they had received while under the FERA's jurisdiction. She placed her concern on production, "standards and procedures of performance," and teaching women good industrial work habits by instilling in them "regular and orderly working habits which would aid them in securing and holding jobs in private industry."[57]

On the national level, Woodward committed her division of the WPA to hiring "every able-bodied employable woman on relief who is the breadwinner for her family or who is dependent on her own efforts for a livelihood."[58] She argued that women should be allowed to do any and all work for which they qualified, including manual labor, and should earn a "man's wages" for doing strenuous jobs. Male leaders on the state level objected and instead dictated that women be restricted to lighter work (which paid less)—clerical jobs for skilled women and sewing work for the unskilled. Woodward also battled local project sponsors from across the country who held "provincial viewpoints" about aiding minorities and employing women, private manufacturers fearing competition, and housewives complaining that their maids were leaving for government jobs, at the same time devising projects to employ women whose work skills varied from virtually existent to professional.[59]

Missing from this discussion were the voices of the sewing room workers themselves. Stevenson claimed to be in contact with these women regularly from 1936 on, and she periodically retyped portions of their letters within the text of her own. According to Stevenson's portrayal, these women were frustrated by the hiring/certification process, conditions in the sewing rooms, and low wages. In essence, these women's goals meshed with those of the capitalist wage system. They conceived of themselves as workers and defined their interests as such, never asking for and in many cases directly refusing to attend domestic classes.[60] There is little evidence from the Atlanta area to corroborate or challenge Stevenson's portrayal of the women's interests, but evidence from other locations, where better documentation exists, suggests that these sentiments were common. Sewing room workers in Tampa, for example, struck over just these issues in 1937.[61] Conditioned by her class background, club work, and passing acquaintance with organized social work, Stevenson did not or would not recognize the ways in which sewing room workers thought of and positioned themselves as workers, deserving of better treatment because of their skill and labor rather than because of their other identities as women and mothers.

Sewing rooms became the major form of work relief for women during the depression largely because such institutions represented a compromise between these various perspectives. For destitute and unemployed women, the projects offered work and cash wages instead of direct relief. Administrators liked the projects because they could operate all year, used skills that women were believed to possess already (or to learn easily), and required limited supervision.[62] Politicians supported sewing because it pleased many constituencies at once. The projects bought up surplus commodities, such as cotton, and therefore soothed business leaders in these troubled markets. The projects may have also quieted legislators, who often felt that states were being forced into taking over relief for unemployables, by providing goods that the state could distribute to the needy. For those who believed that women should be trained to serve in the industrial workforce after the depression, sewing rooms could be seen as a stepping stone into the garment industry, a major industrial employer for women in Atlanta and nationally. But training and the nature of the program also appeased those who wanted to see women returned to their roles as homemakers by keeping women working in tasks that could be read as traditional and domestic. In Georgia, as in most states, sewing rooms provided the great bulk of the work relief for unemployed women, totaling nearly 80 percent of all women's WPA work.[63] By the end of the 1930s, women working in Atlanta-area sewing rooms alone had produced more than four million garments for distribution to the needy.[64]

The range of beliefs regarding women, work, and welfare in the 1930s could coexist relatively peacefully not only because of the compromise nature of the sewing projects but also because questions over how and when women should be aided never became central to popular or administrative debates on work relief. That central territory was firmly held by the unemployed male, or the "forgotten man," as Franklin Roosevelt once named the image.[65] And, as Alice

Kessler-Harris reminds us, "efficiency tried to be sex-blind and sometimes succeeded. Workers and the public fully expected that in a crisis jobs ought to go to male breadwinners; however, efficiency responded to its own imperatives, consistent with its own traditions," and some jobs went to women because the positions were rigidly gendered, economically useful, and pleasing to important constituencies or because some policy makers understood that some women needed to support their families.[66]

The federal government's work-relief programs may have been welfare in that they provided assistance to the destitute and unemployed, but the policies used in these projects were based on a model of male industrial employment. Relief recipients became "workers" and were paid cash wages rather than receiving the surplus commodities or food and rent vouchers associated with direct relief. Unlike recipients under earlier New Deal relief programs, applicants were not means-tested and theoretically needed only to be deemed unemployed to be certified for WPA jobs. This determination, however, was also based on gendered criteria, as individual women who had not previously worked for wages but might have generated income in other ways often had trouble convincing local officials that they should now be considered unemployed. Once on the WPA, women had trouble keeping their jobs. When decreased appropriations mandated removing workers from the WPA's employment rolls, women were the first to go. The WPA also allowed only one job per family. While the language did not specify, assumptions that as breadwinners, men were more entitled than women to jobs translated into more positions for men. Within this structure, voices proclaiming the special needs of women—whether the voices of government outsiders such as Stevenson or of administrative insiders such as Van De Vrede—never predominated, but they also never wholly disappeared.

The balance between various interests under the auspices of sewing projects was an uneasy one, and the periodic release of relief workers as a result of budget cuts in 1936 and 1937 encouraged Stevenson and the GWDC to continue to defend the interests of the state's poor women. "They may not be the Government's 'deserving' clients" Stevenson challenged, "but I do insist that they might have become deserving had the funds provided by the Administration been used to help them in a more intelligent way."[67] In a letter to the president, Stevenson argued that workers were being defined as deserving on the basis of their "docility" rather than their need, accusing WPA administrators of privileging economics over humanity and efficiency over rehabilitation by driving "the young and strong and the old and infirm" to produce the same quotas and using production ability to measure how deserving clients were.[68] "These emergency sewing rooms," she queried, "were never intended to be sweat shops, were they?" "The individual was the important point," Stevenson quipped, "not the number of garments turned out."[69]

Stevenson's sense that the government was beginning to place less importance on relief and more emphasis on a model of production based on efficiency and competition was not entirely inaccurate. In 1939, in an effort to streamline and solidify the WPA as a permanent form of welfare (a move that lost support with the rising economic fortunes brought by World War II), the organization's name changed from the Works Progress Administration to the Works Projects Administration. One account of this change emphasized that it reflected that "emphasis was being shifted to a degree from the viewpoint of the unemployed worker to the satisfactory service rendered to the community."[70] Sewing rooms, in particular, were reorganized and mechanized in the late 1930s so that they functioned more like small factories and less like a sewing circle, the model the club women had preferred. This transition violated the basic views on women and work held not just by observers such as Stevenson but also by many of those in power, including Hopkins. Standardizing and mechanizing production translated into increased treatment of women laboring in the sewing rooms as workers first and women or mothers second.

Despite this shift, women and men never received equal treatment under federal work-relief or direct assistance programs. The policy for these programs did tend to be written in gender-neutral language. The procedures for cutting workers, for example, specified that officials should take "efficiency" and "relative needs" into consideration when making dismissal decisions.[71] What political scientist Suzanne Mettler has labeled administrators' "preexisting inclinations" to channel men and women through distinct programs, however, ensured that the genders were treated differently.[72] With no overwhelming popular or governmental mandate to give women work relief and a direct relief system established under the Social Security Act focused only on the elderly, the disabled, and children, women became neither wholly worthy of work nor entitled to relief.[73] The only exceptions occurred when women served as full-time employees, enabling them to "fit the mold"[74] created around the male breadwinner, qualifying them for unemployment insurance, or when women were heads of households, in which case they might qualify for Aid to Dependent Children benefits under the Social Security program.

In response to these changes and to her inability to gain much influence through more traditional channels, Stevenson steadily distanced herself from the "maternalism" of traditional club work and moved toward an alliance with working-class women on labor issues. She guided her organization into something of an alliance with women relief workers after 1936, and although she never entirely lost her elitist view of women's relationship to paid labor, Stevenson did push her organization and other Atlanta club women to focus more of their efforts on organizing destitute female relief workers and on improving work conditions. Concerns about the conditions under which women labored in the city's sewing rooms, particularly in the downtown project that employed more than a thousand workers, started to rival and then surpassed Stevenson's early focus on the local and state wpa administration. The gwdc's continued investigative visits to area sewing rooms revealed disturbing conditions that eventually prompted the organization to accuse the wpa of running government sweatshops. Women toiled through brutal summers, for example, without fans, water, or a shaded place to eat their lunches. Facilities had poor lighting and heating in the winter, inadequate toilets, and "old-rickety" equipment. Supervisors "using sweat-shop methods" sped up the process by increasing workers' loads.[75] "We had the opportunity to shake hands with some of [the cutters]," the club women reported, "and were shocked at the condition of their hands. Blistered and calloused hands, caused by the poor quality of scissors supplied them, and very tired bodies long standing or bending over tables would suggest that little real thought had been given to them."[76] The gwdc began to advocate improved conditions and better pay for women workers. In stark contrast to their earlier tactic of speaking for the workers, the club women encouraged Hopkins "to work out your plans with the workers themselves."[77]

Stevenson and the gwdc continued their efforts to "improve" the sewing room women, but more than a year of interacting with women on relief engendered a new respect for the skills these women already possessed, the menial and undervalued nature of their work, and their commitments outside of the workroom. The club women came to support officials who treated the sewing women as no "different in any way from other government employees."[78] The club challenged both Franklin and Eleanor Roosevelt to come to Atlanta and spend time with the sewing room workers both on and off the job. "I dare you," Stevenson wrote to the president, "to spend a week in the ordinary sewing room,—go home with those women, and rush with them through their home work."[79] Writing in 1938, Stevenson asked wpa administrators with a good dose of sarcasm and perhaps just a tiny hint of hope, "Do you think Mrs. Roosevelt would consent to try out some of the sewing machines that women are ordered to make 'production' with?"[80] Giving up completely on reaching WPA officials sometime in 1938, Stevenson dismissed the administrators as hopelessly elitist, describing them as those who "live in fair houses and eat dainty food,—and would not sit down with these women in their homes and really know what conditions are."[81]

Stevenson became a voice for workers afraid to raise complaints for fear of losing their positions. Workers and those wanting WPA positions sought out Stevenson in the hopes that she could intercede on their behalf or at least tell their story to administrators without fear of repercussions.[82] In explaining why she had begun to take up the causes of so many individual women in her letters, Stevenson wrote, "The women are afraid to protest because they must not lose the little they are getting."[83] She accused supervisors of "bulldozing" their underlings and taking "the heart out of the upright among the workers."[84] Objecting to the conclusions reached by earlier investigations of sewing room conditions, Stevenson demanded of Hopkins, "Send your next investigator to me and let the desperate women and hungry children speak for themselves."[85]

The GWDC steadily created a new role for itself. The organization no longer sought the role of impartial and privileged observer and adviser to the administration or party; members increasingly came to see themselves as promoters and protectors of working women. The club women intended to use their privileged positions in society to ensure that the voices of these "desperate women" would be heard. Never able completely to escape their own elitism, however, the organization's members continued to "teach" the women how and when to speak and to broker the relationship between the workers and the government. GWDC members attended sewing room workers' meetings and transmitted demands for better conditions, supplies, safety measures, and job security on to Eleanor Roosevelt and Labor Secretary Frances Perkins. Stevenson lobbied the Department of Labor to issue an edict guaranteeing the "right of women to organize" and personally supported the workers' efforts to unionize, believing that doing so would improve self-discipline and morale. Stevenson began to see herself as a crusader for these women, promising to "win for them the consideration they are worthy of receiving."[86] Following this lead, the GWDC even created a "Citizenship Committee," with Stevenson as its head, that reached out to the "Workers' Union" by organizing meetings at which workers could study New Deal legislation such as Social Security and learn about labor issues generally.[87]

Estelle Stevenson and the GWDC had come a long way between 1935 and 1939. The organization, which had begun as little more than a middle-class fan club for the Roosevelts, had turned into a group of labor activists of a sort. These women suffered few direct effects of the depression, though their disappointing experiences with New Dealers and what Stevenson called the "fraud" of the Democratic Party pushed them into a new relationship with the city's unemployed women.[88] An odd sort of sisterhood emerged in which the elite women sought to raise up the working classes but at the same time adopted at least some of the issues and language of organized labor. Running behind this transition and throughout Stevenson's five years of correspondence is a relatively consistent vision of what the government should be doing and how it ought to treat the citizens it governed. The vision changed little over the years, and its hopefulness, liberalism, and enthusiasm go far in explaining to the generations that follow how even critics of the New Deal could have been so positively invigorated by it.

Stevenson envisioned a creative, flexible, honest, and caring federal government. She pleaded for a state that took seriously its responsibilities to its citizens and valued their talents, experiences, and possibilities. Beyond her specific desire to see work-relief programs improve women's home-based skills and provide them with a humane way to earn their welfare, Stevenson also hoped that the WPA would be more than just a temporary or emergency agency. In a letter to Hopkins, Stevenson explained that "as the years pass you naturally expect that those in charge of the welfare of so many human beings and of the spending of so much of the people's money would wish to use every means possible to promote the interest of all."[89] Arguing for the implementation of "better methods" of relief, Stevenson reminded the president, "Your workers can no longer hide behind 'the emergency.'"[90]

Stevenson and club women like her saw that new federal spending created massive opportunities to reinvent the way social work was done in the state and provide "a very great and lasting benefit to these most under-privileged" women if only administrators would stand up for "decency and justice."[91] In taking advantage of these opportunities, she wanted policy makers to apply more creativity in addressing the problems and opportunities created by the depression. In critiquing the programs that New Dealers had used to aid

women, Stevenson queried, "Can't you see that it required no imagination,—
no vision to crowd them into the sewing room?"[92] "The opportunity is so
great," she reminded Hopkins, urging him adopt more idealistic and far-
reaching welfare methods.[93]

Stevenson's idealism was readily apparent in her correspondence: "We were
thrilled and encouraged to hope that our President's New Deal would, indeed
be the beginning of hope for the underprivileged of our country," she wrote
to WPA officials.[94] But she found administrators lacking similar enthusiasm,
leaving her to ask bitterly of the president, "Is there any virtue in your WPA
in Georgia or is it just a racket?"[95] "Back in the old days," she concluded,
"government had a conscience."[96] Stevenson saw the New Deal as missing an
appreciation for the individual—the thread that tied together her advocacy
for domestic education and her advocacy for women's rights—and she still
believed that such an appreciation was possible. She pleaded with officials to
consider the "human element" in their programs and to privilege the worker
over the work, remembering that "each is a 'living soul.'" A welfare program,
according to Stevenson, "must be used intelligently, simplified to suit certain
groups, and given—not as a dose of medicine by clock-watchers, but by those
who value the individual human being."[97] Of the growing tendency to stan-
dardize procedures and emphasize output, Stevenson reminded New Dealers,
"perhaps the work is excellent: but what of the workers?"[98]

The rhetoric of prominent national officials would seem to support at least
parts of Stevenson's vision for government. For example, in arguing for work-
relief programs, Franklin Roosevelt stressed that at least one of their functions
was "to provide a bridge by which people can pass from relief status over to
normal self-support."[99] Hopkins similarly worked to remove the stigma attached to relief by providing the unemployed with jobs that would improve
their self-esteem.[100] "The human being should come first," Hopkins wrote,
"and the serviceability of the economic system in which he functions should
be estimated by the number of persons who share in its rewards." For Hopkins
and others, the depression opened up opportunities to expand the role of government because "new ideas and new solutions to old problems seemed less
alarming under such circumstances."[101] However, Stevenson never saw Hopkins's idealism because New Dealers and elected officials never widely agreed
on this vision, and Hopkins repeatedly compromised it in the effort to build
a permanent welfare state under the Social Security Act.[102]

New Deal administrators on the state, regional, and national levels knew
full well of the truth of many of Stevenson's charges against them. Women

were being worked hard with few breaks in inadequate facilities. Workers with few other options did lose jobs with no warning when relief rolls were cut because of budget shortfalls. Supervisors at times treated their charges with contempt. Local authorities ignored "suggestions" from their superiors, and many administrators chose to overlook local customs in overseeing federal relief efforts. In the end, however, the survival of the program trumped other interests. It was as if administrators such as Hopkins and Shepperson believed that any public relief program coming from the national level was preferable to none at all: protecting the WPA from its liberal friends became nearly as important as heading off its conservative critics.

The responses to and letters about Estelle Stevenson's criticisms contain only one outright dismissal of her and her claims, a late-1937 reference to her as "the prize crank."[103] Officials handled Stevenson's charges with notable care. She had personal visits with state administrators and received numerous letters from national officials. The record suggests that at least three investigations of work-relief conditions in Georgia occurred in response to Stevenson's efforts to improve the sewing rooms. As a result of her work, the WPA altered the administrative structure in some sewing rooms; investigated and, in at least a few cases, rectified individual workers' cases; and tried to break large projects into smaller programs. Stevenson's campaign to fix the WPA sewing rooms and influence the development of the welfare state also revealed a number of issues common to work-relief programs in the 1930s—issues not confined to sewing rooms, to Atlanta, or even to the South. Letters from Americans across the country raised familiar challenges to the New Deal—wages too low, jobs going to those who did not need them, endless red tape, and outsiders receiving aid or holding too much power. Although Stevenson's letters to WPA administrators ceased in 1939, the issues she raised linger even today in discussions of welfare programs.[104] Sewing rooms, which many observers saw as the "lowest form of work relief,"[105] raised some of the most significant challenges to the emergence of a new federally sponsored U.S. social welfare system.

For club women of the 1930s such as those who belonged to the Georgia Woman's Democratic Club, the creation of federal social welfare policies ultimately encouraged a sense of both hope and foreboding. The expansion of the government and the Democratic Party under the New Deal offered some of these women the chance to move into significant positions of power as political appointees and party officials.[106] But this transition forced club women to adopt a different style in promoting their political and reform agendas. Some historians have noted that patronage frequently replaced the club women's traditional nonpartisanship.[107] In the case of Stevenson and the GWDC, investigation and personal appeals to those in power would gradually be replaced by more confrontational tactics. Stevenson in particular never completely abandoned the middle-class progressivism that had ushered her into the world of politics during the 1920s, but her experiences with the New Deal encouraged her to challenge the government and to adopt a new, more assertive definition of citizenship both for her personally and for the working-class women with whom she increasingly allied herself.

Notes

1. GWDC Yearbook, 1940–41, Georgia Department of Archives and History, Atlanta.
2. Stevenson to [Franklin Roosevelt], June 12, 1936, Central Files: State: Georgia, 1935–41, Works Progress Administration, RG 69, National Archives (hereafter cited as WPA).
3. Dewson quoted in Susan Ware, *Partner and I: Molly Dewson, Feminism, and New Deal Politics* (New Haven: Yale University Press, 1989), 198.
4. Talmadge feared losing the power of patronage in crucial rural counties once federal money arrived. He also resented the control a woman, Shepperson, had over federal money in the state, federal interference and spending in a time of depression, race-blind aid programs, and what he felt was excessive aid for urban areas (Douglas L. Fleming, "Atlanta, the Depression, and the New Deal" [Ph.D. diss., Emory University, 1984], 25; James T. Patterson, *The New Deal and the States: Federalism in Transition* [Princeton: Princeton University Press, 1969], 138–39).
5. Speaker Pro Tem Ellis Arnall quoted in "Relief in Georgia," *Atlanta Georgian,* February 11, 1935.
6. Club women's interest in sewing rooms was not confined to Atlanta. In Charleston, West Virginia, for example, the Business and Professional Women's Club challenged local pay scales for women (Jerry Bruce Thomas, *An Appalachian New Deal: West Virginia in the Great Depression* [Lexington: University Press of Kentucky, 1998], 187).
7. Very few records exist to illuminate the background of these women or the organization of the sewing rooms. National studies suggest that most of the women were not drawn from the city's garment trades and had no union affiliation. Reflecting the consumer culture of the early twentieth century, Shepperson observed that "by and large many women did not know how to sew simple seams, much less construct garments" and therefore required substantial training in the government sewing rooms (Shepperson to Woodward, April 6, 1935, Jane Van De

Vrede WPA Records and Other Papers, 1913–73, Georgia Department of Archives and History, Atlanta).

8. Stevenson to [Franklin Roosevelt], June 24, 1936, WPA.

9. Georgina Hickey, "Disease, Disorder, and Motherhood: Working-Class Women, Social Welfare, and the Process of Urban Development," in *Before the New Deal: Social Welfare in the South, 1830–1930*, ed. Elna C. Green (Athens: University of Georgia Press, 1999).

10. Michael S. Holmes, *The New Deal in Georgia: An Administrative History* (Westport, Conn.: Greenwood Press, 1975).

11. George McJimsey, *Harry Hopkins: Ally of the Poor and Defender of Democracy* (Cambridge: Harvard University Press, 1987), 55–60.

12. Patterson, *New Deal and the States*, 74–75, 84. Patterson credits this arrangement as the source of the WPA's ability to keep criticism below levels seen with the FERA.

13. "Conference on Emergency Needs of Women," November 20, 1933, White House Conference, Old General Subject, FERA-WPA Central Files, RG 69, National Archives.

14. Woodward quoted in Martha H. Swain, *Ellen S. Woodward: New Deal Advocate for Women* (Jackson: University Press of Mississippi, 1995), 55.

15. Martha H. Swain, " 'The Forgotten Woman': Ellen S. Woodward and Women's Relief in the New Deal," *Prologue* 5 (winter 1983): 213. Women made up 24 percent of the overall workforce at the time, so their numbers in the WPA did not approach their proportion in the labor force (Winifred Wandersee, *Women's Work and Family Values, 1920–1940* [Cambridge: Harvard University Press, 1981], 97).

16. Both Douglas Smith and Roger Biles note that despite the "newness" of the New Deal, southern cities and their power structures were largely unchanged by the decade of the Great Depression (Smith, "Continuity and Change in the Urban South: The New Deal Experience," *Atlanta History Journal* 30 [spring 1986]: 7–22; Biles, *The South and the New Deal* [Lexington: University Press of Kentucky, 1994]).

17. On Hopkins's social work background, see June Hopkins, *Harry Hopkins: Sudden Hero, Brash Reformer* (New York: St. Martin's Press, 1999). On Hopkins's management style, see McJimsey, *Harry Hopkins*, 55–56.

18. Shepperson quoted in Kathryn W. Kemp and Elaine Kirkland Kemp, "The Gay Bolling Shepperson Papers and Photographs," *Atlanta Historical Journal* 30 (spring 1986): 118.

19. GWDC, "Resolutions: Addressed to the President of the United States and to the Congress," June 1937, WPA.

20. Stevenson to Hopkins, June 25, 1936, WPA.

21. Stevenson to Franklin Roosevelt, April 24, 1936, WPA.

22. Stevenson to Franklin Roosevelt, May 9, 1936, WPA.

23. Stevenson to Shepperson and Van De Vrede, April 17, 1936, WPA.

24. Untitled report enclosed with Stevenson to F. S. Bartlett, December 3, 1936, WPA.

25. Stevenson to Eleanor Roosevelt, April 28, 1938, WPA.

26. Holmes, mistakenly citing an *Atlanta Journal* article of September 14, 1936, seems to be the source of later references to racist motivations of the GWDC (*New Deal in Georgia*, 132).

27. Stevenson to Wolfe, June 8, 1936; see also Stevenson to Ralston, June 24, 1936; Stevenson to Hopkins, June 25, 1936, WPA, for examples of her references to race.

28. Stevenson to Ralston, June 24, 1936, WPA.

29. Stevenson to Bartlett, December 3, 1936, WPA.

30. Stevenson to Hopkins, July 23, 1937, WPA.

31. Stevenson to Eleanor Roosevelt, April 28, 1938, WPA.

32. "Copy for Mr. Hopkins," Stevenson's handwritten notes on Shepperson by Van De Vrede to Stevenson, May 19, 1936, WPA.

33. Stevenson to [Franklin Roosevelt], received April 19, 1938, WPA.

34. Ralston to Woodward, July 28, 1936, WPA.

35. Stevenson to Ralston, June 24, 1936, WPA.

36. GWDC Reporters, "Suggestions Made to the Works Progress Administration," April 1936, WPA.

37. Owens to Van De Vrede, "Background and Set-up of the F.E.R.A. and W.P.A. Sewing Rooms in De Kalb County," July 18, 1936, WPA.

38. Ralston to Woodward, July 28, 1936, WPA.

39. Marie Dresden Lane and Francis Steegmuller, *America on Relief* (New York: Harcourt, Brace, 1938), 10.

40. Shepperson by Van De Vrede to Woodward, December 3, 1936, WPA.

41. Ibid.

42. Stevenson to [Franklin Roosevelt], August 8, 1936, WPA. This particular letter prompted the president's secretary to ask the assistant director of the WPA, Aubrey Williams, to draft a reply to Stevenson.

43. *Atlanta Journal,* September 14, 1936; *Atlanta Constitution,* September 15, 1936.

44. Surviving documents suggest that the GWDC had been the officially recognized Atlanta-area Democratic club but that this relationship was severed sometime in early 1936, perhaps over this issue. See "Lists of Reporters serving in . . ." for the state of Georgia, Papers of the Democratic National Committee, Women's Division, Franklin D. Roosevelt Library, Hyde Park, N.Y. See also Manta Rollison to Wolfe, January 20, 1936, Papers of the Democratic National Committee, Women's Division.

45. Mrs. J. A. Rollison, "The WPA Program for Unemployed Women in Georgia," Georgia State Section, *Democratic Digest,* July 1937, 2.

46. Stevenson to Shepperson and Van De Vrede, March 17, 1937, WPA.

47. "Suggestions."

48. Stevenson to Wolfe, June 8, 1936, WPA.

49. Stevenson to Ralston, June 24, 1936, WPA.

50. Stevenson to [Franklin Roosevelt], September 19, 1936, WPA.

51. Stevenson to [Franklin Roosevelt], August 8, 1936, WPA.

52. Jane Van De Vrede, "Talk Made at WSB Broadcast," May 15, 1937, Van De Vrede Papers.

53. Hopkins quoted in Paul A. Kurzman, *Harry Hopkins and the New Deal* (Fair Lawn, N.J.: R. E. Burdick, 1974), 122.

54. Hopkins, *Harry Hopkins*, 4.

55. Linda Gordon, *Pitied but not Entitled: Single Mothers and the History of Welfare* (New York: Free Press, 1994), 193–94.

56. Shepperson by Van De Vrede to Stevenson, April 17, 1936, WPA.

57. Owens to Van De Vrede, "Background."

58. Woodward quoted in Hopkins, *Harry Hopkins*, 189.

59. Martha H. Swain, "A New Deal for Southern Women: Gender and Race in Women's Work Relief," in *Women of the American South: A Multicultural Reader*, ed. Christie Ann Farnham (New York: New York University Press, 1997), 247, 249–51.

60. Owens to Van De Vrede, "Background."

61. James Francis Tidd Jr., "Stitching and Striking: WPA Sewing Rooms and the 1937 Relief Strike in Hillsborough County," *Tampa Bay History* 11, no. 1 (1989): 5–21.

62. Swain, "Forgotten Woman," 207.

63. Holmes, *New Deal in Georgia*, 132.

64. Swain, "New Deal for Southern Women," 249.

65. Samuel I. Rosenman, ed., *The Public Papers and Addresses of Franklin D. Roosevelt* (New York: Random House, 1938), 1:624. On the gendered iconography of the New Deal, see Barbara Melosh, *Engendering Culture: Manhood and Womanhood in New Deal Public Art and Theater* (Washington, D.C.: Smithsonian Institution Press, 1991).

66. Alice Kessler-Harris, *Out to Work: A History of Wage-Earning Women in the United States* (New York: Oxford University Press, 1982), 265.

67. Stevenson to Shepperson and Van De Vrede, April 17, 1936, WPA.

68. Stevenson to [Franklin Roosevelt], May 9, June 13, 1936, WPA.

69. Stevenson to Eleanor Roosevelt, April 22, 1938, WPA.

70. Georgia Civil Works Administration History, Van De Vrede Papers. This shift was evident in other states as well. See, for example, George T. Blakey, *Hard Times and New Deal in Kentucky, 1929–1939* (Lexington: University Press of Kentucky, 1986), 60–61. The replacement of Hopkins with Francis C. Harrington, an engineer, might help account for the shift in WPA goals and policies. See Swain, *Ellen S. Woodward*, 132–33.

71. Bartlett to Stevenson, November 27, 1936, WPA.

72. Suzanne Mettler, *Dividing Citizens: Gender and Federalism in New Deal Public Policy* (Ithaca: Cornell University Press, 1998), 18.

73. There is growing body of literature on the emergence of the gendered welfare state; see esp. Gordon, *Pitied but Not Entitled*, chap. 7; and Gwendolyn Mink, *The Wages of Motherhood: Inequality in the Welfare State, 1917–1942* (Ithaca: Cornell University Press, 1995), esp. chap. 6.

74. Mettler, *Dividing Citizens*, 26.

75. Stevenson to Works Progress Administration, March 15, 1938, WPA.

76. Stevenson to Shepperson and Van De Vrede, March 17, 1937, WPA.

77. Stevenson to Hopkins, May 17, 1937, WPA.

78. Stevenson, "The Georgia Woman's Democratic Club again asks the Works Progress Administration of Georgia . . ." (enclosure to letter of May 17, 1937), WPA.

79. Stevenson to [Franklin Roosevelt], April 24, 1936, WPA.

80. Stevenson to Works Progress Administration, February 5, 1938, WPA.

81. "Data for Mrs. Roosevelt and Secretary Perkins on Georgia WPA Sewing Room Workers," April 28, 1938, WPA. Also around this time, Stevenson stopped writing to administrators and officeholders individually and instead began to address a single letter to all.

82. Official policy set by Hopkins (in 1938) forbade firings for political reasons, but this seems to have offered little sense of security to women in the city's sewing rooms (Hopkins to "All Project Workers . . . ," May 5, 1938, Central Files: State Georgia, Complaints, WPA, RG 69, National Archives).

83. Stevenson to [Franklin Roosevelt], [1938], WPA.

84. Stevenson to [Franklin Roosevelt et al.], July 9, 1938, WPA.

85. Stevenson to Hopkins, July 23, 1937, WPA.

86. Stevenson to Eleanor Roosevelt, April 22, 1938, WPA.

87. GWDC Yearbook, 1940–41.

88. "Data for Mrs. Roosevelt and Secretary Perkins."

89. Stevenson to Hopkins, [June 1936], WPA.

90. Stevenson to [Franklin Roosevelt], June 24, 1936, WPA.

91. Stevenson to Shepperson and Van De Vrede, April 17, 1936; Stevenson to [Franklin Roosevelt et al.], July 9, 1938, WPA.

92. Stevenson to [Franklin Roosevelt], May 9, 1936, WPA.

93. Stevenson to Hopkins, March 17, 1937, WPA.

94. Stevenson to Hopkins, June 25, 1936, WPA.

95. Stevenson to [Franklin Roosevelt], July 1937, WPA.

96. Stevenson to [Franklin Roosevelt], October 30, 1937, WPA.

97. Stevenson to [Franklin Roosevelt], June 12, 1936, WPA.

98. Stevenson to [Franklin Roosevelt], [ca. 1938], WPA.

99. Lane and Steegmuller, *America on Relief*, 6–7.

100. Kurzman, *Harry Hopkins*, 12–13. See also McJimsey, *Harry Hopkins*, 83.

101. Hopkins quoted in Hopkins, *Harry Hopkins,* 191.

102. Gordon, *Pitied but Not Entitled,* chap. 9.

103. Handwritten note from Howe attached to Woodward to Stevenson, August 7, 1937, WPA.

104. At least until the time of her husband's death in 1946, Stevenson continued to live in Decatur, Georgia, and hold various offices within the GWDC. She applied for a Social Security number sometime thereafter in St. Louis, Missouri. At the time of her death in 1985 at the age of ninety-three, Stevenson resided in Peachtree City, just south of Atlanta. She was buried in St. Louis. My attempts to find out what she did with the second half of her life have garnered no further information.

105. Stevenson to Eleanor Roosevelt, April 22, 1938, WPA.

106. Susan Ware, *Beyond Suffrage: Women in the New Deal* (Cambridge: Harvard University Press, 1981); Frances M. Seeber, "Eleanor Roosevelt and Women in the New Deal: A Network of Friends," *Presidential Studies Quarterly* 20, no. 4 (1990): 707–17; Martha H. Swain, "A New Deal for Mississippi Women, 1933–1943," *Journal of Mississippi History* 46, no. 3 (1984): 191–212.

107. Sarah Wilkerson-Freeman, "From Clubs to Parties: North Carolina Women in the Advancement of the New Deal," *North Carolina Historical Review* 68, no. 3 (1991): 321.

The Farm Security Administration and Rural Families in the South

Home Economists, Nurses, and Farmers, 1933–1946

BRENDA J. TAYLOR

In 1937 the newly created Farm Security Administration (FSA) absorbed the rural rehabilitation work of the Federal Emergency Relief Administration (FERA) and the Resettlement Administration (RA). Franklin Delano Roosevelt's New Deal had instigated numerous programs to assist the almost two million farm families living below the poverty level of fifteen hundred dollars per year.[1] Based on the many studies that had recognized the factors contributing to rural impoverishment, including poor housing, inadequate food, substandard health care, lack of education, and perpetual despair, administrators concluded that successful rural rehabilitation required that policies address not only the farmer but also the farm wife. Furthermore, the farm family's health became an integral part of the rehabilitation process. Farmers and their wives, therefore, became the focus of government services provided by nurses and home economists. To rural inhabitants, these female professionals represented the best in scientific improvement.[2]

Although the New Deal rural programs under the FERA, RA, and FSA varied from newly created resettlement communities to in-place subsistence or industrial rehabilitation, they all revealed similar deficiencies in health conditions and modern scientific planning. Early FERA workers consequently concluded that permanent relocation required that farmers and their families receive subsidized medical care for health reasons and full productivity. In response, FERA settlements (and later those of the RA and FSA as well) employed nurses and created medical cooperatives. Furthermore, whereas many displaced workers relocated to farms often lacked critical agricultural knowledge, many women were seen to be deficient in "modern" homemaking techniques.

Government planners also believed that successful rehabilitation necessitated administrative supervision. Home economists subsequently began to fill "home supervisor" positions within these New Deal agencies.[3] This chapter will consider the impact of home supervisors on southern farm families, demonstrating that New Deal agents (much like social workers in other areas) utilized their positions of authority to reshape rural family life. Focusing on health and hygiene, home supervisors attempted to bolster middle-class cultural norms in southern farm families. Consequently, the New Deal worked to rehabilitate not only farming families but also the culture and values of the rural South.

As New Deal agencies began staffing home supervisor positions in the 1930s, they discovered an available contingent of professional home economists, although such would not have been the case just a few decades earlier. The field of home economics had multiple origins, with some adherents tracing their lineage to Socrates' discourse on home and farm management. Coincidentally, New Deal agencies profited from recent trends in education. In the United States during the second half of the nineteenth century, the need for an appropriate academic field for women and the application of scientific progress to household problems coincided with reform movements to develop home economics at the college and university level. By 1905, twenty-two colleges had four-year home economics programs offering courses in three major divisions: college instruction, extension service, and experiment stations. Moreover, in 1914 the federal government funded its first adult-education program under the Smith-Lever Act, elevating home economics to the same importance as agricultural work. This legislation also authorized agricultural extension work in cooperation with the U.S. Department of Agriculture (USDA) to spread "useful and practical" knowledge concerning farming and homemaking to rural citizens. Only one year later, all states had adopted the extension program. By 1923 the USDA had expanded its role in home economics to such an extent that it created the Bureau of Home Economics to continue research and education. In the 1930s, almost every agricultural county hosted an extension worker, and almost 50 percent boasted a home economist. The federal government, therefore, had employed many university-trained home economists prior to their hiring by the New Deal resettlement agencies. In fact, many of the resettlement supervisors were former extension officers.[4]

By the time the FSA acquired the resettlement communities of its predecessors in 1937, home management was already a critical component of rural rehabilitation. The FSA's Rehabilitation Division had multiple tasks, one of which especially concerned home economists. Although successful rehabilitation required financial aid, farmers and their wives needed assistance in preparing farm and home plans that would earn income for a "healthful" standard of living. Working under the Home Management Section, employees created policies to enhance home management and promote food production, conservation, and storage. According to the FSA manual *Toward Farm Security*, a home supervisor was "usually a woman, trained in home economics," who worked in tandem with the rural rehabilitation supervisor in implementing Washington's plans to improve health and diet and provide adequate clothing. Home supervisors also collaborated with the Resettlement Division and sanitation engineers to improve housing and sanitation. These workers, furthermore, assisted farm supervisors and families in community education and recreation as well as in farm and home planning and record keeping.[5]

Toward Farm Security asserted that farm and home planning was the "hub" of the FSA program. Washington policy makers insisted that farm supervisors (always male) and home supervisors (always female) had the greatest responsibility for the success of rehabilitation: "Any mistakes or weaknesses in this plan will affect the family adversely and retard its rehabilitation." The completed plan used all family and community resources, unifying the farm and home. Furthermore, the manual insisted that supervisors work with each husband and wife in creating and applying the plan. An analysis of assets included the family's health, labor resources, agricultural and managerial skills, and cooperative attitude and industry as well as land, buildings, equipment, furnishings, and operating capital. Supervisors encouraged farmers to view their farm- and home-management plans as flexible guides for the "best possible living" rather than as rigid schemes. The assistant regional chief of home management in North Carolina, Martha E. Smith, wrote to her employees, "Families should be made to understand that *their* farm plan is *their* schedule of operation." The FSA also determined that a year-end report was an essential tool for success. A properly kept record also revealed the plan's strong and weak points.[6]

Farm and home plans opened a window into the rehabilitation family's life. Although the FERA, the RA, and the FSA used several different forms, supervisors first took inventory of households and recorded personal histories. After determining the number of family members, the supervisor noted those able to perform farm labor or housework. The survey then determined the "recommended" annual food supply and counted the family's stores. Later recommendations advised that the farm grow at least half of the food necessary in the first year, with that number eventually increasing to 75 percent. In addition to nutritional assets, the report described available clothing, household items, and furniture. Effective planning mandated that clothing, the second-largest expenditure after food, be sufficient to "meet the needs of health, warmth, and the standards of the community." Supervisors also helped families allot spending for personal-care items such as toiletries. The listing of items such as undergarments, napkins, and spoons illustrated the thoroughness of the report and economists' dedication to accuracy.[7]

Evaluations of the clients' homes were guided also by the FSA's view that families should be not only healthy but "wholesome." The home supervisors' reports described the interior and exterior of the farm home, counting rooms, screens, and closets. Encouraging privacy, guidelines insisted that children over the age of two sleep away from parents and have their own beds to prevent suffocation. Believing that adolescents were capable of building furniture, the USDA provided cabinet and bed blueprints, thereby encouraging older boys and girls to design their rooms. Home supervisors also noted the existence of heating and storage within the home and the availability and location of freshwater in relation to sanitation outside the structure. Supervisors also recorded the presence of poultry houses or gardens. The report concluded with a health history of the family, listing tuberculosis, cardiac trouble, venereal disease, paralysis, cancer, "feeblemindedness" (both "suspected" and "diagnosed"), and insanity, among many other maladies. After carefully observing the family's work ethic, the home supervisor endorsed or denied rehabilitation.[8]

Home economists' monthly reports subsequently cited continuing difficulties with clients. Ida Mae Knight, a North Carolina home economist, wrote between November 1938 and 1940 that a principal problem in home visits was the "need for instruction in budgeting, need for instruction in making Farm and Home Plans." In addition to listing educational and training duties, reports also depicted home supervisors' heavy record-keeping workload. In 1936 the thirteen hundred county home supervisors spread across forty-eight states had an average caseload of 142 rehabilitation families and an additional 125 emergency clients. Moreover, in addition to completing new client inventories, supervisors were required to visit each of their families every six weeks.[9]

Home-management workers, however, did not view the heavy caseloads as the only hindrance to successful rehabilitation. In February 1935 Associate Director Anna M. Boggs, writing from Morgantown, West Virginia, noted several difficulties in a report to her regional chief in Raleigh, North Carolina.

Only half of her supervisors had been on the job for at least five months. A shortage of experienced home economists in West Virginia complicated the situation as most of the "girls" needed additional training. Second, but more difficult to overcome, the supervisors had to contend with extreme weather conditions. Temperatures twenty-five degrees below zero had contributed to impassable roads, five automobile wrecks, and stockings that had frozen while their wearers were walking in snowdrifts. One home manager had suggested that the only solution was to "Tar and Feather the Weather Man." Boggs also cited declining morale as pay envelopes had been delayed for weeks and travel expenses for months. Short of cash, supervisors reported that they could not leave the office until they had checks, and one lamented, "If I don't get [a check] by Saturday, the finance company is repossessing my car." Boggs concluded that morale was the home supervisors' greatest hindrance.[10]

Despite reporting problems, supervisors cited improvements in several critical areas. A 1936 Tennessee summary emphasized that the home-management program centered on food production and conservation. In addition to adequate diets being one of the primary rehabilitation goals, the family's food supply formed the largest single budgetary component. Each farm and home supervisor had a goal for a year-round garden and feed for livestock. As fifty-three Tennessee counties suffered from drought, only a few families reached their goals. Food supply increased significantly, however, for some families. The W. P. Perciful family in Dyer County reported only seventy-two quarts of canned goods, with six varieties, in 1936. Six months later, Mrs. Perciful's canning record listed almost four hundred quarts, with twenty-four varieties. Additionally, the garden had furnished the family with ten different vegetables during the previous summer.[11]

In addition to dietary improvements, the FSA records contained many reports prepared by home economists concerning health problems. A 1937 memo from North Carolina home-management supervisor Kathryn M. Ware to Region IV Assistant Director J. B. Slack bemoaned her clients' illnesses. Ware reported that abscessed teeth and other dental problems needing immediate attention plagued rehabilitation clients. Eye problems included vision correction, corneal ulcers, and damage from accidents. In one instance, a piece of steel had flown into a worker's eye. Because the eye did not receive proper treatment, infection had caused a loss of sight; without surgery, the man faced blindness in the remaining eye. In another case, flu afflicted all nine members of a Richmond, Virginia, family, leaving three children needing surgery for inflamed adenoids and tonsils. The family's seventeen-year-old son developed inflammatory rheumatism from flu complications, and doctors hospitalized him for an entire summer. Although the county welfare worker had assisted and the FSA made grants toward food and clothing, the family faced the loss of its home because of mounting doctor and hospital bills. These insurmountable problems prompted Ware to ask, "Can't something be done?"[12]

Another home-management supervisor, L. O. Browning, located in Fredericksburg, Virginia, further expressed the FSA workers' frustration about health problems: "Often I have said, and am convinced beyond a doubt in my own mind, that if our families could be on productive land and could be *physically fit,* the whole world would be astonished at the results obtained under our supervision." Browning reported that more than 75 percent of her clients needed dental care, and most of those over age forty-five had few teeth. The few who retained their teeth complained that they "don't hit." At least 25 percent needed tonsillectomies, and a minimum of 20 percent of the women suffered from varicose veins. Although counties held tuberculosis clinics, those diagnosed did not receive proper care because of the lack of sanatoriums. Browning also lamented that "nothing was being done" to treat clients with venereal disease in her district.[13]

Browning attributed her clients' health problems both to ignorance and to lack of money. She asserted that supervisors recognized more fully than did the "folks" the need for better health before rehabilitation could be successful. Farm problems, Browning claimed, overwhelmed supervisors and clients alike, making it difficult to teach even the basic health-care program, much less "figger" (as her clients put it) how to provide medical care. One family's dental care alone required more than one hundred dollars. In another instance, a mother of four needed insulin twice each day, dental extractions, dentures, and surgery. The family was unable to borrow money for the mother's care, and Browning insisted that the woman would not be able to "live to old age and suffer as she does." Who would then care for the children left behind? Browning ended her report seemingly engulfed by the futility of her work: "If she was our only problem, we might manage, but there are others and others *and* others."[14]

Home supervisors also oversaw the selection process for the resettlement communities. In the Texas settlement of Ropesville, home-management supervisor Helen Johnson and other RA officials interviewed applicants for the first farms. In addition to appraising overall suitability for farming, the panel examined each family's health. Doctors gave each family member a physical and looked for diseases such as tuberculosis, pellagra, and cancer. Although rehabilitation officials sought to improve the general welfare of rural inhab-itants, the ability to repay FSA loans was a vital factor in client selection. As a result, officials bypassed petitioners such as A. F. Allred of Lindale, Texas, whose wife had been recently released from a tuberculosis sanitarium, in favor of healthier applicants. Home supervisors also educated farm families in san-itation. Home-management supervisors, therefore, cited the hiring of nurses in resettlement communities as crucial to better health and worked closely with both project and county nurses.[15]

Therefore, when the FSA inherited the RA's resettlement communities in 1937, nurses were already the health program's centerpiece.[16] The Interior De-partment's Division of Subsistence Homesteads had placed nurses in some of its communities, a practice the RA expanded by hiring public-health nurses in larger projects. The RA established several guidelines for nurses' employment. Salaries adhered to each state's department of health pay scale but were not to exceed eighteen hundred dollars per year. Although the RA required each nurse to have an automobile, the administration reimbursed up to six hun-dred dollars in travel expenses. Each state, furthermore, selected and certified public-health nurses for RA approval. The medical director of the RA's Public Health Section, Robert Oleson, asserted that the nurses' presence prevented illness, improved homesteaders' morale, aided in rendering health care, and improved the relationship between the RA and local and state health officials.[17]

FSA supervising nurse Matilda Ann Wade evaluated the agency's nursing program in a 1942 article, "Community Nursing—FSA Style." She declared that the 148 projects scattered across the country provided farmers a new way of life. She also commended planning that recognized that "neighborliness," although desirable, also fostered the spread of communicable diseases. Wade recounted that 45 FSA projects had community-nursing services to address health problems. Although no two were exactly alike and each was adjusted to fit the community's needs, most included some form of clinic facility, educa-tional programs, and inoculations. Nurses also coordinated screening exami-nations and medical treatment with local public-health officials.[18]

At Dyess Farms in Arkansas, the Mississippi County Association (an RA medical cooperative) hired a project nurse to supplement its physician ser-vices. Dyess Farms, built by the FERA, was one of the few projects that con-structed a full-service hospital within its boundaries. Although the nurse did not have duties at the hospital, she coordinated her work with the project physician. In August 1941 she reported supervising nine cancer-education meetings with an average of thirteen participants and training seventy-one women in the use of artificial respiration, first-aid-kit preparation, and home-accident prevention. She also held two bedside demonstrations of how to deliver babies and made four prenatal and nine postnatal visits.[19]

Wade also applauded FSA measures to address a 1934 Bureau of Agricultural Economics report on rural housing that revealed that 27 percent of farm homes lacked window screens. The agency had provided eleven dollars per house for screens at its project in Ropesville, Texas. The project's home-management supervisor, Helen Johnson, reported holding seven meetings at Ropesville's community center in 1939, teaching fifty women to build fly traps, eliminate insect breeding grounds, and properly dispose of garbage. Although cost prohibited a sewage system, Ropesville planners built sixty-nine sanitary privies. These improvements in Ropesville and other FSA projects improved health significantly as well as enriched farm life.[20]

Despite this RA and FSA commitment to better health, nurses confronted almost insurmountable problems. Prior to the twentieth century, rural residents were healthier than urban dwellers, with a lower incidence of fatal diseases and premature deaths. In 1900, the average life span for a rural white male was 10 years longer than that of his urban counterpart, while the average white female lived 7.5 years longer in the country than in the city. Between 1900 and 1939 however, the average length of life increased by 40 percent in the city, whereas that of the rural citizen grew by only 19 percent. The military's 1943 rejection of 49.4 percent of rural draftees but only 46.5 percent of urban men awakened policy makers to the situation; for farmers, the fitness failure rate was even higher, at 56.4 percent. Improvements in health resulting from vaccines, antiseptics, and medical training clearly were not reaching rural citizens.[21]

Surveys by public-health officials and benevolent associations such as the Rockefeller Foundation had revealed for three decades the poor health conditions in the Cotton Belt. A Works Projects Administration monograph, *The Plantation South, 1934–1937,* identified conditions including decrepit housing, poor or nonexistent sanitation, deficient diets, and ignorance that contributed to the South's label as the "Nation's Number One Economic Problem." The study directly linked the want of the simplest household equipment and plumbing to the spread of communicable diseases. Remote areas operated under the handicap of fewer doctors and hospitals, and more than three-quarters of rural residents resided in areas without public-health controls. Prominent among the regions' maladies was the "southern trilogy of 'lazy diseases,'" or the "scourge of the South"—hookworm, pellagra, and malaria. These illnesses especially debilitated farmers, robbing them of energy that could be applied in the field. A final group of diseases, although not endemic to the region, still held sway in the South and included diphtheria, whooping cough, tuberculosis, syphilis, and various gastrointestinal afflictions.[22]

To determine more closely its clients' health needs, the FSA conducted studies in 1940 of more than ten thousand low-income farm families in twenty-one representative counties in seventeen states. A survey in Worth County, Georgia, of both white and black clients illustrated the extent of physical impairment and reflected most southern rural areas: only 4 percent were healthy, 96 percent had one of more defects, and disease afflicted more women than men in many categories. Women, for example, were more likely to be overweight or underweight than males. Women had higher incidence of anemia, tonsillitis, hemorrhoids, varicose veins, and intestinal parasites. Men exceeded women in heart defects and hernias. Other maladies cited included rickets, skin disease, defective vision, otitis media, and syphilis. Children suffered from severe weight deficiencies, ongoing tonsillitis, and high rates of intestinal parasites.[23]

Maternal and child health, in fact, was as much a concern as men's health. Although the farmer's health influenced his ability to work, the overall family condition equally concerned reformers. Maternal and child health affected the family greatly because farm wives and children contributed labor in the home and in the field. One rehabilitation report praised the "hard-working" farm wife of a "hopeless invalid" for performing most of the housework and looking after the cows, hogs, chickens, and vegetable gardens.[24]

Anecdotal evidence concerning women's health proliferated during the 1930s, although hard statistics remained unavailable. Dr. Blanche M. Haines, director of the Division of Maternal and Infant Hygiene, surveyed eighteen counties in the South for a 1933 Children's Bureau report. In Robeson County, North Carolina, she blamed maternal health problems on the use of open wells for private water supplies, the unavailability of sanitation systems, and the lack of gardens for fresh vegetables. Furthermore, the drastic cutbacks in funding because of the depression had limited personnel, especially public-health nurses. Although prenatal care in Robeson County fell far short of standards, Haines praised the county's work within its limited budget. She concluded by recommending both federal and state subsidies to improve maternal care in the region.[25]

Renewed funding for the Children's Bureau was not imminent, however. Congress had passed the Sheppard-Towner Act in 1921 at the urging of women voters. The legislation initially appropriated $1,240,000 for the "Advancement of Maternity and Children's Welfare." In addition to $50,000 allocated for

Children's Bureau administrative expenses, each state received $5,000, and an additional $5,000 was earmarked for matching funds. Forty states signed on in 1922, with only Massachusetts, Connecticut, and Illinois failing to participate. Although states spent millions, the sum was negligible when compared to the needs of American women, especially rural southerners, and after powerful lobbying by the American Medical Association, Congress defunded the work in 1928.[26]

The 1940 FSA community-health studies had clearly revealed that rural inhabitants continued to suffer disapportionately despite earlier spending. In addition to contracting most maladies at a rate similar to or higher than that of men, rural women bore particular problems associated with childbirth. The Worth County study revealed that women suffered from many preventable childbirth-related defects, including prolapsed uterus, laceration of the cervix, and perineal damage. Another FSA study conducted in southeast Missouri found that 74.7 percent of white women needed perineal repairs and found a hemorrhoid rate twice that of the Worth County women.[27]

Although the exact number of corrective measures performed was unavailable, reports to various officials indicated that the FSA determined that 10 percent of the Worth County clients had correctable major defects and that between 30 and 50 percent had lesser problems needing treatment. In the summer of 1941, Worth County farm supervisor Joe H. Wilder and home supervisor Marie M. White obtained grants for tonsillectomies, hemorrhoidectomies, and hernia repairs. The cost estimates did not distinguish patients' gender, but it can be assumed that women comprised a significant proportion of the first two categories, and the six recipients of perineum repair were definitely female. Although documentation existed for the expenditure of $660 in these six cases, no notation surfaced concerning any treatment rendered for the remaining sixty defects of the uterus, cervix, and perineum mentioned in the report. The supervisors also advised regional health specialist T. A. Prewitt Jr. that little of the remaining work was "*urgent,* however, we had planned to have around 28 or 30 cases of Cervix Cauterization done during May and June which would amount to around $250.00 to $300.00." The availability of funds obviously determined the "urgency" surrounding treatment.[28]

The Worth County study also revealed several other problems faced by farm wives. Many suffered from venereal disease, and in most cases their husbands were also infected, although some women tested positive when their husbands did not. In two families where the mother was syphilitic, thirteen-year-old children, one female and the other male, also had positive Wassermann tests. In addition to the lack of prenatal and postnatal care, farm women also endured repeated pregnancies that severely hindered their health. The farm economy depended heavily on children's labor, and social conditioning encouraged large families. Rural women also did not have knowledge of or access to effective birth control. Several examination records recommended birth control for "spacing." One doctor commented that a patient's cervical laceration was "probably due to the fact that this individual has had 13 children and is only 38 years of age." Another report advised birth control for a forty-year-old mother and her forty-seven-year-old husband who had had twelve successive pregnancies resulting in ten children in the household between six months and twenty years of age. Another recommendation focused on the seventy-four-year-old matriarch, who appeared underweight. In addition to prescribing cataract treatment, the doctor poignantly advised, "Rest from her labors." [29]

Besides providing medical treatment, in April 1938 southern FSA staff received training in contraceptive techniques from the predecessor of the Planned Parenthood Federation of America (which came into existence in 1942). By March 1939 350 FSA county workers had been "equipped to distribute contraceptives." The program faltered, however, for several reasons. Many pharmacists refused to dispense the foam powder prescribed. The program also was so popular with clients that funds ran out. Finally, because controversy surrounded government support for or provision of birth control measures, Washington FSA officials forbade publications or administrative reports from acknowledging the FSA's participation in such programs. [30]

Other education measures, however, stirred less debate. Monthly and annual reports illustrate that nurses as well as home supervisors addressed women's problems in particular through nutritional education and prenatal care. Katherine F. Deitz, regional educational and community activities director in Atlanta, responded to Emory professor Dr. Ralph Wager's inquiry concerning health conditions in the rural South health by saying that "health education and prevention should be our first rather than our last consideration." Deitz advised Wager that most of the projects in Alabama, Georgia, Florida, and South Carolina had a full-time nurse who focused on education and immunizations rather than on bedside nursing. Piedmont Homestead nurse Elizabeth Branham, for example, requested an "immunization outfit" and syringes for additional syphilis testing in June 1939. Rosa Young, a registered nurse at Prairie Farms, thanked Deitz in the same month for a "blood pressure machine and nursery scale," reporting that twenty-eight children had attended a well-baby clinic. [31]

From 1933 until after the beginning of World War II, home economists and nurses thus labored in New Deal resettlement agencies, albeit in traditional domestic-sphere roles. The FSA attempted to ensure pay equity between blacks and whites. Records do not reveal the hiring of a black senior nurse at the top annual salary of $1,620 with a travel allowance of $40 per month, but both white and black junior nurses were paid $1,440 a year with a $30 per month allotment. Parity was not accorded to men and women in similar professional positions, however. The agency recognized male regional administrators with the title of regional director, whereas the female head of the entire FSA nursing service was only "nursing supervisor."[32]

Women also gained opportunities in nongovernmental peripheral hiring. The Dyess Farms hospital, for example, hired a seventeen-year-old project resident, Patsy Pierce, in 1943, between her junior and senior years of high school. Pierce began on-the-job training with Dr. Gervas F. Hollingsworth, assisting as a scrub nurse in surgery and delivery as well as stoking the fire at night and washing the linens. Pierce continued full time at the hospital until her marriage in 1949. From 1950 to 1953 she worked part time, resigning only for the birth of her son. The hospital closed the next year. In a 1996 interview, Pierce related that her father, Chester E. Pierce Sr., had moved his family to Dyess Farms in 1936 at the age of fifty-three. The senior Pierce farmed into his seventies and did "well enough to feed his family." Pierce took pride in her early career in nursing despite her lack of formal training.[33]

From 1933 until 1946 the medical and resettlement programs hired economists, nurses, and untrained young women such as Pierce to improve the health and livelihood of thousands of farm families. However, FERA, RA, and FSA programs suffered from infighting among USDA policy makers over conservative, laissez-faire agrarian policy and the liberal bent of New Deal social welfare experimentation. On the one hand, conservatives, including those involved in the farm extension programs, were the proponents of the family farm, fostering education and tariffs to perpetuate the middle-class yeoman farmer. These traditional agrarians strongly believed that country life was central to the survival of U.S. democracy. The reformers, on the other hand, considered themselves advocates for sharecroppers and tenants, a segment of the population that had little political clout.[34]

Moreover, rural medical programs had emanated from the field and lacked wide philosophical support. Free-market economists, supported by the American Medical Association, disagreed with progressive social reformers concerning the provision of government-subsidized medical care, decrying "socialized medicine." By the U.S. entry into the war, congressional opposition to Roosevelt, calls for decreases in nondefense spending, and growing opposition to New Deal "sociological experimentation" had all contributed to the collapse of FSA support. Beginning with fiscal year 1942, Congress reduced the FSA's appropriations. The effect was a mortal wound from which the agency did not recover. The final slash of the knife was delivered with the March 1943 creation of the U.S. House Select Committee to Investigate the Activities of the Farm Security Administration. In August 1946 President Truman signed a bill abolishing the FSA and creating its successor, the Farmers Home Administration. Anti–New Dealers had put to death the last of the radical agricultural New Deal agencies. By this time, the medical program was already lifeless.[35]

Although short-lived, these resettlement agencies offered home economists, nurses, and rural women numerous advancements. Because FSA resettlement projects were rural by design, opportunities especially grew in farming areas. Although the United States was primarily an urban nation by 1920, the southern states remained mostly rural through the 1940s. Furthermore, more than half of the nation's farmers—twenty-six million people—lived in the South. Therefore, although the FSA built projects across the United States, the South had the largest number of counties with medical projects and provided female home economists and nurses increasing employment. Still, despite these measures, many needs remained. The South, with 43.5 percent of the population, hired only 18.3 percent of the nation's nurses in 1940. FSA nurses did not reach administrative parity with their male colleagues, and black nurses were not appointed to the senior nursing position. Female professionals experienced only temporary advancement in hiring during the New Deal and World War II, gains not solidified until the women's movement of the 1970s.[36]

Furthermore, despite several polls taken during the depression and through 1945 demonstrating that Americans believed that the government should assist citizens in attaining health care, and despite the 1948 United Nations declaration that "Everyone had the right to a standard of living adequate for health and well-being of himself and of his family, including . . . medical care," more than one-sixth of Americans were still excluded from health insurance coverage and another sixth were underinsured as late as the 1990s. In 1993, President Bill Clinton failed to influence Congress to pass a broad-based medical-coverage program although he had made the issue a focal point of his campaign.

And what of the New Deal resettlement programs and their focus on farm lives and health care? What success did they have? Just as it is difficult to measure the impact of contact with professional home economists and nurses on the individual farm woman's view of women's roles, much of the measurement of the efficacy of FERA, RA, and FSA medical and home programs is anecdotal. With these programs' abrupt end, little "before and after" data exist. Olaf F. Larson of the Bureau of Agricultural Economics used surveys conducted between 1936 and 1939 to measure the improvements in client families. Larson's *Ten Years* concluded that suffering and hardship declined and that farmers made gains in income. Families also obtained better health and attained a "socially desirable level of living." Finally, farmers and their wives made "spotty gains" in "becoming full participants in a democratic way of life." Home supervisors and nurses clearly contributed to these gains and, in some measure, made gains themselves in democratic participation and in employment opportunities.[37]

Moreover, through the New Deal's rural-rehabilitation programs, professional standards from the fields of home economics, trained nursing, and professional social work were spread to the South's rural families. Home supervisors, visiting nurses, and home demonstration agents focused their attentions on farm wives and in the process acted as de facto rural social workers. With activities that frequently mirrored those of caseworkers, home supervisors brought new standards of hygiene, self-sufficiency, morality, and productivity to southern farm families. Those heavily gendered lessons, taught by a newly professionalized generation of female bureaucrats, served to bring the South's rural families closer to the mainstream of American middle-class culture.[38]

Notes

1. Histories of the FSA include Brian Q. Cannon, *Remaking the Agrarian Dream: New Deal Rural Resettlement in the Mountain West* (Albuquerque: University of New Mexico Press, 1996); Denise Montgomery, Louis Schmier, and David Williams, "The Other Depression: A Farm Security Administration Family in Carroll County," *Georgia Historical Quarterly* 77, no. 4 (1993): 811–22; Michael J. Grant, "Down and out on the Farm: Borderline Farm Families and Rural Rehabilitation in the Great Plains, 1929–1945" (Ph.D. diss., University of Kansas, 1998); *History of the Farm Security Administration* (Washington, D.C.: Farm Security Administration, 1940). Much recent work has focused on the photography of the FSA. See, for example, Nicholas Natanson, *The Black Image in the New Deal: The Politics of FSA Photography* (Knoxville: University of Tennessee Press, 1992). One of the few monographs to consider rural health in the New Deal is Michael R. Grey, *New*

Deal Medicine: The Rural Health Programs of the Farm Security Administration (Baltimore: Johns Hopkins University Press, 1999).

2. Franklin D. Roosevelt, *Looking Forward* (New York: John Day, 1933), 265; Brenda Jeanette Taylor, "The Farm Security Administration: Meeting Rural Health Needs in the South, 1933–1946" (Ph.D. diss., Texas Christian University, 1994), v–vii; Joseph Gaer, *Toward Farm Security* (Washington, D.C.: U.S. Government Printing Office, 1941), 5–6.

3. Brenda Jeanette Taylor, "Farm Security Administration," vi–vii.

4. Mildred Thurow Tate, *Home Economics as a Profession* (New York: McGraw-Hill, 1961), 325–37, 374–86; Gaer, *Toward Farm Security*, 159. See also Sarah Stage and Virginia Bramble Vincenti, eds., *Rethinking Home Economics: Women and the History of a Profession* (Ithaca: Cornell University Press, 1997); Marilyn Irvin Holt, *Linoleum, Better Babies, and the Modern Farm Woman, 1890–1930* (Albuquerque: University of New Mexico Press, 1995); Amy Elisa Ross, "Every Home a Laboratory: Arizona Farm Women, the Extension Service, and Rural Modernization, 1932–1952" (Ph.D. diss., Arizona State University, 1998); Ann Elizabeth McCleary, "Shaping a New Role for the Rural Woman: Home Demonstration Work in Augusta County, Virginia, 1917–1940" (Ph.D. diss., Brown University, 1996).

5. Gaer, *Toward Farm Security*, 127, 192–93.

6. Ibid., 98–100. Important works on farm women include Rebecca Sharpless, *Fertile Ground, Narrow Choices: Women on Texas Cotton Farms, 1900–1940* (Chapel Hill: University of North Carolina Press, 1999); Katherine Jellison, *Entitled to Power: Farm Women and Technology, 1913–1963* (Chapel Hill: University of North Carolina Press, 1993); Joan M. Jensen, *Loosening the Bonds: Mid-Atlantic Farm Women, 1750–1850* (New Haven: Yale University Press, 1986).

7. "Household Inventory and Personal History," box 22, "Plans and Forms" file, E 59, RG 96, Farmer's Home Administration, National Archives–Southeast Region, East Point, Ga. (hereafter, FHASE); Gaer, *Toward Farm Security*, 73–74.

8. "Household Inventory"; Gaer, *Toward Farm Security*.

9. "Status of Home Management Plans of Farm Security Projects," June 1–30, 1938; November 1–30, 1938; May 24–June 24, 1940, box 5, "Farm and Home Plans" file, E 59, FHASE; Rena B. Maycock, "Home Economic Work in the Resettlement Administration," *Journal of Home Economics* 27 (October 1936): 561. Maycock, chief of Region IX, including Arizona, California, Nevada, and Utah, was one of twelve chief home economists.

10. Boggs to Helen Estabrook, February 15, 1936, box 2, unmarked file, E 77, FHASE.

11. "Home Management Program in 1936," box 1, "Home Management" file, E 76, FHASE.

12. Ware to Slack, October 13, 1937; George S. Mitchell to Will W. Alexander, October 16, 1937, box 1, "Health" file, E 61, Correspondence File of James S. Heizer, 1937–39, FHASE.

13. Browning to Slack, September 25, 1937, box 1, "Heizer" file, FHASE.

14. Ibid.

15. Paul Conkin, *Tomorrow a New World: The New Deal Community Program* (Ithaca: Cornell University Press, 1959), 187; Jerry Beth Shannon, "History of the Ropesville Project," 16–17, 48, Southwest Collection, Texas Tech University, Lubbock; petition from A. F. Allred, March 13, 1934, box 11, "Letters Concerning Ropesville Community," file, Lubbock Chamber of Commerce Papers, Southwest Collection.

16. On public-health nursing during the New Deal, see Marlene Hockenberry Cianci, "Public Health Nursing during the Great Depression: The Maryland Experience" (Ph.D. diss., George Mason University, 1997); Rose Broeckel Cannon, "Georgia's Twentieth Century Public Health Nurses: A Social History of Racial Relations" (Ph.D. diss., Emory University, 1995); Margaret Ellen Kidd Parsons, "White Plague and Double-Barred Cross in Atlanta, 1895–1945" (Ph.D. diss., Emory University, 1985).

17. Correspondence between Oleson and Rexford Tugwell's office, February 20, 1936, box 71, "Medical Services" file, E 13, General Correspondence of the Resettlement Division, RG 96, Farmer's Home Administration, National Archives, Washington, D.C. (hereafter, FHA).

18. Matilda Ann Wade, "Community Nursing—FSA Style," *Public Health Nursing* (February 1942): 1–7. Although Wade reported that the resettlement projects employed only forty-five nurses in February 1942, the "Annual Report of the Office of the FSA Chief Medical Officer, 1940–1941" indicated that fifty nurses served in rural homestead communities as of June 1941 ("Annual Report," box 71, "Medical Services" file, E 13, General Correspondence of the Resettlement Division, 1935–42, FHA). Resignations or reassignment of nurses because of the war effort could explain the difference.

19. "Region VI Summary of Activities of Community Nurses, August 1941," box 22, "Reports" file, E 13, General Correspondence of the Resettlement Division, 1935–42, FHA.

20. Shannon, "History of the Ropesville Project," 13–14; memo concerning housing estimates, box 7, "Ropesville Farms Project" file, E 106, Region VIII Project Records, RG 96, National Archives–Southwest Region, Fort Worth, Tex.; Project Records, 1935–40, FHA; "Report of the Interbureau Coordinating Committee on Rural Housing," box 7, E 25, RG 83, Bureau of Agricultural Economics Papers, National Archives, Washington, D.C.

21. Charles Reagan Wilson and William Ferris, eds., *Encyclopedia of Southern Culture* (Chapel Hill: University of North Carolina Press, 1989), 1144–45; Carl C. Taylor, ed., *Rural Life in the United States* (New York: Alfred A. Knopf, 1949), 157–58.

22. Carl C. Taylor, *Rural Life*, 41–44; Gaer, *Toward Farm Security*, 70–71; William C. Holley, *The Plantation South, 1934–1937* (Washington, D.C.: Works Projects Administration, 1940), 60; John Duffy, *The Sanitarians: A History of American Public Health* (Urbana: University of Illinois Press, 1992), 229–33, 65. See also John Ettling, *The Germ of Laziness: Rockefeller Philanthropy and Public Health in the New South*

(Cambridge: Harvard University Press, 1981); Elizabeth W. Etheridge, *The Butter-fly Caste: a Social History of Pellagra in the South* (Westport, Conn.: Greenwood, 1972).

23. Frederick D. Mott and Milton I. Roemer, *Rural Health and Medical Care* (New York: McGraw-Hill, 1948), 124–30.

24. "Farm and Home Plan," October 4, 1940, box 4, E 59, Region IV General Correspondence of the Regional Office, 1935–41, FHA.

25. "Maternal and Infant Study, 1933," box 209, Information File, 1914–68, RG 102, Records of the Children's Bureau, National Archives, Washington, D.C.

26. Duffy, *Sanitarians,* 247–48. On the Children's Bureau, see esp. Kriste Lindenmeyer, *"A Right to Childhood": The U.S. Children's Bureau and Child Welfare, 1912–1946* (Urbana: University of Illinois Press, 1997); and Robyn Muncy, *Creating a Female Dominion in American Reform, 1890–1935* (New York: Oxford University Press, 1994). On earlier maternal and infant health crusades, see Richard M. Meckel, *"Save the Babies": American Public Health Reform and the Prevention of Infant Mortality, 1850–1929* (Baltimore: Johns Hopkins University Press, 1990); and Alisa Klaus, *Every Child a Lion: The Origins of Maternal and Infant Health Policy in the United States and France, 1890–1920* (Ithaca: Cornell University Press, 1993).

27. Mott and Roemer, *Rural Health,* 130.

28. "Narrative: Physical Defects Found by the General Medical Examinations of Farm Security Administration Clients of Worth County, Georgia," November 1939, and Wilder and White to Prewitt, box 206, E 7, Records of and Relating to Cooperative Associations, 1935–54, FHA.

29. "Narrative"; Wilder and White to Prewitt, box 206, E 7, Records of and Relating to Cooperative Associations, 1935–54, FHA.

30. James Reed, *From Private Vice to Public Virtue* (New York: Basic Books, 1978), 264–67.

31. Deitz to Wager, January 17, 1939, monthly report from Branham, June 23, 1939, monthly report from Young, June 24, 1939, box 12, "Health" file E 93, Region V General Correspondence of the Director, FHASE.

32. Memo from Roy Reid, March 10, 1939, box 71, "Medical Services," file, E 13, General Correspondence of the Resettlement Division, 1935–42, FHA.

33. Patsy Pierce Carmichael, interview by Brenda Taylor, March 1997, Dyess, Ark.

34. Brenda Jeanette Taylor, "Farm Security Administration," 171–86.

35. Ibid.

36. Mott and Roemer, *Rural Health,* 6–14, 192–96.

37. Sidney Baldwin, *Poverty and Politics* (Chapel Hill: University of North Carolina Press, 1968), 211–12.

38. See esp. Daniel J. Walkowitz, *Working with Class: Social Workers and the Politics of Middle-Class Identity* (Chapel Hill: University of North Carolina Press, 1999).

"Hopeful People on the Move"

The Urban South and the Transient Problem during the Great Depression

JEFFREY S. COLE

Referring to transiency as a "national growing pain," a 1930s Works Projects Administration publication entitled *Depression Pioneers* insisted that the quest for greener pastures "is as American as baked beans."[1] Indeed, transiency was not new, but the economic conditions of the Great Depression exacerbated it. As the "pioneers" of the early 1930s left the familiar to escape the tyranny of economic adversity, most only increased their misery by setting out on the highways and byways of the land of opportunity. Despite the romanticism portrayed by this publication, the men, women, and children who took to the nation's rails and roads during the 1930s found themselves unwelcome in cities and towns across the country. Commonly considered a parasitical nuisance, those who chose the pioneering life were not helping to build a new nation or to fill jobs in factories booming from prosperity but rather were threatening to take away precious relief from local citizens. Once privately funded organizations faltered under the burden of mounting demands for relief during the Hoover years, charities and citizens turned to municipal governments for help. As the depression deepened, localities often experienced financial difficulties and implemented austerity measures that limited relief.

Transiency became an acute problem in many southern states between the close of 1929 and early 1933, particularly in cities and towns convenient to major rail lines and highways. Because urban areas throughout the South struggled to care for their local needy, they rarely extended the proverbial southern hospitality to transients. The New Deal's Transient Division (1933–35), initiated under the auspices of the Federal Emergency Relief Administration, proved a mixed blessing for the urban South and transients. Most communities accepted the presence of federal transient bureaus out of necessity. Washington's efforts removed the burden of caring for nonresidents but also, some local leaders argued, attracted transients and encouraged wandering. This study of transiency, however, reveals that many communities initially opposed to the federal program quickly recognized the practicality of it and strongly protested its liquidation in 1935. In fact, community leaders across the South argued that the federal government had a duty to continue its work among transients because wandering was a national problem. An examination of the course of the program demonstrates that a social welfare policy intended as a temporary expedient became ingrained in southern communities because it removed a scourge and at the same time brought financial rewards. A regional survey of the short-lived program also demonstrates that the New Deal's successful endeavor failed to alter deep-seated social welfare policies that discriminated against Americans who roamed.

Prior to the onset of the Great Depression, seasonal workers and professional hobos comprised the vast majority of the transient population.[2] The economic ravages of the early 1930s significantly altered the traditional profile, however. The reasons for transiency varied widely but were most often associated with unemployment, adventure seeking, boredom, personal or family problems, inadequate relief, or a combination of these factors. Okies deserted the Dust Bowl in search of work and a new life, as John Steinbeck movingly portrays in *The Grapes of Wrath*. Curious teenagers, in the spirit of Horatio Alger novels, abandoned their homes in pursuit of adventure. The nomads, young and old alike, held to the hope that a different locale might provide a respite from the despair they fled. The desperate gravitated toward urban centers because they believed that an abundance of factories implied job opportunities. Unfortunately, they quickly discovered that conditions elsewhere differed little from those they fled. Lorena Hickok, an aide to President Franklin Delano Roosevelt's chief relief administrator, Harry Hopkins, traveled the nation and kept her boss informed of her discoveries. Of the nation's horde of wanderers, she wrote, "This transient thing is funny. Men unable to get work in California and en route to the Kansas wheat fields, actually meet up in Denver with men unable to get work in the Kansas wheat fields and on their way to California."[3] A 1933 Texas study confirmed Hickok's intimation that the grass always seemed greener elsewhere, concluding that "the flow of transients has a wide and varied source and that it is difficult to assign any particular reason for any certain territorial origen [sic]."[4]

During the early depression years, when Herbert Hoover extolled the virtues of self-sufficiency and advocated reliance on local and private charitable efforts, transients usually found towns and cities inhospitable. A meal or two, accommodations for one night (often at the town jail), and an invitation to leave at their earliest convenience was all the hospitality most wanderers received. Some localities required their guests to pick cotton or fruit or to milk cows before sending the migrants on their way.[5] Until the establishment of the federal Transient Division, the unofficial policy that prevailed in Flomation, Alabama, was common: "Keep the transients off the streets . . . and move them along as soon as possible."[6] Strangers found receiving communities hostile not only because the burden of caring for their own neighbors strained diminishing resources but also because American ideas about relief were securely rooted in English poor laws, which assigned responsibility for assistance to the transients' home communities.[7]

Because cities and towns found themselves inundated with migrants in need of work and relief, localities did not bother to count the new arrivals but focused on dealing with the emergency. Estimates of the size of the transient population during the Hoover years vary from four hundred thousand to more than two million persons.[8] Individuals and families left the familiar for the unknown not in great droves at the same time but gradually, as work ran out, living expenses depleted savings accounts, banks repossessed homes and farms, and the prospects for local relief deteriorated.

Although the transients' numerical strength remains a mystery, their characteristics are well defined. The population encompassed couples, a small percentage of women, and families with children, called by their contemporaries "rubber tramps," "gasoline gypsies," or "tin-can tourists" because they often traveled by automobile, usually their last vestige of social prestige.[9] White males traveling alone, however, comprised the majority of the nomadic army.[10] A federal study conducted during 1934–35 found that the average white single male transient was between the ages of twenty and forty-five, had completed the eighth grade (at least), was willing and able to work, was unskilled or semiskilled, and hailed from an urban area.[11] Although not the customary clan of drifters, the recently displaced group associated with hobos, tramps, and bums on trains and in "jungles" where the habitual migrants congregated. Troubled by the moral effects of migration on temporary wanderers, a Salvation Army official stated, "We are alarmed to find that . . . the roving life is having serious effect upon the characters of the men themselves. Through hunger and deprivation a large number of them are becoming beggars and petty thieves." Although the majority of the depression's migrants were men who sought work, the Salvation Army worried that the transients might "lose the work habit and technical skills acquired by training and so deteriorate in character as to constitute a menace to society for years to come."[12] The men's health also concerned relief agencies. Exposure to the elements, especially during cold weather, and the unsanitary conditions in which they traveled nourished dysentery, tuberculosis, influenza, pneumonia, colds, and other maladies. A diet of soup, beans, bread, and coffee also contributed to precarious health. An investigator posing as a transient in Alabama and Florida found that the "Sallys" (Salvation Army workers) regularly served such a diet and sometimes a couple of slices of tomato.[13]

Teenagers and young men in their early twenties comprised a significant portion of the male transient population. Although some sought work or hit the road to escape unhappy homes, many set out in search of adventure. Investigators in St. Louis spoke with a fatherless eighteen-year-old who had been away from his hometown of Houston for three weeks. He was out "to see the world" but, in the investigators' opinion, was "picking up the ways of the road entirely too fast for his own good." The interviewers presented a seventeen-year-old boy from Georgia as "rather typical" of transients. He "did not know where he was going and did not care. He explained that he did not have a trade and did not know where he could get work so he was just drifting around. . . . He has decided that he can get just as much work while drifting around and can have a change of scenery along with it," they reported. Another Georgia teen headed for Kansas City left home "just for the fun of it" and was tired of life on the road after a week.[14]

While some men found hitchhiking convenient, many male migrants rode the rails because they provided the fastest and most independent means of travel. In the South, which had great stretches of thinly populated territory, railways were the preferred mode of transportation. Few depression-era drifters had the resources to purchase a ticket for a Pullman car, so most instead stole away on freight trains. Testifying before a Senate subcommittee investigating transiency, an agent with the Missouri Pacific Railroad reported that the number of persons traveling illegally on the line increased more than tenfold between 1929 and 1932. Because the problem was so acute, the Missouri Pacific stopped arresting and fining the trespassers and merely escorted them off of railroad property. Other railroads ignored the drifters traveling on freight trains but ejected stowaways from passenger trains. Rather than remove transients, the Missouri Pacific often permitted them to ride its afternoon "fast freight" from St. Louis to Texas. By September 1933, authorities estimated that some three thousand free riders arrived in St. Louis daily by rail.[15] Officials not only sympathized with the plight of the depression's pioneers but also found arresting trespassers futile because the drifters desired the accommodations and meals local police supplied.[16] "Dad" Moore, a "yard policeman" at the L&N freight yards in Mobile, Alabama, told an investigator that he did not arrest wanderers unless they committed serious crimes. Mobile officials instructed him not to bring transients to the city jail because the municipality could not afford to feed them.[17]

Even if a locality had the means to provide for transients, it certainly did not wish to advertise its generosity for fear that its benevolence might bring more gypsies to its gates. A resident of Texarkana, Texas, remarked, "I live near the intersection of two national highways and the back doors in our neighborhood are beginning to need repairs from the constant hammering by the . . . indigent wayfarer who never bothers with the organized charities but prefers to depend on the ever ready sympathies of the housewife."[18] Many communities referred transients to the Salvation Army or other private relief organizations. Across the South, Sallys found themselves inundated with wanderers and patched together assistance as best as possible. In Richmond, Virginia, investigators discovered conditions they labeled "the worst we have ever seen." The facilities were crowded and unsuitable, the superintendent incompetent, and the men had nothing to do but loaf all day. In Roanoke, state investigators lamented that men often had to sleep two to a bed in a "cheerless [building] with no refinements of home-life."[19] Most Salvation Army facilities did the best they could with available funds collected from local drives but not supplemented by local government money.

Taxpayers also did not want to help drifters, whom the sedentary population believed brought crime and disease. Testifying before a Senate committee in January 1933, a California official declared, "It is our feeling that the nonresident transient man is one of the greatest problems we have to contend with in the state." Approximately one hundred thousand men had entered the state during the final month of 1932 without money and in search of work. California's situation was not unique. Southern states with salubrious climates also attracted transients and found their resources stretched to the limits.[20] Florida, Texas, and Louisiana were among the states that received the largest number of wanderers as the federal transient program commenced.[21] Texarkana, a rail and highway juncture located on border between Texas and Arkansas, for example, hosted 10,198 transients between February 1 and July 7, 1933. The United Charities called this "a startling number" because it equaled one-third of Texarkana's population. Furthermore, the organization estimated that only half of those who passed through Texarkana bothered to register. The wanderers hailed from every state as well as Europe, Latin America, Canada, and Hawaii. When asked where they were headed, the transients cited all of America's states except Delaware. Some even claimed to be headed for South and Central America, Canada, Cuba, and Hawaii.[22]

State and local government officials, private relief agencies, and transients themselves believed that only action by the federal government could ameliorate the economic and social difficulties caused by transiency, a problem of national proportions.[23] In the storm of legislation that accompanied the initial hundred days of the Roosevelt administration, Congress approved the Federal Emergency Relief Act, which created the Federal Emergency Relief Administration (FERA), the New Deal's first effort to address the problems of unemployment through public relief measures. Congress financed the stopgap agency with a five hundred million dollar appropriation and allocated fifteen million dollars for transient relief. Like many of the other problems the president and his advisers addressed, dealing with transiency meant entering "uncharted and hazardous territory." Hopkins noted that the federal government did not possess an accurate picture of the size of the transient population and was "confused as to whether transiency should properly be treated as an evil to be suppressed or as a necessary function of our economy to be rendered as painless as possible."[24] Providing transients with the right to relief was also treacherous political territory for Washington, given the strong public sentiments against wanderers during a time of severe economic difficulty.[25]

In late July 1933, Washington encouraged states to begin planning for the care of nonresidents (those residing in a state for less than a year). The FERA's Transient Division began to function in late August 1933 and funneled money to states as they presented their plans to the federal government. Although transiency presented serious problems to localities, Washington found it necessary to expend great effort to motivate states to submit plans for nonresident care. Urban leaders believed that transient bureaus would serve as magnets for undesirables. Federal officials discovered that enabling the program to work required overcoming "deep-seated prejudices" toward transients. By the close of the year, however, forty states and Washington, D.C., had received approval for their programs and established 261 transient bureaus and 63 work camps. The South had 81 of the bureaus and camps, led by Texas (with 15 camps),

Missouri (8), and Virginia (8).[26] The state bureaus operated under the direct supervision of the state relief administrations, which functioned under the FERA's guidance.

Under the FERA, funding for some programs depended on matching moneys from the states, but the federal government alone bore the financial burden for the transient bureaus because most localities did not have the means to aid indigents or refused to help them. As the FERA's Transient Division supplied the means for the care of the nation's homeless, the wanderers gained the right to relief rather than expulsion from the localities they entered.[27] Comparing the depression's pioneers with those in America's past, Hopkins argued that helping transients "in their search for re-establishment is just as logical as when the government encouraged the settlement of the West by grants of homesteads to hopeful people on the move."[28] With the commencement of the federal transient program, which relied on state and local administrative apparatus for its operation, the government replaced traditional methods of dealing with wanderers (such as the "passing-on" system) with programs that sought to diminish drifting.

Although Washington mandated standards for state transient programs, great variety existed, in large measure because of the need to take drastic measures to deal with an emergency situation. Florida's transient system, although much more extensive than that of most states, provides an example of the apparatus southern states devised. Twenty-two Florida localities had facilities that cared overnight for wanderers. After a brief stay at one of these centers, drifters were transferred to an urban bureau, the focal point of transient care operations. These were located in six Florida cities: Jacksonville, Pensacola, Ocala, St. Petersburg, Tampa, and Miami. Social workers at these sites interviewed the transients; passed them on to doctors and nurses, who performed medical evaluations; provided clothing; and either kept the migrants at the urban bureaus or sent them to nearby work camps. Florida established camps for men outside Jacksonville, Tampa, and Miami. Work teams from the urban bureaus constructed a national cemetery at St. Petersburg's veterans' hospital, operated Miami's city farm, and finished building the Pensacola municipal airport, a project abandoned by the Civil Works Administration. The bureaus required each able man to work thirty hours a week. The transients usually earned an allowance of ninety cents weekly but were eligible for increases if they proved themselves dedicated to their assigned tasks.[29] The number and type of shelters in a state such as North Carolina reflects the nature of the transient population throughout the South. By the summer of 1934, the Tarheel

State had six shelters for white men, two for African Americans, and one for women.[30] Transient females provided bureaus with special challenges. Such women at times were housed in shelters; at other times, they were referred immediately to the Travelers Aid Society (as in Nashville, Knoxville, and Chattanooga) and returned to their permanent residences, if possible.[31] Few surviving documents provide adequate descriptions of the efforts dedicated to the female transient population. Women presented "complicated" problems, according to a Florida observer, but documents rarely indicate what those were.[32] One observer wrote that she believed that "women are not wanderers fundamentally. If plans were made for them locally, few would go on the road."[33] No matter the state, the Transient Division focused on unattached men and boys.

The emergency nature of the transient problem necessitated converting existing structures to housing and office space as quickly as possible. As a result, many bureaus across the nation had inadequate facilities for transient care. In a 1934 publication, the National Association for Travelers Aid and the Transient Service warned against sheltering men in buildings not "originally constructed for human habitation." While the association realized that buildings previously devoted to commercial activity might provide more space, the structures usually did not have appropriate safety features (such as fire escapes) or "adequate plumbing and heating facilities." The publication advised administrators to consider the feelings of potential residents when searching for structures to house and care for indigents, noting that a former warehouse, factory, or store might foster "an atmosphere of bleakness and a feeling among the residents of being an outcast group."[34] As men pursuing lodging, meals, and work entered localities across the nation in droves, however, finding a convenient, serviceable shelter, not the mental state of wanderers, was the foremost consideration. Meeting physical needs came first. Writing later in the decade, Hopkins characterized the makeshift accommodations as "thinly disguised flophouses."[35] San Antonio's clients lived at the County Farm in a building that had previously housed juvenile delinquents.[36] Greensboro's bureau originally operated in an old post office.[37] The Memphis bureau accommodated boys in a "swanky building" that was formerly home to a medical fraternity.[38] The Knoxville, Tennessee, bureau was located in two old apartment buildings.[39] Richmond's shelter for blacks was located in a building abandoned by a black college.[40] In Lynchburg, Virginia, workers transformed a former business college and Oakland car dealership on the outskirts of the downtown business district into a dormitory for male wanderers. The Transient Division's greatest tragedy occurred at the Lynchburg facility on March 24, 1934, when an early morning kitchen fire rose through the building's abandoned elevator shaft, sending smoke and flames to the upper floor, where 107 black and 83 white males were housed in a segregated sleeping area intended for 100. City residents gathered on the icy street below and watched in horror as men jumped from second-story windows, many of which had been boarded up to provide the transients with privacy. The facility's fire extinguishers had been locked up for the night in a room to which the sleeping night watchman had the key. The structure had no fire escapes because the city's building code did not require the safety devices on structures under three stories. The grease fire claimed the lives of 19 men and left 70 others with severe burns and fractures.[41]

Because the Transient Division operated as a partnership among the federal government, states, and localities, each bureau had an advisory committee comprised of citizens from the community. These boards were vital to the Transient Division's initial success because of many communities' opposition to the presence of bureaus. Trying to patch together programs for transients, states and localities found it vital to educate citizens about the value and type of work to be done among the wandering population. A report from Virginia noted, "Through these committees the relationship [between Washington and the localities] has been made quite successful. In the beginning some communities felt uncertain as to the merits of transient work. They appeared to feel that such an agency would attract undesirables or 'hoboes' to the city."[42] Sentiments in Lynchburg were similar: "No less than a dozen intelligent lay persons," one official observed, "have expressed their disapproval to the too benevolent government program."[43] Because transients often received better care than those who remained at their legal residences, some people saw the road as a viable and better alternative. The urban centers were established to address wanderers' immediate needs. Meeting more than the physical needs of transients was at first a secondary concern. Casework, medical attention, education, recreation, and work projects were added as time and resources permitted. A North Carolina official described what she termed the "Center Program," which consisted of "rest, play, medical treatment, plenty of nourishing food three times daily, frequent showers and clean clothing with regular work on some approved Project suitable to the physical and mental equipment of the client while former employer, family, or friends are reached by wire, telephone or letter in an effort to re-establish or secure employment." She described the work as "a united effort to aid lonely, homeless, wandering humanity in finding themselves and fitting into a place where they may take their share of the World's work and carry on in Peace."[44]

Ranald Savery, an investigator with the Alabama Relief Administration who posed as a transient, reported that the men he observed were not provided with enough activities to fill their time. "I think this is one of the most important problems of relief for the transients," he commented. "They live in a world by themselves and, psychologically, have no chance to get out of it."[45] Administrators at urban centers found it necessary to create or find jobs for transients or to devise ways for them to fill their time and help contribute positively to society. Some established shoe repair shops and barbershops; put men to work improving the facilities, cooking, or performing administrative duties; or provided recreational opportunities. Transient helping transient was the approach to relief taken by many bureaus. In Salisbury, North Carolina, supervisors found that putting men to work aiding each other helped transients feel as if they were not a burden to society.[46] Educational opportunities abounded at most centers. The slate of offerings at the Georgia bureaus was typical. Depending on the skills of transients, some centers offered business arithmetic, typing, foreign languages, and vocational classes in electricity, plumbing, brick making, and blueprint reading.[47] The Baton Rouge bureau enrolled youth in local public schools as well as in courses offered at Louisiana State University. The Lone Star State located one of its bureaus at Texas A&M University, where the men were reported to be "working above average."[48] There, two hundred young transients took vocational courses or enrolled in college classes while working on campus projects.[49] The New Orleans facility boasted tremendous success with its youth population. Officials claimed that 97 percent of those registered at the shelter attended classes weekly. As was typical across the South, however, courses for black transients had yet to be organized nearly a year into the program.[50] The arts flourished at many bureaus. Tennessee reported that some transients had formed glee clubs or orchestras, and others performed minstrel and vaudeville shows.[51]

An activity common to many bureaus and camps was the publication of a newsletter. Residents at some two hundred locations across the nation published journals funded with profits from transient-operated canteens.[52] Bryan J. Boyle, the editor of St. Petersburg's *Windjammer*, recognized the publications' long-term value: "We feel that our transient publications of today will become important source documents for the historians who will some day write a comprehensive history of this important period. We wish to put into *The Windjammer* enough of the color and interest accompanying our social position to make it of more than temporary value."[53] The diversity of the transient population fostered interesting publications that reflect transient life and, indeed, reveal much about the people who traveled America during the depression. Originally intended for leisure reading at the shelters where they were published, the uncensored and unofficial publications circulated across the United States and gave rise to friendly competition. Each included sections offering praise and helpful criticism to other newsletters. Two of Tennessee's publications, for example, were labeled "high-brow."[54] Others were praised for their editorials or informed that they needed to include more art. Their titles reflected their authors' creativity: Atlanta had the *Pilgrim's Progress;* Louisville published the *Crossroads* and Lexington the *Ark;* Amarillo, Texas, had the *Panhandle.*

Even though the New Deal guaranteed transients the right to relief, it could not guarantee positive community response to the presence of a shelter or to the transients themselves. Rather than looking beyond the unshaven travelers' dirty, tattered clothes and seeing recently productive members of society temporarily down on their luck, sedentary citizens often passed moral judgment on transients, labeling them lazy, disease-ridden persons who depended on handouts for their livelihood. A government publication, however, insisted that "there was evidently nothing habit-forming in federal transient aid," because only "about 10 percent of the migrants appeared again and again at one point or another asking for help."[55] Nevertheless, transients remained unpopular. Harry J. Early, the director of Louisiana's Emergency Relief Administration, informed Hopkins that "the transient operations are in every way undesirable from the standpoint of local citizens" and painted a sinister picture of the transient. "Inevitably," Early wrote, "these people roaming the community become a cause for alarm for the reason that it is commonly known that transient operations provide a means for persons of doubtful character, communistic and otherwise, to temporarily reside in as transients but who, in many cases, have other and ulterior purposes to serve." He suggested an end to the transient program in his state.[56] A Florida community petitioned Washington to place a transient camp elsewhere because the locality "had all the crime [it] could handle."[57] Texas officials noted similar problems early in the program's tenure: "There was on the part of the general public, police forces, and other organizations a feeling that there would be brought into the community a concentrating point for undesirables."[58]

Through the establishment of "forceful and constructive" programs in most states, however, bureaus worked to improve relationships with the communities they served.[59] The director of the Kentucky Emergency Relief Administration took to the airwaves during the first year that the state's five urban transient centers and five camps operated and assured citizens of their necessity and usefulness. He also invited Kentuckians to visit the center or camp nearest them.[60] More than six hundred people in Lexington accepted his invitation. Workers there reported, "In many instances individuals have expressed that they have changed their opinion in connection with transients and transient service after personal visits to our facilities, not only in the observation of the way the service is conducted but in the control of men, their conduct, desire to work and various individual backgrounds on the part of the transients."[61] In Corbin, Kentucky, officials visited "luncheon clubs" in an effort to familiarize citizens with the local bureau's work. The relationships between transients and the citizens of Salisbury, North Carolina, were especially cordial. On one occasion, a transient spoke to a local citizens' group about the use and abuse of alcohol. The bureau also cooperated with churches to get men involved in Sunday services. Members of the First Methodist Church even provided transportation for the men during the winter. When Catawba College presented Gilbert and Sullivan's *Mikado,* residents picked up transients and took them to the theater. The bureau's motivation for all of these activities was to "establish personal contact" between Salisbury's citizens and transients. Contacts between the black community and black transients were not as extensive as between white transients and the white community, but officials made educational and religious programs available to African American wanderers.[62]

Relationships in some communities were strained. In Louisville, for example, local newspapers regularly "harassed the Bureau" and its officials and helped perpetuate a negative tone toward the organization's work in the community.[63] In Miami, despite the bureau's efforts, the police department continued to follow its pre–New Deal policy of loading transients on trucks and dropping them off at the county line.[64] One night in late November 1934, the police chief of Asheville, North Carolina, arrested all of the city's bureau residents except an ill wanderer on trumped-up vagrancy charges. From the beginning, citizens living nearby had lodged a variety of complaints against the shelter's inhabitants. The facility was located in a nice residential section of the city and next door to an upscale apartment building. Area residents complained that begging was frequent, told of robbery attempts and of men who insulted female passersby, and complained that transients "sat on the front porch on Sundays in an unholy manner, while people went to the three churches surrounding the Center." The area's denizens also noted seeing men walking around naked in the basement, drinking on the fire escape, and picking produce from residents' gardens. The arrests confirmed what citizens of Asheville suspected: there were many undesirables among the bureau's population. Nineteen of the fifty-four men arrested had criminal records. Many of the problems, though, were attributable to the shelter's poor management, the tactlessness of its director, a lack of communication and cooperation with the community, and poor site selection. Despite the problems, however, the raid was illegal: the police chief admitted this fact to a federal investigator but stated that he was forced to take the action in light of the volume of complaints the police received about the bureau.[65]

The location of the Big Spring, Texas, bureau fostered ill will within that community. The bureau was situated across the street from the Howard County Relief Board, and when the locality was unable adequately to meet the needs of the local population, citizens wondered aloud why the transients should live so well at the hands of Uncle Sam. Ongoing hostility toward the bureau and its residents led state officials to convert it to a facility that provided only overnight care. The bureau transferred the remainder of the transients to a nearby Civilian Conservation Corps camp.[66] Tennessee reported similar problems, observing that local "relief agencies continue to be jealous because it has been possible to do certain things for the transients that have not been done for the [local] residents."[67] In an attempt to justify dedicating more funds to transient cases than local citizens on relief received, a Florida official wrote, "Those who feel that the transient is receiving favored consideration, should pause to think that for three long years of the depression, the transient, without any relief, has been battered about until his character and resources have reached the zero point. While cities, counties and states provided for their families and resident people, the transient was unrecognized." He also explained that the twin goals of relief and rehabilitation were more costly than relief alone.[68] The economic benefits of the transient bureaus, however, kept complaints in most southern communities to a minimum.

Although the FERA's policies provided access to relief no matter one's skin color, segregation was the order of the day in the South. A 1934 evaluation of the Federal Transient Program reported stronger feelings against black wanderers than against whites. The investigators discovered that some centers in the South did not have any black applicants, a phenomenon they attributed to the desire of "colored applicants" to stay out of harm's way as well as their ability to secure lodging in black neighborhoods. Memphis, Fort Worth, and many other southern municipalities had separate shelters for blacks, which evaluators found less desirable than institutions for white transients.[69] Montgomery and Birmingham had Alabama's largest populations of black transients and employed a staff of black caseworkers to serve that group. The bureaus processed whites and blacks in the same office, and a Montgomery official noted that "not a complaint or an instance of friction" resulted from the arrangement. "It is the known policy of the bureau," he noted, "that everyone is human and each individual is due courtesy and humane treatment."[70]

Officials in Jacksonville claimed severe problems with black transients who sent their children to rummage through garbage bins of the city's grocery stores. Of greater concern was the nationwide reputation that the city earned during the 1920s as the murder capital of the world. Authorities found that blacks were involved in the majority of the homicides and maintained that black transiency exacerbated the problem. Thus, the desire to establish a "Negro Transient Bureau" in Jacksonville was particularly strong. At the bureau, the indigents received food, clothing, shelter, and medical care, but educational, recreational, and arts programs took longer to come than those established at centers for whites. Florida organized a camp for blacks just outside of the city.[71] Until March 1934 the Lynchburg, Virginia, bureau served whites and blacks at the same location but provided separate sleeping areas on the upper floor and separate staircases leading to the dormitories. Partial segregation was not uncommon even in shelters throughout the North and West.[72]

The Transient Division's immediate goals were to relieve the localities of the burden of caring for the nomads and to provide them with food, clothing, shelter, and medical assistance. Washington's goal was not to end transiency, a task it admitted was impossible, but to "lessen the evils of transiency."[73] The federal government tried to prevent wandering by discouraging hitchhiking and freight train riding and sought to stem the regular practice of "back-door begging," an annoyance in many communities.[74]

January 1934 marked an important point in the federal transient program because it signaled the onset of a concerted effort to clamp down on transiency. As 1933 came to a close, Washington directed bureaus to inform transients that after the new year they were to remain where they were. Hitchhiking was to be discouraged, and bureaus posted signs and distributed bulletins announcing the new policy. In addition to a focus on the bureaus, the government asked railroads to stop transients from catching rides on trains.[75] The policy necessitated the continued establishment of transient centers across the nation and helped increase the importance of transient camps. Developed concurrently with the urban bureaus, the camps were designed to deal with the long-term problems associated with transiency and to keep people in one place as long as possible. Most urban bureaus had direct ties to camps nearby and sent men to them regularly. By encouraging transients to remain in one place, Washington not only increased the wanderers' chances of returning to a sedentary life but also promoted better health while improving morale and self-esteem.

In 1935 Congress approved the Works Progress Administration (wpa) and returned transient care to states and localities. Washington ordered federal transient centers to stop accepting transients on September 20 and closed the bureaus on November 1. Roosevelt and Hopkins disliked the dole and preferred work relief. In his January 1935 State of the Union Address, fdr pronounced the death of the Transient Division and other emergency agencies that focused on relief: "The lessons of history . . . show conclusively that continued dependence upon relief induces a spiritual and moral disintegration fundamentally destructive to the national fibre. To dole out relief in this way is to administer a narcotic, a subtle destroyer of the human spirit. . . . It is in violation of the traditions of America. Work must be found for able-bodied but destitute workers. The Federal Government must and shall quit this business of relief."[76] Hopkins also disliked the practice of isolating drifters from society, believing that the separation was "bad, both from the point of view of the men themselves and its effect on the public reaction to the Work Program." He recognized, however, the value of maintaining camps and transient projects already under way to complete projects that localities or other federal agencies could not complete.[77] With the liquidation of the fera and its Transient Division, Washington believed that wanderers could be integrated into federal work projects under the wpa. Authorities advised transient center officials to encourage transients to return to their legal residences so that they would have a better chance to be absorbed into the wpa's work programs.[78]

The federal transient bureaus benefited southern cities because they removed from localities the burden of caring for outsiders. When Hopkins decided to close the centers in 1935 and transfer the residents to camps or wpa projects, many of the same cities and towns that originally protested the placement of bureaus in their communities petitioned Washington to keep the institutions open. Hopkins received hundreds of telegrams and letters from across the nation protesting the Transient Division's liquidation. Nashville's

Council of Social Agencies complained that the municipality was "totally unprepared" to care for the three hundred wanderers who were released from
the bureau. The council's leaders were particularly concerned that the bureaus were closing in the fall, because the autumn and winter months usually
brought more wanderers to the city.[79] Atlanta's Social Welfare Council also announced that it was "totally unprepared" and asked Hopkins to delay the liquidation of the transient program.[80] The Chamber of Commerce in Meridian,
Mississippi, recounted the three hundred thousand hours of community service performed by transients.[81] Amarillo's Community Chest asked Hopkins
to reconsider his order to close the bureaus, calling them "one of the greatest
pieces of social work done in the relief plan of the Federal Government."[82]
Richmond's Council of Social Agencies argued that the success of the federal
transient program demonstrated that because local transient policy varied,
only Washington could bring consistency to transient care, and New Orleans's
Joint Anti-Begging Committee voiced similar concerns.[83] Washington, however, explained that closing the program was "part of the plan of discontinu-
ing federal relief as announced by the President early in 1935."[84] Richmond's
Transient Committee complained that it was "unfair to take from the local
people of Richmond the funds raised for them, in order to provide care for
transients . . . most of whom have come to the city as a result of the Transient
program . . . which was made by the Government without consultation with,
or consideration of, the programs and needs of local agencies and the resident
indigent."[85] When localities, like Richmond, complained that municipal social agencies and citizens once again had to shoulder the burden of care for
outsiders, federal officials sternly reiterated that "each state and community
contributes its share of transients elsewhere."[86] The official who responded
to the Richmond Transient Committee's communication cited a federal survey conducted on March 31, 1935, that found that while Virginia was caring
for 2,885 people from forty-seven states, those states were caring for 3,602
Virginians.[87]

Law enforcement officials in Jacksonville, Tampa, and St. Petersburg claimed
that the Florida Transient Service's work had brought about a 60 percent
decrease in petty crime.[88] Police throughout Georgia agreed that the state's
bureaus helped curtail panhandling and petty crime, and citizens noticed a
reduction in "back-door begging."[89] In Lexington, Kentucky, the police and
courts "constantly [expressed] their appreciation of the service" and wanted
to make it a permanent feature of the municipality.[90] In a letter to the state's
emergency relief administrator, Tampa's mayor wrote, "The maintenance of

the Transient Camp in Tampa has relieved, in a large measure, our citizens from the annoyance of the pan-handlers and has also had a great deal to do with keeping our community from being afflicted with petty thievery and other lawlessness." He admitted that although he had initially opposed the camp, he soon became convinced that it was useful.[91]

In urban areas across the South, the cessation of federal transient activities brought a return to the conditions that had prevailed prior to the establishment of the bureaus. Even under the WPA, the local needy came first, and transients often received work only when all other potential laborers had been serviced. Transients once again became the "pariahs of organized relief."[92] The federal transient program failed to alter localities' entrenched and easily justifiable concern with their own needy.[93] After federal transient work ended in Alabama, former residents of the Birmingham bureau found themselves at the mercy of local agencies, which refused to help them. The conditions outlined by a local relief administrator were reminiscent of the pre–New Deal period because the city lacked the funds to support transient care and believed that the community should not bear responsibility for caring for wanderers.[94] The problem for many former bureau residents was that the WPA allotments in urban areas were not adequate to absorb the local needy and the former transients. Hopkins received a letter from one man denied work with the federal agency who stated that he believed that he and others soon might be forced once again to "become a public nuisance . . . to keep us from starving."[95]

Throughout American history, localities have instituted laws that favor the rights of citizens over transients. The New Deal marked the federal government's initial efforts systematically and effectively to address transiency. In most respects, the transient problem in the South was unexceptional. The region's cities and towns protested the opening and closing of facilities, just as localities in the rest of the nation did. The placement of bureaus throughout the country reflected administrators' need to find inexpensive facilities convenient to railways and well-traveled roads. Cities across the nation experienced similar problems and successes with the program. Although segregation of transient facilities was an issue elsewhere, it presented special problems in the South. Segregation existed, but not to the extent one would expect in a region where it was both a de facto and de jure reality. The emergency nature of the transient program often overrode concerns about segregation. As the program established itself and the immediacy of the transient crisis subsided, a move toward greater segregation occurred. By 1935, most cities had at least one separate shelter for blacks.

Recognizing the value of America's pioneers to the development of the nation, one Florida transient official suggested that discouraging transiency was inappropriate. He asked, "Is it not possible that in doing so we are not only attempting the impossible, but we are helping in the destruction of an urge that is inspirational, creative, and productive of much that is beautiful and good?" The outcome of his utopian vision for a permanent transient care system would be "that prejudice and intolerance, provincialism and ignorance would tend to disappear and be replaced by breadth of vision, tolerance, and comprehension, and a joy in the complex structure of civilized living."[96] Such, of course, never came to pass, and the federal transient effort produced mixed results. An informal survey conducted among drifters in Kentucky indicated that nearly two-thirds believed that the bureaus had helped reduce transiency, although most thought that the proliferation of the shelters had encouraged boys to hit the roads.[97] Louisiana's chief relief administrator blasted the transient program. "He seems to have no doubt whatever," wrote a federal investigator, "that we are . . . nurturing a more serious problem than that which we found when we began. Because we are providing a high standard of relief, we are encouraging migration; we are encouraging people of relief to pack up and join the transients."[98] But such sentiments, especially in 1935, were uncommon.

The New Deal's transient program promoted changes in southerners' views of welfare. Initial disdain for the federal bureaus turned to acceptance in many urban communities. This change in attitude cannot be attributed to a miraculous alteration in public social consciousness. Rather, as with other popular programs such as the Civilian Conservation Corps, economic and social benefits motivated many citizens to support the New Deal's efforts. Washington's bureaus helped reduce panhandling, lowered crime in some areas, and kept drifters contained and occupied. Most importantly, in the eyes of many localities, the president's transient program kept outsiders off local relief and made them wards of the federal government while communities cared for their own needy residents. The complaints that reached Washington concerning the cessation of the program focused on economic concerns, not humanitarianism.

The transient program, although ultimately terminated, was not a failure. In 1933, Roosevelt's goal was to provide a temporary solution to a pressing problem and to relieve localities of the burden that drifters placed on their limited resources. Despite the emergency, states and localities, in cooperation with the FERA, established a system of acceptable, consistent care for wanderers. The president did not seek to alter entrenched social policies and attitudes concerning America's indigent, although some local officials worked toward that end. The purpose of their public relations efforts was to smooth the way for the presence of bureaus in communities, not to encourage citizens to embrace transients if Washington decided to end its work. FDR and Hopkins failed transients and communities across the South when they closed the Transient Division. Reflecting on the situation in 1937, the Committee on Care of the Transient and Homeless, in a terse statement, observed, "There is neither relief nor security as things now stand."[99] After a two-year respite, the Roosevelt administration, with admirable intentions, dismantled a workable system and left America's transients once again at the mercy of inhospitable communities and left communities at the mercy of shifting economic conditions that encouraged hopeful people to move.

Notes

1. Works Progress Administration, *Depression Pioneers,* Social Problems no. 1 (Washington, D.C.: U.S. Government Printing Office, 1939), 6–7.
2. Emily M. Bullitt, "The Transient Drama," *Florida Transient Review* 1 (April 1935): 56–57.
3. Leonard Leader, *Los Angeles and the Great Depression* (New York: Garland, 1991), 195.
4. "A Study of 10,198 Transients Registering at Texarkana U.S.A., February 1 to July 7, 1933," box 29, "Reports, 1933" folder, Works Projects Administration, Records of the Federal Emergency Relief Administration, Transient Division, Record Group (RG) 69, National Archives (hereafter, Transient Division Records).
5. Studs Terkel, *Hard Times: An Oral History of the Great Depression* (New York: Avon Books, 1970), 58.
6. Ranald Savery, Transient Bureau of the Alabama Relief Administration, "Flomation Field Report," October 10, 1933, box 29, "Reports, 1933" folder, Transient Division Records.
7. See Michael B. Katz, *In the Shadow of the Poorhouse: A Social History of Welfare in America* (New York: Basic Books, 1986), 13–21.
8. Ronald Edsforth, *The New Deal: America's Response to the Great Depression* (Malden, Mass.: Blackwell, 2000), 83; T. H. Watkins, *The Great Depression: America in the 1930s* (Boston: Back Bay Books, 1993), 60; Ellen C. Potter, *After Five Years: The Unsolved Problem of the Transient Unemployed, 1932–1937* (New York: Committee on Care of Transient and Homeless, 1937). 4. See also Harry Hopkins, *Spending to Save: The Complete Story of Relief* (New York: W. W. Norton, 1936; reprint, Seattle: University of Washington Press, Americana Library, 1972), 129–37.

9. Robert S. Wilson, *Individualized Service for Transients* (New York: National Association of Travelers Aid Societies, 1934), 59.

10. Works Progress Administration, *Depression Pioneers*, 12.

11. Transient profile compiled from John N. Webb, *The Transient Unemployed: A Description and Analysis of the Transient Relief Population* (Washington, D.C.: Works Progress Administration, Division of Social Research, 1935; reprint, New York: Da Capo Press, 1971), 24–87.

12. Ranald Savery, Transient Bureau of the Alabama Relief Administration, "Pensacola Field Report," October 9–10, 1933, box 29, "Reports, 1933" folder, Transient Division Records.

13. Ibid.

14. Department of Delinquency and Its Prevention, St. Louis Community Council, "Report of Committee on Migrant Boys," September 20, 1933, box 29, "Reports, 1933" folder, Transient Division Records.

15. Ibid.

16. William H. Mullins, *The Depression and the Urban West Coast, 1929–1933: Los Angeles, San Francisco, Seattle, and Portland* (Bloomington: Indiana University Press, 1991), 20.

17. Ranald Savery, Transient Bureau of the Alabama Relief Administration, "Mobile Field Report," October 3–5, 1933, box 29, "Reports, 1933" folder, Transient Division Records.

18. "Study of 10,198 Transients."

19. Helen C. Mawer, "Report on Transient Activities, State of Virginia," December 15, 1933, box 29, "Reports, 1933" folder, Transient Division Records.

20. Webb, *Transient Unemployed*, 94; U.S. Senate Committee on Manufactures, *Relief for Unemployed Transients*, 72d Cong., 2d sess., January 13–25, 1933, 3.

21. William J. Plunkert to Hopkins, March 30, 1934, box 29, "Memorandum A to H" folder, Transient Division Records.

22. "Study of 10,198 Transients."

23. U.S. Senate Committee on Manufactures, *Relief*, 144–45.

24. Hopkins, *Spending to Save*, 129–30.

25. The Agricultural Adjustment Administration (AAA), also born of the legislation that Congress passed during the initial hundred days, exacerbated transience. In an effort to raise prices for agricultural goods, the AAA compensated farmers for cutting production. Rather than share "the rewards of the program with their tenants, . . . landlords often evicted tenants and sharecroppers and hired labor by the day," thus displacing some of the nation's poorest workers. People whose subsistence depended on the cultivation of cotton were particularly hard hit because the South's major crop was the only commodity plowed under during 1933. The Bankhead Cotton Control Act and the Kerr-Smith Tobacco Control Act of 1934 imposed monetary penalties on farmers who produced more than their quota of the

region's most important crops. See Cindy Hahamovitch, *The Fruits of Their Labor: Atlantic Coast Farm Workers and the Making of Migrant Poverty, 1870–1945* (Chapel Hill: University of North Carolina Press, 1997), 155; and David M. Kennedy, *Freedom from Fear: The American People in Depression and War, 1929–1945* (New York: Oxford University Press, 1999), 204–20.

26. "Summary Report of the Transient Division for Period Ending December 31, 1933," January 5, 1934, box 31, "General" folder, Transient Division Records.

27. Webb, *Transient Unemployed,* 11–12; Joan M. Crouse, *The Homeless Transient in the Great Depression: New York State, 1929–1941* (Albany: State University of New York Press, 1986), 201; Josephine Chapin Brown, *Public Relief, 1929–1939* (New York: Henry Holt, 1940), 260–61.

28. Hopkins, *Spending to Save,* 132, 137.

29. Henry Redkey, "What the Transient Service Is Doing," *Florida Transient Review* 1 (January 1935): 14–16.

30. M. Pearl Weaver, "Transient Bureau Report on Activities January through June 1934," North Carolina Emergency Relief Administration, box 30, "North Carolina" folder, Transient Division Records.

31. Elizabeth J. Scheiblich, "Report of Transient Activities, October 1933–August 1934," August 23, 1934, box 30, "Tennessee" folder, Transient Division Records.

32. Redkey, "What the Transient Service Is Doing," 15.

33. Bullitt, "Transient Drama," 61.

34. Robert S. Wilson and Dorothy B. de la Pole, *Group Treatment for Transients* (New York: National Association for Travelers Aid and Transient Service, 1934), 39.

35. Hopkins, *Spending to Save,* 133.

36. Memorandum to Morris Lewis, November 20, 1933, box 29, "Whitney Reports" folder, Transient Division Records.

37. "Greensboro Transient Center," 1934, box 30, "North Carolina" folder, Transient Division Records.

38. Irving Richter to Elizabeth Wickenden, January 29, 1935, box 52, "Richter" folder, Transient Division Records.

39. Frances K. Strong, "Narrative Report," October 1–February 1, [ca. February 1934], Knoxville Transient Bureau, box 32, "Tennessee" folder, Transient Division Records.

40. Helen C. Mawer to Plunkert, November 26, 1934, box 31, "General" folder, Transient Division Records.

41. Code of the City of Lynchburg (1931), sec. 417; "Fourteen Dead, Seventy Hurt in Holocaust," *Lynchburg (Virginia) News,* March 25, 1934; "Death Claims Eighteenth Victim, Others Dangerously Ill," *Lynchburg (Virginia) News,* March 28, 1934; "Rites for Transient Dead on Saturday," *Lynchburg (Virginia) News,* March 30, 1934.

42. "Virginia Report," 1934, box 30, Transient Division Records.

43. Helen C. Mawer, "Lynchburg Transient Bureau: Report of Work Done since Monday," March 28, 1934, box 59, "Lynchburg Fire" folder, Transient Division Records.

44. Weaver, "Transient Bureau Report."
45. Ranald Savery, "Montgomery Field Report," October 11–12, 1933, box 29, "Reports, 1933" folder, Transient Division Records.
46. "Salisbury, North Carolina Report," September 17, 1934, box 30, "North Carolina" folder, Transient Division Records.
47. "Report of First Year's Activities of the Transient Program in Georgia, September 1933 to July 1934," box 30, "Georgia Report" folder, Transient Division Records.
48. Marshall B. Thompson to Plunkert, October 10, 1934, box 32, "Texas" folder, Transient Division Records.
49. Mr. Alsberg to Wickenden, September 12, 1934, box 29, "Memorandum A to H" folder, Transient Division Records.
50. "First Annual Report of the Bureau of Transients, Louisiana Emergency Relief Administration," August 1, 1934, box 30, "Louisiana Report" folder, Transient Division Records.
51. Scheiblich, "Report, October 1933–August 1934."
52. Robert Cornwall, "Voice of the Transient," *Florida Transient Review* 1 (April 1935): 62.
53. Ibid., 63.
54. Scheiblich, "Report, October 1933–August 1934."
55. Works Progress Administration, *Depression Pioneers,* 8–9.
56. Early to Hopkins, November 26, 1934, box 31, "Louisiana" folder, Transient Division Records.
57. "Florida Transient Program," 1934, box 30, "Florida Report" folder, Transient Division Records.
58. "Texas Report," 1934, box 30, Transient Division Records.
59. Ibid.
60. Herman M. Pekarsky, "A Fifteen Minute Radio Address," September 6, 1934, box 31, "Kentucky" folder, Transient Division Records.
61. Ibid.
62. "Salisbury, North Carolina Report."
63. Herman M. Pekarsky to Plunkert, August 13, 1934, box 30, "Kentucky Report" folder, Transient Division Records.
64. "Florida Transient Program."
65. Mawer to Plunkert, December 19, 1934, box 32, "North Carolina" folder, Transient Division Records.
66. "Texas Transient Bureau: Summary Report," August 1934, box 30, "Texas" folder, Transient Division Records.
67. Scheiblich, "Report, October 1933–August 1934."
68. Redkey, "What the Transient Service Is Doing," 17.
69. Ellery F. Reed, *Federal Transient Program: An Evaluative Survey, May to July, 1934* (New York: Committee on Care of Transient and Homeless, 1934), 26–27.

70. "Alabama Transient Bureau," 1934, box 30, "Alabama Report" folder, Transient Division Records.

71. William B. Nesbitt, "The Negro Transient," *Florida Transient Review* 1 (April 1935): 50–51.

72. Reed, *Federal Transient Program*, 27.

73. Redkey, "What the Transient Service Is Doing," 17–18.

74. Ibid., 13.

75. Maryland State Transient Division, "Bulletin #3," December 11, 1933, box 29, "Reports, 1933" folder, Transient Division Records.

76. Samuel I. Rosenman, ed., *The Public Papers and Addresses of Franklin D. Roosevelt*, vol. 4, *The Court Disapproves, 1934* (New York: Random House, 1938), 19–20.

77. Hopkins to Harold L. Ickes, March 12, 1936, box 51, "Agriculture (National Park Service) Transient Camp Material" folder, Transient Division Records.

78. J. Arthur Flynn, memorandum, July 13, 1935, box 51, "General" folder, Transient Division Records.

79. Mary Leigh Smith to Hopkins, October 11, 1935, box 56, "Approval of Closing" folder, Transient Division Records.

80. Mrs. Arthur I. Harris to Hopkins, September 13, 1935, box 56, "Protests Answered" folder, Transient Division Records.

81. Meridian Chamber of Commerce Resolution, October 3, 1935, box 56, "Closing of Program" folder, Transient Division Records.

82. Amarillo Community Chest to Hopkins, October 3, 1935, box 56, "Approval of Closing" folder, Transient Division Records.

83. Richmond Council of Social Agencies, "In view of the national character of the transient problem . . . ," 1935, box 56, "Approval of Closing" folder, Transient Division Records; Emil W. Leipziger, Joint Anti-Begging Committee Resolution, 1935, box 56, "Protests Answered" folder, Transient Division Records.

84. Charles H. Alspach to Fred E. DeCoster, December 31, 1935, box 56, "Approval of Closing" folder, Transient Division Records.

85. Mimms W. Lee to William A. Smith, September 26, 1935, box 56, "Approval of Closing" folder, Transient Division Records.

86. Alspach to DeCoster, December 31, 1935, box 56, "Approval of Closing" folder, Transient Division Records.

87. William A. Smith to Lee, September 28, 1935, box 56, "Approval of Closing" folder, Transient Division Records.

88. "Florida Transient Program."

89. "Report of First Year's Activities of the Transient Program in Georgia."

90. Pekarsky to Plunkert, August 13, 1934, box 30, "Kentucky Report" folder, Transient Division Records.

91. R. E. L. Chancey to Conrad von Hyning, October 1, 1935, box 55, "Protests Answered: Public Officials" folder, Transient Division Records.

92. Gertrude Springer, "Step-Children of Relief," *Survey* 69 (1933): 212–13.

93. Works Progress Administration, *Depression Pioneers,* 8–9.

94. [illegible] S. Addams to H. W. Winning, November 12, 1935, box 55, "Protests Answered, Transient Committee" folder, Transient Division Records.

95. William Jones to Hopkins, October 23, 1935, box 55, "Clients Not Answered" folder, Transient Division Records.

96. Robert C. von Riggle, "Pumpkin into Coach," *Florida Transient Review* 1 (January 1935): 21.

97. "Transient Bureaus," *Louisville (Kentucky) Cross Roads* 2 (October 14, 1935).

98. Richter to Wickenden, January 12, 1935, box 52, "Richter" folder, Transient Division Records.

99. Potter, *After Five Years,* 10.

Gender, Jim Crow, and Eugene Talmadge

The Politics of Social Policy in Georgia

ANN SHORT CHIRHART

From January 9 to January 23, 1934, Lorena Hickok, former reporter for the Associated Press and friend of Eleanor Roosevelt, drove across Georgia. Hired by the Federal Emergency Relief Administration (FERA), Hickok toured the nation to report to Harry Hopkins, the agency's head, about conditions in various regions and what Americans had to say regarding Franklin Delano Roosevelt's New Deal. In Georgia, Hopkins gave Hickok a specific political agenda, discovering who the Roosevelts' allies were, given Governor Eugene Talmadge's hostility to federal relief programs.[1] What really struck Hickok during her traverse across Georgia's pine barrens, foothills, mountains, and Piedmont regions was something more than the condition of the unemployed. "Oh, this *is* the damnedest state!" she wrote. "I just itch to bring all the unemployed teachers and doctors and nurses and social workers in the North down here and put them to work!"[2]

In less than two weeks, Hickok learned about one of Georgia's chronic shortfalls—the lack of public funding, administrative support, and personnel for social policies, notably education. Public education seemed to recede. Many teachers, most of whom were black and white women, taught without pay; children left school to find work to support their parents; schools stayed in session for little more than six months. During winter, leaky roofs in rural, segregated schools allowed rain to drip onto students, both black and white, as they sat on wooden benches or at broken-down desks. Some students missed weeks of school because of poor roads or lack of buses for transportation.[3]

Ten years later, Georgia had become a modern, centralized state with a bureaucratized public school system accessible to more Georgia youths than ever before. Although still plagued by unequal funding for black teachers and students, schools had longer terms, black and white teachers earned better salaries, students received free textbooks, and the state enforced compulsory attendance. Coming on the heels of northern philanthropic assistance and aid from the Extension Service of the U.S. Department of Agriculture (USDA), the New Deal and World War II's push for central and efficient administrations, trained workers, and educated youths forged a modern public education system.[4] Rather than relying on local authorities' whims that financed schools for white middle- and upper-class children, state and federal government funding attempted to equalize schools across states, at least for whites, in accordance with the state and federal educational guidelines that supplanted the district school boards' rule that had begun in the late nineteenth century.

The New Deal and World War II compressed Georgia's modernization into approximately fifteen years, a remarkable period of change. For most historians, the highlights of this period include political turmoil, economic and social upheaval, and cultural renegotiations. From 1930 to 1945, Georgia voters vacillated between Talmadge's efforts to preserve traditions and reject New Deal reforms and Governors E. D. Rivers and Ellis Arnall's moderate reforms. Georgia's tenants and sharecroppers left the land for wage labor in towns and cities, while large landholders switched to agribusiness and mechanized methods. Families and churches lost local control of institutions such as schools to the state and federal governments. Black and white women tossed aside aprons and hoes and redefined feminine authority in professional careers as teachers, nurses, and government administrators. African Americans organized and intensified the attack on Jim Crow that denied them access to political and social rights.[5]

Georgia's development of public education exemplified the contested and contentious transition to modernity that swept across the South. Through a complicated and often convoluted process of action and reaction, accommodation and opposition, Georgia finally assembled a modern—albeit segregated—public school system by 1946. At times unintentionally, educational reform cut through the quagmire of conflicting cultural and social values as political leaders, reformers, and parents debated what should be taught, who should teach it, and how it should be taught. At the end of World War II, a new generation of Georgians defined an education as an integral means of improving their lives. They could make better salaries and buy consumer goods; they could gain social status or "cultural capital" with a high school diploma; they could escape what they now saw as tawdry and backbreaking rural labor and culture.[6] What it meant to be an adult by 1946 had less to do with what one did at church or in the family and community than how much education one had and the job one held.

The more education came to define an individual's worth, the more it fractured class, race, and gender boundaries. Improved schools for all Georgians promised equalization among individuals, an escape from poverty and dependency, an end to the appalling disparities between black and white and rural and urban education. African Americans saw education as a means to resist racist assumptions about inferiority and flee the cycle of dependency on whites. However unrealistic these hopes were, the fact that education became a key issue in elections, legislation, and reform attests to the power all Georgians attributed to it during the first half of the twentieth century. A centralized educational system cracked the framework of localism that had, along with Georgia's conservative constitution, allowed white county officials an extraordinary amount of authority over political appointments, school policies, and most social policies. Losing this authority, some parents and communities raged against the changes.[7] Public education, now cut from local control, released the deepest fears about modernity. Clashes reverberated across the state from the interplay between facets of modernity (industrialization, individualism, public roles for women, the potential for equality between races, impersonal bureaucracies, self-serving consumption, and secularization) and inherited values such as conservative evangelical Protestantism, a white neopaternalistic hierarchy, self-sufficiency, and interdependence. These tensions between tradition and modernity tore political and social relations from county power brokers and granted authority to state and federal agencies.[8] Even as federal policies encouraged the state's school expansion in the 1930s and 1940s, most Georgians favored their state's right to determine funding and policy regulations.

Building this modern, consolidated school system with professional teachers was fraught with obstacles. In 1930, Georgia's population numbered three million and was 31 percent urban and 69 percent rural. Two-thirds of the population was white, with one-third African American, one of the nation's largest black populations. Georgia not only faced economic problems because of a low tax base but tried to fund a hodgepodge of school systems for black and white children and rural and urban children. The state's illiteracy rate stood at 9.4 percent.[9] The crisis in public education strangled rural schools. Only 14.7 percent of all black students who attended first grade reached seventh grade, and most of them were female. Only half of the white students enrolled in first grade made it through fourth grade.[10] Slightly more than one-third of rural white children attended school past seventh grade, as did 44 percent of urban white children.[11]

Moreover, Georgia paid its teachers less than most states, spent less per black or white student than all but three other southern states, and provided only 14 percent of the funds required to finance eight black colleges and universities.[12] About half of 1 percent of black students between the ages of fifteen and twenty-four (a mere 1,289 out of almost 250,000) attended private colleges and universities heavily endowed by churches, the General Education Board (GEB), and the Julius Rosenwald Fund (JRF), although the state also had three poorly funded public higher-education institutions that had 234 enrolled blacks.[13] In a 1933–34 study of salaries for black and white teachers in the South, the National Association for the Advancement of Colored People (NAACP) discovered that Georgia paid white teachers an average of $793.29, while black teachers received $269.53. Only Alabama, Arkansas, Mississippi, and South Carolina paid white teachers less, and only South Carolina's black teachers received less pay. Georgia's black teachers received an average of 47 percent of white teachers' salaries in 1930.[14] Part of the problem was that even though Georgia gave authority for teacher certification to the state department of education in 1934, counties continued to issue local certificates until after World War II because of the lack of trained teachers and tenacious grip of localism. Even so, the state and many counties performed mind-boggling feats of accounting. Some Georgia counties diverted more than $1,150,000 designated for black schools to white schools or other projects. Georgia's white children received approximately 252 percent more funding than black children did. The state offered no graduate programs for black students: all such programs were offered by southern black private schools or by northern universities and colleges.[15] And from the late 1920s through the 1930s, the state never paid its full appropriation for schools or teacher salaries.[16]

From its earliest efforts to establish a public school system, Georgians faced political, economic, and cultural conflicts. Georgia's 1877 constitution originally denied state funds for schooling beyond grade seven, leaving additional school support in the hands of counties. From the late nineteenth to the early twentieth century, the state's basic source of income was a general property tax. Following World War I, the Georgia legislature passed a sales tax on fuel oil in addition to a motor vehicle registration fee. As historian Numan Bartley states, these taxes provided the core of state revenue by 1930.[17] Still, between 1920 and 1930, state revenues increased but public school allocations decreased, as

Georgia focused on funding highway construction and pushed local school districts to increase property taxes to fund education. Because the constitution also restricted communities' abilities to raise school taxes by requiring that two grand juries and two-thirds of all registered voters approve the changes, cities, county seats and small towns formed their own school districts to increase the tax base for their schools. Drawing from wealthier property tax bases and circumventing state law, these city and town school districts, which numbered more than one hundred by 1920, provided the best education for Georgia's white children.[18] The result was a conglomeration of school districts that fed localism. In 1930, predominantly rural counties with ten thousand residents, such as Forsyth and Heard, relied on county and state property taxes that provided approximately forty-two thousand dollars for their schools. In contrast, the seat of Hall County, Gainesville, had a population of 8,624 and spent more than forty-four thousand dollars on its schools—funds obtained from state, county, and municipal appropriations and taxes.[19] For African Americans, the best higher education was offered by private philanthropic organizations such as the American Missionary Association and the GEB, which established several schools, including, among others, the Knox Institute in Athens, Atlanta University, and Fort Valley Normal and Industrial School.

As in other southern states, debates about what kind of public school system should be funded, who should teach, and what should be taught to whom were circumscribed by inherited beliefs in localism. Localism reinforced cultural values in four ways. For white Georgians it underscored the traditional authority of parents, churches, school trustees, and communities to determine school policies without intervention. Confronted with the possibility of educated blacks, localism justified racist practices of minimal funding for black schools. Facing the increasing number of black and white women who wanted to teach, localism allowed white male community leaders to determine which women would teach the area's children and what the students would learn. And localism drew from the independent congregational emphasis of conservative evangelical Protestant denominations such as the white Missionary Baptists, the Primitive Baptists, the black Independent and Missionary Baptists, and the black and white Methodists, who insisted that teachers instill fundamental beliefs including the inerrancy of the Bible and Christ's salvation.[20]

So white school trustees hired black and white female teachers who exemplified community standards of church attendance, respectable appearance, and moral behavior—avoiding alcohol consumption, playing cards, and dancing those insidious modern jazz steps. "When you taught under the trustees, you

knew your trustees and they knew you," recalls white teacher Ruth Smith Waters. "They inquired. They knew your background. They knew your grandpa
and grandma. They knew if you went to church, but they wouldn't tell you you
had to go."[21] Black women teachers also needed to espouse Booker T. Washington's belief in industrial training and follow similar behavioral codes, but,
most, like Beulah Rucker Oliver, taught black history and literature and encouraged their students to become teachers or learn a trade.[22] By 1920, black
and white women comprised more than 70 percent of teachers, a number that
increased to more than 80 percent by 1930.[23] Both black and white Georgians
believed that evangelical Protestant women made better teachers as a result of
gendered constructions of women as family nurturers and educators. Teachers
espoused traditional cultural beliefs such as hard work, self-sufficiency, and
community interdependence, although black and white women used these
values for different ends in their respective communities.

Most women had other reasons for becoming teachers. African American
women used schools to promote racial uplift, embodying what historian
Stephanie Shaw calls "social responsibility."[24] As Oliver often stated, most of
her life was spent lighting a torch of instruction for her race.[25] For some white
women, teaching provided a chance to leave the tedious farm labor they, like
black women, watched their mothers perform.[26] "My mama," stated Leona
Clark Williams, "didn't have time to do a whole lot because [she had] twelve
children. . . . She'd go and hoe or plant or anything there was to do. She canned
and dried fruit and made all our clothes for us. I never did stay home and
knit. . . . I have never been attracted to that sort of thing."[27] Other women
needed salaries to support their parents. White teachers Nelle Still Murphy
and Florrie Still initially taught because they needed the money and could
help their family.[28] Oliver used her salary to support not only her family but
also her school in Gainesville, Georgia. For most women, black and white,
teaching fulfilled desires for professional work that promised respectability,
fulfilled ambitions to escape rural labor, and served the community.[29] At the
same time, women created their classrooms as a feminine realm of authority
circumscribed by a white, male hierarchy. For white women, their feminized
domain allowed them to reinforce conservative rural values at the same time
that they assumed some independence. Teaching permitted black women to
challenge racist assumptions of black mediocrity, promoted self-pride, and
helped improve black community life.

By 1920 educational funds from northern philanthropic organizations and
the USDA poured into Georgia, and most Georgians welcomed this assistance

as long as it conformed to local community standards and relied on county officials for implementation. The GEB, a philanthropic fund established by John D. Rockefeller Sr., joined Georgia reformers and teachers in the push for a modern, public school system. Early GEB members favored different standards for African American education and white education, but the GEB nonetheless provided funds for black education, whereas white Georgians frequently chose to allocate nothing. Even so, Hickok's 1934 assessment echoed what some GEB representatives had said of Georgia in 1921. To Jackson Davis, "There was a deep seated notion that education was a matter for the family and the individual to look after, and any attempts for public support and control were branded as unwarranted invasions of individual liberty, socialism, and at best, as an expedient for the education of the poor." [30] As one father told white teacher Florrie Still, "I didn't go to school, and I've worked hard all my life. [My children are] no better than I am. They're my children. I'll do what I please." [31]

At the same time, localism never meant a complete rejection of state, federal, or northern philanthropic funds and regulations. From 1910 to 1920, Georgia increased funding for white public schools and allowed counties to pass higher tax levies for education. [32] The federal government provided public funds for industrial education with the 1917 Smith-Hughes Act and for agricultural education with the 1914 Smith-Lever Act. African Americans gained financial support from the JRF, named for a stockholder in the Sears and Roebuck Corporation who, after meeting Booker T. Washington, provided matching funds to black communities for elementary schools. From 1917 to 1932, Georgia African Americans built more than two hundred schools, aided by $247,569 from the JRF. [33] The Anna T. Jeanes Fund, administered by the GEB, funded black teaching supervisors for counties with more than fifteen black teachers and contributed more than $8,000 for twenty-six Jeanes teachers in 1930. [34] By 1930, Georgia received more than $300,000 annually from Smith-Lever and Smith-Hughes funds. [35] Because of the Smith-Lever Act, the USDA joined the choirs of reformers and organizations in Georgia by using public schools to spread their gospel of better cotton production and home improvement methods. To extension service agents, "the trained teacher in the community organization is invaluable; and can be brought about only by making the school house the community center for meetings of the various clubs even when the school is in session." [36] As with northern philanthropy, extension service work more often than not conformed to local boundaries. Black agents' reports throughout the 1920s read like copies of previous years as they repeatedly detail inadequate diets for black sharecroppers and tenants, poor living conditions, and lack of schools.[37] Although some projects gave black and white students scholarships to attend vocational or agricultural schools, most agents accepted conventions of what white and black children should learn.

Still, the combination of the USDA's extension service, northern philanthropy, and teachers' methods relocated the structure of community authority, the webs of social training and decision making. Children were now learning how to live and succeed from teachers in addition to parents and ministers. And what the students were learning from teachers was a decisive shift from parental expectations for the future. Here lay the precise dangers of education that some Georgians had feared for decades. The political possibilities of education spread from classrooms to communities and households, challenging traditions of respectability, identity, and power. Even though some children could ill afford new clothing styles or movies, they learned how modern, fashionable families lived from teachers and extension service representatives. Aware of consumer goods such as radios and appliances, many children began to consider possibilities for life outside of their rural communities, a world that certainly seemed more exciting than attending square dances or revivals. For example, Oliver taught her black students how to set a proper dinner table with dishes and silverware, settings that few of them saw outside the school. Black and white teachers such as Oliver and Waters modeled professional attire to many barefoot children clad in clothing made from feed sacks. Teachers and USDA agents unintentionally represented the world of consumption, that self-serving aspect of modernity that began to shatter patterns of interdependence and self-sufficiency.

Even as the social and cultural structure of Georgia's cotton culture began to crack, so did its economic foundations. The price of cotton fluctuated until it finally plummeted to five cents a pound in 1932. Facing economic disaster, closing schools, unpaid teachers, and increasing relief lines, most Georgians voted for Franklin Delano Roosevelt's promise of a New Deal at the same time they elected former state agricultural commissioner Eugene Talmadge as governor. While the men seemed to be strange bedfellows, Georgians' political choices reflected their uneasiness about their circumstances. FDR's programs might help the nation, but in Georgia, one of their own would guide them.[38]

Talmadge's stock racist and antiurban slogans appealed to farmers as he reassured them that the cotton culture remained viable. At other times, his policies belied his rhetoric. His supporters included the Georgia Power Company, textile companies, and other industries as well as white owners of large tracts of land, economic powers that doted on his hands-off policies toward big business and large landholders.[39] Farmers saw Talmadge thumbing his galluses at city people and modernity as he insisted that Georgians knew how to take care of their own. He heartened Georgia's white men and rural residents by recalling traditional white masculinity as he caroused with his cronies—the man who still wore the pants in the family and ran the show.[40]

Never oblivious to Georgians' plight, Talmadge established the Georgia Relief Administration (GRA) in January 1933 to distribute state relief. The GRA, headed by Talmadge supporter Herman De La Perriere, used political patronage as a main criterion for county and state appointments and made little effort to investigate how state funds were distributed within counties.[41] From the outset, federal supervisors from the Reconstruction Finance Corporation objected to the GRA's lack of investigation and urged Talmadge to appoint trained workers from Georgia's Department of Public Welfare, which was headed by Gay Bolling Shepperson.

Born in Charlotte County, Virginia, in 1887, Shepperson devoted her life to social work after she attended the New York School of Social Work in 1923. Working for the American Red Cross as a field-worker in Alabama and Louisiana, she switched to welfare work in St. Louis before leaving in 1928 to assume the directorship of Georgia's Children's Bureau, part of the state's Department of Public Welfare. By 1933 she was the executive secretary of the department.[42] Like teachers and home demonstration agents, Shepperson represented the professional woman who circumscribed her public career and ambitions with gendered definitions of community service, social welfare, and education.[43] Always a professional social worker, Shepperson demanded detailed investigative reports before granting requests for relief and fought to distribute funds equitably. She also knew how to maneuver around the land mines in white male political culture.

Shepperson gained a powerful ally when President Roosevelt appointed Hopkins as head of the FERA in May 1933. Hopkins, a former social worker from Iowa, knew Shepperson from their days in the American Red Cross and trusted her opinions. By the end of the summer of 1933, Talmadge's attacks escalated as he opined that the National Recovery Act and the Tennessee Valley Authority were "all in the Russian primer and the President has made the statement that he has read it twelve times."[44] A staunch supporter of Franklin and Eleanor Roosevelt, Hopkins tolerated few attacks. When Shepperson suggested that the Department of Public Welfare administer relief in Georgia to avoid the taint of political cronyism, Hopkins agreed. In September 1933, FERA representative Alan Johnstone and Talmadge signed a proposal to establish the Georgia Emergency Relief Administration (GERA), with Shepperson as director and De La Perriere as adviser.[45] Shepperson immediately appointed social workers—predominantly women—as county administrators to investigate applications for relief. Talmadge countered by insisting on signing every paycheck and attacking GERA personnel.

If Talmadge objected to federal regulations and investigators in Georgia as early as the days of the RFC, the governor's opposition to FDR's New Deal programs only intensified. A woman now directed relief funds and projects in his state, and Talmadge could do little to stop her. Then she had the temerity to appoint more women, and social workers at that, as county administrators of relief. Yet Talmadge's conflicts with FDR, Hopkins, and Shepperson had more to do with preserving localism and traditions. Talmadge sought appointees who were allied with his political positions. This meant that out-of-state funds, whether from northern philanthropists or the federal government, were welcome as long as the state and counties controlled the distribution of the money.

But the FERA shredded localism in four ways. It promoted modern constructions of gender by allowing Shepperson and her appointees to answer to the federal government rather than to state and local officials. The FERA threatened to upset Jim Crow's separate and unequal principles by paying blacks $3.20 a day, more than they ever made picking cotton. It usurped county officials' power by granting federal funds to black and white schools. Moreover, it supported urban residents, whom Talmadge viewed as nothing more than "bums and loafers."[46] The governor believed that farmers needed relief more than city folks did, and Talmadge had a point. Georgia's small farmers, tenants, and sharecroppers, both black and white, bore the brunt of cotton's collapse. Yet Talmadge had little use for these people. He wanted relief for the white owners of large amounts of land who had voted him into office.

What relief began to tear, therefore, was the fabric of relations between large landholders and dependent farmers, upper-class whites and working-class blacks and whites, white men and all women—the complex webs of neopaternalism's dominance and dependency relations in rural cotton culture. Consequently, Talmadge's diatribes addressed the New Deal's potential to overturn class, race, and gender roles. Worse still, to Talmadge and his supporters, these FERA demands came from non-Georgians, outsiders. He repeatedly objected to "the employment of men and women from out of the State, utterly unfamiliar with the people and conditions of this State," who were largely "responsible for the condition in Georgia."[47] Relief, Talmadge inveighed, created only a class of people permanently dependent on government assistance.[48] Talmadge's solution was to "get back to fundamental principles. . . . Go back to your Bible . . . get back out in the country; do not let the old schoolhouse and church rot."[49] At the heart of the confrontation between Talmadgism and FDR's New Deal lay the contested terrain between traditions and modernity.

If Talmadge believed that most Georgians supported his attacks on federal relief, and it seems that he did, he stunningly misjudged their plight. Loss of income meant lower tax revenues, which cut public school funds. Despair and determination fed teachers who taught without pay or at reduced salaries and swept through schools and into the homes of parents and children struggling to keep schools open for at least six months out of the year. The white Georgia Education Association (GEA) and the black Georgia Teachers and Educators Association (GTEA) repeatedly asked for state funds that the legislature had magnanimously appropriated but amazingly misplaced.[50] But Talmadge was more concerned with cutting taxes and claimed that education "ain't never taught a man to plant cotton."[51] Too much education threatened to destroy traditional constructions of identity and traditional beliefs.

Many Georgians disagreed with their governor. Hundreds of black and white Georgia teachers, like teachers across the nation, wrote to President Franklin Roosevelt and First Lady Eleanor Roosevelt, asking for items from clothing to books to teaching materials. The writers described clothing and shoes with holes and tears and worried that their reduced pay made survival and family support impossible. Black teachers wrote of salaries as low as thirty-five dollars a month while teaching as many as fifty students per class in dilapidated buildings.[52] Mothers insisted that "our boys and girls of today must be educated to bring our State up to a high standard," an impossible achievement for most rural children.[53] Localism and community networks cracked.

These letters mark shifting gender constructions across the nation as well as in Georgia. Responding to Eleanor Roosevelt's radio addresses and columns, in which she asked Americans to write to her about their problems, women, children, and young adults saw the president's wife as someone who could understand their plight because she was a mother, a wife, and a public advocate of social reform and education. The more Eleanor talked about the need for education, the more Georgians and other American women wrote to her "because I believe you will understand my problems and because I know you can help me solve it."[54] Women from every state viewed the First Lady as representing feminine ambition, social policy reforms, and the possibility of new higher-education goals for young people and women, public policies with which women increasingly identified. Teachers laid the foundation for women's public work; women such as Shepperson and Roosevelt then reinforced and strengthened that foundation. But even Eleanor Roosevelt could do little about the turmoil at the GERA.

After the signed agreement of September 1933, Shepperson, Johnstone, Hopkins, and Talmadge battled again over one of Shepperson's appointments —not surprisingly, a woman, Jane Van De Vrede, a nurse and Red Cross worker who became director of women's work. Exasperated by Shepperson's female GERA appointments, Talmadge fired Van De Vrede in December 1933 as a warning to Hopkins and Shepperson that the governor must approve state appointments. Outraged at Talmadge's actions, Johnstone demanded that Van De Vrede, who knew Hopkins from New Orleans, be reinstated and recommended that Hopkins federalize the GERA because "joint administration of these [federal] funds seems impracticable."[55] Hopkins agreed and federalized Georgia's relief administration on January 5, 1933. Now one of the most powerful people in Georgia, Shepperson controlled the distribution of federal funds in the state.[56] One of the few women FERA administrators and the only female Works Progress Administration (WPA) administrator ever chosen by Roosevelt and Hopkins, Shepperson carried women's political clout to the highest level yet in Georgia.[57] Insisting on professional training for female teachers and social workers and then placing them in administrative positions where they could act without answering to local officials, Shepperson struck at the core of Talmadgism.

Shepperson immediately set to work on Georgia's schools and illiteracy. She used $1.6 million in FERA money for teachers' salaries in 1934. She hired unemployed teachers as literacy and vocational education instructors at FERA centers across the state. But in March 1935, teachers again faced a spring without pay. Talmadge and Georgia State School Superintendent M. D. Collins asked Shepperson for another FERA grant of $1.8 million to keep the schools open. Shepperson and Hopkins sympathized with the teachers but knew that Talmadge could obtain money for teachers' salaries either by taking money from the state highway department, which always had a surplus, or by borrowing against the next year's tax revenues. So Shepperson and Hopkins refused the request. Hopkins wanted Talmadge to take the blame for the situation and repeatedly told Shepperson to make sure the press understood what the governor was doing. "We certainly told them we wouldn't do it," Hopkins said to Shepperson on April 22, "so if the teachers take it up tell them to go see Governor Talmadge. That is the real thing and I think somebody is going to have to say it."[58] Shepperson and Hopkins also had evidence that Talmadge and some county officials had misused the 1934 FERA loan for purposes other than teachers' salaries. In the end, teachers and students were pawns in political posturing. Each side wanted to blame the other for the lack of money for salaries, and both refused to budge. Caught in the middle, teachers taught with sporadic pay until the 1940s. Some counties closed schools. Some priorities of the past remained—education was dispensable when political stakes were high.

Joining Talmadge in the spring of 1935 were some Georgia legislators, including future governors Rivers and Arnall, who publicly denounced Shepperson as a danger to local traditions and state authority.[59] Arnall accused Shepperson of hiring "non-resident persons, for the most part of the Republican and progressive party affiliation, notwithstanding the fact that capable Georgians . . . are available for this work."[60] According to Arnall, Shepperson was an outsider and condoned teachings of racial equality and Yankee Republican carpetbag rule. Shepperson countered by releasing the facts about her staff, noting that the GERA's division of social service lacked enough professional social workers to fill all its positions.[61] No Georgia public college or university had a school of social welfare because social workers were seen as meddling, intrusive busybodies in men's private households. Florrie Still recalled that social workers were "dirty words. Goodness, the Talmadges would have blown their tops [if a school of social work had been created in Georgia]. They'd put an end to that right there. Being a social worker meant you believed in people—if they were black, you know? Even one of the state board members told me one day, 'You and your crowd are getting people in school that ought to be in the cotton patch.' "[62] To some Georgians, social workers supported giving women more authority to intervene in family rules or racist practices that pulled children from school and sent them to cotton fields or textile mills. Even so, Shepperson had hired out-of-state social workers only after hiring all available Georgians. Of the thirty-nine hundred relief workers in Georgia, 94.2 percent had been on Georgia relief rolls.[63]

This attack on Shepperson used the old refrain that outsiders or carpetbaggers were interfering in local affairs, cloaking fears of shifting cultural values, fears of what educated women or African Americans might do, fears of what a centralized state bureaucracy might mean. Here were white women running

FERA programs across the state, answering to no one but federal authorities. Blacks were earning more money as workers on federal relief projects than they had earned picking cotton. After Shepperson released data about FERA employees, Johnstone met with Georgia's representatives in Washington, D.C. After Shepperson proved that her employees were predominantly Georgians, Johnstone described what the FERA could do for the state. When Georgia's delegation learned how much money Georgia could get, several members, including state legislators Arnall and Rivers, left Talmadge's camp. Rivers then learned how state legislation could circumvent Georgia's constitutional restrictions on raising taxes.[64] Because the FERA provided funds in proportion to a state's ability to pay tax revenues to the federal government, Georgia alone, of eighteen eligible rural states, failed to receive federal education aid. FERA required states to match federal funds with state tax funds, but Georgia's constitution prevented the state from borrowing more than 7 percent of total county tax values, and Georgia thus rarely met FERA's requirements.

Rejected by Talmadge and his supporters, Rivers's proposals became the platform for his 1936 gubernatorial candidacy. His proposed "Little New Deal" for Georgia included free textbooks, a seven-month school year, and better pay for teachers. Of course, the reforms targeted white schools, but black schools also would benefit from free but used textbooks and longer terms. That Rivers chose educational reform as the cornerstone of his campaign indicated the issue's importance to many Georgians. But after trouncing Talmadge's ally in the race, Governor Rivers failed to solve Georgia's constitutional deterrents against borrowing money.[65] By 1940, the state was bankrupt, schools closed again across the state, and teachers worked without pay or hoped that local banks would honor vouchers. Rivers's programs, while clearly an effort to modernize Georgia's social policies, cost him Georgians' support and paved the way for Talmadge's reelection in 1940.[66]

Still, the National Youth Administration (NYA), a popular New Deal program established during Rivers's administration, changed the way many Georgians defined the role of education as well as who should be educated. Prompted by Eleanor Roosevelt, Hopkins, and Aubrey Williams, a white social worker from Alabama, FDR created the NYA by executive order in 1935 as a branch of the WPA. Because thousands of students across the nation left school to support families, the NYA offered financial aid to college and high school students.[67] FDR appointed Mary McLeod Bethune to head the Negro Division of the NYA, an appointment that proclaimed that the NYA would give equal pay to blacks and whites, men and women. All students receiving NYA funds had to work fifteen to twenty hours a week.[68] During the program's first year, 9,900 Georgia high school and college students received financial aid.[69] Twelve percent of students enrolled at forty white colleges and thirteen black colleges earned fifteen dollars per month. Blacks never received a proportion of aid commensurate with their percentage of Georgia's population. Nonetheless, at the high school level, aid to Georgia's black students compared favorably with that given to white students. For example, in October 1937, 1,897 white students received financial aid, as did 1,082 black students. The difference between funding for black and white students was readily apparent at the college level, however, where 1,551 white youths received aid, compared to only 168 black students.[70] The problem here was the lack of public colleges and universities for black students in Georgia.

Furthermore, like established guidelines from the USDA's extension service work, northern philanthropy, and WPA projects, gender conventions determined NYA jobs for girls and boys. Girls did sewing, clerical, or library work, while boys labored as masons or carpenters or repairing roads.[71]

For NYA participants, high school education became something that all young people should have, a necessity for becoming a member of the middle class.[72] Watching families toil for a fickle crop that barely fed and clothed them, Georgia's next generation wanted to become part of the modern world, where different job opportunities and consumer goods were available. In addition to providing financial aid to high school and college students, the NYA sponsored live-in training camps that taught skills to students who had left school after eighth grade. Unlike the WPA sewing rooms in Georgia, which had neglected vocational training for poor women on relief, the camps provided training for a future as a wage laborer.[73] Although such training was available to both boys and girls, the skills offered followed traditional gender lines. Boys learned auto or aviation mechanics, carpentry, construction trades, and better farming methods. Girls attended courses on sewing, planning menus and diet, hairstyling, or clerical skills. The training camps reinforced some class and race boundaries as well: black boys never learned aviation mechanics, and black girls tended to learn domestic skills. But most participants were eager to learn almost anything except farming—endless, isolated work that represented what they had left behind rather than what they wanted for the future.

But learning a trade or attending school was only part of the NYA's program. Participants also learned social skills and how to prepare for a job interview. Camp residents worked, ate, and slept with others their own age. Case after case describes how a boy or girl's social skills and personality improved during training, thereby increasing chances of success in the modern world. John Henry, "a reticent boy" from Fulton County, learned metal crafts, but "the most interesting part of this boy's story . . . is the complete change" in his personality. After working in the NYA craft shop, he "now mingles with the rest of the class, dresses in a clean, neat manner, and feels himself a part of society, where before, he was a backward, nondescript type of boy."[74] At nineteen Alice Main "was a headstrong Negro girl with a disagreeable disposition" and two children. Learning modern cooking and domestic skills, she obtained a position as a cook and a maid. She had become "a different girl" who was "neater in her appearance, worked more pleasantly with other girls on the project, really put forth an effort to win the praise of her supervisor."[75]

Thus, the NYA taught a wide variety of skills. Just like black and white teachers and home demonstration agents, NYA instructors taught students what the modern world required for jobs and success. Who would hire a surly maid or a disagreeable mechanic? How to dress and interact with others was part of learning to live in a changing world. Girls learned how to use makeup and wear fashionable hairstyles and clothing. Becoming a consumer was part of the NYA curriculum, a particular accomplishment for rural students who had either never bought makeup or been forbidden to use it. All participants learned to manage their personal finances and acquired skills needed for urban industries, such as filling out payroll forms or using a time clock. Obtaining a high school, vocational, or college education relocated Georgia boys' and girls' career and material expectations beyond their parents' rural lives. White Georgians acquired the ability to negotiate a world of new skills, better education, and individualism within a shifting social hierarchy. For African Americans, the NYA promised better educational opportunities after decades of racist practices. Led by Aubrey Williams and Bethune, the NYA directors encouraged black and white boys and girls to stay in school, learn a skill that would get them off the farm, and use consumer goods for their goals. Like most New Deal programs, the NYA sought to create future consumers, not to redistribute income.[76] Education, marketable skills, and personal style created the path to modern success.

NYA programs intentionally boosted the NAACP's equalization campaign for southern schools.[77] As the NYA's programs began, the NAACP, the JRF, and the GEB studied each state's tax system and the percentage of taxes received by public schools. Their discoveries were telling. Part of the problem with southern schools, in addition to racism and localism, was the South's low tax base. Even if white southerners had wanted to fund black and white schools equally, which they obviously did not, the South collected lower property tax revenues, although it contributed as large a proportion of this tax to schools as other states did. If the NAACP, along with the support of the JRF and the GEB, decided to push for the actual practice of separate and equal as established in *Plessy v. Ferguson*, federal funds would have to equalize the states' financial support for schools.[78]

Beginning in 1931, before the Legal Defense Fund was established, the NAACP investigated and detailed unequal funding for black schools across the South in a report that was finally released in 1939. Even with federal funds from FERA, the WPA, and the NYA, black schools continued to receive less money than white schools.[79] Arguing that current salaries had a "demoralizing influence" on black teachers, the NAACP targeted these salaries for improvement to keep professionally trained black teachers in the South.[80]

Georgia paid all teachers according to their training and experience, but some black teachers received as little as $175 for seven months of work because they held county rather than state licenses. Some white female teachers in Georgia were paid less than black teachers in North Carolina. A black woman teaching in Georgia who had a two-year degree earned 75 percent of what a white teacher with the same degree received.[81] Contemporary logic told black and white reformers that better teachers and more educated students meant a more prosperous South.

At the same time, some members of the U.S. Congress realized the benefits of the New Deal's educational programs and acted in 1936. Senators Pat Harrison of Mississippi and Hugo Black of Alabama and Representative Brooks Fletcher of Ohio introduced what became known as the Harrison-Fletcher-Black Bill, which provided three hundred million dollars in federal aid to public education in any state where schools were in session for at least 160 days each year. According to the original draft of the bill, in states where separate schools existed for black and white children, the funds could be divided between black and white schools in proportion to the number of black and white inhabitants between five and twenty years old. States retained the right to allocate federal funds as they deemed fit.[82]

The NAACP campaigned to "insure that Negro schools (in those states where Negroes are forced by law to attend separate schools) would get their equitable share of such appropriations."[83] Initially, the NAACP and other African American leaders opposed the bill because it contained "no safeguards against racial discrimination."[84] Congress amended the legislation to require that distribution of federal funds would be supervised by the U.S. commissioner of education, who would report any problems to Congress and the secretary of the interior. With these changes, the NAACP chose to support the bill, noting that it was not foolproof but offered a minimum guarantee.[85] However, W. E. B. Du Bois, representing the GTEA, insisted "that the control of these funds be transferred from the legislature of Georgia, none of whose members my people elect, to the Congress of the United States, many of whom my people elect."[86] The battle over the bill and its amendments continued through the 1940s, but the legislation represented a sincere effort to equalize funding between the public schools of different states. And support from many southern members of Congress, including Georgia Senators Richard Russell and Walter George, demonstrated the growing belief that education was the means by which the next generation (at least of whites) could increase their income and purchasing power and become better citizens. Still, no federal legislation was ever passed to equalize school funds because of religious and regional disputes among members of Congress: some representatives wanted parochial schools included, while others feared the loss of local and state authority over schools once the federal government began to reach into the politicized and hierarchical means of educating children.

The NAACP's pending court cases regarding the equalization of teachers' salaries in Virginia and Maryland no doubt prodded many white Georgians to look for federal aid. The GEA rarely carried the banner for black educational reform and consistently adhered to Jim Crow principles. The state could barely afford to pay whites' salaries, so how could it possibly increase black teachers' pay? The GEA insisted that equalization funds had to come from the federal government, which provided yet another reason for Georgians to support the Harrison-Fletcher Bill.[87] White women teachers agreed that salaries needed to improve and used their expanding political clout to publicize all schools' needs for federal funds. Among many others, Leona Clark Williams, Florrie Still, and Ruth Smith Waters supported the GEA's efforts to equalize salaries.[88]

At the same time, Georgia's white educators knew that after the U.S. Supreme Court ruling in *Missouri ex rel. Gaines v. Canada* in 1938, black higher education had to be upgraded. And additional funds were desperately needed for black schools. Since the late 1920s, the GEB and the JRF had urged the state to assume more financial responsibility for black colleges.[89] Now came a Supreme Court mandate to provide equal higher-education facilities for blacks. Between 1936 and 1939, the Georgia State Board of Education negotiated the purchase of Fort Valley State College from the American Church Institute, a deal that was consummated only because the JRF added fifty thousand dollars to the thirty-four thousand dollars provided by the state.[90] At last, the state had a public college that offered a four-year degree to black teachers.

Educational policy had clearly moved to the forefront of political debates. Merit displaced kinship and community ties in many school appointments. Some parents and children began to look to teachers as experts on what children needed to succeed, thereby increasing teachers' public authority. State and federal educational bureaucracies increasingly determined what children should know and who should teach them. Faced with the breakdown of localism, some Georgians turned to the man who had always assured them that their traditions were noble—Eugene Talmadge.

In the wake of Governor Rivers's financial disasters, Talmadge easily won the 1940 gubernatorial election by denouncing the New Deal as an assault on Georgia's traditions of femininity, Jim Crow, and the poll tax. His first target, to him a cesspool of modernity, was the University of Georgia's Department of Education. Between 1938 and 1941, the department's dean, Walter Cocking, sponsored conferences with the support of the GEB and the JRF on Georgia's education problems. The conference reports came as Talmadge and many other Georgians were debating how much change they wanted in their public schools. An ex-officio member of the university's Board of Regents, Talmadge attended a May 30, 1941, meeting and promptly fired Cocking, accusing him of using "Jewish money" or the JRF to support integrated education. One woman, a distant relative of Talmadge, accused Cocking of advocating biracial education at a training school in Athens. Because of Talmadge's autocratic actions, which occurred against the board's advice, the Southern Association of College and Secondary Schools yanked Georgia's accreditation, and the GEB and the JRF pulled almost three million dollars for education from the state.[91]

On the surface, the issue appeared to be fear of integrated schools. But it was more than that. Traditional rural values of localism and family and church authority collided with secular, individualistic values in the centralizing state.[92] Talmadge accused Cocking of representing "foreign ideas . . . being taught in our universities" and specifically attacked the JRF as an agency that advocated racial integration or "Jew money for niggers."[93] Talmadge's actions embarrassed other Georgians. William Fowlkes, an editorial writer for the *Atlanta Daily World,* explained that for white Georgians, the issue was not "the race equality issue, but . . . the democracy issue."[94] Countless black and white Georgians compared Talmadge's attacks on Georgia blacks to Hitler's attacks on Jews. Talmadge was now perceived as another fascist dictator. University of Georgia students, who had come of age during the New Deal and under-stood that an education definitely taught them more than how to pick cotton, marched against Talmadge.[95] Talmadge had unwittingly handed Arnall the is-sue that would win the 1942 governor's race.

During the white Democratic primary campaign, Arnall supported sepa-rate schools and Jim Crow, but he insisted that democracy required better-educated citizens. In an ad that appeared in the *Georgia Education Journal* before the primary, Arnall promised teachers "a public school system and a university system freed from the slimy hands of dictatorial policies."[96] Black teachers, most white teachers, and most state newspapers endorsed Arnall's candidacy. While Talmadge still had the support of the Georgia Power Com-pany, textile owners, highway contractors, and many farmers, Arnall gained the endorsements of banking and insurance companies, all universities, oil companies, the Coca-Cola Company, and most urban residents and educa-tors.[97] How could Georgia attract modern industries, including World War II defense contracts that required new skills, without better schools? The *Atlanta Daily World* urged Georgia's blacks to pay their poll taxes and register to vote to support Arnall.[98] Arnall won a landslide victory.

Georgia voters approved Talmadge's constitutional amendment that allowed Georgia governors to serve a four-year term rather than two consecutive two-year terms. But Ellis Arnall, not Talmadge, won the distinction of being the first governor to achieve this. For the next four years, Arnall's administra-tion followed moderate policies while preserving aspects of the old order. Key policy changes included fundamental educational reforms. Yet changing ed-ucational policies required a quick solution to the problem of Georgia's debt, which reached almost thirty-six million dollars in 1942. The state's income came primarily from the fuel tax, so coffers dwindled as a result of wartime gas rationing.[99] Refusing to raise property taxes or pass a sales tax, Arnall abruptly stopped all new highway construction and placed new highway contracts in the lap of the federal government. State revenues never declined as much as Ar-nall feared; in fact, because of wartime construction, revenues increased, and the debt was paid off. Georgia also gained additional income when Arnall's revenue commissioner, Melvin Thompson, raised the state's warehouse liquor fee from fifty cents to three dollars a gallon. These funds provided Arnall with the means he needed for educational reform.[100] By 1946 the state allocated 41 percent more funds for public schools than it had during Talmadge's admin-istration.[101] Georgia's colleges and universities were reaccredited, the Board of Regents was reorganized, the Georgia Constitution was rewritten, the poll tax was removed, teachers won a retirement plan in 1945, black and white teachers' salaries became more equitable, and a bachelor's degree was required for all teachers. The seven-month school year, free textbooks, and a compulsory school-attendance law became realities.

Arnall also supported the pending but never enacted federal legislation to equalize schools across the nation and encouraged industrial growth in the state.[102] State and federal funding for vocational instruction soared from $209,769 in 1930 to almost $900,000 in 1941.[103] And more one- and two-teacher schools for whites consolidated into institutions with twenty or more teachers: between 1930 and 1941, the number of such schools rose from 62 to 133. For black schools, however, the numbers remained dismal: only 8 consolidated schools were built for blacks during the same period.[104] More significantly for the purposes of modern state building, Georgia assumed central authority for financing and implementing a public educational system after relying primarily on county and district taxes to fund schools for more than seventy years.

But in the wake of the U.S. Supreme Court's 1944 ruling in *Smith v. Allwright* that the white primary was unconstitutional, most Georgians panicked over the possibility of blacks registering to vote. Although some Georgians had already written Eugene Talmadge's political obituary, in 1946 he again ran for governor as the savior of the white race and a bulwark against communism and outsiders. He won the election but died before taking office. Even Talmadge could not have stopped the gains that women, African Americans, and some rural residents had made over the previous fifteen years, gains that had been made possible by education. As some turn-of-the-century reformers recognized, education beckoned to the disenfranchised—blacks, women, the poor—offering hope and opportunity to those who wanted a better life. Education constituted a means by which African Americans could resist Jim Crow. Education provided hundreds of female Georgia teachers with an opportunity for an independent and public life even if they remained in their original communities. At the same time, education reform by itself could never redeem society, for it also carved a path for self-serving consumption and modern bureaucracies. It removed parents and communities from decisions regarding their schools. But during the 1930s and 1940s, it was the most useful tool for change that blacks and women had.

Returning to Virginia in December 1939, Shepperson must have watched these events with mixed emotions. Part of her legacy was the promotion of education and professional training for women and African Americans using FERA and WPA funds. She demonstrated how federal funds could benefit the state. Arnall instituted change at the state level, however moderate it may seem today. Four years later, Georgia's politicians retrieved racist fears and communist monsters from their campaign files and trounced reformers again and again for the next twenty years. Still, New Deal programs gave women and blacks ideas for the future, teaching them that with enough determination and resolve, they could effect change. Having won battles for better schools, salaries, and conditions, blacks now had the courage to face the larger and more costly battles to kill Jim Crow once and for all. And female teachers and social workers gained resolve and confidence to continue to fight for even better schools, improved social conditions, and professional respect.

Notes

1. Hickok to Hopkins, January 11, 1934, box 57, "Georgia—Field Reports" folder, Papers of Harry Hopkins, group 24, "FERA-WPA Narrative Field Reports," Franklin Delano Roosevelt Library, Hyde Park, N.Y. (hereafter, Hopkins Papers).

2. Hickok to Hopkins, January 23, 1934, Hopkins Papers.

3. Leona Clark Williams, interview by author, June 13, 1991, Buford, Ga.; Ruth Smith Waters, interview by author, June 28, 1991, Flowery Branch, Ga.; Dorothy Oliver Rucker and Carrie Oliver Bailey, interviews by author, May 6, 19, 1993, Gainesville, Ga.; Sanford Byers, interview by Lu Ann Jones, April 20, 1987, Gainesville, Ga., Oral History of Agriculture Collection, National Museum of American History, Smithsonian Institution, Washington, D.C.; Aubrey and Ina Belle Benton, interview by Lu Ann Jones, April 28, 1987, Commerce, Ga., Oral History of Agriculture Collection; Walter Cocking, *Report of the Study of Higher Education of Negroes in Georgia* (Athens: University of Georgia, 1938); Georgia Fact-Finding Committee, "Georgia—Education," 2–3, box 203, folder 8, Julius Rosenwald Fund Papers, Fisk University, Nashville, Tenn. (hereafter, JRF Papers); Numan Bartley, *The Creation of Modern Georgia* (Athens: University of Georgia Press, 1990), chaps. 6, 8.

4. Oscar Joiner, ed. *A History of Public Education in Georgia 1734–1976* (Columbia: R. L. Bryan, 1979), chaps. 4, 5; "Present State of Rural Education in the South," March 5, 1943, ser. 1.2, box 211, folder 2036, General Education Board Files, Rockefeller Archive Center, Pocantico Hills, N.Y. (hereafter, GEB Files); Harold Paulk Henderson, *The Politics of Change in Georgia: A Political Biography of Ellis Arnall* (Athens: University of Georgia Press, 1991); U.S. Bureau of the Census, *Seventeenth Census of the United States, 1950: Population*, pt. 2, vol. 2 (Washington D.C.: U.S. Government Printing Office, 1952), 11–6, 11–8.

5. On southern agriculture, see Pete Daniel, *Breaking the Land: The Transformation of Cotton, Tobacco, and Rice Cultures since 1880* (Urbana: University of Illinois

Press, 1985); Jack Temple Kirby, *Rural Worlds Lost: The American South, 1920–1960* (Baton Rouge: Louisiana State University Press, 1972). On southern labor, see Jacquelyn Dowd Hall, James Leloudis, Robert Korstad, Mary Murphy, Lu Ann Jones, and Christopher B. Daly, *Like a Family: The Making of a Southern Cotton Mill World* (New York: W. W. Norton, 1987): Bryant Simon, *A Fabric of Defeat: The Politics of South Carolina Millhands, 1910–1948* (Chapel Hill: University of North Carolina Press, 1998). On African Americans, see Harvard Sitkoff, *A New Deal for Blacks: The Emergence of Civil Rights as a National Issue* (New York: Oxford University Press, 1978); Patricia Sullivan, *Days of Hope: Race and Democracy in the New Deal Era* (Chapel Hill: University of North Carolina Press, 1996). On localism in the South, see William A. Link, *The Paradox of Southern Progressivism, 1880–1930* (Chapel Hill: University of North Carolina Press, 1992). On women and the New Deal, see Susan Ware, *Partner and I: Molly Dewson, Feminism, and New Deal Politics* (New Haven: Yale University Press, 1987): Jacquelyn Dowd Hall, *Revolt against Chivalry: Jessie Daniel Ames and the Women's Campaign against Lynching* (New York: Columbia University Press, 1979); Blanche Wiesen Cook, *Eleanor Roosevelt: The Defining Years, 1933–1938.* (New York: Penguin Books, 1999).

6. Pierre Bourdieu, *Distinction: A Social Critique of the Judgement of Taste,* trans. Richard Nice (Cambridge: Harvard University Press, 1984). On individualism and modernity, see Elizabeth Fox-Genovese, *Feminism without Illusions: A Critique of Individualism* (Chapel Hill: University of North Carolina Press, 1991).

7. For the mixed results of school reform, see William A. Link, *A Hard Country and a Lonely Place: Schooling, Society, and Reform in Rural Virginia, 1870–1920* (Chapel Hill: University of North Carolina Press, 1986); James Leloudis, *Schooling the New South: Pedagogy, Self, and Society in North Carolina, 1880–1920* (Chapel Hill: University of North Carolina Press, 1996); James D. Anderson, *The Education of Blacks in the South, 1860–1935* (Chapel Hill: University of North Carolina Press, 1988).

8. Jack Temple Kirby, *The Countercultural South* (Athens: University of Georgia Press, 1995); Simon, *Fabric of Defeat;* Bartley, *Creation;* Hall et al., *Like a Family;* Jimmy Carter, *Turning Point: A Candidate, a State, and a Nation Come of Age* (New York: Three Rivers Press, 1992).

9. "A History of the Georgia Civil Works Administration, 1933–1934," 2–3, Gay Bolling Shepperson Papers, box 1, folder 1, Atlanta History Center, Atlanta (AHC).

10. Cocking, *Report,* 15–18; Georgia Fact-Finding Committee, "Georgia—Education," 2–3.

11. U.S. Bureau of the Census, *Sixteenth Census of the United States: 1940 Characteristics of the Population,* vol. 2, pt. 2, Florida–Iowa (Washington, D.C.: U.S. Government Printing Office, 1942), 202.

12. Leo M. Favrot, "Negro Public Education in the South," 1925, 3, ser. 1.2, box 315,

folder 3297, GEB Files; Jackson Davis, "Recent Developments in Negro Schools and Colleges," exhibit A, p. 1, ser. 1.2, box 315, folder 3296, GEB Files. See also Louis R. Harlan, *Southern School Campaigns and Racism in the Southern Seaboard States, 1901–1915* (New York: Atheneum, 1968); Bartley, *Creation;* James D. Anderson, *Education of Blacks.*

13. Fred McCuistion, *Higher Education of Negroes (A Summary)* (Nashville: Southern Association of Colleges and Secondary Schools, 1933), 18; U.S. Bureau of the Census, *Fifteenth Census of the United States: 1930 Population,* vol. 3 (Washington, D.C.: U.S. Government Printing Office, 1932), 456.

14. "Average Annual Salaries of White and Negro Teachers, Principals, and Supervisors, 1933–34," Campaign for Educational Equality, 1913–50, pt. 3, ser. A, reel 3, NAACP papers.

15. "Inequalities in Expenditures for Public Schools," 3, Campaign for Educational Equality, 1913–50, pt. 3, ser. A, reel 3, NAACP papers.

16. Georgia Department of Education, *Sixtieth and Sixty-first Annual Reports of the Department of Education to the General Assembly of the State of Georgia for the Biennium Ending June 30, 1932* (Atlanta: State Printing Office, 1932), 6.

17. Bartley, *Creation,* 160.

18. Ibid., 158.

19. Georgia Department of Education, *Sixtieth and Sixty-first Annual Reports,* 100; U.S. Bureau of the Census, *Fifteenth Census,* 494, 502.

20. George M. Marsden, *Fundamentalism and American Culture: The Shaping of Twentieth Century Evangelicalism, 1870–1925* (New York: Oxford University Press, 1980); Mark A. Noll, *A History of Christianity in the United States and Canada* (Grand Rapids, Mich.: Eerdmans, 1992).

21. Waters, interview.

22. Ann Short Chirhart, " 'Gardens of Education': Beulah Rucker and African-American Education in the Georgia Upcountry," *Georgia Historical Quarterly* 82 (winter 1998): 829–47; Glenda E. Gilmore, *Gender and Jim Crow: Women and the Politics of White Supremacy in North Carolina, 1896–1920* (Chapel Hill: University of North Carolina Press, 1996); Adam Fairclough " 'Being in the Field of Education and Also Being a Negro . . . Seems . . . Tragic': Black Teachers in the Jim Crow South," *Journal of American History* 87 (June 2000): 65–111.

23. Georgia Department of Education, *Thirty-ninth Annual Report of the Department of Education to the General Assembly of the State of Georgia for the School Year Ending December 31, 1910* (Atlanta: Charles Byrd, 1911), 255, 387–88; Georgia Department of Education, *Sixtieth and Sixty-first Annual Reports,* 148, 179.

24. Stephanie J. Shaw, *What a Woman Ought to Be and to Do: Black Professional Women Workers during the Jim Crow Era* (Chicago: University of Chicago Press, 1996); Gilmore, *Gender and Jim Crow;* Chirhart, "Gardens of Education."

25. Beulah Rucker Oliver, *The Rugged Pathway* (n.p., 1953), 3.

26. On rural women, see Mary Neth, *Preserving the Family Farm: Women, Community, and the Foundations of Agribusiness in the Midwest* (Baltimore: Johns Hopkins University Press, 1995); Rebecca Sharpless, *Fertile Ground, Narrow Choices: Women on Texas Cotton Farms, 1900–1940* (Chapel Hill: University of North Carolina Press, 1999).

27. Williams, interview.

28. Nelle Still Murphy and Florrie Still, interview by author, May 9, 1997, Gainesville, Ga.

29. Ann Short Chirhart, "Torches of Light: African American and White Female Teachers in the Georgia Upcountry, 1910–1950" (Ph.D. diss., Emory University, 1997), chaps. 3, 4.

30. Jackson Davis, "State Normal Schools and Agricultural and Mechanical Colleges for Negroes, 1912–1922," ser. 1.2, box 313, folder 3267, GEB Files.

31. Murphy and Still, interview.

32. Chirhart, "Torches of Light," chap. 3.

33. Report of Committee on School Plant Rehabilitation, *Improvement and Beautification of Rural Schools* (Nashville: Julius Rosenwald Fund, 1936), 5, RG 12, ser. 62, box 2, Georgia Department of Education, Division of Negro Education, Georgia Department of Archives and History, Atlanta (hereafter, GDAH).

34. Georgia Association of Jeanes Curriculum Directors, *Jeanes Supervisors in Georgia Schools: A Guiding Light in Education* (Athens: Graphic Composition, 1975), 35; Georgia Department of Education, *Fifty-eighth and Fifty-ninth Annual Reports of the Department of Education to the General Assembly of the State of Georgia for the Biennium Ending June 30, 1930* (Atlanta: State Printing Office, 1930), 40.

35. Georgia Department of Education, *Sixtieth and Sixty-first Annual Reports*, 208.

36. "Report Home Demonstration Work Georgia, 1917," Extension Service Annual Reports Georgia, 1909–44, RG 33, reel 2, 1916 (Gordon County)—Director 1918, National Archives Center, College Park, Md. (hereafter, USDA). See also "Annual Report of Home Demonstration Work for Women and Girls Calendar Year 1919, Jackson County, Lurline Collier," RG 33, reel 3, 1918 (Home Demonstration Leader)—1920 (Veterinary), USDA; Daniel, *Breaking the Land*; Neth, *Preserving the Family Farm*; Sharpless, *Fertile Ground, Narrow Choices*.

37. "Report of Negro Home Demonstration Agent of State by Camilla Weems," RG 33, reel 31, Georgia 1909–44, 1928 (County Agent Leader—Chatham County), USDA.

38. William Anderson, *The Wild Man from Sugar Creek: The Political Career of Eugene Talmadge* (Baton Rouge: Louisiana State University Press, 1975), chap. 5. See also Simon, *Fabric of Defeat*; and Bartley, *Creation*.

39. William Anderson, *Wild Man*; Bartley, *Creation*; Calvin Lytle and James A. Mackay, *Who Runs Georgia? A Contemporary Account of the 1947 Crisis That Set the Stage for Georgia's Political Transformation* (Athens: University of Georgia Press, 1998).

40. William Anderson, *Wild Man*, chap. 8. See also Simon, *Fabric of Defeat*; and Ted Ownby, *Subduing Satan: Religion, Recreation, and Manhood in the Rural South, 1865–1920* (Chapel Hill: University of North Carolina Press, 1990).

41. Michael S. Holmes, *The New Deal in Georgia: An Administrative History* (Westport, Conn.: Greenwood Press, 1974), chap. 1.

42. "Summary of Gay Bolling Shepperson," Shepperson Papers.

43. See, for example, Gilmore, *Gender and Jim Crow*; Robyn Muncy, *Creating a Female Dominion in American Reform, 1890–1935* (New York: Oxford University Press, 1991); Sarah Wilkerson-Freeman, " 'The Woman Who Beat the Governor': Gay Shepperson of the Georgia New Deal vs. Eugene Talmadge and the Old Order," paper presented at the annual meeting of the Southern Historical Association, Fort Worth, Tex., November 1991.

44. Roger Biles, *The South and the New Deal* (Lexington: University Press of Kentucky, 1994), 64.

45. "Federal Emergency Relief Administration," September 29, 1933, signed by Eugene Talmadge and Alan Johnstone, "Confidential Political File, 1933–38," box 40, folder T, Hopkins Papers; Johnstone to Hopkins, September 18, 1933, box 40, folder Sa–Sl, Hopkins Papers; Holmes, *New Deal*, chap. 1.

46. Johnstone to Hopkins, September 18, 1933, box 40, folder Sa–Sl, Hopkins Papers.

47. Talmadge to Franklin Roosevelt, January 10, 1934, "Confidential Political File, 1933–38," box 40, folder T, Hopkins Papers.

48. Johnstone to Hopkins, September 18, 1933, box 40, folder Sa–Sl, Hopkins Papers; see also box 1, folder 2, "Business Correspondence 1933–45," Shepperson Papers.

49. William Anderson, *Wild Man*, 95.

50. "History of the Georgia Civil Works Administration," 58.

51. Quoted in William Anderson, *Wild Man*, 209.

52. "Material Assistance Requested," Papers of Eleanor Roosevelt, ser. 150, Franklin Delano Roosevelt Library, Hyde Park, N.Y. (hereafter, ER Papers). See also Robert Cohen, ed., "Public Schools in Hard Times: Letters from Georgia Educators and Students to Eleanor and Franklin Roosevelt, 1933–1940," *Georgia Historical Quarterly* 82 (spring 1998): 120–49.

53. Mrs. J. W. Sharp to Eleanor Roosevelt, March 9, 1934, ser. 150, "Material Assistance Requested, 1934," boxes 2202–2203, folder Sh–Sn, ER Papers.

54. Varina Edwards to Eleanor Roosevelt, June 11, 1934, ser. 150, "Material Assistance Requested, 1934," boxes 2192–94, folder E–Ha, ER Papers.

55. Johnstone to Hopkins, January 19, 1934, "Confidential Political File, 1933–38," box 40, folder T, Hopkins Papers.

56. In addition to Georgia, Hopkins federalized the relief administrations in Oklahoma and Louisiana during the 1930s. See Biles, *South and the New Deal*, 64–65.

57. Holmes, *New Deal*, 22–23.

58. Hopkins and Shepperson, April 22, 1935, FERA-WPA Transcripts of Telephone

Conversations: Alabama–Kansas, boxes 71–74, "Transcripts of Telephone Conversations, Georgia–Illinois" folder, Hopkins Papers.

59. "News Clippings Notebook," box 1, folder 4, Shepperson Papers; Johnstone to Hopkins, March 6, 1935, box 22, "FERA Procedural Issuances, 1933–35" folder, Hopkins Papers.

60. "Relief in Georgia Hit in Resolution Offered in House," *Atlanta Journal,* February 10, 1935, "News Clippings Notebook," box 1, folder 4, Shepperson Papers.

61. Lee S. Polansky, " 'I Certainly Hope That You Will Be Able to Train Her': Reformers and the Georgia Training School for Girls," in *Before the New Deal: Social Welfare in the South, 1830–1930,* ed. Elna C. Green (Athens: University of Georgia Press, 1999).

62. Murphy and Still, interview.

63. Tarleton Collier, "Behind Headlines: The GERA and State Politics. Some Facts for the Probe," *Atlanta Georgian,* February 20, 1935, "News Clippings Notebook," box 1, folder 4, Shepperson Papers.

64. Johnstone to Hopkins, March 6, 1935, "Confidential Political File, 1933–38," box 40, folder T, Hopkins Papers.

65. See Georgia Department of Education, *Sixtieth and Sixty-first Annual Reports,* 6. See also Walter B. Hill Jr. to S. L. Smith, March 16, 1929, box 337, folder 10, JRF papers.

66. Bartley, *Creation,* chap. 8.

67. Hill to Clark Foreman, February 15, 1934, record group 33-1-41, box 44, GDAH. See also Dillard Lasseter, "Report on the National Youth Administration in Georgia, June 26, 1935 to December 31, 1938," RG 119, box 55, National Youth Administration Processed and Printed Materials, National Archives, Washington, D.C. (hereafter, NYA).

68. Lasseter, "Report"; William Shell, "The Negro and the National Youth Administration in Georgia, Bulletin 13, 1939," RG 119, Georgia box 35, NYA. See also Florence Fleming Corley, "The National Youth Administration in Georgia, a New Deal for Young Blacks and Women," *Georgia Historical Quarterly* 77 (winter 1993): 728–56; Sitkoff, *New Deal.*

69. Inez Oliveros, "Final Report, National Youth Administration for the State of Georgia, June 1935–July 1943," 14, RG 119, box 1, Final Reports of Forty-Six States with NYA Offices, NYA.

70. "National Youth Administration of Georgia Monthly Narrative for Month ending October 31, 1937," and "Final Report," 28, RG 119, Final Reports of the Division, 1936–39, box 1, Georgia 1936–37, NYA.

71. Richard A. Reiman, *The New Deal and American Youth: Ideas and Ideals in a Depression Decade* (Athens: University of Georgia Press, 1992).

72. Grace Palladino, *Teenagers: An American History* (New York: Basic Books), 38–46.

73. For a comparison of New Deal programs for women in Georgia, see Hickey in this

volume. Shepperson may have been reluctant to implement vocational training in the sewing rooms in part because of the harsh criticism she faced from the time she became head of Georgia's WPA programs. Because the NYA was administered at the federal level, it was less susceptible to local attacks.

74. Dillard Lasseter, "Youth Case Histories from Georgia," October 25, 1939, 5, Group 58, National Youth Administration, box 15, "Miscellaneous NYA Reports (Printed) and Final Reports," folder "Georgia Youth—Lasseter," Papers of Aubrey Williams, FDR Library, Hyde Park, N.Y.

75. Ibid, 81.

76. David M. Kennedy, *Freedom from Fear: The American People in Depression and War, 1929–1945* (New York: Oxford University Press, 1999), 368–80.

77. Sullivan, *Days of Hope*, 42–44.

78. Jerome Robinson, Alton Childs II, J. Garfield Dashiell, and Charles Lawrence, "A Comparative Study of Teacher Salary Differentials in Georgia, Tennessee, and North Carolina," 1939, 1–4, Campaign for Educational Equality, pt. 3, ser. A, reel 3, NAACP Papers.

79. Fred McCuiston, *The South's Negro Teaching Force* (Nashville: Julius Rosenwald Fund, 1931); Favrot, "Negro Public Education"; U.S. Office of Education, *Availability of Education to Negroes in Rural Communities* (Washington, D.C.: U.S. Government Printing Office, 1935).

80. Robinson et al., "Comparative Study," 6.

81. Ibid.

82. "A Bill to Promote the General Welfare through the Appropriation of Funds to Assist the States and Territories in Providing More Effective Programs of Public Education," Senator Pat Harrison, June 20, 1936, Campaign for Educational Equality, pt. 3, ser. A, reel 3, NAACP Papers.

83. "Amend or Defeat the Harrison-Black Bill," Campaign for Educational Equality, 1913–50, ser. A, pt. 3, reel 3, NAACP Papers.

84. Walter White to Agnes Samuelson, December 31, 1936, Campaign for Educational Equality, pt. 3, ser. A, reel 3, NAACP Papers.

85. "Some Questions Regarding the Harrison-Fletcher Bill for Federal Aid to Education," 1–4, Campaign for Educational Equality, pt. 3, ser. A, reel 3, NAACP Papers.

86. "House Committee on Education Holds Hearing on Twice-Amended Federal Aid to Education Bill," April 2, 1937, Campaign for Educational Equality, ser. A, pt. 3, reel 3, NAACP Papers.

87. "Opinion," *Georgia Education Journal*, November 1941, 10.

88. Williams, interview; Waters, interview; Still, interview.

89. "General Education Board Negro Education Meeting," November 17, 1927, ser. 1.2, box 315, folder 3295, GEB Files.

90. Steadman Sanford to Edwin Embree, March 18, 1939, Horace Mann Bond to Sanford, June 17, 1939, RG 33–1–51, box 52, GDAH.

91. Fred Wales to Embree, June 26, 1941, box 204, folder 2, JRF Papers; Harmon Caldwell to A. R. Mann, June 9, 1941, ser. 1.1, box 56, folder 497, GEB Files; William Anderson, *Wild Man*, chap. 16; Henderson, *Politics*, chaps. 2, 3; Bartley, *Creation*, 193–95.

92. William Anderson, *Wild Man*; Henderson, *Politics*.

93. Quoted in William Anderson, *Wild Man*, 200, 197.

94. William A. Fowlkes, "Seeing and Saying," *Atlanta Daily World*, July 15, 1941.

95. Henderson, *Politics*, 42, 46; Anderson, *Wild Man*, 212; newspaper clippings from *Atlanta Constitution and Atlanta Journal*, n.d., box 204, folder 2, JRF Papers.

96. *Georgia Education Journal*, August 1942, 12–13.

97. Henderson, *Politics*, 44–46.

98. "Talmadge Is Right," *Atlanta Daily World*, July 6, 1942, 4.

99. Henderson, *Politics*, 97.

100. Ibid., 100.

101. Ibid.

102. Ibid. See also Joiner, ed., *History*, chaps. 4, 5.

103. Georgia Department of Education, *Sixtieth and Sixty-first Annual Reports*, 208; Georgia Department of Education, *Seventieth and Seventy-first Annual Reports of the Department of Education to the General Assembly of Georgia for the Biennium Ending June 30, 1942* (Atlanta: State Printing Office, 1942), 252.

104. Georgia Department of Education, *Sixtieth and Sixty-first Annual Reports*, 212; Georgia Department of Education, *Seventieth and Seventy-first Annual Reports*, 258.

In the Public Interest?

*The Social and Cultural Impact of the
Blue Ridge Parkway, a Depression-Era
Appalachian "Public-Works" Project*

TED OLSON

The Blue Ridge Parkway is the most visited unit of the U.S. National Park Service, with approximately eighteen million "visits" per year during the 1990s. This figure not only accounts for use by local residents but also reflects the parkway's popularity among millions of urban and suburban dwellers from the eastern megalopolis.[1] Two scholars, Harley Jolley and Anne Mitchell, have thoroughly explored the parkway's political history.[2] In numerous books and articles dating back to the 1960s, Jolley has characterized the parkway as having been constructed in the public interest; Mitchell, in a more recent revisionist study, has challenged this view, suggesting that the promoters of the parkway had ulterior, private motivations. Whatever their merits, Jolley's and Mitchell's works focus primarily on political concerns. Neither author adequately explores the question of whether the Blue Ridge Parkway bettered social and cultural conditions for the majority of the people whose lives that depression-era project directly affected. This chapter will attempt to correct that oversight.[3]

A public-works project from President Franklin Delano Roosevelt's New Deal, the parkway emerged out of the confluence of two seemingly contradictory national socioeconomic movements. The first, initially promoted by conservationists but embraced by the mavens of tourism, was the post–World War I campaign to establish national parks in the eastern United States. One of this movement's long-range objectives was to reconstruct in that part of the nation some semblance of the natural environment and the cultural milieu of frontier America for the purpose of preserving traces of that heritage for posterity.

The second movement, promoted by the automobile and tourism industries as well as by federal and state governments, involved the development, mostly in rural areas, of "scenic highways" to serve the recreational needs of urbanites and suburbanites, many of whom were eager to explore the countryside by car. Although a number of scenic highways (later referred to as *parkways*) were planned during the economic boom of the 1920s, few were built because of high costs. Ironically, rather than curbing progress toward the development of parkways, the nationwide economic decline of the early 1930s fostered the ideal political climate for a deepened commitment to that type of road. Governments—at both the federal and state levels—made available generous amounts of funding to sustain such projects. Spending on public-works projects could easily be justified to depression-era Americans, as the building of parkways was then widely deemed to be an ideal way to benefit disfranchised Americans in economically distressed sections of the nation; at the same time, parkways created new recreational opportunities for upper- and middle-class Americans.[4]

While the New Deal provided much of the funding for depression-era parkways, Roosevelt was in fact furthering a mission begun during the previous presidential administration. One of the earliest and best known of the government-sponsored parkway projects, Skyline Drive (located in the northern Virginia Blue Ridge within Shenandoah National Park), despite being built largely under Roosevelt's watch, was a legacy of President Herbert Hoover. In 1930, believing that a scenic highway project in the newly created Shenandoah National Park would generate jobs for some Americans while facilitating recreational opportunities for all Americans, Hoover helped to pass legislation and to secure funding for Skyline Drive, and construction began the next year. Unfinished at the beginning of the New Deal, Skyline Drive became one of Roosevelt's initial public-works priorities. In 1933 the nation's first Civilian Conservation Corps camps were positioned in Shenandoah National Park in order to complete the Skyline Drive project.[5]

Also in 1933, witnessing the realization of Skyline Drive, government officials and agents of tourism launched campaigns for similar projects elsewhere in the southeastern United States. Encouraged by the availability of extensive federal funds for public-works projects through the National Industrial Recovery Act of 1933, a number of promoters of Skyline Drive (initially a collection of disparate individuals, including U.S. Senator Harry Flood Byrd of Virginia, rather than an organized, unified group) planned another parkway project to connect Shenandoah National Park with Great Smoky Mountains

National Park, both of which had recently been added to the National Park Service system. Aware that New Deal public-works money was overtly intended to fund projects that would generate jobs for unemployed Americans, promoters' official statements about this particular parkway project, later called the Blue Ridge Parkway, accentuated job creation as their primary motivation, declaring that the construction of a new scenic highway in the Virginia and North Carolina Blue Ridge had the potential to improve conditions for people living in Appalachia, an economically distressed region. Furthermore, promoters promised that the construction of the Blue Ridge Parkway would directly improve the region's economy by drawing tourists. Promoters' self-professed altruism was subsequently reinforced by the media, which in its coverage of the parkway in the 1930s tended toward romanticization, stressing the road's potential social benefits and rarely addressing other motivations for its construction.[6]

Parkway promoters were politically savvy to suggest economic empowerment as a justification for their project: despite the considerable amount of funding required for its completion, few Americans would then doubt that a goodwill, public-works project was a legitimate recipient of public money. Most Americans of that era would not have questioned a scenic highway's impact on local society and culture, since the Blue Ridge was part of Appalachia, a region that many depression-era Americans believed to be remote, isolated, and backward. Many Americans viewed residents of Appalachia as "mountain people" in need of outside assistance.

Although such negative attitudes people would today be considered uninformed, they predated the parkway. During the first half of the twentieth century, stereotyped representations of Appalachian people were common among outsiders and even appeared among some elite insiders, generally those who lived in valleys and who thought themselves to be of a higher class than their hillside neighbors. Significantly, insiders stood to gain more than outsiders did from an Appalachia-based economic-development project. Despite the extensive involvement of state and federal governmental officials, the most passionate parkway promoters were members of local elites. As Mitchell persuasively argues, the parkway's promoters were not entirely altruistic philanthropists seeking to improve life for the people of the Blue Ridge; rather, proponents were also well aware of the economic boon the parkway might bring to many people, including themselves and their peers in the tourism industry. Before Mitchell, scholars who studied the Blue Ridge Parkway (particularly Jolley) had overlooked the more self-interested motivations of promoters and instead had viewed the parkway exclusively as a beneficent public-works project.[7] Asserting that the parkway has had "a complex and conflicted history much more directly related to the development of [the regional] tourist industry than . . . imagined," Mitchell contends that parkway promoters were as motivated by personal gain as by possible public benefit; thus, Mitchell invalidates the romanticized characterization of the parkway (generated by the park's promoters, the media, and earlier scholars) as having been primarily a depression-era goodwill gesture from federal and state governments to the American people.[8]

The Blue Ridge Parkway was the second of four scenic highways across the United States to receive designation as a "national parkway" and became a distinct park unit within the National Park Service system.[9] The longest national parkway, the Blue Ridge Parkway extends for 469 miles from Rockfish Gap, Virginia, to Cherokee, North Carolina. Approved for construction on June 16, 1933, the parkway was incorporated into the National Park Service system in 1936. In 1934, a sustained public debate took place over whether the parkway would be built in Virginia and North Carolina or in Virginia and Tennessee. Elites from both western North Carolina and eastern Tennessee realized that the reward for winning the parkway extended beyond jobs and prestige to include countless possibilities for enduring tourism. In November of that year, U.S. Secretary of the Interior Harold Ickes, who also headed the Public Works Administration, proclaimed that the parkway would be routed through Virginia and western North Carolina. Ickes defended his decision by asserting that Tennessee was already receiving federal support for various Tennessee Valley Authority projects.[10]

The building of the parkway posed problems beyond the road's length and route. From 1933 to 1936, the road—officially named the Blue Ridge Parkway in 1936—received extensive federal funding channeled through the Public Works Administration. After 1936 the parkway was financed directly by Congress. Construction companies hired by the Bureau of Public Roads built the road itself (including tunnels and bridges); contractors had to carve out a modern two-lane paved road (carefully banked for the safety of motorists) along the remarkably rugged mountain crest of the easternmost range in Appalachia. Since the parkway was mandated by law to be a scenic rather than conventional highway, private contractors were obligated to heed strict aesthetic and engineering standards. Works Progress Administration and Civilian Conservation Corps workers were responsible for the parkway's landscaping, signage, visitor centers, hiking trails, roadside parks, campgrounds, museums, and scenic overlooks. The parkway traversed the Blue Ridge through dense forest as well as across cultivated fields; some of the land sought for the parkway's right-of-way was already publicly owned, but most of it was privately held. To prevent future development alongside the parkway, surveyors sought a scenic easement, a buffer zone approximately one thousand feet on either side of the road. Since by the 1930s much of the Blue Ridge had been environmentally abused by overfarming and logging, most of the parkway's scenic easements would receive decorative landscaping by the National Park Service, with the goal of giving the visual landscape a pre–twentieth century appearance. Landowners were prohibited from building structures on easements, and commercial advertisements such as billboards were restricted.

Building the road required rights-of-way and easements from many individual property owners. During discussions regarding the distribution of financial responsibilities for the parkway, the U.S. government and the governments of Virginia and North Carolina had mutually resolved that the two states would obtain the rights-of-way and easements and donate them to the federal government, which would subsequently construct and manage the parkway. Virginia's and North Carolina's efforts to obtain land were soon stymied by the reality of state government coffers depleted by the depression. In some cases, the two states bought parcels of land outright from landowners; more often, however, the states sought to obtain rights-of-way and scenic easements at considerably less than full cost. To acquire easements, the two states paid landowners a portion—generally between 40 and 75 percent—of a given property's full value. While technically allowing the original landowner to retain ownership of a piece of property, the concept of a scenic easement was soon questioned. Blue Ridge residents began to balk at the fact that landowners were unable to do whatever they pleased on a portion of their own property.[11] Edward H. Abbuehl, a landscape architect during the early years of the parkway, recalled that landowners in the 1930s often expressed to him their disdain for the scenic-easement policy, fearing that they would lose control over their fates. As one Blue Ridge resident told Abbuehl, "If it was a mortgage on the land, I could hope that I might live long enough to be able to pay it off, but with this here scenic easement, there is nothing I can do as long as I live."[12]

The parkway's first superintendent and resident landscape architect, Stanley W. Abbott, acknowledged in 1958 that the establishment of the parkway interfered with the Blue Ridge people's relationship with the place that had sustained them and their ancestors: "The scenic easement is a comparatively sophisticated idea that was difficult to explain to the Scotch-Irish mountaineer, who could not quite conceive how you could own land and not own it outright, in every regard to do with it as [you] might wish."[13] In an attempt to ameliorate the situation, Virginia and North Carolina began to offer Blue Ridge landowners a less extreme form of easement known as a fee simple. However, landowners still felt that they lost much and gained little for surrendering the use of their land for the parkway.[14]

Furthermore, North Carolina's Highway and Public Works Commission rarely contacted individual landowners directly to negotiate mutually acceptable property settlements; instead, that agency, wielding absolute yet faceless authority, posted at county courthouses maps that identified the properties to be condemned for the parkway.[15] According to William Hooper, an agronomist during the early years of the parkway, the North Carolina lands were "acquired just by deed of acquisition, all in one parcel. No individual deeds [were] recorded."[16] Witnessing such treatment, some resentful Blue Ridge landholders in both North Carolina and Virginia refused to negotiate with parkway representatives. In those cases, the states resorted to condemning private properties through the legal mechanism of eminent domain. For their condemned properties, landowners were entitled by law to receive financial compensation, but state government officials generally attempted to bargain down the price of properties. For example, Bernard Turner, a native of Henry County, Virginia, who worked on the parkway in the 1930s, recalled that he and his brothers received only six dollars each for the condemnation sale of his family's Virginia Blue Ridge landholdings, which stood in the way of a planned government-sponsored dam's backflow.[17] Aware that the properties chosen for the parkway varied widely in terms of location, elevation, and environmental condition, the two states maintained an official silence regarding the prices to be paid for land. North Carolina Governor J. C. B. Ehringhaus mandated that the state Highway and Public Works Commission not publicly disclose such information so that the state might retain the upper hand in negotiations. The commission, however, granted special favors to certain landowners. For example, North Carolina paid an average of between thirty-three and thirty-five dollars per acre (and sometimes a lot less) for other properties intended for the parkway, but the state spent fifty dollars per acre for land obtained from the Linville Company, a resort cooperative owned by politically well connected outsiders.[18]

Many Blue Ridge residents whose lands were obtained by the two states (whether through negotiation or condemnation) were dealt the additional indignity of not being compensated in a timely manner. As a result of the states' failure to provide sufficient and/or prompt payment for properties taken from landowners, many Blue Ridge residents refused to leave their houses. The two states mandated the removal of people who remained on previously negotiated or condemned parkway landholdings, thereby engaging in a practice similar to the National Park Service's contemporaneous yet more systematic and larger-scale displacement of residents from Shenandoah and Great Smoky Mountains National Parks. Those two parks were attempting to construct eastern "wildernesses," though the true aboriginal Appalachian forests had long since been cut down by settlers or by logging and mining companies. According to Mitchell, "Unlike the process involved in creating the great western parks, the development of the new eastern parks involved removing most traces of the years of human habitation and use (farming, logging, even tourism) in new park areas, which were not the isolated and pristine paradises they were touted to be."[19] Hence, as part of the effort to manufacture "wilderness" within those two parks, the federal government sometimes authorized forced removals of human residents from within the parks' boundaries. The governments of Virginia and North Carolina, constructing the parkway through the inhabited Blue Ridge, likewise forced some people from their homes and farms. Displacement was particularly traumatic and alienating for the many Blue Ridge families that had resided in the same locales for several generations (in some cases, for nearly two centuries).

Although the parkway's relatively narrow corridor permitted many Blue Ridge residents to remain on their rural farms, those residents were forced to heed restrictions on the activities that they could conduct on their properties' easement sections. For example, Hooper related that the purchased easements destroyed existing agricultural fence lines; maintained for generations, those lines had been integral to many farmers' livelihoods, allowing the raising of livestock.[20] Some Blue Ridge residents expressed anger that the parkway was built between them and their familial churches and cemeteries, physically separating them from the sources of their spiritual renewal. Furthermore, the National Park Service limited access to the parkway and banned commercial traffic: local residents could not use the parkway to transport farm products to market. (The new road's higher speed limit would have caused conflicts between tourists and the slow-moving farm vehicles and ox-drawn carts employed by Blue Ridge farmers in the 1930s.) Turner acknowledged that the parkway was dangerous in its early years: locals driving on the parkway would sometimes "run into something."[21]

Documentary evidence from the first three decades of the twentieth century suggests that before the establishment of the parkway, many people in the Blue Ridge had maintained a largely traditional, regionally specific way of life that depended little (if at all) on paved roads. This way of life was flexible, involving complex traditional elements. At the time of the parkway's construction, many Blue Ridge residents were remarkably self-sufficient, practicing small-scale farming while complementing their diets with wild plants and with meat from wild animals. Homer Reeves, a native of Sparta, North Carolina, and a construction worker on the parkway, remembered that during his youth, people "had plenty of time to fish and hunt. And there was plenty of fish and plenty of game."[22] While virtually all Americans during the 1930s were affected to some degree by the depression, Blue Ridge residents as a whole were less seriously influenced than most Americans and certainly less harmed than people living in more industrialized parts of Appalachia, such as in the eastern Kentucky coal fields. Abbott conveyed in 1958 that Blue Ridge residents had maintained a self-sufficient way of life into the 1930s:

> The people along the parkway, its immediate neighbors, . . . are distinctly country folk, of limited horizons. . . . In the early days—and of course all this has changed slowly—they looked with distrust on people who came in from the outside, from whatever direction. One of the sure things, . . . they had an isolated economy, for the most part a hand-to-mouth living; the more backward [people of the Blue Ridge] existed, rather than lived; it was a matter of very few cash crops. In the early depression days they must have felt something of the nation's wide downturn, though far less, comparatively, than the people of other parts of the United States.[23]

Until parkway-related right-of-way and scenic easement negotiations and condemnations upset the continuity of traditional life, many residents on small farmsteads maintained a way of life radically different from that found in mainstream America. Abbott acknowledged the Blue Ridge people's self-sufficiency, stating, "The people along the parkway, in the very early days before the grapevine had worked fully, resented our coming, [our] interfering with accustomed privacy, or [our] stumbling on a pile of leaves and uncovering one of their stills, or otherwise disturbing them in their perfectly sufficient, agreeable, and pleasant life in the mountains."[24] Some Blue Ridge counties were so rural during the 1930s that the parkway constituted the first paved road constructed within their boundaries.[25] Recalling life in the Blue Ridge before the arrival of the parkway, Buren Ballard of Weaverville, North Carolina, said, "We didn't have no electricity, no Frigidaire or nothing. And we had to cook on a wood stove. And keep our milk and butter in the spring. [We] didn't buy no produce. 'Course . . . everybody had a cow and had a chicken. Didn't have to buy nothing."[26] Even Blue Ridge town dwellers lived differently from their contemporaries in small towns in other American regions. According to parkway landscaper Ted Pease, "You couldn't get fresh meat [in Sparta, North Carolina]. You couldn't get fresh vegetables in the store [because] everybody had a garden."[27]

Tourists viewed residents, who had surrendered much of their ancestral rural economic and cultural autonomy for the sake of the parkway, as embodiments of the Appalachian hillbilly stereotype rather than as models of good citizenship, as loyal Americans who had, willingly or grudgingly, sacrificed their resources for a larger national mission. Some nonnatives who worked on the parkway side by side with natives also projected stereotyped, paternalistic attitudes toward locals and their culture.[28] From this perspective, parkway promoters—whether private citizens, business leaders, or government officials—assured the region's people that the project would bring economic empowerment. Yet in their obeisance to the elite values of positivistic social science, those promoters did not adequately address the profound social and cultural changes that economic development would necessarily force on Blue Ridge residents, endangering their distinctive traditional regional culture. Raleigh Hollefield, a contract laborer and native of Little Switzerland, North Carolina, remembered his 1930s employment with the parkway as having severed him from his father's more self-directed life of small-scale agriculture: "That's all I've ever done, construction work. . . . We didn't have time to enjoy nothing. We left at daylight and come back at dark. [On weekends I] didn't do too much of anything but rest. You needed it [after working fifty-five hours each week]."[29]

Parkway promoters and the media during the 1930s ignored the fact that Blue Ridge residents were considerably self-sufficient economically and self-assured culturally. Drawing on the poor and passive characterization that has historically been at the core of the hillbilly stereotype, the project's supporters paternalistically suggested that the parkway's mission was to empower economically disadvantaged Appalachian mountain people. Dillard Teer, whose father owned the company responsible for constructing some of the earliest stretches of the parkway, betrayed the degree to which the road's promoters and the media projected a distorted picture of the traditional Blue Ridge way of life as a life of poverty: "Mr. Roosevelt [and] Mr. Ickes decided they were going to help out the Appalachian area of North Carolina. [The people there] were so poor, they were . . . dirt poor. Some of them didn't even have heat in their houses, except for an old stove, and half [the time] it didn't work."[30]

Parkway proponents ignored the fact that constant interaction with local ecosystems had resulted in a regionally specific practice of land stewardship. The region's residents had learned through trial and error how to coexist with the forces of nature in their particular place. Over time, Blue Ridge dwellers had developed a sophisticated set of agricultural traditions. However, the depression's mounting economic impact meant that many able-bodied Blue Ridge men accepted the opportunity to earn extra cash by working on road construction. The parkway led to a general escalation in the cost of living in the Blue Ridge. According to Turner, "I guess it increased the value of the place."[31]

While quick to discuss positive contributions, parkway supporters rarely acknowledged any negative consequences of the road. Interestingly, though Abbott recalled that many people in the Blue Ridge were living self-sufficiently in the 1930s, Samuel P. Weems, the parkway's second superintendent, felt that the road offered only benefits to the region:

[The parkway] had been a boon to them, because [it] came along right after the chestnut was killed, in the mid-twenties. The mountain people used to gather chestnuts for a cash crop. . . . When the chestnuts were killed through the mountains, . . . they only had sawmill employment to keep them going. Well, when the depression hit, there was no market, hardly, for the lumber; then all the sawmills were practically shut down, so the mountain people . . . were desperately in need of employment. But it certainly paid off, because the whole economy of the country changed after we got the parkway going and these people got employment. They spruced up their houses, they started mowing their grass; they saw what we were doing on the parkway and they took pride in trying to keep their places somewhat along the lines of good maintenance that we had been doing.[32]

Jolley, who strongly influenced the contemporary attitude toward the parkway, shares Weems's wholly positive perspective toward the parkway, as evidenced by Jolley's statement that "the possibility of a paved road through the mountains, as began to be rumored in late 1933, stimulated hopes of ending [Blue Ridge residents'] isolation and improving their economy."[33] Of course, any assessment of the Blue Ridge way of life as isolated and in need of "improvement" is inherently subjective. The loss of the chestnut and the decline in lumber sales during the 1930s were not as catastrophic as Weems contended—they were simply new developments in a long series of environmental and economic changes affecting the Blue Ridge region.

The Blue Ridge Parkway was another such development, one that symbolized a sudden yet emphatic readjustment in the balance of political, economic, social, and cultural power within the region. The tourism industry that sprang up around the parkway soon resulted in radical changes, bringing in droves of outsiders. As William Pruitt, a native of Alleghany County, North Carolina, and a former parkway worker, declared, today "everybody wants to live on this mountain when they come through." [34] As the parkway became a reality, inhabitants of the Blue Ridge became increasingly dependent on money, and their mostly self-sufficient way of life began to disappear. As the parkway increasingly encouraged the rise of a money-based economy, many people had no choice but to leave the region to find work. Dean Richardson, a longtime parkway ranger, recalled witnessing this predicament during the 1940s: "You'd drive along and see these little farms, and these old houses. . . . Those people were there when the parkway came. . . . Well then, so what has come of the children that was raised up there? [A] lot of them left. . . . There wasn't much money for them to make, living out there along the Blue Ridge. So they had to move off. . . . The land was for sale. 'Cause they couldn't afford to put a house on it." [35]

In the span of a few years, the parkway not only opened the rural Blue Ridge to millions of outsiders but also transformed the consciousness of the region's people from traditional to modern ways of living and thinking. Teer recalled that in the 1930s many "mountaineers . . . didn't have cars. And some of those people walked fifteen miles a day to get to work [on the construction of the parkway]." [36] In addition, the traditional concept of land use long practiced by Blue Ridge residents—that of individuals as stewards of their own property—was now obsolete, as externally imposed governmental policies controlled everyday activities.

When Blue Ridge farmers realized that the loss of their land to the parkway threatened their agricultural livelihoods, the National Park Service, in an ironic gesture of "goodwill," leased farmland within parkway easements back to its former owners. Although the fees for such leases were modest, farmers were expected to adhere to agricultural practices imposed by a professional agronomist hired by the park service. [37]

While many insiders welcomed the employment generated by the road and while countless outsiders appreciated the recreational opportunities it afforded, the Blue Ridge Parkway accelerated the decline of certain aspects of traditional culture. As the region's residents grew accustomed to the increased presence of commercial goods within their communities and to the growing regional reliance on a money-based economy—modernizing trends accelerated by the parkway's arrival—many of their folkways gradually fell into disuse; before long, some of the more time-consuming and labor-intensive aspects of their regional folklife were neglected, since self-regulated time and labor became increasingly scarce facets of everyday life. William Pruitt's wife, Marie, confessed, "We've got a lot we need to do [on our farm]. It used to be [that] you'd find somebody to do it. Now, you can't get nobody to do it. I don't know when we're gonna do it."[38]

Conversely, the parkway's popularity has ensured the survival of certain other regional traditions, particularly performance activities that appealed to visitors (such as fiddle playing, blacksmithing, and Appalachian traditional dancing) and material-culture traditions that outsiders esteemed as folk art (such as quilting and basket making). In essence, the parkway served as a catalyst in the natural selection of Blue Ridge culture: the road transported residents from a situation of unself-consciousness regarding their cultural worth to an unshakable feeling of discomfort about their regional identities. Illustrating this natural selection, Richardson stated that when land was purchased for the parkway, government officials "put an easement, saying that you couldn't have a sawmill, you couldn't cut any material timber, you couldn't put [out] a sign, you couldn't put [up] a building. But you could keep cattle in it. . . . That's what the Park Service wanted—maintain the scene."[39]

In many areas, the parkway was the first major manifestation of modernization. The early 1940s brought the spectacle in many locales of tourists driving the ultramodern parkway while mountain people traveled along parallel dirt roads in handmade, ox-drawn wagons. This interaction between traditional and modern value systems appealed to urban and suburban tourists, who saw their excursions along the parkway as offering nostalgic retreat from the complexities of modern civilization. For their part, residents accepted—in many cases, welcomed—the new economy. Yet the steady accretion of modernization into previously isolated sections of the Blue Ridge rendered the region's traditional folkways increasingly obsolete. Frequent exposure to outsiders brought self-consciousness and cultural commodification. Property taxes increased, straining the resources of those who had previously survived via small-scale agriculture but could no longer do so. And hunting was no longer permitted in the vicinity of the parkway, depriving area residents of one of their main food sources.

By the 1940s, just as the parkway made travel into and out of the Blue Ridge much more feasible, the war effort demanded the displacement of many people from the region. Those who left the Blue Ridge at this time either did not return or came home utterly changed by their experiences outside their native region. Life was not the same in the Blue Ridge, even for those who had never left. Residents no longer controlled their own destinies, having grown dependent on external economic support.

The parkway belongs to all Americans. Many Americans think that the Blue Ridge itself also belongs to them, in that the region hosts their vacations and/or retirements. Reflecting on the parkway's role in changing human history within the Blue Ridge, Abbuehl identified an overarching irony: in the eighteenth century, "people came down from Pennsylvania and found it was good living [in the Virginia and North Carolina Blue Ridge]. The high altitude, the cool summers. And they could grow wonderful crops. And that's the thing that people are finding out now, wanting to build houses with the Blue Ridge Parkway as their frontage."[40]

Beyond their initial modest financial compensations for rights-of-way and scenic easements on their properties, the people who provided the land on which the parkway was built benefited relatively little from the road. Curtis Evans, a Glade Valley, North Carolina, native and a contract laborer during the early years of the parkway, reflected that "we'd have been better off if it never came through. It took up a lot of land. . . . And you can't do nothing on [the parkway], you can't [use] commercial vehicles. . . . There's just sight-seeing. And it brings stuff in from every part of the country into this country. . . . We'd have been better off without [the parkway]. 'Course I, I enjoyed the money I got out of it, and the job. But we'd [have] been better off in the long run if it [had] never come through."[41]

Notes

1. Dwight F. Rettie, *Our National Park System: Caring for America's Greatest Natural and Historic Treasures* (Urbana: University of Illinois Press, 1995), 51.

2. Anne Virginia Mitchell, "Parkway Politics: Class, Culture, and Tourism in the Blue Ridge" (Ph.D. diss., University of North Carolina at Chapel Hill, 1997); Harley E. Jolley, *Blue Ridge Parkway: The First Fifty Years* ([Boone, N.C.]: Appalachian Consortium Press, 1985); Harley E. Jolley, *The Blue Ridge Parkway* (Knoxville: University of Tennessee Press, 1969). See also Ethan Carr, *Wilderness by Design: Landscape Architecture and the National Park Service* (Lincoln: University of Nebraska Press, 1999).

3. Other aspects of Appalachian culture and history are considered in Phillip J. Obermiller, Thomas E. Wagner, and Edward Bruce Tucker, *Appalachian Odyssey: Historical Perspectives on the Great Migration* (Westport, Conn.: Praeger, 2000); and Sandra Barney, *Authorized to Heal: Gender, Class, and the Transformation of Medicine in Appalachia, 1880–1930* (Chapel Hill: University of North Carolina Press, 2000).

4. See Donald Edward Davis, *Where There Are Mountains: An Environmental History of the Southern Appalachians* (Athens: University of Georgia Press, 2000); C. Brenden Martin, *To Keep the Spirit of Mountain Culture Alive: Tourism and Historical Memory in the Southern Highlands* (Chapel Hill: University of North Carolina Press, 2000); Carr, *Wilderness*.

5. Other treatments of New Deal projects for the Appalachian region include Melissa Walker, *All We Knew Was to Farm: Rural Women in the Upcountry South, 1919–1941* (Baltimore: Johns Hopkins University Press, 2000); Keller Easterling, *Organization Space: Landscapes, Highways, and Houses in America* (Cambridge: MIT Press, 1999); Jerry Bruce Thomas, *An Appalachian New Deal: West Virginia in the Great Depression* (Lexington: University Press of Kentucky, 1998); Paul Salstrom, "Appalachia's Path toward Welfare Dependency, 1840–1940" (Ph.D. diss., Brandeis University, 1988).

6. Mitchell, "Parkway Politics," 4–7.

7. Ibid.

8. Ibid. In a 1969 book-length history of the parkway, Jolley had tagged the road "a godsend for the needy" (*Blue Ridge Parkway,* 50).

9. Skyline Drive was not officially recognized as a national parkway because it was located entirely within Shenandoah National Park. The other "national parkways" are George Washington Memorial Parkway (located in the Washington, D.C., area and originally authorized in 1928 as the Mount Vernon Memorial Highway); the Natchez Trace Parkway (which stretches through Mississippi, Alabama, and Tennessee; was authorized in 1934; and was acquired by the National Park Service in 1938); and the John D. Rockefeller Jr. Memorial Parkway (dedicated in 1972 and located in Wyoming). Several other U.S. roads were also called parkways and received federal or state support but were never authorized as separate National Park Service units, either because they were incorporated into larger park service units

or because they were deemed not to have sufficient cultural or natural significance for inclusion in the National Park Service system.

10. Jolley, *First Fifty Years,* 15.

11. Ronald A. Foresta, *America's National Parks and Their Keepers* (Washington, D.C.: Resources for the Future, 1984), 243.

12. Edward H. Abbuehl, interview by S. Herbert Evison, 1971, National Park Service, Harpers Ferry, W.Va., 17.

13. Stanley W. Abbott, interview by S. Herbert Evison, 1958, National Park Service, Harpers Ferry, W.Va., 29.

14. Recent work on Appalachian culture includes Benita J. Howell, *Culture, Environment, and Conservation in the Appalachian South* (Urbana: University of Illinois Press, 2002); Bill Leonard, *Christianity in Appalachia: Profiles in Regional Pluralism* (Knoxville: University of Tennessee Press, 1999); Carolyn Neale Hickman, "What to Throw Away, What to Keep: Mobilizing Expressive Culture and Regional Reconstruction in Appalachia" (Ph.D. diss., University of North Carolina at Chapel Hill, 1998); Ted Olson, *Blue Ridge Folklife* (Jackson: University Press of Mississippi, 1998).

15. Mitchell, "Parkway Politics," 161.

16. William Hooper, interview by Julie Mullis, 1996, Blue Ridge Parkway Headquarters, Asheville, N.C., 2.

17. Bernard A. Turner, interview by Alicia Gallant, 1996, Blue Ridge Parkway Headquarters, Asheville, N.C., 11.

18. Mitchell, "Parkway Politics," 164–66.

19. Ibid., 169.

20. Hooper, interview, 9.

21. Turner, interview, 15.

22. Homer Reeves, interview by Alicia Gallant, 1996, Blue Ridge Parkway Headquarters, Asheville, N.C., 8.

23. Abbott, interview, 44.

24. Ibid., 15.

25. Jolley, *Blue Ridge Parkway,* 11.

26. Buren Ballard, interview by Sarah Ramirez, 1996, Blue Ridge Parkway Headquarters, Asheville, N.C., 11, 14.

27. Ted Pease, interview by Julie Mullis, 1996, Blue Ridge Parkway Headquarters, Asheville, N.C., n.p.

28. William Van Hoy, interview by Alicia Gallant, 1996, Blue Ridge Parkway Headquarters, Asheville, N.C., 4.

29. Raleigh Hollefield, interview by Sarah Ramirez, 1996, Blue Ridge Parkway Headquarters, Asheville, N.C., n.p.

30. Dillard Teer, interview by Julie Mullis, 1997, Blue Ridge Parkway Headquarters, Asheville, N.C., 1.

31. Turner, interview, 15.

32. Samuel P. Weems, interview by S. Herbert Evison, 1971, National Park Service, Harpers Ferry, W.Va., 51–52.

33. Jolley, *Blue Ridge Parkway*, 11.

34. William Pruitt, interview by Alicia Gallant, 1996, Blue Ridge Parkway Headquarters, Asheville, N.C., 9.

35. Dean Richardson, interview by Alicia Gallant, 13, 1996, Blue Ridge Parkway Headquarters, Asheville, N.C.

36. Teer, interview, 4.

37. Samuel P. Weems, interview by S. Herbert Evison, 1975, National Park Service, Harpers Ferry, W.Va., 35–39.

38. Pruitt, interview, 10.

39. Richardson, interview, 14.

40. Abbuehl, interview, 4.

41. Curtis Evans, interview by Alicia Gallant, 1996, Blue Ridge Parkway Headquarters, Asheville, N.C., 5.

PART 2

. . . and Beyond

Racial Segregation in Southern Hospitals

How Medicare "Broke the Back of Segregated Health Services"

JILL QUADAGNO AND STEVE MCDONALD

In Charlotte, North Carolina, in the 1950s, there was a tacit agreement among the hospital, city police, and ambulance operators that whenever Negro citizens were injured or ill, they were carried to the inferior all-Negro Good Samaritan Hospital. One night, thirty-nine-year-old Hughie David, an African American man, complained of a severe headache. David was a patient of Richard James, a white physician, who sent David to the emergency room at Charlotte Memorial, the white hospital. There James examined his patient and concluded that he needed immediate hospitalization for a subarachnoid hemorrhage. When the hospital admissions office told James that no Negro beds were available, David was sent to Good Samaritan hospital. But James did not have staff privileges at Good Samaritan, which lacked the facilities to perform an angiogram and had no neurosurgeon on staff. David died the following morning, more a victim of the segregated health-care system that flourished in the South until 1966 than of a brain hemorrhage.[1]

The legal basis of racial segregation in health care derived from *Plessy v. Ferguson,* the 1896 Supreme Court ruling that "separate but equal" facilities were constitutional. At the local level, separate but equal was maintained by oppressive racial codes that permeated all southern institutions and their agents in the legal system and the local welfare system.[2] At the national level, southern congressmen maintained the racial state by using their seniority to block any legislation that might allow federal authorities to intervene in local political and economic arrangements.[3] The racially segregated health-care system flourished following enactment of the Hill-Burton Hospital Survey and Construction Act of 1946, which provided grants to states for the construction of hospitals.[4] At the insistence of southern congressmen, Hill-Burton included a statute specifying that hospitals were private entities whose operations could be regulated only by the states, not by federal authorities. The provision was written by Alabama Senator Lister Hill, who testified on the Senate floor, "Who shall practice in the hospitals, and the other matters pertaining to the conduct of hospitals, we have sought in the bill to leave to the authority and determination of the States, and not have the federal government, through this bill, invade the realm of the operation and maintenance of the hospitals."[5] To get the bill through Congress, federal officials agreed to allow hospitals to practice racial segregation.[6] As I. S. Falk, a Social Security Administration official, explained, "Those of us who were involved in that bill took the position that if that was the price we had to pay for getting this legislation through, we would pay it."[7]

Federal statutes required that institutions receiving Hill-Burton funds sign a nondiscrimination assurance agreeing to provide a reasonable amount of care to people who were unable to pay and agreeing that care would be available to all persons in the hospital's service area regardless of race, creed, or color. However, section 622 allowed federal funds to be used to construct separate facilities for different population groups as long as the segregated facilities were of equal quality. Section 622 also allowed racial segregation within a hospital as long as no patient was denied admission if beds allotted to the "other population group" were available. Further, doctors and other health-care workers could be denied staff privileges and jobs based on race, because these were issues of internal hospital policy outside the jurisdiction of the federal government.[8]

Between 1947 and 1974, the Hill-Burton program disbursed $3.7 billion to the states, contributing 30 percent of the funds for all hospital projects and generating an additional $9.1 billion in local and state matching funds.[9] Federal funds supported 7,750 hospitals and clinics, of which at least 98 accepted no black patients; many others contained racially segregated wings and wards, with basements and halls reserved for black patients. For example, Alabama used Hill-Burton funds to construct racially segregated or separate facilities in sixty-five of its sixty-seven counties.[10] Other southern states engaged in similar practices.

Then in a landmark 1954 decision, the Supreme Court effectively overturned *Plessy v. Ferguson* in education. In *Brown v. Board of Education*, the Court declared that the doctrine of separate but equal had no place in public educatin and that segregation deprived the minority group of equal protection of the laws guaranteed by the Fourteenth Amendment. *Brown v. Board of Education* raised the question of whether the separate-but-equal provisions of the Hill-Burton program were constitutional. The Court had indicated that its decision applied to areas other than education, including public housing, public golf courses, and public auditoriums. The issue now was whether federal funds could be used constitutionally to finance hospital-construction projects.

After debating whether to review current policy in the context of the Supreme Court decision, attorneys in the Department of Health, Education, and Welfare (HEW) concluded that the department could not issue new regulations that would contradict the laws of Congress enacted prior to the decision. Although separate but equal facilities might be discriminatory in light of the *Brown* decision, the present statute allowed HEW to continue funding segregated hospitals as long as the separate facilities were "of like quality."[11] HEW refused, however, to evaluate whether segregated hospitals actually were providing similar quality care. As one official explained, "We are not intending to suggest at this time that we are required to be concerned with relative quality of segregated services."[12] HEW attorneys also decided that the federal government had no jurisdiction over any internal hospital policy decisions, such as admission practices or room assignments, that fell under the category of hospital operation.[13] Until it was "definitely established that segregation on the basis of race in public hospitals [was] unconstitutional, the Surgeon General [was] certainly under no statutory mandate to anticipate the outcome of court tests of that issue."[14] When hospital administrators inquired about whether HEW policy would change in light of the *Brown* decision, they were informed that "the propriety of separate hospital facilities for separate racial groups [was] not directly affected by court decisions to date."[15] The school-desegregation decision did not relieve HEW of its responsibility to carry out the Hill-Burton statute as written.[16]

Although HEW remained a captive of southern interests even when legal decisions challenged the constitutionality of its policies, the agency received increasing pressure from the civil rights movement. Encouraged by *Brown v. Board of Education,* civil rights advocates outlined their grievances against racial segregation in health care in a stream of complaints directed at HEW, Congress, and executive-branch officials. The complaints originated from regions where the civil rights movement had extensive grassroots mobilization and a well-organized network of activists.[17] Catherine Patterson, a member of the Congress of Racial Equality and the Gadsden Freedom Movement, complained that the new Baptist Memorial Hospital in Gadsden, Alabama, reserved just twenty-five beds for Negro adults and that the hospital had separate entrances for "colored" and "white" patients.[18] In Atlanta, doctors from Grady Hospital contended that "ambulances are not sent out on emergency calls until the race of the persons needing help has been determined."[19] In Florida, Horace Reed, president of the Volusia County Branch of the National Association for the Advancement of Colored People (NAACP), complained that in the Halifax Hospital, "separate wards were being maintained for Negro and white patients, even the most insignificant equipment [was] labeled 'Negro' and 'white,' Negro employees were required to occupy a segregated area in the cafeteria, and employees were assigned duties on the basis of race."[20] In Wilmington, North Carolina, African American patients were segregated in "old sections" of hospitals, where facilities were poor: "James A. Walker Memorial provided about twenty-five beds for black patients in a ward that had two toilets. The ward was in a building separated from the main hospital so that to reach the operating room, the delivery room, or x-ray facilities, patients were exposed to the elements as they were wheeled across ninety feet of an open yard to the main hospital."[21]

Those who gained entrance to these hospitals were relatively fortunate. The limited availability of beds for blacks at most hospitals meant long waiting lists for admission and great risks to health. David Chisholm was another victim of poor care in Charlotte. On June 28, 1963, his physician referred him to the emergency room at Charlotte Memorial Hospital, but he was denied admission because there were no available Negro beds. Although he required immediate treatment, he was sent to the poorly equipped Good Samaritan Hospital, where he died the following day.[22]

Civil rights activists also engaged in protests and demonstrations against health-care facilities and organizations of health-care professionals. The NAACP joined with the National Medical Association, an organization of black physicians, and picketed white medical societies whose members refused to grant privileges to black doctors or refused to serve black patients. Activists triumphed when several Kentucky hospitals responded to picketing by granting staff privileges to black doctors.[23]

Civil rights activists also mounted a legal battle against segregated health care. Much of the legal pressure came from black doctors who sought to break down the many barriers they faced as professionals. For example, the Old North State Medical Society, which comprised black doctors from North Carolina, pressed for inclusion in the all-white Medical Society of North Carolina and the consequent access to better employment opportunities as well as automatic membership in the American Medical Association.[24] Other civil rights activists focused on the segregation and discrimination that hospital staff faced. Many black doctors, nurses, and other staff were segregated from white health-care professionals. Reports from Atlanta's Grady Hospital indicate that black doctors could treat only black patients and could practice medicine only in certain hospital areas (often those with the poorest facilities); they could not use X-ray machines and were denied various other staff privileges.[25]

In 1956 the NAACP filed the first of a dozen lawsuits against hospitals and other health-care facilities, asking the courts to declare Hill-Burton's separate-but-equal provision unconstitutional and to force the integration of patient-care facilities, student training, and state and local medical societies. Some suits were dismissed; others resulted in incremental changes. For example, one 1959 NAACP suit against the city of Lakeland, Florida, charged that the new Lakeland General Hospital had received Hill-Burton funds to construct a hospital addition that had a wing reserved for black patients.[26] When the new wing became overcrowded, the hospital administrator moved all Negro patients from the new building to the old building.[27] Although the district court dismissed the case for lack of evidence, the hospital attempted to ward off further suits by renovating the old building and admitting patients of both races. The psychiatric and nursery facilities in the new building were also opened to both white and black patients.[28]

Another suit filed in 1962 against Grady Hospital in Atlanta charged the hospital with racial discrimination in staffing practices, patient admissions, and nursing-school admissions.[29] The plaintiffs requested relief in two forms: (1) a declaratory judgment that Section 291(e) (f) of the Hill-Burton Act was unconstitutional, and (2) an injunction against the continued operation and assignment of facilities on a segregated basis. In response to the suit, the hospital opened a psychiatric ward for black patients, improved the black maternity ward, and made plans to open a Negro orthopedic ward. The Fulton County Medical Society admitted to active membership two black physicians who were recent additions to Grady's visiting staff.[30]

Yet hospitals presented a powerful barrier to civil rights objectives, because they remained legally defined as private organizations. Their private status insulated them from the legal prohibitions that applied to public entities, including the equal-protection provision of the Fourteenth Amendment.[31] All activities within the "range of administration, personnel, maintenance or operation of the hospital" were outside HEW's jurisdiction.[32] This included such issues as admission policies, room assignments, and the use of the cafeteria. As the administrator of Charlotte's Presbyterian Hospital explained to a civil rights advocate, his institution was a "private hospital . . . that would continue to discriminate against Negro patients."[33]

A key component of the lawsuits filed against the hospitals was to challenge the definition of *private* that granted immunity from federal oversight. In a suit against the Lynchburg, Virginia, General Hospital, the plaintiffs alleged that even though the hospital had a private board, it fell under the scope of civil rights statutes because it was "almost a wholly tax supported institution with tax money coming from the city of Lynchburg and the state of Virginia."[34] In response to the suit, the hospital's board moved to transfer its assets to a private corporation.[35]

When John F. Kennedy was elected president in 1960, a more liberal Congress took office. Members of Congress now openly challenged HEW's policy position on the distribution of Hill-Burton funds. As Senator Harrison Williams of New Jersey complained to an HEW official,

> Your description is . . . of an agency following a narrow interpretation of the letter of the law and wholly ignoring the intent of the law. By stating that Hill-Burton does not specifically outlaw segregation once the patient has been admitted into the hospital, you are, in effect, adopting the principle of separate but equal facilities. Considering that the United States Supreme Court, in a unanimous decision, declared this doctrine unconstitutional, I find it hard to accept your position. I cannot think that a Federal agency must continue to operate, some eight years after the Court's decision, in a manner that perpetuates this principle.[36]

New staff members appointed by the Kennedy administration also opposed current practices. Lisle Carter, the deputy assistant secretary of HEW, angrily asked whether segregated facilities could ever be nondiscriminatory. Hospitals had, after all, provided assurance that "no person in the area would be denied admission to the proposed facilities as patients because of race."[37] Assistant secretary James Quigley also challenged official policy, arguing that it was imperative that HEW reconsider its position in regard to the Hill-Burton program: "whatever justification there may have been for the original interpretation at the time it was made in the late 1940s, which permitted internal segregation, no such justification exists in 1963." Quigley feared that "if we do not act in this area quickly and effectively, we are going to have pickets outside our door one of these mornings."[38]

Until 1963, court decisions continued to uphold the principle that the Fourteenth Amendment's equal-protection clause did not apply to private institutions. The case of *Simkins v. Moses H. Cone Memorial Hospital* finally overturned these claims. When the hospital applied for a grant from the Hill-Burton program, the plaintiffs asked the court to declare that it was unconstitutional to give federal grants to racially discriminatory hospitals. For the first time, the Department of Justice and Attorney General Robert F. Kennedy intervened on behalf of the plaintiffs, arguing that the government had an obligation to protect its citizens from unconstitutional action made possible by a federal statute. Although the U.S. District Court dismissed the complaint on the grounds that the hospitals were private in character and therefore beyond the reach of the Fourteenth Amendment, the plaintiffs appealed the decision. On March 2, 1963, the Fourth Circuit Court of Appeals ruled that the statute that provided the legal basis for the separate-but-equal clause of Hill-Burton was unconstitutional.[39] Because the hospital received federal funds, it was not a private entity but an "arm of the state" and thus subject to Fourteenth Amendment prohibitions. The decision prohibited internal segregation in any facility on the basis of race, creed, or color; banned hospitals or other health-care facilities from denying staff privileges on the basis of race; and asserted that all benefits associated with staff privileges must be available without discrimination.[40]

The *Simkins* decision challenged the constitutional basis of the practices and procedures that had guided HEW's funding decisions for seventeen years. The civil rights movement had transformed the definition of hospitals from private to public organizations and transformed HEW's policy legacy from condoning to prohibiting racial discrimination in health care. Civil rights leaders now demanded that HEW implement the decision and "enforce to the fullest extent the law that is now at your command."[41]

HEW's first response to the *Simkins* ruling was to issue new Hill-Burton regulations expanding the definition of *nondiscrimination*. The new regulations, which applied to any institution that had received Hill-Burton funds, prohibited hospitals from discriminating in admission, from denying physicians hospital privileges on the basis of race, and from segregating patients by ward or room. Despite these new policies, HEW had little authority to force hospitals to comply. The major impediment was that these regulations applied only to pending applications.[42] Although Hill-Burton projects that had been approved on the basis of separate but equal were now unconstitutional, HEW had authority to take action only against hospitals that sought further federal assistance.[43] Hospitals that violated their nondiscrimination assurances could not be asked to repay federal funds that had been improperly used. HEW's only leverage was to withhold further federal funds for construction of new projects.[44]

In June 1964 HEW surveyed state statutes that were "inconsistent" with the nondiscrimination assurances in the Hill-Burton program.[45] Eleven southern states had statutes mandating the segregation of white and black patients in hospitals and other health-care facilities, separate black and white sanitary facilities and eating places, separate hospital entrances, separate wards within hospitals, and separate training schools for black and white nurses. The statutes were enforced through fines or imprisonment. Although these statutes often violated a hospitals' nondiscrimination assurances, HEW officials decided that they could not intervene unless a court ruled that "the applicable portion of the statute [was] invalid or inoperative." If no court decision existed, then HEW would rely on the opinion of the state attorney general. Although these statutes would eventually be judged unconstitutional, the HEW counsel's opinion could "have little effect on an applicant who may be subject to local enforcement efforts." An agency with deeply embedded ties to local political structures, HEW was forced to leave the resolution of any conflicts to local officials.[46]

The first bill prohibiting federal funding for construction of segregated facilities was proposed in the House in 1957. The bill, which was written by Congressman Adam Clayton Powell of New York, became known as the Powell Amendment. Powell proposed that no funds be provided to any agency that practiced segregation. The measure was defeated by a vote of 123 to 70, as were bills that were introduced in succeeding years.[47] The *Simkins* ruling lent the legitimacy of the courts (and, by implication, the Constitution) to the issue. When Congress passed the Civil Rights Act of 1964, the Powell Amendment became title VI.[48] The 1964 act stated that "no person in the United States shall, on the grounds of race, color or national origin, be excluded from participation in, be denied the benefits of, or be subject to discrimination under any program receiving federal assistance."[49] Any private organization that received federal financial assistance could not discriminate in any program or activity.

Title VI applied to more than four hundred federal programs administered by thirty-three agencies. It was the only title of the Civil Rights Act not delegated to the courts but to the federal bureaucracy. Next to the courts, HEW became the foremost government agent for changing the nation's racial patterns. It became HEW's job to implement the law, a task complicated by the loopholes southern members of Congress had inserted into title VI.[50] One loophole prohibited federal officials from taking any sanctions before demonstrating that compliance could not be secured voluntarily. Other provisions specified that any regulations adopted had to be approved by the president; that unless the proper congressional committee gave consent, funds could not be terminated to a recipient who ignored the regulations; and that the termination be limited to the programs where noncompliance was found. Title VI also excluded employment practices, which were covered by other titles of the Civil Rights Act and thus administered by other federal agencies.[51]

HEW was responsible for coordinating all compliance investigations in all its programs. Each agency in turn was responsible for carrying out day-to-day enforcement activities. Each regional director was assigned a special assistant to help coordinate activities between agencies.[52] This arrangement meant that regional managers and field staff who had complied with local practices that promoted racial segregation now became title VI compliance investigators.

Within HEW, the Public Health Service (PHS) received responsibility for desegregating twenty thousand hospitals, two thousand nursing homes, and more than one thousand home health agencies through a newly created Office of Equal Health Opportunities (OEHO). OEHO's head was Robert Nash, a career service employee who was determined to overturn HEW's historic policies. In his view, the passage of title VI now required a different resolution "in favor of nondiscrimination in the disbursement of benefits."[53] Yet OEHO had a full-time office staff of only thirty-one and a field staff of seventy-two, and its only leverage was its ability to investigate complaints and develop community-wide programs to accelerate compliance.[54] One year after passage of the Civil Rights Act, virtually no progress had been made in desegregating southern hospitals.

The title VI enforcement effort coincided with the enactment in 1965 of Medicare, a program of health insurance for the aged. During congressional debates about Medicare, reformers in the Social Security Administration (SSA) deliberately avoided any mention of civil rights. As SSA Commissioner Robert Ball recalled, "We didn't want it brought up legislatively. It would have been a big barrier to passage in the Senate, particularly if it had been clear that this was going to be applied. I think everyone knew it, but they didn't want to have to go on record about it."[55]

The SSA had just begun planning the process of certifying hospitals and nursing homes for Medicare eligibility, and Medicare was now swept into the title VI compliance efforts. To become eligible for federal funds, hospitals applying for Medicare certification had to prove that they were not discriminating.

In the fall of 1965 representatives from the SSA met with PHS officials to plan how to determine if hospitals were complying with title VI. They agreed that the SSA would contribute staff and help formulate rules and procedures to determine whether hospitals were eligible for Medicare funds. The PHS would take responsibility for large city hospitals and university hospitals. The SSA would assume the more complex task of confronting local racial attitudes, reviewing smaller hospitals, nursing homes, and home health agencies, especially the fifty-five hundred hospitals and nursing homes in the South.[56] The SSA regional offices would then review the compliance reports to see if they were complete and acceptable.

To initiate the process, all hospital administrators received a letter informing them that they could not receive Medicare funds unless they could certify that their hospitals did not discriminate in patient admissions, room assignments, or staff assignments.[57] Then a staff of nearly one thousand people, five hundred from the SSA and five hundred from the PHS, was hastily assembled, including several hundred personnel temporarily reassigned from other HEW programs, medical students on summer internships, and some outside consultants. After a three-week crash training program in civil rights, they were sent south to inspect hospitals and review their compliance reports. Southern district managers from the SSA were assigned the task of surveying the hospitals "to see that they were actually assigning blacks and whites as they came in, and seeing that they were actually in the beds in two bedrooms. . . . I am not sure they were 100 percent enthusiastic about the task. They lived in those communities."[58] According to Richard Smith, a PHS physician involved in the effort, "The most feared investigators were white southerners. They knew what they were looking for. We were dealing with deceit at all levels. They sniffed it out."[59]

The SSA now had the leverage to force hospitals to comply by threatening to withhold desperately needed Medicare funds. On Ball's order, the SSA became proactive on civil rights issues. Staff members were told to welcome public requests to explain the objectives of title VI. Indeed, according to Commissioner Ball, SSA staff had the responsibility to promote "within the communities in which they lived and worked . . . the understanding that is essential to broad public acceptance of the objectives, . . . something employees could do on and off the job."[60]

On July 1, 1966, Medicare went into operation. Some observers have argued that the process of certifying Medicare providers "pushed the HEW bureaucracy to the brink of chaos and encouraged expedient actions and compromise."[61] The president of the American Medical Association suggested that hospitals in communities that opposed integration be allowed to participate in Medicare by "switching the burden of bigotry to the patients. . . . A patient who refused to accept the hospital room offered could be placed in a segregated facility but he would then lose his Medicare payment."[62] According to HEW Undersecretary Wilbur Cohen, however, HEW made no compromises: the signs reading "white" and "colored" were removed from southern hospitals. In one day, "Medicare . . . broke the back of segregated health services."[63] By July 21, 1966, fewer than 0.5 percent of hospitals were not certified for Medicare eligibility. In the South, however, 132 counties had no hospitals approved for Medicare, a total of 320 hospitals.[64] Mississippi and Alabama were slowest to comply.[65] In these counties, compliance was hindered by the difficulty of establishing clear measures of racial integration. For example, inspectors told a hospital in Lynchburg, Virginia, that it could not be certified unless 13 percent of the patients were black. Hospital administrators complained that the quota was too large, given the low percentage of minorities in the service area.[66] Another problem was that eliminating racial barriers did not necessarily lead to integration. Some African Americans refused to enter white hospitals, fearing that they would not receive care.[67] One Arkansas town had two officially desegregated hospitals, but patients black continued to go to one, while white patients went to the other. Administrators complained, "Tell us what we are doing wrong and we will make it right." James Lemons, a black antipoverty worker, told federal authorities, "Give us some guidelines . . . give us time . . . don't shut off our hospital beds."[68]

The most controversial issue was interracial room occupancy. Alabama hospitals refused to make biracial room assignments. As a result, only 5 percent of the estimated 18,600 beds met the compliance requirement.[69] In Mississippi, the only threats of violence were triggered by this issue. The local hospital administrator in Canton received a threatening phone call and was visited by four local Klansmen who told him that they planned to bomb the hospital if patients were placed in integrated rooms. At another Mississippi hospital, FBI agents investigated allegations of civil rights violations. When the local HEW manager entered the hospital in Meridian, Mississippi (site of the murder of three civil right workers), for a minor operation, he shared a room with the head of the local NAACP, an act that was widely criticized by the community. After his release, however, the hospital did make other biracial room assignments. Despite opposition, the majority of the state's doctors participated willingly in Medicare, which would pay them for services they had previously performed for free.[70]

Nursing homes also fell under title VI because they were eligible for federal funds from Medicare and from Medicaid, a joint federal-state program of health insurance for the poor legislated in 1965. Unlike hospitals, where most racial barriers were rapidly eliminated, efforts to integrate nursing homes generally failed. Nursing homes were difficult to integrate because only institutions applying for Medicare eligibility were evaluated for title VI certification.[71] Of the nation's 11,800 nursing homes, only 2,500 were of sufficiently high quality to meet the eligibility criteria for Medicare funds. As a result, most nursing homes were excluded from the evaluation process.

Another problem was timing. HEW did not begin evaluating nursing homes for title IV compliance until August 1966, after the hospital-integration effort was nearly completed. As a result, most of the temporary and summer staff who had been involved in hospital integration had returned to their regular jobs. A much smaller staff had to conduct title VI reviews of a much larger number of nursing homes. Because of the staff shortage, few site visits were conducted. Most nursing home reviews were based almost entirely on signed assurances and compliance reports.[72] As HEW officials admitted, "determinations to accept assurance will in many instances have to be made without a demonstration of performance."[73]

In most cases, nursing home evaluations were turned over to the state agencies that set standards for nursing home care and licensed such institutions.[74] These agencies in turn passed the task of investigating nursing homes to state health departments. The diffusion of responsibility weakened federal oversight of the process. As a result, many nursing homes that should have been evaluated for Medicare certification were not reviewed.[75]

Although the SSA excluded most nursing homes from title VI compliance reviews, many did receive federal Medicaid funds as vendors of state welfare agencies. Reviews of these nursing homes were conducted by another HEW agency, the Welfare Administration (WA). The WA, in turn, handed over to state welfare authorities the task of evaluating compliance forms, performing on-site visits, and certifying nursing homes for title VI. By mid-October 1966, the WA had yet to initiate plans for implementing a compliance program.[76]

Finally, nursing home integration was less successful than hospital integration because nursing homes were organized in a different fashion. Whereas hospitals had a community-wide responsibility and were open to all members of the community, nursing homes were developed to serve a particular segment of the community, such as members of a particular religious or ethnic group or members of a fraternal order. Many nursing homes were for-profit organizations that selected patients by their ability to pay over a long period. Few black families could pay for nursing home care. Further, unlike hospitals, where patients entered and were dismissed on a daily basis, the turnover rate in nursing homes was low. Many areas had a shortage of facilities and long waiting lists.[77] Thus, even if administrators made a serious commitment to compliance, integration was likely to proceed very slowly. As Nash admitted, "Because Negroes are not now and will not be in Extended Care Facilities in any appreciable numbers within the period of this program, it will be difficult to evaluate the effectiveness of a stated policy to assign accommodations without regard to race."[78]

Civil rights advocates also exerted less pressure on nursing homes than on hospitals. The issue of biracial room occupancy in particular raised vexing issues for civil rights advocates. HEW guidelines asserted that patients had to be assigned to all rooms, wards, and floors without regard to race and that patients could not be asked if they were willing to share a room with a person of another race.[79] For an elderly person whose nursing home room was home, however, compatibility was a crucial factor in room assignments. Language, health, income, education, personality, age, cultural background, and individual preferences were all relevant, and in the South, both black and white residents objected to interracial room assignments. As a result, civil rights advocates who were monitoring the hospital-integration effort relented on this issue. As one HEW staff member explained, "While it is not surprisingly the bete noire of southern segregationists, it has become the concern of thoughtful and reasonable people who are dedicated to Civil Rights but who find a slavish insistence that bi-racial room occupancy be demonstrated a quite unsophisticated approach to the basic issue of providing services on a non-discriminatory basis. . . . I am specifically concerned about [nursing homes,] where the stay is longer and where the matter of compatible placement is considered quite important."[80] In response to these objections, HEW relented. New regulations stated that a facility would be in violation of title VI "if Negro patients within the facility [were] clustered in one wing, on one floor, in one or two wards," but "the guidelines do not require that a Negro and a Caucasian, for example, despite obvious incompatibility on other grounds must be placed together regardless of the depth of feeling of the individual." [81]

Twelve years transpired between the time the Supreme Court ruled against racial segregation in public institutions and the racial integration of southern hospitals. Despite the ruling that separate but equal facilities were unconstitutional, HEW continued to provide federal funds to southern hospitals that practiced segregation and discriminated in hiring. The disparate conditions hindered both blacks' access to care and quality of health care they received. These conditions adversely affected the health of blacks throughout the South and sometimes directly led to the death of victims of discrimination. The efforts of civil rights activists and black medical professionals and NAACP litigation exposed but did not remedy these injustices.

The ruling in *Simkins v. Moses H. Cone Memorial Hospital* made segregated facilities illegal in hospitals. However, HEW could withhold funds only from those hospitals applying for federal funds and could do nothing to change the practices of segregated hospitals that had already received such funds. Such hospitals continued to discriminate against African Americans despite the legal precedent set by the court ruling. Then title VI of the Civil Rights Act of 1964 effectively struck down state mandates for segregation and provided the federal government with additional enforcement powers, though the limited resources of the OEHO severely limited the effectiveness of hospital-desegregation efforts.

In 1965, the enactment of Medicare "broke the back of segregated health services." Medicare certification required proof of nondiscriminatory hospital practices with regard to race. With superior enforcement resources, the SSA, the PHS, and staff members within HEW certified virtually all hospitals by the end of July 1966. However, nursing homes did not experience the same successful desegregation. Since only a small proportion of nursing homes were large enough to receive Medicare funds, HEW failed to evaluate and certify most nursing homes. In addition, these evaluations had little federal oversight, as they were conducted by state rather than federal agencies.

The court cases that struck down separate but equal in public facilities in the 1950s and 1960s provided a necessary but insufficient condition for the desegregation of southern hospitals. In the absence of direct federal intervention and certification—despite the threat of withholding federal funding—discrimination persisted in the access and quality of health care southern hospitals provided.

Notes

1. Reginald Hawkins to Alanson Willcox, July 27, 1963, box 7, Hospital Construction, "Segregation and Discrimination" file, Department of Health, Education and Welfare, Records of the Public Health Division, Office of the General Counsel, RG 235, National Archives (hereafter, Public Health Records).

2. David R. James, "The Transformation of the Southern Racial State: Class and Race Determinants of Local-State Structures," *American Sociological Review* 53 (1988): 191–208.

3. Jill Quadagno, *The Transformation of Old Age Security* (Chicago: University of Chicago Press, 1988).

4. Kenneth Wing, "Title VI and Health Facilities: Forms without Substance" *Hastings Law Journal* 30 (1978): 137–90.

5. Willcox to secretary, March 4, 1964, box 7, Hospital Construction, "Segregation and Discrimination" file, Public Health Records.

6. Gladys Harrison to Harold Siegel, January 18, 1954, box 7, Hospital Construction, "Segregation and Discrimination" file, Public Health Records.

7. Isadore S. Falk Oral History, 279, Columbia University Oral History Collection, New York.

8. David Barton Smith, *Health Care Divided: Race and Healing a Nation* (Ann Arbor: University of Michigan Press, 1999), 47.

9. Paul Starr, *The Social Transformation of American Medicine* (New York: Basic Books, 1982), 341, 363.

10. David Barton Smith, "Addressing Racial Inequities in Health Care: Civil Rights Monitoring and Report Cards," *Journal of Health Politics, Policy, and Law* 23 (1998): 75–105.

11. Darrell Lane to Parke Banta, June 10, 1954, January 31, 1956, box 7, Hospital Construction, "Segregation and Discrimination" file, Public Health Records.

12. memorandum from Edward Rourke, October 11, 1961, box 7, Hospital Construction, "Segregation and Discrimination" file, Public Health Records.

13. "Hospital Construction Program—Nondiscrimination—Constitutional Question," November 16, 1956, box 7, Hospital Construction, "Segregation and Discrimination" file, Public Health Records.

14. Harrison to Rourke, November 16, 1956, box 2, Mississippi, Louisiana file, Public Health Records.

15. Harrison to Banta, January 31, 1956, box 7, Hospital Construction, "Segregation and Discrimination" file, Public Health Records.

16. Willcox to Jack Haldeman, February 12, 1963, box 7, Hospital Construction, "Segregation and Discrimination" file, Public Health Records.

17. Aldon Morris, *The Origins of the Civil Rights Movement* (New York: Free Press, 1986), 276–77.

18. Correspondence between Patterson, Burke Marshall, and Willcox, October 4, 23, 25, 1963, State File, box 1, Alabama file, Public Health Records.

19. Margaret Shannon, "Negroes' Suit Demands Full Grady Hospital Integration" (newspaper clipping), June 20, 1962, box 7, Hospital Construction, "Segregation and Discrimination" file, Public Health Records.

20. Horace Reed to T. Fletcher Little, May 2, 1962, box 7, Hospital Construction, "Segregation and Discrimination" file, Public Health Records.

21. Hawkins to Willcox, January 27, 1964, box 7, Hospital Construction, "Segregation and Discrimination" file, Public Health Records; David Barton Smith, *Health Care Divided*, 75–76.

22. Hawkins to Willcox, July 27, 1963, box 7, Hospital Construction, "Segregation and Discrimination" file, Public Health Records.

23. Augustus Jones, *Law, Bureaucracy, and Politics* (Washington, D.C.: University Press of America, 1982), 109.

24. David Barton Smith, *Health Care Divided*, 103.

25. Shannon, "Negroes' Suit."

26. Office of General Counsel to Carl Harper, December 31, 1959, box 7, Hospital Construction, "Segregation and Discrimination" file, Public Health Records.

27. Harper to Rourke, May 4, 1962, box 7, Hospital Construction, "Segregation and Discrimination" file, Public Health Records.

28. James S. Carr to Edward Burke, October 16, 1962, box 7, Hospital Construction, "Segregation and Discrimination" file, Public Health Records.

29. "Negroes' Suit Demands Full Grady Hospital Integration," *Atlanta Constitution*, September 25, 1962.

30. Carr to Burke, October 16, 1962, box 7, Hospital Construction, "Segregation and Discrimination" file, Public Health Records.

31. David Barton Smith, "Addressing Racial Inequities," 143.

32. Hubert Eaton to Boisfeuillet Jones, October 13, 1962, Jones to Eaton, November 13, 1962, box 7, Hospital Construction, "Segregation and Discrimination" file, Public Health Records.

33. Hawkins to Marion Folsom, April 30, 1957, box 7, Hospital Construction, "Segregation and Discrimination" file, Public Health Records.

34. Memo to General Counsel to Marion E. Gardner, *Wood v. Hogan*, Lynchburg General Hospital, June 25, 1962, box 7, Hospital Construction, "Segregation and Discrimination" file, Public Health Records.

35. Virgil A. Wood to Robert F. Kennedy, June 8, 1962, box 7, Hospital Construction, "Segregation and Discrimination" file, Public Health Records.

36. Williams to Haldeman, February 4, 1963, box 7, Hospital Construction, "Segregation and Discrimination" file, Public Health Records.

37. Carter to Willcox, June 18, 1962, box 7, Hospital Construction, "Segregation and Discrimination" file, Public Health Records.

38. Quigley to Willcox, July 10, 1963, box 7, Hospital Construction, "Segregation and Discrimination" file, Public Health Records.

39. Adam Clayton Powell, "Hospital Integration and Job Opportunity: Equality Goals for 1963," *Journal of the National Medical Association* 55 (July 1963): 338–41.

40. Rourke to Luther Terry, April 6, 1964, box 7, Hospital Construction, "Segregation and Discrimination" file, Public Health Records.

41. Hawkins to Willcox, July 4, 1964, box 7, Hospital Construction, "Segregation and Discrimination" file, Public Health Records.

42. Wing, "Title VI and Health Facilities," 158.

43. Willcox to Hawkins, August 20, 1964, box 7, Hospital Construction, "Segregation and Discrimination" file, Public Health Records.

44. Willcox to Wilbur Cohen, August 14, 1963, box 7, Hospital Construction, "Segregation and Discrimination" file, Public Health Records.

45. Harrison to Banta, January 31, 1966, "Appendix I: State Statutes," box 7, Hospital Construction, "Segregation and Discrimination" file, Public Health Records.

46. "Conduct Required under State Statutes Which Is Inconsistent with the Nondiscrimination Assurances in the Hill-Burton, Mental Retardation Facilities and Community Mental Health Centers Construction Programs," June 26, 1964, box 7, Hospital Construction, "Segregation and Discrimination" file, Public Health Records.

47. *Congressional Record,* April 3, 1957, 4480–82; David Barton Smith, "Addressing Racial Inequities," 83.

48. David Barton Smith, "The Racial Integration of Health Facilities," *Journal of Health, Politics and Law* 18 (1993): 851–69.

49. Hugh Davis Graham, *The Civil Rights Era: Origins and Development of National Policy* (New York: Oxford University Press, 1990), 152.

50. Jeremy Rabkin, "Office for Civil Rights," in *The Politics of Regulation,* ed. James Q. Wilson (New York: Basic Books, 1980), 310.

51. Jones, *Law, Bureaucracy and Politics,* 167.

52. Title VI of the Civil Rights Act of 1964, December 14, 1965, box 300, "PA 16 Title VI Compliance" file, Records of the Social Security Administration, Office of the Commissioner, RG 47, National Archives (hereafter, Social Security Records).

53. Nash to James Murray, March 19, 1966, box 300, "PA 16 Title VI Compliance" file, Social Security Records.

54. Rufus E. Miles Jr., *The Department of Health, Education, and Welfare* (New York: Praeger, 1974), 197.

55. M. G. Gluck and Virginia Reno, eds., *Reflections on Implementing Medicare* (Washington, D.C.: National Academy of Social Insurance, 2001), 7.

56. Title VI of the Civil Rights Act of 1964, 1, box 300, "PA 16 Title VI Compliance" file, Social Security Records.

57. "Hospital Application for Participation; Guidelines for Compliance with Title VI," n.d., box 300, "PA 16 Title VI Compliance" file, Social Security Records.

58. Gluck and Reno, *Reflections*, 10.

59. Richard Smith, telephone interview by author, February 17, 1999.

60. Commissioner's Bulletin, box 300, "PA 16 Title VI Compliance" file, Social Security Records.

61. Wing, "Title VI and Health Facilities," 159.

62. "AMA Head Urges Doctors Not to Thwart Medicare Program That Starts Friday," *Wall Street Journal,* June 27, 1966.

63. Edward Berkowitz, *Mr. Social Security: The Life of Wilbur J. Cohen* (Lawrence: University Press of Kansas, 1995), 244.

64. Memorandum from Roy Swift, July 25, 1966, box 298, "PA 16 Hospital Compliance Report" file, Social Security Records.

65. "Title VI Compliance Problems," box 298, "PA 16 Hospital Compliance Report" file, Social Security Records.

66. Swift to Robert Ball, May 27, 1966, box 300, "PA 16 Title VI Compliance" file, Social Security Records.

67. Richard Smith, interview.

68. "Federal Compliance Complaint Is Puzzle for Officials of Two Hospitals in Lincoln," *Elk Valley Times,* June 29, 1966, box 298, "PA 16 Hospital Compliance Report" file, Social Security Records.

69. Murray to Ball, February 15, 1966, box 300, "PA 16 Title VI Compliance" file, Social Security Records.

70. Swift to Ball, October 21, 1966, box 300, "PA 16 Title VI Compliance" file, Social Security Records.

71. Ball to the secretary, November 19, 1965, box 300, "PA 16 Title VI Compliance" file, Social Security Records.

72. Wing, "Title VI and Health Facilities," 160.

73. "Public Health Service Compliance Program for Extended Care Facilities," box 298, "PA 16 Hospital Compliance Report" file, Social Security Records.

74. William Gaskill to Swift, July 20, 1966, box 298, "PA 16 Hospital Compliance Report" file, Social Security Records.

75. David Barton Smith, *Health Care Divided,* 246.

76. Louis Zawatzky to Ball, October 10, 1966, box 298, "PA 16 Hospital Compliance Report" file, Social Security Records.

77. "Nursing Home Compliance Review Program," n.d., box 298, "PA 16 Hospital Compliance Report" file, Social Security Records.

78. "Public Health Service Compliance Program for Extended Care Facilities," July 9, 1966, box 298, "PA 16 Hospital Compliance Report" file, Social Security Records.

79. "Guidelines for Compliance of Extended Care Facilities with Title VI of the Civil Rights Act of 1964," 1964, box 298, "PA 16 Hospital Compliance Report" file, Social Security Records.

80. Tom Parrott to Ball, July 13, 1966, box 298, "PA 16 Hospital Compliance Report" file, Social Security Records.

81. "Sample Policy for a Nursing Home," n.d., box 298, "PA 16 Hospital Compliance Report" file, Social Security Records.

Citizen-Soldiers

The North Carolina Volunteers
and the South's War on Poverty

ROBERT R. KORSTAD AND JAMES L. LELOUDIS

During the summers of 1964 and 1965, more than three hundred college students—black and white, male and female—fanned out across the state of North Carolina in a bold campaign to defeat poverty and, as they saw it, to uplift the poor. They were the foot soldiers of the North Carolina Fund, a pacesetting antipoverty program of the 1960s. The story of those students and their summers of service is important for many reasons, but most especially because it highlights volunteerism's potential to expand the boundaries of democratic participation. That point was driven home for us several years ago when we were approached by a number of young people who were active in the community-service movement, that broad-based volunteer effort initiated during the 1980s by college and high school students who were eager to develop modes of social action appropriate to the challenges of their own time and generation. The young people who came to us had demonstrated a remarkable capacity for leadership—they included the founders of such groups as the Campus Outreach Opportunity League (COOL), Public Allies, and Empty the Shelters—but they also complained of feeling that they were laboring in isolation. How, they wondered, might the past inform contemporary efforts to take their work beyond the walls of the university, to move students from service to a broader civic engagement, and to build new alliances to address enduring social problems: poverty, homelessness, illiteracy, and racial inequality?[1]

Since that encounter, much of our research on the North Carolina Fund and its student volunteers has focused on trying to answer that question. In this chapter, we trace the history of the Fund's Volunteers program, provide an analysis of the contribution that those students made to fighting poverty in

North Carolina, and evaluate the impact of that experience on the lives of the Volunteers themselves. We also consider more broadly the role that the North Carolina Fund played in shaping national antipoverty policy.

The Establishment of the North Carolina Fund

The Fund was established in 1963 by Governor Terry Sanford, who had been elected in 1960 with President John F. Kennedy. When Sanford took office in 1961, North Carolina's factory workers earned some of the lowest industrial wages in the nation; 37 percent of the state's residents had incomes below the federal poverty line; half of all students dropped out of school before obtaining a high school diploma; and one-fourth of adults twenty-five years of age and older had less than a sixth-grade education and were, for all practical purposes, illiterate.[2] Although shocking, those conditions had long been a part of everyday life in the state. Since the turn of the century, North Carolina's political and business leaders had underfunded human-capital development for vast sectors of the population. Public policies such as segregation, disfranchisement, antiunionism, and miserly expenditures on public education effectively maintained a racially divided and low-wage labor force. By the early 1960s, however, poverty was moving from the shadow of neglect to the forefront of public-policy agendas. The civil rights movement, now at high tide, was challenging the nation to fulfill its promise of equality and opportunity. Not since the Civil War and Reconstruction had so many citizens demanded so clearly the full implementation of equal rights before the law. At the same time, technological innovation was revolutionizing both the agricultural and manufacturing sectors of North Carolina's economy. Automation in the textile and tobacco industries and the mechanization of agriculture meant that employers' profits no longer depended so heavily on access to a large pool of unskilled labor. Displaced by these processes, thousands of men and women lacked steady employment, and many were migrating out of the state. North Carolina had a net outmigration of more than 250,000 people between 1940 and 1950. Between 1950 and 1960, that number fell to 30,000, but veiled by such seemingly good news was the fact that North Carolina and the rest of the South continued to lose from 6 to 10 percent of young adults between the ages of twenty and thirty-five.[3]

In this context of upheaval and dislocation, Governor Sanford and others in the liberal wing of North Carolina's Democratic Party sought to "awaken" the state to the human and social costs of poverty and racial inequality.[4] The governor devoted his administration to diversifying the economy, improving public education, and reducing North Carolina's dependence on low-wage manufacturing. He and his supporters also signaled a willingness—indeed, an eagerness—to surrender segregation so long as they could simultaneously control the pace and direction of change. For progressive Democrats, poverty and racial discrimination became pressing concerns both because of the suffering they inflicted and because they threatened to block the path of the state's economic growth. Writing for a national audience in *Look* magazine in 1964, Sanford explained:

> The President's Council of Economic Advisers estimates that racial bias deprives the U.S. of between $13 and $17 billion a year in increases in gross national product. In North Carolina, we know that we are 42nd on the list of states in per capita income because Negroes don't have adequate economic opportunities. If their income equaled that of white citizens, North Carolina would jump to 32nd, at least.
>
> The South badly needs new industry. But what manufacturers would expect to find a worthwhile market in an area where a large percentage of the population is on relief and likely to remain so? What space industry, which must compete mightily for physicists and engineers, would locate in a community ridden with hate and prejudice? The answer to these questions is already being given. In the last several years, new industry has with few exceptions gone most heavily into those Southern states making the most progress in civil rights.

Poverty, Governor Sanford was quick to add, also exacted a terrible human price. "We can measure the costs of lost productivity, of lost purchasing power, and of the relief rolls," he contended. "But how do we measure the cost of a crushed spirit or a dead dream or a long-forgotten hope? What is the incalculable cost to us as a people when the children of poverty become the parents of poverty and begin the cycle anew?" The challenge posed by these observations was obvious but daunting. "How," asked one of the governor's aides, "can we in North Carolina reverse trends, motivate people, reorient attitudes, supply the education and the public services and the jobs that will give all our people the chance to become productive, more self-reliant, and able to compete in the complex but dynamic, exciting but perilous world of today and tomorrow?"[5]

Changing times required innovative strategies for uplifting the state's economically disabled citizens. To that end, the governor and a well-connected coalition of business and educational leaders established the North Carolina Fund in the summer of 1963. They chartered the new agency as a private, nonprofit corporation whose purpose was to "enable the poor to become productive, self-reliant citizens, and to foster institutional, political, economic, and social change designed to bring about a functioning, democratic society." Governor Sanford chaired the Fund and recruited an interracial board of directors that represented all geographic sectors of the state. Daily operations were overseen by Executive Director George Esser, a law and government professor at the University of North Carolina at Chapel Hill, and a small staff of social workers, ministers, journalists, and academics. For its time, that staff was remarkably diverse. At its peak, it included roughly seventy-five employees, at least half of whom were either women or African Americans.[6]

From 1963 to 1968, the Fund drew the bulk of its financial support from the Ford Foundation($7,000,000), which was actively investing in similar social-reform projects elsewhere in urban America and throughout the postcolonial Third World; two local philanthropies, the Z. Smith Reynolds Foundation ($1,625,000) and the Mary Reynolds Babcock Foundation ($875,000), both of which were tied to influential banking and tobacco interests and had records as generous contributors to health and welfare reform; and agencies of the federal government ($7,042,753), including the Office of Economic Opportunity and the Departments of Labor, Housing and Urban Development, and Health, Education, and Welfare. That five-year budget of $16,500,000 roughly equaled the state of North Carolina's average annual expenditure for public welfare during the mid-1960s.[7]

The North Carolina Fund was the only statewide antipoverty agency of its kind and, as such, played a notable role in shaping the Great Society initiatives that became the hallmark of President Lyndon B. Johnson's administration. Both Governor Sanford and Executive Director Esser helped draft the Economic Opportunity Act of 1964, which launched a national assault on poverty, and a number of Fund initiatives served as models for the national effort. Beginning in 1965, for example, the Fund helped establish the Volunteers in Service to America (VISTA) program by training participants from across the country. Because the Fund's statewide assault on poverty began six to nine months before the national campaign, there was considerable interaction between Fund staff and White House aides, and over the next few years, programmatic ideas were regularly passed back and forth between the Fund headquarters in Durham and the Office of Economic Opportunity in Washington, D.C.[8]

Despite this involvement, Sanford helped pioneer the Great Society from a position of relative weakness. By 1963, he had already begun to run afoul of small-town and rural elites who opposed his economic plans and objected to his moderate stance on civil rights. Those men and women depended on existing social arrangements to guarantee their access to cheap labor and to maintain their status and cultural authority. In fact, they would rise up in 1964 to repudiate Sanford by delivering his handpicked successor a bruising defeat in the Democratic primary. Sensitive to that impending backlash, Governor Sanford conceived of the North Carolina Fund as a means of keeping his reform agenda alive. As a private corporation, the Fund did its work with foundation and federal grants rather than state appropriations, and for that reason, it had a unique capacity to bypass hostile conservative lawmakers.[9] Its purpose, as George Esser explained, was "to *create* the possible" by cultivating like-minded reformers on the local level and nurturing experimentation in antipoverty work.[10] In that way, the Fund foreshadowed the proliferation of nonprofit social-service providers, both in the United States and around the world, that today stand alongside government and business as a vital third sector in the development of social and economic policy.[11]

One of the Fund's first—and in some ways definitive—undertakings was its Volunteers program, which for two consecutive summers brought a select group of college students face to face with the realities of poverty. The Volunteers explained their motives for service in lengthy letters of application, and they recorded their experiences, doubts, and discoveries in detailed daily logs. We have worked extensively in those materials and have supplemented them with three dozen oral history interviews and a survey of almost one hundred Fund veterans. Together, those sources highlight the vital role student activists played in shaping both the Fund's work and the general character of the 1960s, demonstrate volunteerism's capacity to influence the trajectory of individual lives, and, most important, reveal the War on Poverty's potential for expanding the boundaries of participatory democracy. In ways that none of the participants fully anticipated, the Fund offered its Volunteers not simply a summer of service but also an opportunity to rethink the meaning of citizenship for both themselves and the people they set out to help.[12]

The Volunteers Program

The North Carolina Volunteers had its genesis in a tutorial program for underprivileged children that Sanford had tried unsuccessfully to persuade the state legislature to support. Inspired by the Peace Corps, the governor was convinced that the program would deliver needed services while cultivating a new generation of enlightened state leaders. When his request was denied, Sanford and Fund officials turned to the U.S. Office of Education, which provided fifty thousand dollars from monies set aside to experiment with the idea of establishing a national service corps. With that grant and fifty thousand dollars from its own resources, the Fund launched its Volunteers program under the direction of Jim Beatty, a national collegiate track star from the University of North Carolina at Chapel Hill.[13]

In March 1964, Beatty and his coworkers blitzed the state with a call for volunteers for the first summer program. Within a matter a weeks, they were inundated with more than five hundred applications. Teams of interviewers then selected one hundred finalists who represented every college campus in the state—small and large, public and private, black and white. Most of the "First One Hundred," as they were dubbed by the state's press and the Fund's publicity office, came from middle-class households—economically secure but not particularly prosperous. Women outnumbered men three to one, reflecting both the gendered character of social service and the fact that Fund recruiters targeted college majors that tended to enroll large numbers of women: education, psychology, sociology, and English. Racial representation in the group roughly reflected the general population. The presence of fifteen African American students flouted the practices of segregation and signaled the Fund's determination to confront the role of racial discrimination in the perpetuation of poverty. The challenge for those chosen to be Volunteers was not simply to serve the poor but also to model for themselves and their society an inclusive notion of public life that otherwise had little currency in the segregated South.[14]

Members of the First One Hundred and the more than 250 students who followed them in 1965 gave a variety of reasons for answering the call to service. In their applications, many of the white students spoke of their religious faith and their desire to practice the principles of Christian brotherhood by venturing across the boundaries of class and race. A junior from Catawba College believed it was his "duty to help those who are oppressed by poverty and ignorance." "I don't mean to sound pious," he added, "but this is the way I think the Christian can . . . fulfill the work of Christ in today's world." A young woman echoed those sentiments and suggested how they might undercut a lifetime of racial indoctrination. "Here in the South," she wrote, "most of us have been taught to think poorly of the Negro. When I look into the eyes of a white child I see no great difference. I see a human being in both." Those sentiments convinced her that the time had come "to do something about the problem of the underprivileged people instead of just thinking about them." Similar concerns pervaded the application essays of African American students, although their writings were shaped in distinctive ways by a firsthand knowledge of poverty and discrimination. A sophomore from historically black Elizabeth City State College wrote, "I was reared in poverty, and to a large extent still live in it. I know what it is to be among the have-nots and to be faced with the fore-knowledge of defeat and rejection." For this young man and other black Volunteers, the Fund's work tapped into a tradition of racial self-help and dovetailed with civil rights activism.[15]

These motivations came together in unique combinations for each individual, but the one theme that resounded in nearly all of the students' writings was a conception of citizenship defined by the militarized culture of the Cold War and President Kennedy's call for patriotic self-sacrifice. In a nation threatened by communism abroad and social strife at home, the Volunteers felt a duty to what they saw as American ideals. "Because I am a concerned American, I think to be able to help others is more than an opportunity; it is a duty that is part of the democratic form of government which we have," wrote Hugh Jones. Battling poverty became a way of advancing the cause of social progress, achieving justice at home, and thus strengthening the nation for the global confrontation with communism. Guided by those principles, the student Volunteers dubbed themselves "citizen-soldier[s]" in what President Johnson had only months before described in his State of the Union address as a national War on Poverty.[16]

In the summers of 1964 and 1965, the Volunteers gathered in early June for a week of training at Duke University. Visiting speakers—sociologists, lawmakers, and administrators from various social-service agencies—said little about jobs, wages, and affordable housing. Instead, they kept a tight focus on the "culture of poverty" and the ways it worked to "twist and deform" the human spirit. As Sharon Young wrote shortly after her orientation, "Lecturers and discussants constantly referred to 'these people.' I was told that they were a people who needed to be given a sense of dignity and pride which was absent from their lives. . . . We, the Volunteers, were . . . to provide the atmosphere that could foster ambition, dissatisfaction, and ultimate change."[17] After three days of such preparation, Young and her fellow students climbed into buses and cars and made their way to host communities chosen to represent the regional and demographic diversity of the state.

Once in the field, the Volunteers performed a variety of tasks. A majority spent their summer of service working with children in educational and recreational programs. In many cases, these interactions in the classroom or on the playground led the Volunteers into the homes and neighborhoods of their young charges, where the Volunteers became immersed in the lives of individual families. The Volunteers tutored adults as well as children, counseled high school dropouts, served as advocates for access to health care and better housing, and in the process became increasingly aware of the complex causes of poverty. Other students took temporary positions in county health departments, where they worked with public-health nurses to conduct dietary surveys, assisted in clinics, renovated homes, installed sanitary privies, and helped develop community water systems. In rural mountain communities, Volunteers drove the bookmobiles that offered residents their only access to public libraries and established local craft cooperatives to provide employment and supplement family incomes. As remuneration for these activities, the Volunteers received $250 plus room and board for a ten-week program.[18]

Almost immediately, the Volunteers encountered scenes so abject as to challenge comprehension. One young woman was stunned by the squalor and deprivation she witnessed in a "shack" not far from the campus of the University of North Carolina at Chapel Hill. She reported the condition in her daily log: "Only five of the children were home. We read to them and played with them. Those children do not know how to even look at a book—Sophia, who is 6 [and] starts to school next year, picked up a book upside down and turned the pages from back to front. . . . The place has a sickening smell—The children have sores and welts from beatings all over them—They also have protruding stomachs." When faced with such suffering, most of the Volunteers turned, at least initially, to explanations that were both familiar and comforting. While never quite blaming the poor for their plight, Volunteers did locate the causes of poverty within a cluster of social and psychological inadequacies. The poor, it seemed, "believed in nothing and [had] little faith in their own capacities." Such views provided both emotional distance from hardship and assurance that the Volunteers could "fix" the people they encountered. "All we had to do was clean up this one generation," a former Volunteer recalled many years later, "educate these people and lift them up, and it would be over with. We really believed that."[19]

A significant minority of the Volunteers never escaped this way of thinking. For most, however, face-to-face encounters made it increasingly difficult to typecast the people they had come to serve. With few exceptions, the Volunteers knew little of the realities of poor people's lives. What the students thought they understood came primarily from newspaper accounts, popular stereotypes, and scholarly abstractions. Over the course of ten weeks in the field, students wrestled with the tension between those "previously-held opinions and recently-gained impressions." One of the most striking features of the daily logs is how characterizations of the poor move grammatically from the third to the first person. As poverty came to have a human face, its afflictions could no longer be ascribed simply to "those people." They were instead the troubles of Pete, a teenager whose anger got him into fights and often landed him in jail, or the struggles of families like the Townsends, known by social workers as the "worst case" in their county but in fact desperate for their children to have an education and the chance of a better life.[20]

Through personal encounters, the Volunteers moved—often haltingly— toward thinking about themselves and the poor in ways that were both new and emancipating. Anne Henderson, a sophomore from the exclusive Saint Mary's Junior College in Raleigh, found it difficult to "explain to . . . friends and classmates . . . that there is so much more to life than the narrow, sterile, prejudiced world that they know and accept." After two months in the North Carolina mountains, she wanted "more than ever . . . to take some real action." Another student who had served in 1964 and who reapplied in 1965 reported that involvement with the North Carolina Fund had marked a turning point in her life. In her 1965 application, she wrote, "The program was one of the most worthwhile things that has ever happened to me. . . . It forced me to look at myself, while I was helping others to look at themselves." Carol Kendall shared that assessment. She described her summer as "the richest and most rewarding" experience of her life. "I find that many of my attitudes about poverty and people in poverty have been drastically changed." Cindy Johnson, a white Volunteer from Stedman, a small town in eastern North Carolina, provided the following assessment: "The experiences of this summer—working, living and playing with fellow Negroes has been invaluable—has begun, I feel, to break a cycle of my own poverty." While the trajectory of these transformations seems clear, their depth is less easily plumbed. Nevertheless, both contemporary and retrospective evidence leaves no doubt that many of the Volunteers found themselves caught up in experiences with a potential to shift their loyalties away from the world of their parents' generation and its established principles of power and privilege.[21]

The Volunteers program was especially effective in exposing the limitations of white students' self-satisfied racial liberalism. Most of the white Volunteers emphasized in their application essays both their capacity to "work with any

ethnic group" and their commitment to interracialism. Putting those principles into practice, however, was often harder than the students had imagined. After all, they came from schools and communities that had undertaken
only the most limited forms of desegregation. In 1965–66, most black students in three of the state's largest urban districts—95.7 percent in Charlotte,
98.5 percent in Raleigh, and 88.7 percent in Winston-Salem—still attended
elementary schools with 80 to 100 percent black enrollment. The Volunteers'
summer experiences forced them to confront the oppressive power of racism,
both their own and that which permeated the society at large. For many Volunteers, the test came in the intimate act of sharing a meal with black teammates or with members of a black community. Such associations violated one
of the South's most deep-seated taboos. A sophomore from a small church-
run college strained against the grip of "southern customs" on her first day
in the field. "Tonight we ate supper in a Negro school," she wrote in her daily
log. "I felt a little nauseated, mainly because I had never before eaten in a Negro school, and I was becoming sick." That reaction so disturbed the young
woman that she resolved to make the examination of her racial phobias one
of her chief projects. "By the end of the summer, I should feel completely
different."[22]

Because the Volunteers lived and worked in integrated teams, race posed
a constant challenge. White students found few escapes from the contradictions of their racial views. One white Volunteer was infuriated when he and
his teammates were "served poorly, ordered around, talked about, [and] called
names" in a segregated restaurant. "Personally, I think that someone ought to
bomb the place," he confided in his daily log. A few weeks later, however, the
same young man reacted with only slightly less anger when a white female
coworker became too friendly with young black men in the neighborhood
to which they were assigned. Such inconsistencies frustrated African American Volunteers. In weekly group meetings, Charlotte Williams demanded to
know why, whenever the team moved into new quarters, she was the last to
get a roommate; she chastised white Volunteers for describing the diet of poor
families as "typical Negro food"; and she insisted that her teammates learn to
pronounce "the word 'Negro' " and abandon the polite disrespect of "Nigra."[23]

Such confrontations demonstrated that habituated ways of thinking and be-
having were not easily changed. Indeed, the white Volunteers' best intentions
were often caught short. A young woman who worked as a teacher's aid in an
all-black elementary school titled an entry in her log, "My most embarrassing
moment as a Volunteer (I forgot my children were Negro)":

Last week I went downtown and bought paint for puppets' faces, and paint for a puppet stage, and yarn to use for puppets' hair. My selections were good, I thought. This morning I went to the room and asked each child to get his puppet. Then I showed them how to put on the hair—paint the face and features. One of the children said, " . . . where is the brown paint?" You see I had purchased "flesh colored paint" and yellow hair, and black and brown hair—and the children wanted to make puppets like themselves. I almost died. I said very quickly, "Children since we are pushed for time we will *not* paint your puppets' skin today. We will just try to get their hair on." (I'm making a[nother] trip downtown before Monday.)

In a similar situation, a group of white Volunteers who worked with a black preschool teacher were at a loss to understand the woman's coolness. One Volunteer wrote that "Mrs. Brown keeps herself very removed from us: She's the boss." The relationship became so strained that the Volunteers mentioned the problem to the local school superintendent, who surprised them by suggesting that they had given offense in ways they never understood. "He thought the reason for our cool relationship . . . was due to the fact that we were white [and the teacher] wanted to show she was perfectly competent and didn't need our help." In such circumstances, the Volunteers had to confront the paternalism that too often characterized their own labors. They learned slowly—and sometimes painfully—the limitations of patron-client relations. Effective reform required instead that the Volunteers engage their hosts as equals, acknowledging the fullness of their claims to citizenship and their capacity for independent action. [24]

As the students began to translate that lesson into practice, they found themselves ensnared by the tangle of connections that tied racism and poverty to political power, class interests, and the privileges of whiteness. The Volunteers experienced some of the stiffest resistance and indifference from where they expected it the least. Poor whites were often deeply suspicious of the Fund and its activities. They had much to gain from the antipoverty program but, in their estimation, even more to lose from the prospect of racial leveling. In one white community after another, Volunteers found themselves rejected as "communists," "freedom fighters," and "civil rights workers." [25] Except in the mountains, where the black population was small and therefore perceived as less threatening than elsewhere in the state, the North Carolina Fund won only limited acceptance in poor white communities.

That rejection of the Fund was reinforced by middle-class business and political leaders, who were equally resistant to lowering the walls of segregation or surrendering the class prerogatives that racial discrimination helped to sustain. Local officials invited the Volunteers into their communities both to secure needed services and to take advantage of the North Carolina Fund's ties to the federal Office of Economic Opportunity. Beginning in 1964, the Fund became a major pipeline for new federal investments in community development and job creation. Yet even as they sought to benefit from that largesse, local leaders often defended established lines of authority, power, and privilege.[26] Sue Hester reported from the small eastern town of Laurinburg that "not one white person has gone out of his way to make us welcome. . . . This very obvious 'snubbing' is beginning to tell on group morale. . . . People here seem to be trying desperately to ignore the fact that we are here, as ostriches with their heads in the sands of their own prejudice. It's as if we're the symptoms of some dread disease they don't want to know they have." Torn between outrage and her own middle-class manners, Hester exclaimed, "It makes me so mad at these self-satisfied, self-righteous whites that I could kick them in the wazoo!"[27]

Local leaders also worried about the potential of the Fund's work to catalyze and legitimate organizing initiatives within poor neighborhoods. Marc White belonged to a team of Volunteers assigned to work with the Parks and Recreation Department in Durham, a tobacco-manufacturing town with a large black community and one in which white politicians and some members of the black middle class shared an interest in limiting independent political activity among poor residents. At first, White felt excited by the promise of the job. After an introductory meeting with "Durham civic leaders," he reported in his daily log that "the upper levels of the Durham bureaucracy are vitally concerned with the problems we have been sent to help out with." But the limits of that concern soon became apparent. White and his teammates grew weary of "keeping order" on ball fields and began organizing parents to build a playground in a poor black neighborhood where the city refused to provide recreational services. That affront prompted a tongue-lashing from the mayor. "The mayor launched a politely-phrased tirade," White reported. "To wit, we, the volunteers, must remember that we were employees (in effect) of the City of Durham, and under the city's thumb. We are here to serve as requested, not to change the requests. In short, we are here to be uncreative, and not to fight poverty, but to play the city's conservative ball game."[28]

In a small farming community south of Durham, town officials took an even more direct approach. They had initially requested assistance from the Volunteers in reopening the public library but were horrified by the way that the young people interpreted their task. "We went in and cleaned and dusted and cleaned some more," recalled Adisa Douglas, who had been one of the first black students to enroll at the University of North Carolina at Chapel Hill. Her interracial team "re-established some order to the books and opened a children's section [with] a reading corner." They then visited "both Black and White neighborhoods" to announce the library's reopening. "Children came in droves," Douglas remembered, "and these were primarily black children. White residents of the town went up in arms. Black children did not use the public library! We were threatened by the Klan and had to withdraw from the town altogether." [29]

When faced with such hostility, teams across the state adopted a common strategy: they hunkered down in black communities where they were welcomed and felt that they could make a meaningful contribution. As several Volunteers explained, they took it upon themselves to set "the pace for integration" and to model for others a vision of what "could be." They had become, in their own estimation, "charter members of an idea." [30] In Durham, Marc White defied the mayor and continued organizing the black community so that the playground would survive his departure and so that neighbors could structure their own recreational programs. In other communities, Volunteers took up similar efforts. One team organized a mothers' club for poor women so that "*they* [might] investigate for playgrounds"; another team helped neighbors in a poor coastal community secure federal money for an after-school tutoring and recreational program that local officials refused to fund; and in yet another community, a group of Volunteers worked with poor parents to turn a summer play school into a Head Start program. Such organizing efforts could go only so far in the course of ten weeks of summer work, but they reflected nonetheless a fundamental change in the students' understanding of citizenship. The Volunteers had come to embrace activism no less than service as an essential element of democracy. The poor, they began to argue, had not only a responsibility to live as productive, self-reliant citizens but also a right to demand in return political rights, higher wages, improved housing, and better schools. [31]

The Volunteers' expanded sense of rights and obligations—both their own and those of the poor—helped steer the North Carolina Fund in dramatically new directions. At the end of a summer of service, many of the students complained bitterly about the ephemeral nature of their work. What good was it to tutor a child or to provide organized recreation, they asked, if those programs would disappear as soon as the summer ended? Others went even further and openly mocked the idea that poverty might be eradicated by rehabilitating the poor rather than addressing issues of politics and economics. "Taught one 7 year-old boy to tie his shoes," a Volunteer quipped in her log. "Very important for breaking the cycle of poverty: if we're to help them lift themselves by their shoe straps, it helps if their shoes stay on."[32]

Those challenges resonated with new voices rising up from within poor communities. In many places where the Volunteers worked, the summer program provided a public stage for indigenous leaders who had their own ideas about how best to fight poverty. In Durham, for instance, the men and women who had worked with Marc White to build the playground moved next to organize a rent strike and to picket City Hall. They insisted that the streets in their neighborhood be paved, that garbage be collected more regularly, and that housing laws be enforced against white realtors and slumlords.[33] Such demands from below worked, in turn, to amplify incentives from above, as the Office of Economic Opportunity coupled federal dollars ever more tightly to the goal of ensuring the "maximum feasible participation" of poor people in the framing and implementation of antipoverty initiatives.[34] By late 1965, Fund officials were ready to shift course. They felt pinched by these pressures and frustrated by the intransigence that had too often greeted their initial efforts. When the summer program ended in August of that year, the Fund disbanded its Volunteers program.

A number of factors contributed to that decision. First, Fund staff had grown increasingly concerned about the safety of the Volunteers, the majority of whom were white women, as the civil rights movement heated up and violence directed at interracial groups intensified.[35] Second, and more important, federal underwriting for the Volunteers program had run out by 1965, and Fund leaders had not been able to locate another source of support. To continue the Volunteers program would have required the Fund to draw more heavily on its own resources at precisely the time when many within the organization were raising questions about the efficacy of spending money on middle-class volunteerism instead of developing the capacities of the poor. "It seems to me that the North Carolina Volunteers have done what they intended to do," observed staff member Betty Ward. "That is, they have demonstrated that college students, with their refreshing idealism and enthusiasm, can show us a different way of looking at the poor." It was now time for something more. Ward and other Fund leaders had come to the same conclusion as many of the Volunteers: "the real issues . . . were issues of power, and . . . not a whole lot was going to change . . . without changing internal power."[36] For that reason, the Fund began in late 1965 to direct its attention toward community organizing. It financed independent poor people's movements and began training former Volunteers and the poor themselves as Community Action Technicians who would live and work full time in the places they served. In eastern North Carolina, for example, the Fund underwrote the People's Program on Poverty, an organization of black sharecroppers, domestic workers, and small farmers. In Durham, the Fund helped to finance United Organizations for Community Improvement, which coordinated rent strikes and led local civil rights protests. The goal in these and other such partnerships was not simply to deliver services but to give the poor the institutional and financial footing from which to press their demands.[37]

Through this shift in tactics, the Fund unleashed a wave of activism in poor communities across North Carolina. As the poor began to organize, picket, and protest, the Fund's opponents became increasingly shrill in their recriminations. One newspaper in the eastern part of the state insisted that the Fund had steered the War on Poverty off of its intended course. The editor saw "no reason why the anti-poverty program should be controlled by the poor any more than social security should be run by the elderly . . . or the draft run by draftees. . . . Congress never intended that the 'poor' should run the anti-poverty war [but only that their views] should be taken into account." Another paper accused the Fund of waging "guerrilla warfare," and in Congress, Representative James Gardner charged that the agency had "redirected the War on Poverty . . . into creating a political machine." At risk, in Gardner's view, were deep-seated notions of civic identity in which race and class had long determined access to the fullness of American citizenship. To work with, rather than for, the poor was to acknowledge not only their humanity but their claim to power and privilege as well. For Gardner and his constituents—many of them still reeling from the assault on the racial foundations of their own status—such a simple precept provoked a flood of anger and anxiety. The North Carolina Fund, in their view, promised not so much economic development as social chaos and disorder.[38]

By 1968, the Fund's future was in peril. The agency had expended its initial foundation grants, which had been awarded for a five-year period, and the national War on Poverty was under siege. When the Fund's philanthropic backers offered to extend their support, its leaders declined. In part, they held to a vision of the Fund as a temporary and experimental agency. The founders had no desire to see their work routinized: to allow such a development, they insisted, would be to sacrifice innovation to the very forms of inertia that had for so long crippled the nation's response to its most needy citizens. Even more crucial were considerations of the changing political climate. In North Carolina, as in the country at large, the political alignments that had made the War on Poverty possible were beginning to dissolve. Liberal Democrats were in retreat by 1968, scrambling to ward off a white backlash against civil rights and to answer charges that they were somehow responsible for the violence and disorder that engulfed many communities across the state and nation in that year. During the spring primaries, a significant minority of North Carolina's white voters rallied behind the presidential candidacy of George Wallace, and in the November elections, Richard Nixon became the first Republican to carry the state since Herbert Hoover in 1928. Like liberals elsewhere in the nation, the Fund's architects saw few options but to settle for what seemed politically viable. They disbanded the Fund and dug in to defend hard-won enhancements of federal transfer payments—Aid to Families with Dependent Children, food stamps, jobs programs, Supplemental Security Income, and Medicaid—which, even though they did little to address the causes of poverty, at least strengthened the safety net for the most vulnerable Americans.[39]

Fund officials did take steps to see that a number of initiatives would be continued. Executive Director George Esser and his staff helped to create three new nonprofit organizations with specific goals: the Foundation for Community Development, which carried forward the work of grassroots organizing among the poor; the Manpower Development Corporation, which focused on job training and rural economic development; and the Low-Income Housing Development Corporation, which promoted the construction of affordable housing. Many people on the Fund staff went to work for one of these organizations, and both the Ford Foundation and the Office of Economic Opportunity continued to provide some support. But with the Fund's demise, the antipoverty effort in North Carolina lost its place at center stage in the state's politics. Indeed, of these three spin-off organizations, only the Manpower Development Corporation survived over the long term.[40]

Lasting Effects of the North Carolina Fund

The North Carolina Fund, like the War on Poverty, fell victim to racial divisiveness and Americans' continuing refusal to come to terms with issues of class in a purportedly classless society.[41] Yet while its programs have been long forgotten by most North Carolinians, its legacies survive in the lives of the former Volunteers. Miriam Dorsey, a Raleigh native, served with the First One Hundred and has since built a career around political activism. At the end of her summer of service, she briefly considered joining the Peace Corps but ventured instead to Washington. She secured a staff position with North Carolina Representative Richardson Preyer and, enticed by a study of wage discrimination in Congress, found her way onto the Capitol Hill Women's Political Caucus during the early 1970s.[42] Dorsey eventually chaired the group and was thoroughly caught up in the women's movement that was taking shape around the country. Her interests brought her back to North Carolina in 1977 to join the administration of Governor James Hunt. She served the governor as executive director of the North Carolina Council on the Status of Women and as his senior policy development analyst and women's policy adviser. In the latter capacity, Dorsey authored landmark legislation on domestic violence in 1979 and spearheaded the unsuccessful campaign to have North Carolina's General Assembly ratify the Equal Rights Amendment during the early 1980s. Today, she credits her work as a Volunteer for giving her life a guiding purpose: "Everything I have done since that summer . . . has been trying to broaden civil rights for different groups of people. Whether it's race or sex or class, civil rights is the basic thing I have been working for all these years."[43]

Emily Coble, who also served during the summer of 1964, has led a quieter but no less committed life. After leaving the Fund, she signed on for two tours with the Peace Corps and then returned to North Carolina to begin work as an elementary school teacher. Today, she runs a bilingual classroom for Spanish-speaking children of migrant farm workers. Just as thirty years ago she delighted in working with the impoverished children in a Fund-supported play school, she now feels a commitment to helping new immigrants make their way in an often hostile and unwelcoming world. A self-described "stranger in a strange land," Coble relies on memories of her summer as a Volunteer to supply her with the ability "to be tolerant, to appreciate, to respect, and to care."[44]

In 1996, Coble and other veterans of the North Carolina Fund gathered for a reunion and conference. Together with more than two hundred grassroots activists, policy makers, and representatives of charitable foundations, they discussed and debated the experiences of the past, the lessons of history, and the challenges of our own time. Even in the 1960s, when the economy was growing and national leaders stood committed to equal opportunity, local communities, as much as the federal government, were key battlegrounds for change. Today, in an age of welfare reform and devolution, that is as true as ever. The story of the North Carolina Fund and its Volunteers, therefore, has much to teach us.[45]

First of all, the story reminds us of the importance of activist citizenship in a diverse democracy. The young people who attended the 1996 conference were intensely concerned about continuing issues of racial justice and economic equality. Nevertheless, they work in an environment that is constrained in powerful and sometimes contradictory ways by the legacies of the past. Lacking either direct experience or deep appreciation for the critical role of community organizing and political mobilization, many of today's young activists see only two viable means of effecting change: as the providers of direct service to poor communities or as power brokers in the public-policy arena. That is, in part, no accident. Today's community-service movement often reflects lessons learned during the 1960s about the political messiness and unpredictability of volunteerism. Much of the literature on service learning, for instance, focuses more on the moral development of volunteers than on the role of service in contesting political power. Similarly, the enabling legislation for AmeriCorps draws a sharp distinction between service and activism. For example, AmeriCorps volunteers can work to winterize the homes of the poor, but they would violate the terms of their contracts by joining with labor unions or other "partisan political organizations" to demand the enforcement of housing codes. One way to break this impasse is to explore the work of the Fund Volunteers and to recover historical memories of their experiences. Social change, they remind us, requires not only good intentions but also a willingness to confront and transform existing social and economic relations.[46]

The recovery of historical memory it not just the work of scholars; it is, perhaps more importantly, the work of ordinary citizens as well. Volunteer programs—ranging from Habitat for Humanity to Teach for America and campus service-learning curricula—have proliferated in recent years. What is striking, however, is how little these undertakings are informed by a knowledge of their predecessors. To fill that void, we need a concerted research effort to explore the history of volunteerism in contemporary America and its effects on individuals, communities, and the larger polity. We also need volunteer and service-learning programs that actively promote an intergenerational dialogue. Only in these ways can we begin to prepare citizen-volunteers who are neither ignorant of the past nor bound by it.[47]

Finally, the story of the North Carolina Fund Volunteers underscores the role of interracial, cross-class alliances in nurturing an inclusive, democratic society. The Fund was surely right in turning its attention after 1965 to the development of indigenous leadership within poor communities, but if the agency made a mistake, it was in setting that goal against a sustained and robust program of student volunteerism. With the shutdown of the Volunteers program, the Fund lost much of its ability to build broad-based support for its work; student activists—both black and white—had fewer opportunities to establish relationships across the racial divide; and the poor found it increasingly difficult to secure the allies they needed to pursue their rights and needs.[48] As William Julius Wilson and others have argued, these are precisely the kinds of coalition-building and boundary-crossing activities that are needed to combat "the rising inequality in American society." "The true task before us," Wilson maintains, is for "the American people, and especially the leaders of the poor, the working classes, the displaced and the marginalized, the downsized and the deskilled, to set aside differences and work together" on a common agenda.[49]

Today, the South—and, indeed, the nation as a whole—faces problems similar to those confronted by Governor Sanford and his colleagues forty years ago: rapid technological change, growing income inequality, smoldering racial hostilities, and a workforce that is increasingly ill equipped to meet the challenges of a global economy. In remarks to the North Carolina Fund conference in 1996, Sanford lamented his generation's inability to address these issues adequately. His colleagues had not lost the War on Poverty, he insisted, "they [had] abandoned the battlefield." He was excited to see young activists committed to the ideals of the North Carolina Fund, and he urged them to be "more persistent" in fighting poverty and racial injustice. For all its limitations, Sanford counseled this new generation of citizen-soldiers, the Fund still offered a model of what "could be."[50]

Notes

1. Claudia Horwitz helped to found Empty the Shelters in 1991 while a student at the University of Pennsylvania. The organization works with young people around the country to teach them to become advocates for the homeless. See Claudia Horwitz, "What Is Wrong with National Service?" *Social Policy* 24 (fall 1993): 37–44. Jason Scott was one of the founders of Public Allies, an organization that "identifies a diversity of talented young adults and creates opportunities for them to practice leadership and strengthen their communities in a new alliance with people from

neighborhoods, nonprofits, business and government." See Public Allies' Web site, www.publicallies.org. Julia Scatliff helped to develop COOL, which works to coordinate community-service programs at colleges and universities around the country. See "A Trek for Voluntarism Links Campus Projects," *New York Times,* September 1, 1985, and Elizabeth Lenhard, "Committed to Community," *Atlanta Journal and Constitution,* March 10, 1996.

2. Billy Barnes to George Esser, ser. 8.2, North Carolina Fund Papers, Southern Historical Collection, University of North Carolina at Chapel Hill (hereafter, NCF Papers). The only overview of the North Carolina Fund and its work is Emily Herring Wilson, *For the People of North Carolina: The Z. Smith Reynolds Foundation at Half-Century, 1936–1986* (Chapel Hill: University of North Carolina Press, 1986), 65–82. Useful descriptions of the Fund's early years are Terry Sanford, "Poverty's Challenge to the States," and George H. Esser Jr., "The Role of a State-Wide Foundation in the War on Poverty," in *Anti-Poverty Programs,* ed. R. O. Everett (Dobbs, N.Y.: Oceana, 1966), 77–89, 90–113.

3. For background on the political economy of North Carolina, see Pete Daniel, *Standing at the Crossroads: Southern Life in the Twentieth Century* (New York: Hill and Wang, 1986); Gavin Wright, *Old South, New South: Revolutions in the Southern Economy since the Civil War* (New York: Basic Books, 1986); Paul Luebke, *Tar Heel Politics: Myths and Realities* (Chapel Hill: University of North Carolina Press, 1990); and Phillip Wood, *Southern Capitalism: The Political Economy of North Carolina, 1880–1980* (Durham, N.C.: Duke University Press, 1986). On outmigration, see C. Horace Hamilton, *Net Migration to and from North Carolina and North Carolina Counties from 1940 to 1950* (Raleigh: Agricultural Experiment Station, North Carolina State College, 1953); C. Horace Hamilton, *The New South: Its Changing Population Characteristics* (Chapel Hill: Carolina Population Center, University of North Carolina, 1970), 8, 75, 76; and Esser, "Role of a State-Wide Foundation," 95.

4. This "awakening" is, in and of itself, fascinating. It suggests, in part, the effects of the cultural and political amnesia created by the 1950s. Southern liberals of the 1930s and '40s often possessed incisive understandings of poverty and offered sophisticated prescriptions for change. Nevertheless, the students and liberals of the 1960s had to "discover poverty" all over again, and they did so within a Cold War and culture-of-poverty framework that was much less useful than the class framework of earlier generations. See John Egerton, *Speak Now against the Day: The Generation before the Civil Rights Movement in the South* (Chapel Hill: University of North Carolina Press, 1994); and Michael B. Katz, *In the Shadow of the Poorhouse: A Social History of Welfare in America* (New York: Basic Books, 1986).

5. Terry Sanford, "The Case for the New South," *Look,* December 15, 1964, 83–84; Sanford, "Poverty's Challenge," 78; and Esser, "Role of a State-Wide Foundation," 96. Excellent discussions of the relationship between white business leaders and the

civil rights movement can be found in Elizabeth Jacoway and David R. Colburn, eds., *Southern Businessmen and Desegregation* (Baton Rouge: Louisiana State University Press, 1982).

6. "Three Years of Change: Narrative History of the North Carolina Fund," A-3, ser. 1.1.1, NCF Papers; Sanford, "Poverty's Challenge," 81–83; Esser, "Role of a State-Wide Foundation," 90–96; Emily Herring Wilson, *For the People of North Carolina*, 73; and "N.C. Fund Yields Legacy of Progress," *Philanthropy Journal* 1 (May 1994): 1. For more information on the Fund's board members and their backgrounds, see Terry Sanford, *But What about the People?* (New York: Harper and Row, 1966), 128.

7. For a detailed breakdown of contributions to the Fund, see Emily Berry, " 'One Building Block in the Battle': The North Carolina Fund and the Legacy of Idealism" (honors thesis, Department of History, University of North Carolina at Chapel Hill, 1996), 5; and "Records of the North Carolina Fund Inventory," 19–20, Southern Historical Collection, University of North Carolina at Chapel Hill. For North Carolina expenditures on public welfare, see *The Budget, 1965–67* (Raleigh: Edwards and Broughton, n.d.), 1:218–21; *The Budget, 1967–69* (n.p.), 1:174–76; and *The Budget, 1969–71* (n.p.), 1:194–97. The role of the Ford Foundation in urban antipoverty efforts is most recently discussed in Alice O'Connor, "Community Action, Urban Reform, and the Fight against Poverty: The Ford Foundation's Gray Areas Program," *Journal of Urban History* 22 (July 1996): 586–626.

8. "Three Years of Change," A-1; Sanford, "Poverty's Challenge," 82; and Esser, "Role of a State-Wide Foundation," 108. The relationship between the Fund and the Office of Economic Opportunity is documented in the extensive correspondence files in ser. 1 of the NCF Papers.

9. Luebke, *Tar Heel Politics*, 158–59. A close account of the 1964 Democratic primary can be found in James R. Spence, *The Making of a Governor: The Moore-Preyer-Lake Primaries of 1964* (Winston-Salem, N.C.: John F. Blair, 1968). The only biography of Sanford is Howard E. Covington Jr. and Marion Ellis, *Terry Sanford: Politics, Progress, and Outrageous Ambitions* (Durham, N.C.: Duke University Press, 1999). On the creation of the Fund and political logic of its establishment as a private, nonprofit corporation, see "Three Years of Change," A-4; and Sanford, *But What about the People?* 125–29.

10. Esser, "Role of a State-Wide Foundation," 92.

11. See Peter F. Drucker, *Managing the Non-Profit Organization* (New York: Harper Business, 1992).

12. The Volunteers' essays and logs, along with our interviews, are on deposit in the Southern Historical Collection, University of North Carolina at Chapel Hill. For comparative purposes, the best work to take up similar issues of volunteerism and social action is Doug McAdam, *Freedom Summer* (New York: Oxford University Press, 1988). The program that most resembled the North Carolina Volunteers was

Volunteers in Service to America VISTA, which was modeled in part on the North Carolina experiment. The Fund's relationship with VISTA is detailed in ser. 3.4, NCF Papers.

13. David Andrew Biggs, "The First One Hundred" (honors thesis, Department of History, University of North Carolina at Chapel Hill, 1992), 30; and "Three Years of Change," A-15. In 1965, the Fund supported the Volunteers program with $274,316 from the Office of Economic Opportunity and $32,444 of its own resources.

14. For a detailed account of the recruiting process in 1964 and a demographic profile of both summers' Volunteers, see Berry, " 'One Building Block in the Battle.' " On the Fund's determination to challenge established forms of volunteerism, see Sanford, "Poverty's Challenge," 81. An interesting discussion of gender and student voluntarism in the 1960s can be found in Doug McAdam, "Gender as a Mediator of the Activist Experience: The Case of Freedom Summer," *American Journal of Sociology* 97 (March 1992): 1211–40. On the Volunteers' nickname, see "The First One Hundred," a documentary film produced by the North Carolina Fund, NCF Papers.

15. Application essays, ser. 2.1.3, NCF Papers.

16. Hugh Jones (pseud.), application essay, ser. 2.1.3, NCF Papers. The term *citizen-soldiers* is from Johnette Ingold Fields, interview, October 18, 1995, Southern Oral History Program Collection, Southern Historical Collection, University of North Carolina at Chapel Hill (hereafter, SOHP). The records of the North Carolina Fund are open to researchers with one important restriction. To protect the Volunteers' privacy, the Southern Historical Collection has requested that pseudonyms be substituted for individual names in published references to application essays and daily logs.

17. Michael Harrington, *The Other America: Poverty in the United States* (New York: Macmillan, 1962), 2; and Sharon Young (pseud.), daily log, August 18, 1964, ser. 2.1.2, NCF Papers.

18. Billy E. Barnes, "The North Carolina Fund: A Progress Report," *Popular Government* 30 (June 1964): 1–5, 22; and "Description of Tasks Performed by the North Carolina Volunteers, Summer, 1964," ser. 2.1.2, NCF Papers.

19. Daily log, August 4, 1965, ser. 2.1.3, application essay, ser. 2.1.3, NCF Papers; Berry, " 'One Building Block in the Battle,' " 50; and Fields, interview.

20. Daily log, June 14–17, July 24, 1964, ser. 2.1.1, and daily log, June 30, July 30, and August 11, 1964, ser. 2.1.2, NCF Papers.

21. Application essays, ser. 2.1.3, and daily log, July 12, 1964, ser. 2.1.1, NCF Papers. A similar learning process took place among student volunteers in eastern Kentucky. See Thomas J. Kiffmeyer, "From Self-Help to Sedition: The Appalachian Volunteers in Eastern Kentucky, 1964–1970," *Journal of Southern History* 64 (1998): 65–94.

22. Application essay, ser. 2.1.3, and daily log, June 22, 1964, ser. 2.1.1, NCF Papers. On the pace of desegregation in North Carolina, see U.S. Commission on Civil Rights,

Racial Isolation within Public Schools (Washington, D.C.: U.S. Government Printing Office, 1965), 1:4, table 1; and William H. Chafe, *Civilities and Civil Rights: Greensboro, North Carolina, and the Black Struggle for Freedom* (New York: Oxford University Press, 1980), 105–6.

23. Daily log, June 25, 1964, and Charlotte Williams (pseud.), daily log, July 1, 1964, ser. 2.1.2, NCF Papers.

24. Daily log, July 30, 1965, ser. 2.1.3, and daily log, July 24, August 26, 1964, ser. 2.1.1, NCF Papers.

25. Daily log, August 16, 1965, ser. 2.1.3, and daily log, July 27, 1964, ser. 2.1.2, NCF Papers.

26. Esser, "Role of a State-Wide Foundation," 105.

27. Sue Hester (pseud.), daily log, August 4, 1964, ser. 2.1.2, NCF Papers.

28. Marc White (pseud.), daily log, June 22, 28, 1964, ser. 2.1.2, NCF Papers.

29. Adisa Douglas, Volunteer survey, in possession of the authors. Volunteers working in the Harnett County town of Coats reported a similar incident of a library closing after they brought in black children. Here, too, Volunteers were forced to abandon their work after Klan threats. See daily log, June 28, July 1, Fund withdrew its Volunteers from Craven County when night riders fired shots into the house where the students were living. See daily log, July 10, 1965, and advisory committee meeting notes, July 12, 1965, ser. 2.1.3, NCF Papers. On the increase of Klan activity in North Carolina in this period, see Oliver Williams, "Rebirth of Klan Counters Moderate Action in State," *Raleigh News and Observer*, August 23, 1964, and "Big Gains Scored by Carolina Klan," *New York Times*, September 6, 1964.

30. Douglas, Volunteer survey; and daily log, July 26, 1964, ser. 2.1.1, NCF Papers.

31. Daily log, June 30, July 7, 1964, ser. 2.1.2, daily log, July 26, August 14, 1965, ser. 2.1.3, and Lynda Ruth Lovett to Jack Mansfield, June 28, 1965, box 34, NCF Papers.

32. Daily log, July 1, 1964, ser. 2.1.1, NCF Papers. Another Volunteer complained openly of superiors and local officials who "appeared to be self-satisfied with the mere fact of the Fund." See daily log, August 19, 1964, ser. 2.1.1, NCF Papers.

33. Chris Gioia, " 'How to Get out of Hell by Raising It': Race and Politics in Durham's War on Poverty" (honors thesis, Department of History, University of North Carolina at Chapel Hill, 1996), 32–54; and Osha Gray Davidson, *The Best of Enemies: Race and Redemption in the New South* (New York: Scribner, 1996), 153–85.

34. The term *maximum feasible participation* was inserted into the language of the Economic Opportunity Act by White House aides who wanted to make sure that poor people, not just politicians and social welfare professionals, were involved in the design and implementation of antipoverty programs. For a critical view of this effort, see Daniel Patrick Moynihan, *Maximum Feasible Misunderstanding: Community Action in the War on Poverty* (New York: Free Press, 1969).

35. See George Esser, interview with Emily Berry, October 17, 1995, Chapel Hill, N.C., cited in Erika LeMay, "Battlefield in the Backyard: A Local Study of the War on Poverty" (master's thesis, University of North Carolina at Chapel Hill, 1997), 23.

36. Betty Ward, untitled manuscript, January 3, 1966, ser. 2.1.4, NCF Papers; and Diane Sasson, interview, October 28, 1995, SOHP. See also Esser, "Role of a State-Wide Foundation," 102.

37. LeMay, "Battlefield"; Gioia, "How to Get out of Hell"; and Lisa Gayle Hazirjian, "The Daily Struggle: Poverty, Power, and Working-Class Life in Rocky Mount, North Carolina, 1929–1969" (Ph.D. diss., Duke University, forthcoming).

38. "PPOP Owes CADA an Apology," *Hertford County Herald*, February 20, 1967; "The Local Poor Have Their Say," *Northampton News*, August 4, 1966; and James Gardner to Esser, November 21, 1967, box 31, NCF Papers. For more on these matters, see LeMay, "Battlefield"; Gioia, "How to Get out of Hell"; and Hazirjian, "Daily Struggle." On the history of race and class in the definition of American citizenship, see Rogers Smith, "American Conceptions of Citizenship and National Service," in *New Communitarian Thinking: Persons, Virtues, Institutions, and Communities*, ed. Amitai Etzioni (Charlottesville: University Press of Virginia, 1995), 237–58.

39. On the guiding vision of the North Carolina Fund as a temporary, experimental agency, see Esser, "Role of a State-Wide Foundation"; Esser memorandum, n.d., ser. 1.2.6, NCF Papers; and "Three Years of Change," A-4. For a general account of the waning of the War on Poverty and sixties-era reform, see Allen J. Matusow, *The Unraveling of America: A History of Liberalism in the 1960s* (New York: Harper and Row, 1984).

40. On the phaseout of the North Carolina Fund, see Esser memorandum, n.d., ser. 1.2.6, and "Transcription of Tapes of Interview of George Esser by Patricia Maloney Alt on January 2, 1970," ser. 5.3, NCF Papers. For information on the continuing work of the Manpower Development Corporation, see its Web site, www.mdcinc.org.

41. See Jill Quadagno, *The Color of Welfare: How Racism Undermined the War on Poverty* (New York: Oxford University Press, 1994).

42. Preyer was the Sanford protégé who was defeated in the 1964 Democratic gubernatorial primary. He was elected to the U.S. House of Representatives in 1968.

43. Miriam Dorsey, interview, March 1, 1996, SOHP.

44. From the text of a speech by Emily Coble, "Presentation on Cultural Diversity," November 16, 1995, cited in Berry, "One Building Block in the Battle," 113.

45. Ben Stocking, "Groundbreaking North Carolina Fund Provides Inspiration," *Raleigh News and Observer*, December 14, 1966.

46. In reflecting on the Fund's work, Sanford emphasized the importance of contesting political and economic power. "The [Fund's] first impact," he wrote, "was to upset the existing power structures within communities so that changes in the status-quo could occur. In most cases, this amounted to radical changes in community relations and activities—but this we did knowingly, realizing that positive results would occur when existing structures are challenged by the new" ("Poverty's Challenge," 82). For a general discussion of community service in the 1990s, see Robert Coles, *The Call of Service* (New York: Houghton Mifflin, 1993). For

the prohibition on political activism in the AmeriCorps program, see U.S. Public Laws, 103d Cong., 1st sess., Public Law 103-82 (H.R. 2010), September 21, 1993, National and Community Service Trust Act of 1993, title 1, section 132. For more on AmeriCorps policies and practices, see also Commission on National and Community Service, *What You Can Do for Your Country* (Washington, D.C.: Commission on National and Community Service, 1993); Corporation for National Service, *Expanding Boundaries: Serving and Learning* (New York: Corporation for National Service, 1996); Jill Zuckman, "Pared Funding Speeds Passage of National Service," *Congressional Quarterly Weekly Report* 51 (August 7, 1993): 2160; Harris Wofford and John P. Walters, "Should the Federal Government Try to Stimulate Volunteerism through its National Service Program?" *CQ Researcher* 6 (December 13, 1996): 1097; and Jim Zook, "National-Service Program Hurt by Politicking over Its Future," *Chronicle of Higher Education,* June 16, 1995, A29.

47. We have much to learn from other volunteer programs created in the 1960s, especially the Peace Corps, VISTA, and the Appalachian Volunteers (AV). Recent studies of all three programs emphasize the strong relationship between voluntarism and citizenship and the role of volunteers both in the United States and overseas in stretching American society's capacity to accommodate the views of the poor. Two recent studies of the Peace Corps are Fritz Fischer, *Making Them Like Us: Peace Corps Volunteers in the 1960s* (Washington, D.C.: Smithsonian Institution Press, 1998); and Elizabeth Cobbs Hoffman, *All You Need Is Love: The Peace Corps and the Spirit of the 1960s* (Cambridge: Harvard University Press, 1998). The story of VISTA and AV volunteers in Kentucky and West Virginia is detailed in Marie Tyler McGraw, "Staying On: Poverty Warriors in West Virginia," *Journal of American Culture* 8 (winter 1985): 93–103; and Kiffmeyer, "From Self-Help to Sedition."

48. A prescient analysis of the need for middle-class volunteers in the fight against poverty is found in Guion Griffis Johnson, *Volunteers in Community Service* (Durham, N.C.: North Carolina Council of Women's Organizations, 1967). The North Carolina Fund sponsored Johnson's study but seems to have largely ignored her recommendations for a continuation of volunteer programs.

49. William Julius Wilson, *The Bridge over the Racial Divide: Rising Inequality and Coalition Politics* (Berkeley: University of California Press, 1999), 1, 128. For the value of community service in addressing the fragmentation of American life, see also Steve Waldman, *The Bill: How the Adventures of Clinton's National Service Bill Reveal What Is Corrupt, Comic, Cynical—and Noble—about Washington* (New York: Viking Books, 1995).

50. Tim Caldwell, "Can the Mountaineer Lead the Nation? The Origins of Community Action and the War on Poverty in North Carolina" (honors thesis, Department of History, University of North Carolina at Chapel Hill, 1995), 53; and Stocking, "Groundbreaking North Carolina Fund."

"They Can Be like Other People"

Race, Poverty, and the Politics of Alienation
in New Orleans's Early Great Society

KENT B. GERMANY

In New Orleans in the mid-1960s, social welfare moved out of the poorhouse. Encouraged by the Great Society, local social-welfare advocates charted antipoverty strategies that elevated the role of social-welfare policy in the city's struggle to adjust to the decline of official Jim Crow. In particular, the Great Society represented a way for local leaders to accommodate African American inclusion, to limit the perceived dangers of poverty, and to enrich the city. Antipoverty strategies from the early Great Society reveal an adherence to some of the traditional functions for social welfare while offering some significant departures. Most local policy participants continued to expect social-welfare policies to relieve the desperate, maintain social order, and shape the labor market. Some of them hoped the War on Poverty would encourage political mobilization and, in a relatively new social-welfare function, fight racial prejudice.[1] This chapter suggests that in New Orleans in the 1960s, most functions fell under two categories. Locals sought social-welfare policies that first preserved social stability and second boosted the economy.

A central theme in the early Great Society was a desire to make the poor—especially the African American poor—more like other people. A considerable number of reformers envisioned that growth, inclusion, and security would come from creating more productive workers, better consumers, and confident citizens. The vision came partly from above as President Lyndon B. Johnson, the President's Council of Economic Advisers, and federal program developers promoted a Great Society that would help the rising tide to lift all boats, turn tax eaters into taxpayers, and defer the "fire next time" to a later date.[2] The vision also drew from social-psychological theories about poverty that were prominent in the social sciences. Locals folded those influences into their own conceptualization of the Great Society. Locally, the search for the Great Society involved building institutions and reforming individuals. In the mid-1960s, the demolition of Jim Crow complicated and intensified the impact, while psychological reasoning and therapeutic thought demonstrated new dimensions of public policy.[3]

In the early Great Society, social-welfare politics reflected New Orleans's civic hopes and anxieties, especially those that arose from the deconstruction of legalized racial segregation. As the inclusion of African Americans into the public sphere moved beyond tokenism, the early Great Society contributed to two broad developments. It helped build an organizational foundation that later grew into a primary institutional base for racial integration, and it encouraged the articulation of an inclusion rationale that underlay the rise of biracial liberalism.[4] Racial liberals associated with the antipoverty movement saw the opportunity to build a post–Jim Crow South as both enticing and befuddling. During the profoundly disruptive period of racial desegregation, they tried to answer a serious question: How could the South fully include African Americans while preserving civic order and sustaining economic growth? In other words, how could the region replace segregation without a dramatic restructuring of local political thought and local government, especially when the traditional levers of power lay in the hands of people who had been quite pleased with Jim Crow? Racial segregation had created a public culture that had severely restricted the participation of African Americans and had ensured their relegation to the economic periphery. The Great Society, for its part, contributed administrative, political, and intellectual components that helped to displace—in increments—the culture that Jim Crow had wrought. The result was a gradual compromise between old New Orleans and a new Dixie.

The structures and ideas mobilized in the local implementation of the Great Society undermined segregation while accommodating three intertwined but frequently conflicting local demands: (1) a powerful push for economic growth, (2) a deep commitment to maintaining civic stability, and (3) an intense black search for power and inclusion. In particular, the Great Society's accommodation offered a new and powerful political outlet for New Orleans's racial progressives. During the first two years of the Great Society, reformers and activists used federal social-welfare experiments to define new public roles for African Americans and to build unprecedented bases for funding, patronage, and political mobilization. Structurally, the Great Society provided the administrative core of a newly developing state apparatus that this chapter calls the soft state.[5] This soft state was a public-private hybrid of nonprofit agencies, charitable institutions, public bureaucracies, and local political organizations that arose in the late 1960s from federal antipoverty grants and programs.[6] A few years earlier, in the mid-1960s, the Community Action Program of the Office of Economic Opportunity (OEO) and other antipoverty programs accelerated the mobilization of the constituent bases of the soft state and the establishment of its bureaucratic imprint. The resulting apparatus became the chief public means for dealing with local African American concerns. The soft state developed into a fast administrative fix to the relative statelessness that had existed for black New Orleans before the civil rights movement.[7] Intellectually, the Great Society served an equally important role. The rationale used by local liberals in the implementation of the Great Society set forth subtle terms for black inclusion that reveal the influence of America's therapeutic culture on public policy. This chapter briefly examines the early structuring of the soft state while taking a deeper look at the role of poverty in shaping local liberal thought.

This chapter posits that the political dialogue stimulated by the Great Society established an intellectual framework for the rise of black political power and hence for the region's first legitimate biracial liberalism. The dialogue suggests that the injection of new liberal, black constituencies proceeded not because an overwhelming number of citizens viewed it as a matter of justice and equality but because they feared the consequences of black alienation and needed economic growth. In the early Great Society, arguments for the expansion of social welfare and of black power often depended on mobilizing anxiety (typically of white progressives and moderates) about the alienation, deprivation, and taxation linked to black poverty. For a few ironic years, poverty empowered the poor, and, oddly, black poverty led to black power. In so doing, however, the politics of the early Great Society ensured that black power often extended from the capacity to alarm white progrowth constituencies and the ability to align bureaucratic influence rather than from blacks being considered full and equal citizens.

Fear of things falling apart helped to sell the Great Society. As it developed, the Great Society represented yet another extension of an American search for order, and it reflected the influence of postwar conceptions of American individualism, 1960s-era social-psychological thought, and civil-rights-movement-based inclusion arguments.[8] Thematically, the political thought that guided the selling of social-welfare policy reflected three major concerns of local liberals: humanitarianism, economic efficiency, and social stability. At a general level, most early supporters defended the Great Society as an altruistic effort to relieve suffering. More common, however, was the depiction of the Great Society as a way to reduce the costs of poverty. In this argument, social-welfare reform provided the chance to streamline approaches to poverty and improve the city's image as a safe, prosperous, and fun place, especially for convention goers and investors. A third appeal was the most prominent and most important, and it explained the Great Society as a way to keep the poor and alienated from hurting the rest of society. To a broad array of local anti-poverty participants, the Great Society offered a cheap way to buy peace and security, especially since the federal government was footing most of the bill. The widespread desire to root out alienation shows that the early War on Poverty developed less as a means to deal with the problems of the poor than as a means to diminish the problems that the poor posed for the rest of the community. The construction of the early Great Society indicates that the push to pacify the so-called ghetto was not a creation of the riots that occurred from late 1965 to 1968. Neutralizing the potentially negative impact of the ghetto was essential to the Great Society from its conception.

As elsewhere in urban America in the mid-1960s, the ghetto in New Orleans bewildered reformers. Great Society proponents faced the challenge of implementing the Community Action Program, Head Start, the Concentrated Employment Program, the Neighborhood Youth Corps, and other education and counseling programs in a city undergoing dramatic changes. New Orleans stood amid two strong historical currents. A city whose residents loved their old things and their old ways had to assimilate the profound changes wrought by the civil rights movement and by the South's post–World War II economic rejuvenation. New Orleans was experiencing a massive outmigration of white residents and was in the early stages of a major building boom that created a new skyline and new transportation routes. Civic boosters lustily hawked the town to whoever would listen. In 1966, they scored a major coup when the National Football League awarded the city an expansion franchise that became known as the New Orleans Saints. Within a decade, the city and state built the Louisiana Superdome—one of the largest open indoor spaces in the world—to house the team. The petrochemical and shipping industries were nesting themselves in new glass towers downtown along the Canal Street and Poydras Street corridors. Architects, engineers, financiers, and developers enjoyed an almost unprecedented heyday. Like countless other American cities, New Orleans was expanding outward and upward. Unfortunately, it had ill-formed plans to account for the deflation that was occurring in pockets isolated from the Sunbelt boom. On top of the financial consequences of the geographic and demographic transformation, New Orleans (and other southern cities) had to alter Jim Crow, which had provided social order, albeit through oppressive means, for nearly a century.

As the city's more progressive leaders had done since the mid–nineteenth century, when they experienced problems too big to handle on their own, they looked to the federal government. Throughout the twentieth century, leaders labored to protect local investment against floods and hurricanes. In a city essentially below sea level, they used the federal government to build faster pumps, bigger expressways, and better levees (and, at least in one 1927 case, to explode levees downstream to relieve pressure on downtown). For the problems associated with the prevalence of urban poverty and the decline of segregation, a loose coalition of social-welfare professionals, rights activists, and business boosters convened once again along the federal pipeline. Whereas federal transportation and housing policies had stretched the city into the skies and the swamps, federal social-welfare policies helped build linkages—though limited—across racial lines at a time when the city was experiencing some of the most intense racially motivated violence since Reconstruction.[9] In a twelve-month period in 1964 and 1965, some of the episodes of white violence included the shooting of a young black man for ordering a hamburger, the firebombing of an African American home in a previously all-white housing project, and the explosion of at least eleven other bombs meant for civil rights activists.[10]

Partly because of this hostile environment, local War on Poverty leaders shied away from direct challenges to the city's color lines. They molded the OEO's Community Action Program to fit this local political requirement. In particular, a target-area approach gave leaders the opportunity to avoid inflaming racial antagonism by adhering to neighborhood lines and residential segregation patterns. In 1965 and 1966, the local community-action agency, Total Community Action (TCA), designated seven target areas.[11] The seven areas accounted for approximately 150,000 of the city's almost 700,000 residents by 1966. Of the 150,000, about 120,000 were African Americans. Those areas included two predominantly white areas known as the Irish Channel and Florida. The areas of Desire, the Lower Ninth Ward, Central City, Algiers-Fischer, and St. Bernard were predominantly African American and generally lay in a basin formed by the slope of the Mississippi River's natural levee. The basin was considerably below sea level and historically had been marginal land (see map).[12] The table provides a comparison of some characteristics of the target areas.

TCA leaders and their chief delegate agency, the Social Welfare Planning Council (SWPC), chose those areas for a variety of reasons. Broadly defined, these administrators followed the liberal strategy of identifying problems, devising feasible plans, and implementing solutions. In the War on Poverty, they pursued a scheme of isolate and conquer. Target-area designation depended on the section's need, the potential for its residents to participate, and the role of existing agencies in the proposed areas. The selection criteria focused on statistical evidence of poverty, racial factors, the ready appearance of social despair, reputations as damaged areas, and existing social-welfare structures.[13] A quick survey of the areas suggests that the concentration of poor residents,

Reference Map of New Orleans's Seven Target Areas

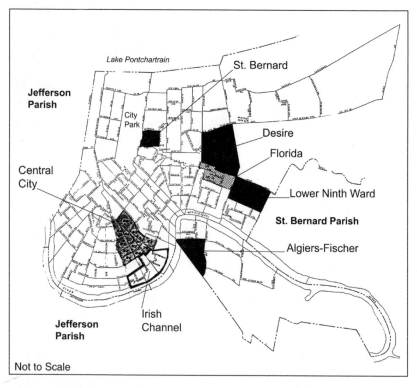

Source: Amended Census Tract Map, box 3, folder 16, Winston Lill Collection, Department of Special Collections, Tulane University Libraries, Jones Hall, Tulane University, New Orleans.

Comparison of New Orleans's War on Poverty Target Areas, ca. 1960

	Population	% White	% Black	% of Families below $3,000 per Year Income	% of Unemployed Males	% of Adults over 25 with 8th Grade or Less Education	% of Families Receiving ADC Payments	Disease Cases per 1,000 Residents
New Orleans	627,525	62.5	37.2	28	6.2	35	1.9	4.7
Desire	17,033	8.7	91.2	61	9.9	52	17.1	6.7
St. Bernard	10,972	4.8	95.1	58	15.2	46	9.4	2.6
Central City	54,252	14.6	83.4	54	9.5	38	15.6	10.5
Lower Ninth Ward	33,001	18.3	81.5	32	8	48	5.3	5.9
Algiers-Fischer	9,177	39.8	60.1	38	5.6	29	14.2	9.5
Florida	10,678	55.6	44.1	44	9.3	24	8.8	3.1
Irish Channel	23,655	87	12.7	35	8.3	47	7.1	7.5

Sources: TCA, "Demographic Information by Target Area" [taken from 1960 Census Tract surveys], box 5, folder 18, Community Relations Council of Greater New Orleans Collection, Amistad Research Center, Tilton Hall, Tulane University, New Orleans; OEO, "Community Profile Project: Orleans Parish, Louisiana," ser. E23, box 202, Records of the Community Services Administration, RG 381, National Archives and Records Administration, College Park, Md.; TCA, "Quick Facts: TCA Target Areas," in Gordon Wilcox, "Inspector's Field Report," July 23, 1966, ser. E75, box 102, "New Orleans" folder, Records of the Community Services Administration; and TCA Research Department, "New Orleans," [1967], box 55, folder 4, National Association for the Advancement of Colored People, Office of Field Director of Louisiana, Records, Amistad Research Center.

the relative homogeneity of the area, and the area's potential for political mobilization were also considerations.

One criterion does not appear prominently in the documents but is an obvious similarity between target areas: the lack of effective public institutional presence. The state's influence was usually represented by welfare caseworkers and the police. The situation was most obvious in the black target areas, which had grossly inadequate street lighting, drainage, schools, public transportation, health facilities, police protection, and political influence—if any at all. Infant mortality there was twice as high as in the rest of the city. Half of the residents of those areas had less than an eighth-grade education, compared to one-third of other New Orleanians. Residents of these areas often traveled unpaved roads and relieved themselves in outdoor toilets. Sixty-one percent of streets in predominantly black sections lacked adequate paving and drainage, with that percentage rising to 86 in the Lower Ninth Ward. Children in those areas typically played on public roads and in vacant lots, the only available recreational space. Combined, the three largest African American areas had a mere 16 acres of recreational space, although the minimum recommended standard for such an area was 202 acres. In the Desire area, one public park served more than 17,000 children. Educational opportunities were at least as constricted. White elementary schools in Orleans Parish averaged 495 students per school, while black schools averaged 892. For white males between ages twenty-five and forty-four, 29 percent had an elementary education or less. For black males of the same age, the percentage was an astounding 69 percent.[14]

The seven target areas accounted for only one-fifth of New Orleans's population. In terms of psychological influence, however, their existence dominated the actions of local and federal leaders. Whether geographically, economically, socially, or psychologically, each of those areas was isolated from the rest of the city. With the exception of the Irish Channel, which was the bastion of James Comiskey, a powerful Irish-American Third Ward tax assessor, they were at least as impotent politically.[15] Using census data and sociological studies, civic leaders identified them as the city's worst areas in regard to crime, disease, illiteracy, and fiscal drain. Statistically, residents of these areas were the least educated, least healthy, least affluent, most violent, and most criminal in New Orleans. In an age of a supposedly overabundant economy, they posed the most serious threat to continued economic growth and social order. The residents of those seven areas, therefore, became the targets of American liberalism.[16] The Great Society joined together the federal government, a small local social-welfare community, civic leaders, and the poor in an ambitious reconstruction of citizenship.

The Great Society's target-area strategy was crucial for the development of a soft state apparatus and the escalation of black political participation. Federal influence and funding pushed the politicization of black neighborhoods at a critical moment in southern politics.[17] The Great Society accelerated the transformation of southern populist-oriented liberalism from what one historian has called the "buccaneering" style of men such as James E. Folsom of Alabama and Earl K. Long of Louisiana to an urban-centered liberalism dependent on biracial coalition and federal involvement, especially in social policy.[18] The efforts of a small group of local progressives created a fragmented yet durable antipoverty structure that speeded the transition. The Great Society served as a catalyst in a process that expanded a neighborhood leadership core that had been roused by the civil rights movement. As a result, federal antipoverty programs and organizing efforts made the Great Society a clear extension of the African American search for inclusion. Newly politicized, semipublic organizations evolved from community action funded by the OEO. Through grants, patronage opportunities, and bureaucratic protection, the War on Poverty underwrote the mobilization of black political leaders and neighborhood-based political cells. Three years after the local War on Poverty began, those leaders and their groups took over the local Great Society from the white liberals and moderates who had initiated it. Five years later, those groups put the city's first racial liberal into the mayor's office.[19]

Great Society–linked groups were successful in preparing the city's post–Jim Crow leadership. In the fifteen-year period after 1964, Great Society programs counted among their former employees or board members at least seven state representatives or senators, four city council members, four mayors (including three in New Orleans), ten high-ranking executives or public officials, dozens of political aides or midlevel bureaucrats, and countless successful business people. TCA's list of alumni (defined as people "affiliated" with TCA for at least ninety days) who later achieved positions of "leadership" ran to more than two hundred people. Its leaders did not exaggerate when they claimed in 1984 that TCA had "served as a launching pad for upward mobility." They were correct in claiming that their former employees comprised a " 'who's who' of the City of New Orleans."[20]

In December 1964, the initial seed that helped produce that list was sown through the founding of TCA. During the first three years of the Great Society, TCA's leadership drew from a cross-section of the city's struggling liberal constituencies. Labor leaders, social-welfare professionals, civil rights leaders, Jewish leaders, teachers, civic activists, and business progressives established the early outlook and objectives of the local antipoverty movement. Their conduct of the War on Poverty depended on several existing social-welfare organizations. The most important of those groups was the swpc, which had specialized in coordinating private social-welfare services for the previous four decades. In 1965, it became tca's chief delegate agency for all target areas except the largely white Irish Channel. Complementing the swpc were the Urban League of Greater New Orleans, Associated Catholic Charities, and several other service providers.

Organizationally, perhaps the most important long-term impact of the antipoverty movement grew from the neighborhood councils that proliferated in the target areas. During this early stage, seven predominantly African American neighborhood groups developed into influential organizations with cadres of rising political talent. Several dozen less-organized entities also forced action from the state. In the beginning, the neighborhood councils were to serve as clearinghouses for community complaints and ideas for reform. They were to function as program consultants and coordinators of community organization. The leaders of one such organization, the Central City Economic Opportunity Committee, claimed that their objectives were to insure "maximum feasible participation" and the directing of War on Poverty money to the poor. They hoped to "unite the citizens of the area to develop an interest in neighborhood development and improvement . . . and provide an opportunity for them to help themselves through self-help programs such as jobs, education, health." The committee endorsed the underlying psychological mission of the Great Society, explaining that members wanted to "involve young people in a social and civic nature, which will be helpful in creating pride, dignity, self-identification and community spirit."[21]

The structure of the local War on Poverty was not completely new. To varying degrees, the seven target areas owed their political power to civic organizations in place prior to the Great Society. Existing neighborhood groups augmented the oeo-developed organizations. In the predominantly white Irish Channel, the organizations were white, church-centered entities whose importance rarely stretched beyond the neighborhoods. Kingsley House (a settlement house founded by the Episcopal Church in 1896 that prided itself on being the "Hull House of the South"), the Irish Channel Action Foundation (founded by a Catholic priest in 1962), several bloc cells largely centered in the channel's St. Thomas housing project, and the tca-led Irish Channel

Neighborhood Development Center wrestled for power. In the Florida area, which was a racially mixed area with a traditionally white housing project, the Florida Area Achievement Group operated briefly as a biracial organization.[22]

In the rest of the target areas, the neighborhood organizations were predominantly African American. In the Desire area, two organizations were critical. The Desire Area Community Council and the Desire Area Economic Opportunity Committee represented dozens of improvement associations and community groups that sprang up in the early part of the War on Poverty. The older areas of Central City and the Lower Ninth Ward had councils that reflected their well-established civic and political leadership. Central City's economic opportunity committee dominated the conduct of the War on Poverty. Its fifty-five members were elected from the area and consisted of teachers, social-welfare professionals, craftspeople, ministers, and other neighborhood residents.[23] In the Lower Ninth Ward, two groups held the most influence. The Ninth Ward Civic Improvement League had been operating as a social relief organization since 1942, and it emerged as a powerful voice under the leadership of longtime civil rights activist Leontine Luke. Complementing the Civic Improvement League and eventually supplanting it in power was the War on Poverty–created Lower Ninth Ward Neighborhood Council.[24] In Algiers, the Algiers-Fischer Community Organization became the most important group. In the St. Bernard area, TCA apparently provided most of the machinery in the early period.[25]

Intended to complement the efforts of SWPC and TCA, the neighborhood councils developed into much more. They became essential liaisons between the neighborhoods and city hall, and their leaders proved crucial to negotiating for federal funding of social-welfare programs and infrastructure improvement. By 1968, the neighborhood councils' power had grown to such an extent that they took over the multimillion-dollar federal community-organizing component (referred to by the OEO as the Neighborhood Development Program) from the SWPC. The neighborhood groups greatly speeded the rise of black political leaders, and a nucleus of those leaders retained power into the next century. In the late 1960s, many of their leaders in Central City, Desire, and the Lower Ninth Ward helped found the Southern Organization for Unified Leadership and the Black Organization for Leadership Development, two of the most powerful black-dominated political machines until the turn of the century.[26] A third such organization, the Community Organization for Urban Politics, also benefited greatly from the antipoverty structure. Those groups became arbiters of the soft state. Their relative durability and influence, however, was offset by their fragmentation. Although the target-area approach quickened black mobilization, it also encouraged territorialism and reduced the incentive for citywide black coalitions.[27]

Political organizations do not, of course, arise in vacuums. They are products of time, place, and circumstance. The development of black and biracial political structures in the mid-1960s occurred amid intense debates about who should fully belong to American society and why. In New Orleans, the War on Poverty's demand for "maximum feasible participation" of the poor in its programs fit dramatically into local debates about including African Americans.[28] The extent of participation by the poor is hard to determine. Richard Haley, the SWPC's director of the Neighborhood Development Program and former southern regional director for the Congress of Racial Equality, estimated the number of community-organization participants at one thousand neighborhood residents. Their socioeconomic backgrounds can only be guessed, but their number certainly included many college-educated activists, teachers, and professionals.[29] More important, however, was the way that maximum feasible participation represented the inclusion agenda. The inclusive thought behind maximum feasible participation became a major part of New Orleans's racial-integration process by encouraging African American involvement in the policy process. Since local and state governments—and most federal programs administered in the city—allowed almost no black participation at a meaningful leadership level, the new Great Society programs illuminated black routes to power. Maximum feasible participation's main importance lay not in turning neighborhood agitators into policy makers but in the trends it represented in American social-welfare policy and southern politics. Those trends made the Great Society more than a collection of bureaucracies, helping to mold a post–New Deal Democratic regime.[30]

One major trend was the fusing of America's expanding therapeutic culture into the American state. Locally, early advocacy for a War on Poverty relied on social-psychological characterizations of poverty. In the mid-1960s, the intellectual tools used by local antipoverty reformers reflected the legacies not of Karl Marx but of thinkers such as Sigmund Freud, Erik Erikson, Oscar Lewis, and John Dewey. Foremost, the local Great Society grew from apprehension about keeping individuals from abandoning the community. Of special concern was the desire to tie into the community those black individuals with few institutions, few economic resources, and—it was feared—few morsels of self-esteem. Evincing a widespread endorsement of the culture-of-poverty theory, a broad array of antipoverty participants focused on the damage caused by poverty and the potential for that damage to perpetuate itself in an endless cycle. Closing the gap between a life of poverty and the "good life" became an exercise in including the excluded and integrating the segregated. Antipoverty leaders searched for ways to make target-area residents more like the rest of the citizenry—and having them feel good about being like the rest—before it was too late. One African American minister in the notoriously impoverished Desire area reflected the hope of the Great Society. He assured a local reporter that the poor in Desire "can climb the ladder. . . . They can be like other people."[31] His statements echoed Michael Harrington, a socialist intellectual whose book, *The Other America,* helped to refocus attention on American poverty. According to Harrington, a great champion of America's poor and a proponent of the culture-of-poverty theory, "The poor are not like everyone else. They are a different kind of people. They think and feel differently; they look upon a different America than the middle class looks upon."[32] Locally, one result of the alienation thesis was its coloring of the politics of inclusion with old white fears of black disorder.

Head Start, adult education, family counseling, Job Corps, the Concentrated Employment Program, and the Neighborhood Youth Corps were programs engineered to help low-income participants gain the attitudes and work skills deemed necessary to fit into the marketplace. Other parts of the War on Poverty took a more comprehensive approach to social amelioration by specifically targeting the political skills of the dispossessed. Great Society officials wanted to encourage the "promotion of untapped leadership" and have community action turn the poor into "positive social forces."[33] In that regard, the League of Women Voters operated a citizenship education program in the Desire housing project and the Irish Channel, while the OEO funded the unprecedented community-organization effort in the city's seven target areas.

The objective common to all of those programs was the transformation of the identity of the poor. The strategy relied on providing target-area residents with tools for full citizenship. In trying to overcome what were ultimately the institutional legacies of segregation—including low wages, union discrimination, inadequate city services, ineffective public schools, discriminatory credit practices, an almost exclusively white and wealthy corporate environment, restricted access to higher learning and skills development, and racialized housing opportunities—the Great Society looked first to the individual. For antipoverty efforts in New Orleans, the key to success lay in rehabilitating and perhaps commodifying the citizens who had been excluded from unrestricted participation in the local marketplace, the local government, and the institutions necessary for access to skilled employment. During the mid-1960s, many reformers saw that the best way to remake the ghetto was from the inside out, one American at a time.

Generally speaking, most antipoverty progressives found the poor (especially the black poor) to be major civic problems. Those progressives tended to defend the War on Poverty as a necessary endeavor to deal with low-income citizens who had been dangerously disengaged from civic participation. In the view of a large number of reformers and sympathetic commentators, poverty had created an alienated minority. They saw a bitter, disconnected group of people who might stray from a commitment to civility and worried that the psychological, political, and economic alienation of the city's poor—especially the increasingly assertive African American poor—was encouraging social fragmentation and civil disorder. Such disorder threatened to interrupt reformers' strident attempts to make the South more American, more worldly, and thereby more prosperous. Perhaps reflecting some of their own regional insecurities, most of their solutions focused on making those poor residents more like other people. Or, as Kingsley House representatives put it, "Until the citizens in the neighborhood are better and happier citizens, we cannot have a better state or nation or world."[34]

The liberal concern for the minds of the poor was not merely a product of fears within the white professional class but also was an outgrowth of a widespread vision of individualism and inclusion. Local liberals' vision drew heavily from the traditional liberal American ideal of the individual as an independent, hardworking, intelligent, and logical being whose capacity to contribute to society sustained the civic culture.[35] Premised on the idea that the best and most stable America depended on strong individuals who bolstered the community, this vision simultaneously demanded that the community nurture all of its individuals. In the context of America—and New Orleans—in the 1960s, this conception implied that exclusion of African Americans and poor people from the American good life was economically inefficient and socially counterproductive. Adherents to this view generally agreed that poverty and segregation were bad for business, bad for innovation, bad for efficient institutional development, bad for education, bad for consumerism, and ultimately bad for democracy. Their model for the more perfect union required social equilibrium and improved productivity. The dilemma was how to accomplish that feat amid social chaos and tight budgets. Local antipoverty crusaders attempted to do so by articulating the severity of the problem of poverty and developing strategies to convince the poor that they had a stake in the status quo.

The early Great Society emerged from political and social thought that was both roseate and cautionary. It contained a hope for a cost-effective regeneration of allegedly damaged individuals that was simultaneously balanced by a fear of calamity if nothing were done. A leading local antipoverty organization endorsed a definition of community that clearly expressed the dual nature of liberal inclusionism. In the conception endorsed by the swpc, community growth depended on individual growth. The council accepted a definition of a community as a "living thing" that was "born when people live together" and "grows when it attracts more people unto itself." "The more adequate [the members of the community's] lives are," it followed, "the better the community is. And, in like manner, when the lives of its people are restricted, the whole community suffers." Highlighting the roseate and the cautionary more clearly, the swpc's model for community action contended that "when people in a given community are seriously deprived—deprived in terms of their religious, economic and social being, the community becomes blighted and deforms the larger society of which it is a part. The blight that overtakes one community threatens to spread to other parts of the body politic." A community "prospers," the definition continued in the logic of liberal inclusionism, "when its citizens work together. It suffers illness and disease when parts of its physical being are impaired or deteriorate or when its people are set off against one another. It grows old in body when its buildings age, and old in spirit when its residents no longer care. It may even die, if all its people entirely lose that sense of unity which makes an aggregation of people become an entity unto itself."[36] A report on poverty and health policy put the dilemma more succinctly. "The obvious point" to the need for inclusion was "that while killer diseases may get started among lower-income families, epidemics . . . are no respectors [*sic*] of zoning ordinances or income levels."[37]

The Great Society became an exercise in containing alienation. As articulated by many local antipoverty reformers, the War on Poverty offered programmatic opportunities to help the poor conquer their supposedly internalized social and economic deprivation. The reformers' search for stability drew from the pervasive influence of therapeutic psychological analysis. Viewed from the long perspective of social-policy development, the antipoverty movement represents an important intellectual transformation. The use of social welfare to make better citizens was nothing new, but the psychological areas into which the Great Society hoped to travel substantially complicated matters.[38] Regarding the poor, attitudes and identity had become at least as important to reformers as patriotism, Americanness, education, and work skills. In fact, local Great Society liberals saw self-esteem, skill sets, and productivity as parts of one larger phenomenon. Consequently, the despair of the poor became a politically potent element.[39] By selling despair and emphasizing psychological renewal as evidence of civic belonging, local social-policy professionals, social workers, and volunteer activists helped define the criteria for integrating the poor (especially African Americans) into effective citizenship. Ironically, this focus on the psyche of the poor perpetuated a sense that they were "damaged" people who were alienated because of something inescapable. In the years to come, when civil disorder dominated racial politics and social-welfare discussions, those perceptions of alienation took on a more devastating meaning.

Several local progressives emphasized the social and psychological consequences of continued poverty and exclusion—limiting progress, undercutting stability, and costing taxpayers money. Gillis Long was a leading white Louisiana progressive who had recently lost his congressional seat and a bid for governor partly because of his level of support for civil rights legislation. From 1964 to 1966, he served as an assistant director of OEO. In 1964, Long argued that the chief threat to stability and growth came from the persistence of black poverty. "Negroes are certainly not the only poor," he contended, "but they are the most costly . . . in terms of crime[,] disease, illiteracy . . . and most important of all, productivity."[40] Hale Boggs, the longtime moderate to liberal New Orleans congressman, deemed poverty to be "America's most expensive luxury," which the nation could no longer "afford . . . from a financial point of view." Boggs argued that a war on poverty would dramatically help America because it could include people who had been wastefully excluded from the marketplace and, most important, because it would increase "PURCHASING POWER." In an earlier document, J. Harvey Kerns, an African American who headed the Urban League of Greater New Orleans, also lobbied for something like the Great Society as a means to eliminate poverty and stimulate growth. His arguments reveal the inseparable connections among the civil rights movement, the growth ethos, and the antipoverty movement.[41] John J. Stretch, a professor of social work at Tulane University, contended that poverty was most dangerous to America because it was a national problem that manifested itself in the personalities of the poor. Poverty was "the new enemy of society," Stretch explained, that "surely and steadily robs a nation of its full productive power." Poverty's legacy included "shame, misery, despair, loss of . . . self-esteem" and wore "a bigger price tag than money."[42] Poverty damaged the self and society, the poor and the nonpoor. According to the liberal vision, poverty's perpetuation of alienation denied full citizenship and corroded American democracy.

Alienation frightened Maurice Anderson, chairman of the swpc's Youth Committee and onetime president of the swpc Board of Directors. In December 1963, five months before President Johnson invoked a call for a renewal of community in a Great Society speech at the University of Michigan, Anderson delivered a report that explained how the problems affecting low-income youth were becoming problems to him and men like him. He viewed integrating the young poor into the community's social, economic, and political functions as an essential part of the search for the Great Society. Anderson reasoned that the city could not "afford" to lose people "who are talented and capable of contributing greatly to our society." Everyone needed to participate in society. The great danger was "the creation of disenfranchised individuals, condemned to personal dissatisfaction, who do not have a stake in our society as full-fledged, functioning citizens." The dissatisfied citizenry posed "not only an economic loss and burden, but also a physical danger to our society." Alienated and poorly educated citizens were "a decided threat to good government." He warned that "large numbers of alienated persons . . . trapped in poverty for lack of education, without a stake in society and without a sense of belonging, can obviously jeopardize the welfare and future of our community and the physical safety of the population."[43]

Democracy required inclusion and participation. Without it, Anderson implied, New Orleans was endangering itself and potentially creating the conditions for future upheaval. He recommended that reformers remedy the deterioration of civic contribution by giving the poor reason to want to contribute more. Local progressives worried that economic and psychological alienation threatened stable society, encouraged corruption, and discouraged the rehabilitation of the poor. According to the rationale expressed by Anderson and other progressives, New Orleanians—and Americans—had a choice. They could deal with their social problems by creating systems that encouraged stable individuals with a deep commitment to the community; otherwise, they could expect the poor to continue to cost more than they contributed. To highlight the benefits of dealing with poverty, antipoverty progressives often dwelt on the most obvious ways that the poor posed threats to other people. Such explanations of why poverty was a problem show how the well-meaning liberal project for inclusion rested on emphasizing the ways that the poor were separated from the rest. According to local War on Poverty program proposals and assessments, racial discrimination and restricted economic opportunity had crippled the poor, especially African Americans. Those sources portrayed the poor as damaged people who were dangerously unattached to the community. The irony was that the target areas' greatest power flowed from the problems they posed to the larger society. At a time when the poor in America had the best chance to reshape the conditions that limited their lives, their greatest source of political power was the public perception of them as damaged goods. During the early antipoverty fight, liberal reformers asked the poor to cast down their buckets to forge new opportunities and to seize full citizenship. In so doing, reformers required the poor to use their limitations as tools of liberation.

By articulating carefully how the poor differed from others, reformers were not merely participating in age-old paternalistic rhetoric but were acting from their training and perceptions of the American way. By placing emphasis on reforming the individual, local and national antipoverty leaders followed their instincts. They saw themselves as healers, and they sought to heal the poor and the city. Many of the city's antipoverty administrators had backgrounds in social work and, therefore, brought a casework perspective to their view of social reform. They were trained to diagnose problems in individuals and to chart solutions on an individual basis. To leaders reared in a culture of therapy, it made sense to want to put the poor on the equivalent of a psychiatrist's couch.[44] In addition, reformers were also operating in an intellectual context framed by the civil rights movement and the Cold War. Expecting antipoverty reformers to build the Great Society as a massive assault on structural elements of America's political economy is questionable. In this regard, as in so many other areas, the antipoverty movement followed the lead of the civil rights movement, whose activists and theoreticians often depicted segregation as a moral problem to be resolved by individual choices. Antipoverty reformers might well have applied Gunnar Myrdal's famous formulation of the American dilemma to the poor as well as to the segregated. The Cold War, however, narrowed the breadth of analytic and political options.[45]

Two specific influences on local progressives' thinking stand out. One influence involved the culture-of-poverty theory associated with anthropologist Oscar Lewis.[46] A second influence was a broader but equally prominent fixation on the minds of the poor. Examples of the use of psychological interpretation or the culture of poverty abound. Two documents illustrate some of the major themes. The pathologies of poverty and the dangers of alienated minds ran through an evaluation of an adult literacy program by a social science student at the predominantly black Southern University at New Orleans and an OEO grant proposal by the New Orleans branch of the National Association of College Women (NACW). In the assessment of the adult literacy program known as Operation Upgrade, Mary Balthazar revealed how deeply psychoanalysis and the culture-of-poverty theory influenced social reform. The program's value, she argued, was in preventing poverty from warping personality. Adult illiterates were not able to "represent themselves." They lacked "dignity." They were shamed, "forgotten people who have been driven like animals into the slums and other poverty-stricken areas of the cities. They have been the ones who were unable to make their silent cries heard because of their inability to verbalize their desires, their frustrations, and their fears in a hostile world." They were people "whose souls were bruised, whose minds were naked, whose aspirations were blocked, and whose hearts were hungry for kindness and recognition." Endorsing theories about the culture of poverty and the debilitating impact of exclusion, she explained that "offsprings [*sic*] become trapped in the ongoing vicious circle, become virtual slaves to a society which isolates them in an alien world outside the mainstream of life." Operation Upgrade offered a chance to keep the poor from being trapped for "generations to come."[47]

Another document revealing the obsession with the psyche of low-income African Americans was an NACW proposal to the OEO. The NACW described the black single mother as the most alienated of all citizens. She was a "victim" and a "social problem" who was "too often unproductive, unacceptable and a social outcast from the mainstream of our modern day society." Society had deformed her personality and her capacity to fit in. Her distorted sense of self came from the "triple jeopardy" of being black, poor, and socially deviant. She suffered from "racial bias" and, most debilitating in postwar America, from "insufficient class mobility." That triple jeopardy had limited her "opportunities for a decent job, training, equal education, and housing." Those problems had produced a group of people "ill-prepared to participate productively in an affluent society—let alone be acceptable to the masses." These women were "characterized by limited motivations, expectations, and abilities because of all-ready defective family, peer group, cultural and sub-cultural preparation to fulfill acceptable adult or pre-adult roles in this society." The NACW argued that black single mothers needed help to develop personality traits that could overcome the lack of social privilege and the realities of racial exclusion.[48]

A broad assortment of social-welfare professionals and activists endorsed the belief that racial prejudice and poverty had made the poor (again, particularly the black poor) different from the rest of society. The director of the New Orleans Department of Welfare explained to the OEO that the poor were "sullen, suspicious, ignorant, and resentful," lived in a "constant state of crisis," and were rarely able to keep up "even the minimum standards expected by the larger cultural group in hygiene, health-care, child rearing and education."[49] According to the SWPC, a group whose leaders worried about the dangers of stigmatizing the poor, New Orleans's target-area residents "feel forgotten, bitter and helpless." Many residents had "given up—they no longer believe life could be better."[50] A community-organization supervisor for Kingsley House stated that "feelings of isolation, hopelessness and defensiveness" pervaded the residents of public housing in the Irish Channel area.[51] Proponents of the Volunteers in Service to America (VISTA) program believed that "many target area residents" lacked "confidence and hope" for any "improvement of their condition." Desolation and racial segregation in the target areas had encouraged "defeatist attitudes," "lack of 'self-esteem,' " and "hostility toward society, its representatives and spokesmen."[52] One social worker saw "a climate of hostility and distrust on the part of residents toward the wider community and the representatives of its institutions and agencies." In one example, one worker reported that "adults systematically drill into the minds of their children not to trust 'others—they are only out to harm you.' "[53] Similarly, the coordinator of the Irish Channel Neighborhood Development Center contended that poverty had a "demeaning effect on human character" and made the poor "either thoughtlessly aggressive or submissively passive."[54]

A VISTA volunteer in the Desire area—a self-professed radical who had been a member of Students for a Democratic Society—explained that Desire residents lived in a "snake pit." Poor residents there had difficulty in fully participating in American society because of "psychological problems" and "problems of alienation." Echoing the claims of more moderate SWPC leaders, he claimed that, like African Americans everywhere, Desire residents were "cut off from American Society, and culture. They have no relationship with it, they have no stake in it, they are disenfranchised."[55] The local Urban League explained that historical neglect from city government had caused many residents to feel "rejection, suspicion and isolation."[56]

The solutions to poverty and alienation pursued by many War on Poverty officials called for a better-organized community, a better-integrated individual, and a better-realized self. In one proposal for community action, the SWPC advocated "intensive educational and community service efforts so that the chain of poverty which sometimes stretches from generation to generation can be broken."[57] Programs sought to make the poor become part of society. Program developers hoped to "show that the 'consumer' of services . . . can be helped to reach a level of civic capacity and responsibility to make significant contributions to community improvement programs." In arguments that reveal the therapeutic perspective of reformers, swpc program developers blamed "environmental social problems" for producing "added personality stresses which, in turn, tend to lead to poor functioning and create maladaptive coping mechanisms."[58]

The poor needed help to be like others. Clark Corliss, the swpc's director, explained the vital need to treat the psyche of the poor to preserve stability. The "poverty stricken for some time often feels defeated. He may withdraw from normal contacts, or become ill, or take to flight, or turn to alcohol or narcotics or steal or do any one of the many things defeated people do to protect the little ego they have left. From a therapeutic standpoint, the problem then is one of helping to restore self-respect."[59]

The swpc planned to help by providing "social and recreational" services to "create a social climate more conducive to better individual and group functioning." Through community organizing, the council planned to initiate a "process which will reorient perceptions, attitudes and behaviors." swpc members expected that over the proposed five-year community-organization program, target-area residents would learn enough to take over operations. As part of the effort to coordinate the efforts of the Housing Authority of New Orleans (hano), the Tulane University School of Social Work, the State Departments of Hospitals and Public Welfare, the Urban League of Greater New Orleans, and the New Orleans Recreation Department, the swpc wanted to turn residents into "community partners" and show them the program would not be run by "distrusted 'outsiders.' "[60] The swpc expected community members to participate in planning for health services, day care, counseling, recreation, and rehabilitating families on public assistance. Above all, according to Corliss, the swpc would "instill confidence that the goals which are consistent with their capabilities are attainable." The group banked on citizen participation and community organization to bring success, "helping people to help themselves," with citizen participation resulting "in better self-images for the resident" in addition to material and health benefits.[61]

Others echoed the swpc's objectives of reducing alienation and expanding productivity. A Kingsley House organizer provided his interpretation of the objectives of the antipoverty movement. Programs needed to assist target-area residents in beginning "to deal with the feelings of isolation, hopelessness and defensiveness," helping "these individuals maintain and build upon an attitude of self-respect and independence, while at the same time, demonstrating that they are members of this community and do have a role to play and a responsibility for their neighborhood."[62] The NACW wanted to use its program for unmarried mothers to help them "to participate actively in the more productive and economic aspects of their communities." The collegiate women hoped that "perhaps a few attitudes might be changed in the process from negative and punative [sic] to positive and constructive."[63]

Infusing the Great Society with the perceived despair of the poor did create a well-honed sense that poverty was bad for the rest of society. It cast the antipoverty crusade as a way to heal America by starting with its most psychologically imperiled people. Although much of the depiction of the poor as damaged entities was done with compassionate intentions, it helped construct a sense that exclusion had turned the poor (especially blacks) into ineffective Americans who were perhaps unworthy of the full benefits of American life. This politics of personal despair ensured that the War on Poverty relied on instilling a sense of crisis and desperation to remain politically viable. In a political culture rooted in reverence for expansive individualism, this approach emphasized the idea that the poor's alienation limited them as individuals. This contradiction underlay the emergence of liberalism in New Orleans. By imbuing the political justification for and thereby the institutions of the Great Society with a separate conception of civic belonging for the poor, such an attitude contributed to a political consciousness built on sympathy and horror. In an age of optimism, the Great Society's political appeal ultimately lay in pessimism. Because the Great Society helped to structure the new political order, that contradictory conception fused with the rise of black political power. The participation of the poor was essential for the new liberalism in New Orleans, but, ironically, the tactics of liberal inclusionism cast the poor as possibly being unable to be like other people.

Considering the deficiencies of the local welfare state and the violent white reaction to sharing public space with African Americans, it is no wonder that Great Society leaders crept with cat's feet in the fight against poverty. By focusing on the individual, Great Society reformers absolved themselves of the sticky problem of fundamentally reforming separate and unequal public institutions. Individual-based strategies in the target areas allowed for reform efforts that adhered to politically acceptable traditions and values while channeling the growing energy of black southern neighborhoods into a governable phenomenon. Combined with New Orleans's racially bifurcated civic culture, this muddled liberal legacy turned the anticipated social-welfare revolution into a gradual mediation of segregation and a triumph of the therapeutic. Locally, the implementation of the early Great Society reflected a drift in the politics of social welfare away from questions of wealth distribution and more toward personal identity and citizenship. In the post–Jim Crow South, social-welfare policy showed that citizenship involved explicitly psychological elements. The effectiveness of including the excluded could not be fully measured in income-transfer tables, by cost-benefit ratios, or through racial-balance formulas. The soft spaces of the government and the psyche became proving grounds for the new biracial liberalism.

Despite a dependence on fears of black alienation, the early Great Society still had a more impressive impact than anything preceding it. From 1964 to late 1967, the War on Poverty established the rudiments of a liberal antipoverty bureaucracy, encouraged the growth of neighborhood organizations, and initiated a strategy for the poor to structure their own autonomy in the political and economic marketplace. Although the politics of despair circumscribed the antipoverty effort, it had pushed forward an irreversible search for community and power. Considering the impediments facing inclusionists, the early Great Society should be identified as truly a remarkable moment in southern history. At a time when segregationists tended to dictate discourse, the political subtlety of the target areas' rejuvenation roused a quiet yet incomplete changing of the guard.

Notes

1. In *In the Shadow of the Poorhouse: A Social History of Welfare in America* (New York: Basic Books, 1986), Michael B. Katz contends that social welfare has served five purposes in American history: (1) relief of misery, (2) preservation of social order; (3) regulation of the labor market, (4) mobilization of political entities, and (5) confrontation of racism (as a result of the civil rights movement).

2. The administration's conceptual blueprint for a broadly defined War on Poverty was put forward in *The Annual Report of the Council of Economic Advisers, from U.S. President, Economic Report of the President to the Congress* (Washington, D.C.: U.S. Government Printing Office, 1964), 74.

3. The shift toward the therapeutic was not original to the War on Poverty. Jennifer Mittelstadt's examination of the Aid to Dependent Children (ADC) program in the postwar period identifies a policy shift in the 1956 Social Security amendments that pushed the program toward a mission to rehabilitate ADC clients. Ten years later, the prevalence of therapeutic, rehabilitative thought at almost all levels of New Orleans's early Great Society suggests that the shift to rehabilitation ran deeper than policy. It reflected a popular understanding of poverty and disorder. See Jennifer Leigh Mittelstadt, "The Dilemmas of the Liberal Welfare State, 1945–1964: Gender, Race, and Aid to Dependent Children" (Ph.D. diss., University of Michigan, 2000), 3–5.

4. The term *liberal* is often vague and illusory, dependent on context for its meaning. This essay uses it interchangeably with the terms *progressive* and *reformer*. The meaning of liberalism here is specific to the region and the 1960s. The labels *liberal, progressive,* and *reformer* apply to people or groups that demonstrably supported major parts of the integrationist agenda and, in most cases, were willing to use governmental means to achieve their goals. In the South, this categorization involves fewer people but includes a broader range of people than one might define as liberal in other regions.

5. The soft state continued the tradition of fragmented social policy. When compared to other industrial nations, America's response to poverty has been hesitating, inconsistent, and grudging. In addition, it has reflected racial and ethnic cleavages in American society. Michael B. Katz has characterized the American welfare state as a "semi-welfare state." The origins of that welfare state lay in the federal effort to provide pensions to Civil War veterans and in state efforts to provide pensions to widowed mothers. The welfare state took shape partly during the Progressive era in the form of legislation designed to aid women, children, and workers. Its chief formative moment came with the New Deal, especially the 1935 Economic Security Act that created contributory social-insurance programs mainly for white male workers and state assistance for others. According to Jill Quadagno and others, this phenomenon reflected racial and sexual divisions in American society and helped create a dual welfare state. Southerners played a key role in excluding domestic and agricultural workers from Social Security, which perpetuated black dependence on the plantation system and on white officials. The War on Poverty inherited this system, and although not by intent, continued some programs on a relatively segregated basis. See Katz, *In the Shadow of the Poorhouse;* Katz, *Poverty and Policy in American History* (New York: Academic Press, 1983); Quadagno, *The Transformation of Old Age Security: Class and Politics in the American Welfare State* (Chicago: University of Chicago Press, 1988); Quadagno, *The Color of Welfare: How Racism Undermined the War on Poverty* (New York: Oxford University Press, 1994); James T. Patterson, *America's Struggle against Poverty, 1900–1994* (Cambridge: Harvard University Press, 1994); Theda Skocpol, *Protecting Soldiers*

and Mothers: The Political Origins of Social Policy in America (Cambridge: Belknap Press of Harvard University Press, 1992); Charles Noble, *Welfare as We Knew It: A Political History of the American Welfare State* (New York: Oxford University Press, 1997); and William R. Brock, *Investigation and Responsibility: Public Responsibility in the United States, 1865–1900* (Cambridge: Cambridge University Press, 1984).

6. This soft state developed from the OEO's Community Action Program, Head Start, the Model Cities program, the food stamp program, VISTA, various job-training programs, and urban renewal projects. Some of the corresponding local bodies were Total Community Action, the Social Welfare Planning Council, the New Orleans Legal Assistance Corporation, the New Orleans Human Relations Committee, the City Demonstration Agency, HANO, and the Community Improvement Agency. Besides the OEO, the U.S. Departments of Labor, Agriculture, Housing and Urban Development, and Health, Education, and Welfare were the chief federal institutions involved. At varying times, other important organizations contributing to this soft state were the Urban League of Greater New Orleans, the Stern Family Fund, Kingsley House [Settlement], Associated Catholic Charities, Tulane University, Xavier University, Loyola University, the League of Women Voters, the National Council of Jewish Women, the Orleans Parish School Board, the Greater New Orleans Chamber of Commerce, the Community Relations Committee, the NAACP, the New Orleans Recreation Organization, state and local departments of welfare, several economic opportunity committees, several neighborhood councils, multiple grassroots community organizations, a selection of local churches, and a number of political organizations founded in the late 1960s.

7. For the white population, the state in New Orleans was relatively small. Outside of a limited city hall, its most prominent features came from a few boards and commissions begun in the Progressive era and the labyrinth of programs linked to the New Deal. For black residents, the state was severely deficient and primarily served a coercive role. The most important representatives of that state were police officers, judges, and social-welfare caseworkers. Other parts of the state came in a rudimentary education system that offered limited opportunities beyond the elementary level, some seriously deficient sanitation services and infrastructure, and some menial public jobs. This lack of a beneficial state for blacks was related to the weak structures that had formed historically to deal with the poor. An 1880 poor law left poverty relief up to parish-level police juries until the New Deal. (Louisiana is organized into parishes instead of counties.) In 1904 Louisiana did start an ineffectual Board of Charities and Corrections. In 1932, New Orleans ranked last among thirty-one American cities in spending for public relief. The city government offered virtually no relief for the blind, for poor mothers, or for indigent families and none for poor blacks, something that even Birmingham, Atlanta, Charleston, and Memphis provided. With the New Deal, the federal government

forced the development of new institutions. According to one study, the federal government provided 98.5 percent of public relief funding in Louisiana in 1933–34. During the rest of the 1930s, the New Deal provided jobs, established critical social-insurance programs (primarily for whites), created means-tested public assistance, poured millions into the city for public works, and helped energize the southern economy. Federal involvement led to the creation of New Orleans's first Department of Public Welfare in 1934 and a state-level one in 1936. The Economic Security Act of 1935 anchored social-welfare policy for the next thirty years. Until the 1960s, these agencies and programs offered important improvements in services but retained characteristics of segregation in their structures. See Elizabeth Wisner, *Public Welfare Administration in Louisiana* (Chicago: University of Chicago Press, 1930); Elizabeth Wisner, *Social Welfare in the South from Colonial Times to World War I* (Baton Rouge: Louisiana State University Press, 1970); Robert E. Moran Sr., "Public Relief in Louisiana from 1928–1960," *Louisiana History* 14 (winter 1973): 369–70; Priscilla Clement, "Children and Charity: Orphanages in New Orleans, 1817–1914," *Louisiana History* 27 (fall 1986): 337–51; Betty Field, "The Politics of the New Deal in Louisiana" (Ph.D. diss., Tulane University, 1973); Alan Stuart MacLachlan, "Up from Paternalism: The New Deal and Race Relations in New Orleans" (Ph.D. diss., University of New Orleans, 1998); Douglas Smith, *The New Deal in the Urban South* (Baton Rouge: Louisiana State University Press, 1988); Bruce Schulman, *From Cotton Belt to Sunbelt: Federal Policy, Economic Development, and the Transformation of the South, 1938–1980* (New York: Oxford University Press, 1991); and Quadagno, *Transformation.*

8. The influence of the social and behavioral sciences on public policy has attracted a growing literature. See Ellen Herman, *The Romance of American Psychology: Political Culture in the Age of Experts* (Berkeley: University of California Press, 1995); Andrew Polsky, *The Rise of the Therapeutic State* (Princeton: Princeton University Press, 1991); Alice O'Connor, *Poverty Knowledge: Social Science, Social Policy, and the Poor in Twentieth-Century U.S. History* (Princeton: Princeton University Press, 2001); and Daryl Scott, *Contempt and Pity: Social Policy and the Image of the Damaged Black Psyche, 1880–1996* (Chapel Hill: University of North Carolina Press, 1997). An examination of the therapeutic in the voluntary social welfare sector is Andrew Morris, "Selling Service: Charity, Therapy, and Welfare in the Late 1940s," paper presented at the annual meeting of the Organization of American Historians, Los Angeles, April 27, 2001.

9. James G. Hollandsworth Jr., *An Absolute Massacre: The New Orleans Race Riot of July 30, 1866* (Baton Rouge: Louisiana State University Press, 2001). In the 1866 riot, forty-eight people died and more than two hundred were injured. Another important event was the September 1874 Battle for Liberty Place, where casualties from the battle between white supremacists and Republican supporters reportedly ran to more than one hundred.

10. "Protest Unprovoked Attack on Negroes; Police Chief, D.A. and FBI Told of Continuing Attacks by Whites," *Louisiana Weekly,* September 26, 1964; "Vandals Hit 'Mixed' Housing Unit Area; Family near St. Thomas Project 'Fire Bomb' Target," *Louisiana Weekly,* May 8, 1965; "Three White Youths Held in Four 'Fire-Bombings'; Police Solve Cases in Project Area," *Louisiana Weekly,* May 15, 1965; "2 More Bombings Reported, LCLU Chief's Car, Uptown Church Struck," *Louisiana Weekly,* May 22, 1965; "These Bombings Are Real," *Louisiana Weekly,* May 22, 1965; "New Orleans Office Fire Bombed, City's 12th Fire-Bombing since March," *Louisiana Weekly,* July 31, 1965; "Alert Police Nab Ex-Con in Rivers Frederick Shooting, Shot Twice in Near Fatal 'Right' Tiff," *Louisiana Weekly,* August 18, 1964; and " 'Rights' Shooting Victim Tells 'His Side,' " *Louisiana Weekly,* August 29, 1964.

11. The Community Action Program was one of several parts of the Economic Opportunity Act that President Johnson signed into law on August 20, 1964. The OEO developed as the administrative arm of that act. As a new bureaucracy, the OEO somewhat bypassed structural constraints in the Department of Agriculture, Department of Labor, and the Department of Health, Education, and Welfare that had dogged antipoverty and civil rights reform. Perhaps most important, most of the OEO's grants sidestepped Louisiana's state government and New Orleans City Hall, thereby giving antipoverty leaders slightly more flexibility. Other important components of that act included Job Corps, Head Start, and VISTA.

12. See Harmon Gilmore, "The Old New Orleans and the New: A Case for Ecology," *American Sociological Review* 9 (August 1944): 386.

13. Clark Corliss to TCA Board of Directors, January 18, 1965, box 55, "TCA 2" folder, Community Services Council Collection—Accession Number 34, Department of Special Collections, Earl K. Long Memorial Library, University of New Orleans, New Orleans (hereafter, CSC).

14. J. Harvey Kerns, "Facing the Facts of the Racial Relations Dilemma in New Orleans, Louisiana, 1964," box 64, "ULGNO Serials" folder, CSC; and SWPC, "Report of Findings and Action Recommendations: School Dropout and Youth Employment Committee," December 1963, unprocessed box 30, unlabeled green folder, CSC.

15. See Eric Wayne Doerries, "James E. Comiskey, the Irish Third Ward Boss: A Study of a Unique and Dying Brand of Politics" (bachelor's honors thesis, Tulane University, 1973).

16. VISTA Proposal by SWPC, July 1965, box 66, "VISTA 1964–65" folder, CSC; Allen Dowling to Paul Sanzenbach, January 16, 1968, unprocessed box 22, "Housing Authority of New Orleans" folder, CSC; and Newell Schinler, "Public Housing with a PLUS Factor," *New Orleans Clarion Herald,* March 24, 1966.

17. "6 Community-Wide TCA Programs Win Approval," *Louisiana Weekly,* October 9, 1965; and Lee Lendt to Theodore M. Berry, August 6, 1965, box 4, ser. 1030-CAP, Office Records of the Director, State Files 1965–68, RG 381, Community Services Administration, National Archives and Records Administration, College Park, Md.

In the first year, the War on Poverty provided almost two million dollars (almost ten million in current dollars) for antipoverty efforts.

18. Numan V. Bartley, *A History of the South,* vol. 11, *The New South, 1945–1980: The Story of the South's Modernization* (Baton Rouge: Louisiana State University Press and the Littlefield Fund for Southern History at the University of Texas, 1995), 24–31, 209–13; Michael L. Kurtz and Morgan D. Peoples, *Earl K. Long: The Saga of Uncle Earl and Louisiana Politics* (Baton Rouge: Louisiana State University Press, 1990); and Carl Grafton and Anne Permaloff, *Big Mules and Branchheads: James E. Folsom and Political Power in Alabama* (Athens: University of Georgia Press, 1985). For the difficulties faced by southern liberals prior to the 1960s, see Morton Sosna, *In Search of the Silent South: Southern Liberals and the Race Issue* (New York: Columbia University Press, 1977); Patricia Sullivan, *Days of Hope: Race and Democracy in the New Deal Era* (Chapel Hill: University of North Carolina Press, 1996); David L. Carlton and Peter A. Coclanis, "Another 'Great Migration': From Region to Race in Southern Liberalism, 1938–1945," *Southern Culture* 3 (winter 1997): 37–62. In the immediate postwar era, New Orleans had something of a progressive city hall. See Edward R. Haas, *DeLesseps S. Morrison and the Image of Reform: New Orleans Politics, 1946–1961* (Baton Rouge: Louisiana State University Press, 1974).

19. In 1970, Maurice E. "Moon" Landrieu, one of the city's leading racial liberals, won election as mayor largely by gaining the support of almost 100 percent of African American voters. His base in African American communities flowed through the Great Society. In 1971, many of the groups that had supported Landrieu eventually backed Edwin W. Edwards in his gubernatorial victory. See James Chubbuck, Edwin Renwick, and Joe E. Walker, "The Emergence of Coalition Politics in New Orleans," *New South* 26 (winter 1971): 17; and Maurice E. "Moon" Landrieu, interview by author, New Orleans, June 4, 2001.

20. TCA, "Employment and Leadership: Alumni List," [1984], box 3, folder 15, Winston Lill Collection, Department of Special Collections, Tulane University Libraries, Jones Hall, Tulane University, New Orleans; TCA, "Total Community Action: 20 Years of Community Service," box 3, folder 15, Lill Collection; Joan Treadway, "Poverty Agency Marks 20 Years," *New Orleans Times-Picayune,* March 4, 1985.

21. "Your Economic Opportunity Committee," Central City Economic Opportunity Committee Records, Amistad Research Center, Tilton Hall, Tulane University, New Orleans.

22. Corliss to TCA Board of Directors, January 18, 1965, box 55, "TCA 2" folder, CSC; minutes of SWPC Citizen Participation Committee, July 6, 1965, box 28, "IC CDC" folder, CSC; "Memorandum of Understanding of Cooperation in Community Organization Responsibilities for Irish Channel Economic Assistance Program, 1965–66; By Joint committee of Kingsley House and Irish Channel Action Foundation, Inc.," June 30, 1965, box 30, "Kingsley House" folder, CSC; minutes of Kingsley House Board of Directors, June 23, 1965, box 28, "IC CDC" folder, CSC.

23. "Your Economic Opportunity Committee."

24. Minutes of meeting, February 15, 1966, box 47, "Ninth Ward Civic Improvement League" folder, CSC; and Richard Haley to Philip Ciaccio, September 20, 1967, unprocessed box 24, "SWPC Neighborhood Centers, 1966–68" folder, CSC.

25. Areas of the city with significant concentrations of poverty that did not receive the target-area designation were Girt Town (also spelled Gert and Gurt, depending on the source) in the Carrollton area, Tremè, which abutted the French Quarter, and Mid-City. See TCA, "Community Action Agency Plans and Priorities," October 1968, box 15, "Total Community Action" folder, Mayor Victor Schiro Collection, City Archives and Louisiana Division Special Collections, New Orleans Public Library, New Orleans; minutes of Carrollton Central Steering Committee, January 15, 1969, box 8, folder 42, League of Women Voters Collection, Department of Special Collections, Howard-Tilton Memorial Library, Tulane University, New Orleans; League of Women Voters, "Background of the Carrollton Project," n.d. [after July 1969], box 8, folder 39, League of Women Voters Collection.

26. James Singleton, interview by author, New Orleans, July 23, 2001.

27. On the issue of fragmentation, Oretha Castle Haley, perhaps the city's best-known civil rights activist, told *New Yorker* magazine in 1964 that the black community was "split in so many different ways. We don't have just Negroes. We have our Catholic Negroes and our Protestant Negroes, our downtown Negroes and our uptown Negroes, out light Negroes and our dark Negroes. And we have too many Negroes who don't think they're Negroes" (quoted in Calvin Trillin, "A Reporter at Large: The Zulus," *New Yorker,* June 20, 1964, 66).

28. The requirement for "maximum feasible participation" was quite vague and led to uncertainty within the War on Poverty. The title of Daniel Moynihan's harsh early assessment of community action summarized some of the resulting disillusionment: see Moynihan, *Maximum Feasible Misunderstanding: Community Action in the War on Poverty* (New York: Free Press, 1969).

29. Haley, "Observations," February 22, 1968, box II C, "Board of Directors 1967–68" folder, CSC. The number of participants does not include children in Head Start, people who received social services, or residents in jobs programs.

30. David Plotke, *Building a Democratic Political Order: Reshaping American Liberalism in the 1930s and 1940s* (New York: Cambridge University Press, 1996).

31. Newell Schindler, "Poverty: The Problems, the Promises," *New Orleans Clarion Herald,* May 13, 1965.

32. Michael Harrington, *The Other America: Poverty in the United States* (1962; New York: Penguin, 1981), 146.

33. "Memorandum of Understanding of Cooperation."

34. Jean F. Craddock, John Wall Jr., Frances K. Burke, and Maurice Stern to Corliss, May 3, 1965, box 30, "Kingsley House" folder, CSC.

35. For a discussion of this ideal, see Rogers M. Smith, *Civic Ideals: Conflicting Visions*

of Citizenship in U.S. History (New Haven: Yale University Press, 1997), 470–506. In *The Masterless: Self and Society in Modern America* (Chapel Hill: University of North Carolina Press, 1994), Wilfred McClay has argued for the Great Society as an effort to maintain social cohesion. In *Beloved Community: The Cultural Criticism of Randolph Bourne, Van Wyck Brooks, Waldo Frank, and Lewis Mumford* (Chapel Hill: University of North Carolina Press, 1990), Casey Nelson Blake argues that Progressive-era intellectual Randolph Bourne's vision of a beloved community premised that the fulfillment of the self would solidify democratic culture (2–9, 51).

36. "Definition of Neighborhood Council," box 79, "Neighborhood Council" folder, CSC.

37. TCA Research Department, "New Orleans," [1967], box 55, folder 4, National Association for the Advancement of Colored People, Office of Field Director of Louisiana, Records, Amistad Research Center.

38. A constant theme in the history of American responses to poverty has been that the poor have posed a serious threat to community stability. For an argument that the search for moral order was the central focus of urban reform efforts, see Paul Boyer, *Urban Masses and Moral Order in America, 1820–1920* (Cambridge: Harvard University Press, 1978). Nathan Huggins's *Protestants against Poverty: Boston's Charities, 1870–1900* (Westport, Conn.: Greenwood, 1971) argues that social reform efforts were a conservative response to social change. Boston charity leaders used their efforts to protect their vision of proper society and culture. This work claims that Boston's charity leaders failed to view the poor on human terms, seeing them more as social problems than as functioning decision makers. Ruth Crocker's *Social Work and Social Order: The Settlement Movement in Two Industrial Cities, 1889–1930* (Urbana: University of Illinois Press, 1992) found that "second-tier" settlement houses in Indianapolis and Gary, Indiana, were set up to maintain social order and reflected business interests. Other important works that explore that issue are Robert Bremner, *The Discovery of Poverty in the United States* (New Brunswick, N.J.: Transaction, 1992); John F. Kasson, *Amusing the Millions: Coney Island at the Turn of the Century* (New York: Hill and Wang, 1978); Katz, *In the Shadow of the Poorhouse;* Kathleen D. McCarthy, *Noblesse Oblige: Charity and Cultural Philanthropy in Chicago, 1849–1929* (Philadelphia: University of Pennsylvania Press, 1990); and Mimi Abramovitz, *Regulating the Lives of Women: Social Welfare Policy from Colonial Times to the Present* (Boston: South End Press, 1988).

39. In *Contempt and Pity,* Scott provocatively argues that postwar liberals used a "damage imagery" (ix) concerning black Americans because it was the easiest way to create social policy acceptable to a majority of Americans. This usage, he claims, was a substitution of political expedience for justice and "black dignity" (185). It also perpetuated white beliefs in black inferiority. Scott also provides a well-balanced analysis of Moynihan's controversial work about the disorganization

of the black family (U.S. Department of Labor, *The Negro Family: The Case for National Action* [Washington, D.C.: U.S. Government Printing Office, 1965]).

40. Rosemary Powell, "Census Data Bares Blight: City and State Declared Poverty War Battlefield," *New Orleans States-Item*, n.d., box 55, "TCA-newspaper clippings" folder, CSC.

41. Boggs, "Speech for the Executive Club in N.O.," April 30, 1964, box 5, Speaking Engagements, Hale Boggs Collection, Department of Special Collections, Howard-Tilton Memorial Library, Tulane University, New Orleans; and J. Harvey Kerns, *The Negro in New Orleans: A Statistical Analysis of Population Trends and Characteristics, Their Effect on the Economic, Social, and Civic Life of the Community* (New Orleans: Urban League of Greater New Orleans, 1959).

42. John J. Stretch, "What Makes a Man Poor: Loss of Income and Lack of Opportunity," box 80, "Poverty Social Welfare Planning Commission" folder, CSC. Other parts of Stretch's article indicate that, wittingly or not, he seemed to have been influenced by the opportunity theories of Richard A. Cloward and Lloyd E. Ohlin: see Cloward and Ohlin, *Delinquency and Opportunity: A Theory of Delinquent Gangs* (Glencoe, Ill.: Free Press, 1960).

43. SWPC, "Report of Findings and Action Recommendations."

44. See Philip Rieff, *The Triumph of the Therapeutic: Uses of Faith after Freud* (1966; Chicago: University of Chicago Press, 1987).

45. Gunnar Myrdal, Richard Sterner, and Arnold Rose, *An American Dilemma: The Negro Problem and Modern Democracy* (New York: Harper, 1944).

46. The history of the culture-of-poverty theory stretches back to the anthropological studies of E. Franklin Frazier, Charles S. Johnson, John Dollard, Allison Davis, and others during the 1930s and 1940s. The theory flowered, however, in the postwar period. The articulation of the theory that had the most impact on the Great Society came from Lewis, whose study of a poor family living in Mexico City concluded that the family's poverty was linked to more than low income, that its poverty stemmed from environmental determinants, which Lewis identified as traits, passed down culturally from ancestors. Accordingly, a culture of deprivation built poverty conditions over several generations and reinforced the isolation of the poor in capitalist societies. The more recent underclass theories are arguably offspring of Lewis's work. Its practitioners contend that in post–World War II America, a permanent underclass developed in American cities as a result of a web of cultural factors, racial and ethnic prejudices, welfare state inadequacy, family disorganization, and the dislocation of employment opportunities for residents. Recently, it has become a serious target for scholars, some of whom dismiss its validity as a term. For a discussion of the development of the culture-of-poverty theory, see O'Connor, *Poverty Knowledge*, 74–123; Scott, *Contempt and Pity*, 142; and Michael B. Katz, *The Undeserving Poor: From the War on Poverty to the War on Welfare* (New York: Pantheon Books, 1989), 16–35. See also

Oscar Lewis, *The Children of Sanchez: Autobiography of a Mexican Family* (New York: Random House, 1961); Oscar Lewis, *Five Families: Mexican Case Studies in the Culture of Poverty* (New York: Basic Books, 1959); Oscar Lewis, *La Vida: A Puerto Rican Family in the Culture of Poverty—San Juan and New York* (New York: Random House, 1966); William Julius Wilson, *The Truly Disadvantaged: The Inner City, the Underclass, and Public Policy* (Chicago: University of Chicago Press, 1987); William Julius Wilson, *When Work Disappears: The World of the New Urban Poor* (New York: Knopf, 1997); Enzo Mingione, ed., *Urban Poverty and the Underclass: A Reader* (Oxford: Blackwell, 1996); Michael B. Katz, ed., *The Underclass Debate: Views from History* (Princeton: Princeton University Press, 1993); James Q. Wilson, "Culture, Inaction, and the Underclass," in *Values and Public Policy*, ed. Henry Aaron, Thomas E. Mann, and Timothy Taylor (Washington, D.C.: Brookings Institution, 1994); Jacqueline Jones, *The Dispossessed: America's Underclass from the Civil War to the Present* (New York: Basic Books, 1992); William Kelso, *Poverty and the Underclass: Changing Perceptions of the Poor in America* (New York: New York University Press, 1994); Herbert S. Gans, *The War against the Poor: The Underclass and Antipoverty Policy* (New York: Basic Books, 1995); Christopher Jencks, *Rethinking Social Policy: Race, Poverty, and the Underclass* (Cambridge: Harvard University Press, 1992); and Christopher Jencks and Paul E. Peterson, eds., *The Urban Underclass* (Washington, D.C.: Brookings Institution, 1991).

47. Mary Balthazar, "No Greater Need: An Early Assessment of Operation Upgrade," and Balthazar to Irene C. Howard, May 13, 1966, box 26, "Guste Home, 1966" folder, CSC.

48. New Orleans Branch, NACW, "The Unmarried Mother: A Demonstration Project," April [1967], box 23, "Desire 63–66" folder, CSC.

49. Mildred Fossier, proposal, 1964, box 32, "Welfare" folder, Schiro Collection.

50. SWPC, "Social Welfare Planning Council's Desire Area Work Program, section 205 of Title II A of Economic Opportunity Act," [1965], box 23, "Desire, 1963–66" folder, CSC. Albert Rosenberg, associate executive director of the SWPC, reasoned that if the residents are "identified with crime, immorality, etc., it will be extremely difficult, if not impossible to engender a sense [of] community responsibility and willingness to participate in improvement efforts." See Rosenberg to Winston Lill, January 18, 1965, box 55, folder TCA 2, CSC; and Dowling to Sanzenbach, January 16, 1968, unprocessed box 22, "Housing Authority of New Orleans" folder, CSC.

51. Gerald Bonnaffons to Dowling, September 1966, unprocessed box 22, unlabeled HANO folder, CSC.

52. Ibid.

53. VISTA Proposal by SWPC, July 1965, box 66, VISTA 1964–65 folder, CSC.

54. Arthur Cooper, "Statement of Community Workers Group RE: Role of the Community Organizer," [1966], box 28, "Irish Channel Community Development Center" folder, CSC.

55. Robert Warshawsky, weekly report, December 13–19, 1965, February 16, 1966, unprocessed box 25, "Warshawsky, Robert (Desire) VISTA" folder, CSC. Warshawsky declared with good intentions that "these people cannot speak to a large extent, with any semblance of how the English Language is to be spoken. This is in direct conflict with Negro advancement." They needed to learn "pronunciation."

56. Urban League of Greater New Orleans, "A Community Organization Project—9th Ward," October 20, 1965, box 64, "ULGNO, 1960–71" folder, CSC.

57. Corliss to TCA Board of Directors, January 18, 1965, box 55, "TCA 2" folder, CSC.

58. "Proposal Background," [1965], box 23, "Desire, 1963–66" folder, CSC.

59. Corliss to TCA Board of Directors, January 18, 1965, box 55, "TCA 2" folder, CSC.

60. "Proposal Background." For the most part, the Urban League's early community-organization contribution consisted of helping create community groups, beautification campaigns, Boy Scout troops, and jobs for teenagers. See Urban League of Greater New Orleans, "A Community Organization Project—9th Ward."

61. Corliss to TCA Board of Directors, January 18, 1965, box 55, "TCA 2" folder, CSC.

62. Bonnaffons to Dowling, September 1966, unprocessed box 22, unlabeled HANO folder, CSC.

63. New Orleans Branch, NACW, "The Unmarried Mother: A Demonstration Project."

More Than a Head Start

The War on Poverty, Catholic Charities, and
Civil Rights in Mobile, Alabama, 1965–1970

SUSAN YOUNGBLOOD ASHMORE

The story of the War on Poverty in Alabama is one of struggle—between administrators of a liberal president and state bureaucrats of a reactionary governor, between federal government initiatives and states' rights traditions, between white municipal power structures and African American grassroots organizations. No other governor had as contentious a relationship with President Lyndon B. Johnson and his Great Society programs as Alabama's George Wallace. Although the famous segregationist tried to hold back the tide, the South was bound to reconcile its racist ways in the wake of landmark civil rights legislation. What remained unclear was just how that reconciliation would begin.

In Mobile, Alabama's second-largest city, the Catholic Church stood uniquely poised to serve as an agent for change through the federal antipoverty campaign. Archbishop Thomas J. Toolen maintained a powerful position as the conservative leader of close to 40 percent of the port city's citizens. At the same time, the archbishop backed the Head Start Program administered through the Catholic Charities Office because he had traditionally supported initiatives to assist impoverished Alabamians. Thus, when the Church sponsored Project Head Start in Mobile, Wallace hesitated to stand in the way.[1]

Compared to other places in Alabama, Mobile had a reputation for being a moderate city, one that had smoothed the hard edges of Jim Crow segregation. The Catholic Church had built a hospital, children's homes, churches, and parochial schools for African Americans. Spring Hill College, a Jesuit-sponsored four-year institution, even began to integrate its student body in 1947, completing the process fully by 1954. After World War II, the city made some adjustments to its racial caste system by negotiating with a handful of African American leaders and hiring black policemen to patrol black neighborhoods, designating segregation on city buses with an adjustable line, and equalizing the salaries of black and white teachers. Although forward-looking for the time, especially compared to Birmingham, Montgomery, and smaller towns across the Black Belt, most of these compromises did not undermine the tenets of white supremacy but merely papered over the injustice of racial segregation and the underlying divisions that existed between the races and between the less well-off and the upper and middle classes.[2]

By the 1960s an undercurrent of resentment began to pulse through parts of the black community as the pace of change lagged behind rising expectations. What had seemed progressive in the mid-1940s and 1950s now appeared patronizing, paternalistic, and increasingly untenable. An urban-renewal program had relocated many people out of the inner city to make way for a new city auditorium, increasing racially segregated housing as whites flocked to the suburbs and black Mobilians moved to African American neighborhoods. Even a 1963 school-desegregation lawsuit did not bring relief. Instead of fostering hope, what became known as the *Birdie Mae Davis* case nurtured bitterness because the board of school commissioners resisted integration, allowing only a few black students to enter formerly all-white schools. This court action dragged on for more than twenty years. After the passage of landmark civil rights legislation, the cracks hidden by this old system could no longer be disguised, especially when one city commissioner endorsed the new laws. As a result, by the late 1960s, the turmoil Mobile's leaders had been avoiding finally came to the surface, giving them some common ground with their more famous neighbors in Birmingham, Montgomery, and Selma.[3]

In addition to the upheaval created by the changing racial environment, Mobile's Catholic citizens also encountered the aftershocks associated with the Second Vatican Council. By calling the gathering, which met in Rome off and on from 1962 until 1965, Pope John XXIII hoped for a complete renewal of the faithful by bringing the Church up to date. After the four-year convocation, the Church published sixteen documents explaining the reforms. One of the constitutions, *Gaudium et Spec,* called for "a profound engagement with the reality of the world's experience." In this treatise, the Church appealed for improvement of the social order: "Excessive economic and social disparity between individuals and peoples of the human race is a source of scandal," the council proclaimed, "and militates against social justice, equity, human dignity, as well as social and international peace."[4]

From the perspective of the pew, the most glaring changes associated with Vatican II were the alterations in the liturgy, use of the vernacular during Mass, and modification of rituals that were centuries old. But for those within the Church hierarchy, more was afoot than moving the altar, leaving Latin behind, and dropping the requirement of meatless Fridays. In addition to these important revisions, there was also a loosening of authority, an ecumenical reaching out, and a renewed sense of participation in the world. For some younger priests, nuns, and brothers working in Mobile in the 1960s, the civil rights movement and the War on Poverty offered new ways to reform the Church by helping the city come to terms with its racist traditions. Nevertheless, this newfound activism inevitably shook the traditional understanding of the roles of clergy and other Church representatives in their religious community.[5]

President Johnson's antipoverty campaign entered this fractious environment in 1964 and therefore reflected the problems associated with Mobile's changing society. At first glance, the War on Poverty waged there appears to have been barely a skirmish. It took two years of negotiating to overcome state and local political infighting before the Mobile Area Community Action Committee formed. And by the time that agency finally received support from Washington, Congress had cut back on federal funds to new communities that wanted to join in the fight against poverty. Hamstrung by the shortage of money and, more importantly, by staff capabilities, this new poverty-fighting organization lacked the ability to develop creative programs that would address the needs of the city and county's poor.[6]

On closer examination, however, the struggle against poverty in Mobile did provide a new mechanism that could address some of the underlying problems associated with poverty and racial discrimination. Instead of entering the city through the local community-action agency, the fight against poverty came through the doors of the Catholic Charities office under the sponsorship of Archbishop Toolen's Anti-Poverty Committee (ABTAPC). The archbishop had desegregated the city's parochial schools in 1964, thereby enabling the diocese to sponsor Project Head Start the first summer it became available. Operating as the Mobile area's only integrated public-education program, this child-development effort made real strides in confronting problems related to early childhood poverty. Head Start also introduced those affiliated with the Catholic Charities office to new realms of the city's problems, especially those associated with a renewed grassroots civil rights movement.[7]

A study of the antipoverty effort in Mobile provides an example of how the programs sponsored by the Office of Economic Opportunity (OEO) interacted with the larger issue of racial justice in the South, thereby enriching knowledge of the circumstances involved in changing the region. On the national level, the OEO intentionally included civil rights enforcement as part of its marching orders. In Alabama's port city, this policy would advance as well as hinder progress because more than race was involved; class also mattered, and the OEO was not always equipped to deal effectively with these distinctions. On the state level, looking at Mobile helps to clarify Governor Wallace's role in thwarting federal initiatives in Alabama. His interference slowed down the larger antipoverty effort in Mobile, but his actions also opened the way for the ABTAPC's involvement. At the local level, an understanding of how the various players waged the War on Poverty underscores the divisions within the African American community that had been submerged. In the end, the approaches taken by both traditional integrationists and insurgent black-power advocates were needed to attack the problems left over from Jim Crow's departure. The antipoverty programs supported by Washington and sponsored by the Catholic Church gave assistance to this struggle in Mobile.

President Johnson's domestic war clearly did not eradicate poverty from the city by 1970. Nevertheless, if that is the only criterion for evaluating the antipoverty campaign, important conclusions about the federal program will be missed. Not only did Project Head Start provide a concrete example of what was possible in a city unwilling to embrace fully school desegregation, but the frustrations of the city's less fortunate encouraged many to seek ways of gaining more than a head start for themselves.

Washington Links Poverty with Fighting Racial Discrimination in the South

In many ways, members of the task force responsible for writing the economic opportunity bill in the winter of 1964 had the South in mind when they formulated pieces of the antipoverty legislation. The Community Action Program (CAP), which became title II, served as the focal point of the act. Instead of the federal government developing projects from Washington, the drafters wanted CAPS created on the local level to suit the local situation. Initially, the program's formulators envisioned federal funds supporting a community-action agency (CAA) composed of city government representatives and poor people working together to design alternative programs to counter the traditional way of delivering services to the poor. But when discussing how this would work in the South, officials wondered how poor black southerners could be guaranteed involvement in a segregated society. The struggle for civil rights undermined trust in the southern states. "We had a problem," William Cannon explained. "We knew we couldn't get community-action agencies in the established governmental structure in the South." As a result, the legislation stated that CAAs could be established by the local government or by nonprofit agencies.[8]

The framers of the legislation further guaranteed that the poor in general and minorities in particular could not be excluded from participating in the CAP by incorporating the phrase "maximum feasible participation of the residents served," into title II. Daniel Patrick Moynihan, as the Department of Labor representative on the legislative task force, said that he agreed to the inclusion of this idea in the bill because he "saw it as a way of ensuring that the Southern black poor would not be denied any of the benefits of the poverty legislation." In this provision resided the concept of participatory democracy that had provided much of the current to the civil rights movement. With this requirement, poor people would be involved in the development, conduct, and administration of programs. The poor could serve on CAA boards, participate on policy committees for the agency, work as subprofessionals on antipoverty projects, and operate neighborhood councils to advise CAAs. Believing that the poor knew what they needed, what worked best, and what new techniques could succeed, many task force members argued that more effective programs would be developed if the poor participated in planning and carrying out projects on their own behalf. If the requirement to include local residents in the program became part of the law, then Washington could intervene if the preconditions of the legislation were not being met.[9]

When the bill went to Congress for hearings and debate in both houses, the title II program ran into some trouble. South Carolina Senator Strom Thurmond warned that CAPs would allow the federal government to establish direct control over local programs. He waved the anti–civil rights banner when he said, "Under the innocent sounding title of 'Community Action Program,' the poverty czar would not only have the power to finance the activities of such organizations as the National Council of Churches, the NAACP, SNCC, and CORE, but also a SNOOP and a SNORE which are sure to be organized to get their part of the green gravy." Thurmond bemoaned the fact that the economic opportunity bill addressed issues that touched on racial discrimination. Referring to the new Civil Rights Act, he said, "I naively thought the Congress had finished with legislation on racial matters last month."[10]

In an effort to keep the omnibus legislation intact, the White House negotiated a deal with reluctant southern senators to enable governors to veto title II programs. Florida Senator George Smathers offered an amendment that called for the OEO director to establish procedures to "facilitate effective participation of the States in Community Action Programs." It would not allow grants to be made to private institutions or nonprofit organizations within a state, "except when said institution operate[d] in conjunction with or under authority of a public agency, unless a plan setting forth the proposed program has been submitted to the Governor of the State, and he has not disapproved by thirty days of submission." Sargent Shriver, the director of the president's task force on the war against poverty, talked to Georgia Senator Herman Talmadge, who told him that such an arrangement would allow southern senators to tell their constituents that they had upheld the states' rights doctrine. Shriver remembered that Talmadge also predicted that the veto would not be used. "They're not going to disapprove of many of them," the senator reasoned, "because the governors all want to have the money come to their states." During the House debates on the legislation, representatives agreed to accept the Senate version of the bill, with the governor's veto intact. This would create another challenge for the federal program's fight against poverty, especially in Alabama, where Wallace would use this provision in his attempt to dominate the antipoverty effort.[11]

The OEO, the federal agency President Johnson created to oversee his War on Poverty, could not escape the connections between poverty and racial discrimination. LBJ signed the Economic Opportunity Act of 1964 seven weeks after the Civil Rights Act passed and almost a year before the Voting Rights Act became law. As a result, it is not surprising that in addition to providing the framework for fighting the War on Poverty, the antipoverty legislation also furthered the civil rights movement's objectives, especially in the South. So, the desires of the task force members who planned the Economic Opportunity Act were linked to the new civil rights legislation, creating a strong mandate for the OEO to confront both poverty and racial discrimination.

The agency opened officially on October 8, 1964. Becoming a part of the federal bureaucracy after the 1964 Civil Rights Act, it had to incorporate civil rights compliance into its antipoverty strategies. The Civil Rights Act required departments that distributed federal funds to formulate rules, regulations, or orders to meet the conditions of the legislation. As a result, not only would fighting poverty compel the OEO to concern itself with the needs of the nation's impoverished minority population, but federal legislation would require the agency to obey the law to ensure that no one received discriminatory treatment. Several departments within the OEO, particularly the General Counsel's

Office, the Office of Inspection, and the Civil Rights Division, made it a priority to keep the agency within the letter of the law.[12]

In February 1965, Stephen Pollack, a Department of Justice official working in the Civil Rights Division, warned Shriver, now the director of the OEO, about the difficulties of fighting poverty in the South: "Southern Negro poverty involves problems having nothing to do with race—the whole question of the rural farm, education, job skills, motivation, etc.—but race is at the bottom." Pollack knew the antipoverty agency's predicament and hoped it could meet the challenge. "To constructively remedy this would tax the skill of persons dedicated to the proposition that whites and Negroes should be treated as one," he advised. "There are hardly any white southerners who feel that way and they are rarely in a position to work their will. It will take constant supervision from Washington for any worthwhile results." As the white power structure continued to erect barricades of defiance, OEO officials would have to alter their plans to implement effectively federal poverty programs.[13]

The War on Poverty became a vehicle for change in the South through programs starting in late 1964 and early 1965. As spelled out in the legislation, the OEO managed the Job Corps, Community Action, and the Volunteers in Service to America (VISTA). No Job Corps centers were located in the southeast region as a result of the governor's veto provision in the Economic Opportunity Act. With the requirement of integrated housing and working conditions, southern governors did not want Job Corps facilities in their states. Conceived as a national Peace Corps, VISTA volunteers received a small government stipend to live and work in the communities they served. Just as local groups in the CAAs had to discover the best ways to solve the problems associated with poverty, VISTA volunteers had to create their own assignments based on their understanding of communities and their needs. The national volunteer program, however, never got very big—especially in the South—and consequently did not have a large effect across the region as a whole. Governors had the right to approve VISTA activity in their states, which kept the program weaker in some southern states than in others. Mississippi did not have a single volunteer working there throughout the history of the OEO, while North Carolina had eighty-six volunteers in 1967.[14]

Without the Job Corps or a strong VISTA presence, CAP provided the greatest opportunity for assisting the South's poor. As the heart of the Economic Opportunity Act, CAP offered something new in the fight against poverty. Local people would assess the problems in their community that fostered poverty, develop ideas and projects to solve those problems, and apply for funds from Washington to accomplish these tasks. The CAA became the structure that would mobilize the poor to develop and implement plans to combat poverty and coordinate local antipoverty resources at all levels. OEO staff members hoped that the CAA would speak on behalf of the poor to focus different approaches and resources simultaneously on the multifaceted problems of poverty while reorienting existing programs to meet more effectively the needs of low-income people.[15]

Getting Started in Mobile: Community Action, 1964–1965

Even before LBJ had signed the Economic Opportunity Act, Mobile had leaders who wanted to establish antipoverty programs as soon as possible. Mayor Joseph N. Langan received a copy of Johnson's proposed program in March 1964 and hoped that the city's participation in the War on Poverty would be a way to develop a combination job training/school-dropout-prevention program. He envisioned a city works project with an educational component. Langan reasoned that if members of the black community increased their ability to participate in the city's economic life, racial tensions would be eased. On later reflection, he thought that economic disparity was the "underlying problem of race relations" with "one offsetting the other." Moving quickly, Langan called a public meeting on September 1, 1964, to begin coordinating the activities of various agencies within Mobile County to prepare a grant application to the OEO. Three days later, he contacted Shriver to schedule a meeting to discuss establishing programs in Mobile.[16]

It was not surprising that Langan would show interest in seeking federal funds to fight poverty. A New Deal Democrat, he was confident in the government's ability to assist those in need. The "government is the only agency that has the scope to do it," he told one newspaper reporter in 1965. A devout Catholic and graduate of Spring Hill College, he had earned a reputation as a racial moderate over the course of his political career, first as Mobile's state senator in the mid-1940s and later as a city commissioner beginning in 1953. Under his watch, the city first black policemen was hired in 1954. Two years later, he formed a human-relations committee after observing Montgomery's troubles during its bus boycott. Langan wanted this group to study housing, recreation, education, and political rights, but with the idea of maintaining the "separate but equal" concept. Taking even these small steps made him an easy mark for racist reactionaries. He became the target of a White Citizens' Council "Joe Must Go" campaign, but the attack failed to keep Langan from winning reelection in 1961.[17]

Unfortunately for the city's poor, Langan would not be the only commissioner interested in the new federal antipoverty program. Over the next six months, competing groups would appear like new shoots of kudzu, choking off any possibility of the War on Poverty following a clear path in the region. By mid-March an OEO investigator found seven different groups vying for the opportunity to become the city's CAA. Commissioner Charles S. Trimmier led one of these groups.[18]

The competing groups were a product of the structure of Mobile's city government. The city commission comprised three commissioners elected at large and serving four-year terms. The specific responsibilities of each position were not assigned by law. As a result, the commissioners would decide among themselves who would oversee the various functions of city government. Each commissioner served as the city's mayor for one year. Although the system was viewed as a progressive form of government when the city established it in 1911, flaws surfaced when the commissioners were at odds with each other. This was the case after the 1961 election, in which Trimmier barely defeated Charles Hackmeyer by tapping into white fears of racial change. Trimmier had accused the incumbent of holding onto his seat by virtue of the "bloc-vote," a euphemism for the black voting strength of Mobile's African American political wards. George McNally also won a position on the commission, the first Republican elected in Mobile since Reconstruction. Under this new configuration it was often two against one, with Langan the odd man out.[19]

With the turn of the new year, Trimmier moved into the mayor's seat; he would be up for reelection in August 1965. He stood on shaky ground as he faced a possible federal income tax indictment and realized he had alienated the black vote in his last bid for office. In an effort to repair the breach and to appear to be an effective commissioner, he established himself as coordinator of the Mobile Area Economic Commission. Trimmier formulated a biracial executive committee that included power brokers from the black community, including Clarence Montgomery, the current president of the Mobile National Association for the Advancement of Colored People (NAACP); Bishop William Smith of the African Methodist Episcopal Zion Church; and John LeFlore, a caseworker for the Non-Partisan Voters League, a Mobile organization created after Alabama banned the NAACP in 1956. Trimmier's group also included white labor and business representatives. In March Trimmier headed to Washington to meet with OEO officials, hoping to gain their favor for his plan. The mayor made a good impression on Bill Haddad, inspector general of the OEO. "He says that the political situation is such that Wallace won't veto," Haddad told CAP director Theodore Berry. "Board looks good (negro, poor) and the money requested ($50,000) is modest enough. His attitude, too, seems okay." Just to be sure, the inspector general decided to send two investigators to Mobile to verify Trimmier's claims. They were in for a surprise.[20]

Larger forces were at work against the mayor's efforts. After he invited County Commissioner LeRoy Stevens to participate in this antipoverty initiative, the mayor learned that the county planned to organize its own agency, with the blessing of the governor. Wallace had asked Stevens to set up a board to serve as the only community-action agency in Mobile County. Following OEO directives, the county commissioner established a biracial group, but the twenty-seven-person committee had only four African American members. With this ratio, independent black initiatives could easily be overruled. The *Mobile Register,* whose editor was a known Wallace supporter, had reported that Trimmier's autonomous efforts had minimized the governor's role. This was a shot across the bow. Wallace envisioned the War on Poverty as a form of patronage for his statewide political machine, not as a program to empower the poor to change their living standards by implementing programs developed from their own ideas. Trimmier's independent activities ran counter to this plan. By early April, the governor made it clear that he backed the Stevens committee. In an attempt to influence the OEO's decisions, he wrote to Shriver, offering support for the county group: "I will be willing to waive the thirty-day waiting period set up under section 209c when the application has been accepted by you and has been sent to me for my action."[21]

This type of meddling was nothing new for Wallace. When Birmingham civic leaders—who were not politically affiliated with him—began to make independent arrangements to form a CAP in March 1965, Wallace brought in Jefferson County officials who were his allies in an effort to dilute the potential for change that a federal antipoverty program could bring. He took the same approach in Mobile. The heavy hand of the governor's office did not go unnoticed. The OEO began to suspect his actions in late March, and a federal employee in Alabama alerted members of President Johnson's staff to Wallace's plans: "It appears that the poverty program in Alabama is being organized along strictly political lines with 100% Wallace forces as co-ordinators in every case and with most executive committee members being Wallacites," he warned. "We have been told by certain key Wallace supporters that only a co-ordinator acceptable to Wallace will be placed on the payroll."[22]

While this jockeying for position was taking place, other Mobilians had been organizing on their own, outside of Wallace's purview. On October 22, 1964, the Catholic Archbishop of Alabama and North Florida, Thomas J. Toolen, hosted a statewide meeting to discuss the new antipoverty program. The director of the diocesan's Catholic Charities office, the Reverend Thomas M. Nunan, planned and organized the gathering. He had been an active board member of National Catholic Charities and had heard about the Economic Opportunity Act through this work. "The word was very clear coming from the national office," he later explained. The Catholic leaders realized that the antipoverty effort was going to be something new. Nunan remembered being told that "any group . . . is a legitimate contender . . . for funds from this." He also knew that the Catholic Charities office provided an existing forum from which to begin developing antipoverty programs.[23]

More than one hundred pastors, heads of charitable institutions, and hospital and school personnel gathered in Montgomery to hear Maurice Hartmann of the National Catholic Community Service in Washington explain how Catholic clergy and laypeople could get involved. Hartmann suggested that Alabama Catholics form a group to coordinate diocesan projects, and he offered suggestions for how parish priests could serve in the effort by opening their facilities to the community, identifying people in need of assistance, and encouraging parishioners to get involved. Rev. Nunan viewed the federal programs as "a practical means of spreading God's kingdom on earth."[24]

The week after the statewide meeting, the Mobile participants began forming a diocesan antipoverty committee led by Nunan. By November, this group called itself Archbishop Toolen's Anti-Poverty Committee. Father Nunan worried that the archbishop would not endorse the program wholeheartedly and therefore named the organization after Toolen, hoping to seal his support. In preparation for a meeting to seek approval of his plans for Mobile, Nunan gave Toolen a draft with the name of the organization printed at the top of the document. "Everyone's got an ego," Nunan later explained. "It was deliberate, and whether it helped or not, I will never know." After their discussion, Archbishop Toolen authorized Nunan to move ahead and said that his efforts would be supported.[25]

One program Nunan hoped to bring to Mobile was the newly formed Project Head Start. As the infighting between the city and county groups vying for recognition as Mobile's CAA revealed, not every community was up to the challenge of creating its own solutions to relieve the plight of the less fortunate. As it turned out, the strength of community action—developing locally controlled responses to poverty—also became its Achilles' heel, leading some OEO officials to believe this requirement had slowed down the overall antipoverty initiative. In an effort to jump-start the idea of community action, the OEO turned to what became known as "national emphasis programs"—such as Project Head Start, Legal Services, Upward Bound, and Foster Grandparents —to serve as building blocks for CAP. These programs became a hybrid of the original community-action idea and the more traditional federal approach to welfare distribution. Originating in Washington instead of on the local level, these programs still required the "maximum feasible participation of the residents served." Shriver and some of his advisers thought that these programs would assist communities in starting the War on Poverty in areas that had not generated any activity. Many hoped that once a national-emphasis program got going, it would serve as a catalyst for more antipoverty ventures. The CAP director, Berry, reasoned that by beginning with a single-purpose CAA organized around a program such as Project Head Start, the concept of community action would make more sense to the community and could ultimately be applied to other programs.[26]

Plans for Head Start began in the winter of 1965 for an eight-week summer project intended to prepare impoverished children for school. Instead of a day-care program, the OEO wanted to follow a comprehensive curriculum that included education, medical care, social services, and nutritional help to meet the complete needs of the poor child. Jule Sugarman, one of the developers of Project Head Start, explained that they wanted the program to "intervene at a point in the life of the child in ways which would keep deficits from developing in that child, . . . mak[ing] it possible for him to achieve his maximum potential in later life." Just like other CAPs, local communities organized and administered Project Head Start. Parents were essential for a successful venture—working as teachers' aides, taking special courses to improve the home environment, or advising in the development and administration of programs. In most cases, the OEO covered 80 percent of the cost for a Head Start program, and the local community funded the balance.[27]

In the South, Project Head Start ran head-on into the fallout from the 1965 Elementary and Secondary Education Act. This education-relief bill provided federal spending on public education in the country based on the number of poor people living in a school district. To receive the aid, school boards had to comply with the Civil Rights Act, which was Washington's way of seeing that school integration moved forward at a more rapid pace. Even though Head Start was not a program of the Department of Education, some southern leaders recognized that it could foster acceptance of desegregation. Shriver initially hoped the child-development program would be the key to the OEO's entrance into Dixie: "Basically I thought that Head Start would be a terrific way to get into the South in a non-confrontational mode and begin to do something very beneficial for the poor whites and the poor blacks who are a huge proportion of the poverty population in the South." He concluded that southerners "had friendly feelings toward little black children," which would enable the OEO to "cut across a lot of the opposition which would otherwise exist in the South to anything we did to help poor people." Friendly feelings aside, some southern communities did not embrace Head Start without trying to manipulate it to fit in with the region's social mores. All across Dixie, what some officials claimed to be an integrated program looked like segregation from the perspective of Washington, D.C. This caused the Office of Inspection, the Civil Rights Division, and the Office of the General Counsel of the OEO to work closely with the people approving Head Start grant proposals to verify that programs did not operate in a segregated manner.[28]

The OEO issued guidelines to make clear its stand on funding only those projects that met the agency's nondiscriminatory conditions. These regulations encompassed all aspects of the program, including the location of the Head Start Center, the eligibility of participants, the recruitment and placement of staff, transportation, program publicity, and who would be responsible for carrying out these prerequisites. There would be no mistaking who would answer to the OEO. The guidelines stated unequivocally, "The burden shall be on the applicants and sponsor to take such measures as may be necessary to insure the program is operated in a completely nondiscriminatory manner." The Office of Inspection set up a special Head Start task force to conduct field inspections on complaints of discrimination and to telephone applicants where there was reason to believe that segregated practices might prevail. In the spring of 1966, the OEO inspection division recruited twenty-five law students to work as summer Head Start inspectors. Their findings resulted in the denial of fifty-nine applications for failure to comply with civil rights requirements.[29]

The Office of the General Counsel also became involved in setting policy to ensure that Head Start programs complied with the Civil Rights Act. The OEO lawyers knew that following the procedures of title VI of the 1964 Civil Rights Act as it applied to schoolchildren would not be effective for Head

Start. If the violating project asked for the full hearing process required by law, the summer would be over before a decision had been made. The OEO's attorneys took a different approach, focusing on the hiring policies of Head Start faculty and citing the discrimination occurring against the student as a beneficiary instead of against the teacher as an employee. OEO lawyers also broadly interpreted civil rights compliance. They held prospective grantees to a higher standard beyond ending segregation. Head Start projects would have "an affirmative duty" to recruit minorities for service on governing boards and provide enrollment on an integrated basis. The OEO legal staff sought to end de facto segregation in OEO-sponsored programs even where no deliberate local policy of segregation existed.[30]

Finally, the General Counsel's office made sure that the separation of church and state would not hinder the financial support of OEO programs. Instead of distributing funds for general aid to education, which the federal government prohibited, Congress allowed the antipoverty agency to offer "special, remedial and non-curricular educational assistance." With this limited aid, the federal government could help children regardless of where they received their education, thereby enabling the OEO to support programs operated by private entities such as parochial schools. This interpretation had significance in the South. When a school district declined to sponsor a Head Start program or when a school board had been denied funds because it refused to comply with the Civil Rights Act, a private nonprofit organization could operate the child-development program.[31]

Project Head Start in the South provided many opportunities for people to confront problems associated with segregation in the classroom as well as in the community. Although this was a prepackaged program created in Washington, it did have the capacity to organize those on the local level who were interested in opposing the established caste and class system that had developed since the turn of the century. This new national-emphasis program also provided the federal antipoverty agency with the opportunity to beat Wallace at his own game. CAP officials in Washington decided that the "OEO must avoid publicly or in actuality involving itself in any degree with Wallace or his state coordinator." When such a situation was unavoidable, the OEO wanted to make sure it never gave "public evidence within one situation of yielding to the governor." Setting up single-purpose agencies when there was no CAA available seemed to be one way of accomplishing this goal. One official rationalized that this would pit Wallace against local antipoverty groups instead of against Washington, which would be less fulfilling for him politically.[32]

Head Start as a Way in, Summer 1965

To get people interested in starting Head Start projects, the oeo mailed out cards across the country to various organizations and public entities that had a connection to early childhood development and education. The antipoverty agency anticipated supporting three hundred communities that would assist 100,000 children for the summer of 1965. But to the oeo's surprise, thirty-three hundred communities wanted to sponsor programs, and 560,000 children participated. Two groups responded in Mobile—the Board of School Commissioners of Mobile County and the ABTAPC. The oeo funded both.[33]

While the squabbling among the various groups seeking community-action funds continued, in mid-April the Mobile County school commissioners unanimously voted to authorize the superintendent to file an application for a summer Head Start grant. The board signed the civil rights compliance form, stating that the school system was already under a court order to desegregate the schools as a result of the *Birdie Mae Davis* case, which had been filed two years earlier. It became clear early on that the oeo planned to scrutinize closely the Mobile program because the agency asked for a revised civil rights compliance form offering further assurances. At this point, the board took a new look at the program and agreed to move forward by a three-to-two vote. The split indicated the commissioners' reluctance to face more federal investigations over the pace of school desegregation.[34]

As plans progressed over the spring and early summer, the oeo made sure everyone understood the duty to enforce the program's civil rights component. The agency mailed a "Supplemental Non-Discrimination Conditions" form to all Head Start sponsors, making it clear that every classroom and center had to be open to anyone regardless of race, color, creed, or national origin. "There shall be no recruitment, selection, or assignment of children or staff on any basis or in any manner which results in segregation or discrimination," the oeo warned. Then on June 17, Shriver wrote a letter to all grantees, stating that "the principle of equal treatment for all our citizens is at the very heart of Project Head Start." He went on to say that the oeo could not and would not support programs in which "racial discrimination or other invidious treatment of children or staff" was allowed. Further, he advised sponsors to withdraw themselves from Project Head Start before the program began if they felt they could not ensure such conduct.[35]

The Mobile County Board of School Commissioners must have felt confident about following the letter of the law, because Head Start classes began June 29 with a $143,000 grant to support eighteen centers serving 1,419 children. After closer inspection, one center had to be closed because too many of its students lived above the designated poverty line. The commissioners clearly viewed the program as a benefit for the African American community, which blinded them to the need to comply with the OEO's civil rights demands. Sixty-two black teachers and three white teachers, assisted by sixty-four black teacher's aides and one white teacher's aide, worked in seventeen centers with an enrollment of 1,106 black children and 41 white children. Fifteen centers were located in black neighborhoods, one in a mixed section of town, and one in a white part of the city. The school superintendent reported that federal investigators began reviewing the Mobile County school system's Project Head Start from its inception. At an early Head Start staff meeting, an OEO inspector told the teachers that the program violated the contract signed by the board of school commissioners. Two weeks into the summer program, the OEO notified Superintendent Cranford Burns that the segregation of his Head Start faculty was not meeting the civil rights compliance requirements. One teacher later said she was afraid to speak out. "You don't know how things are here," she told a reporter. "If we had tried to do anything, we wouldn't have had jobs in the fall." [36]

By July 8, the OEO insisted that Mobile was operating a completely segregated program on the basis of its faculty and stated that unless conditions changed, the grant money would be withheld and termination of the entire program would begin. The school superintendent responded immediately, explaining the school system's good-faith effort to comply. Using the same standard of neighborhood schools used in the *Birdie Mae Davis* case, he told OEO attorney James Heller, "Assignments of teachers and aides were made on the basis of proximity of residences of applicants to Head Start centers." He justified this on the premise of "minimizing transportation problems and cost and compensating for low salaries; and on the basis of previous teaching assignments, thus capitalizing upon staff acquaintance with parents and the sociology of the community." He complained that shifting faculty at this point in the program would only disrupt Head Start and prevent it from "achieving its objectives." In closing his letter a typographical error spoke volumes on what was really happening: "Mobile as a community has a distinguished record of good race relations and a record of cooperation in observing to the letter all instructions given in desegregation programs. Mobile in many instances has taken the initiative in eliminating many forms of Integration." [37]

By the end of the month, the OEO had run out of patience and threatened to cut off funds on July 30. Burns had made some minor adjustments to the faculty—three black teacher's aides had been moved to the centers in predominantly white neighborhoods, one white teacher was relocated to a majority black center, and the central staff employed three black workers. Nevertheless, this left fourteen Head Start centers with all-black staffs. "Several white teachers who did apply refused assignment to centers serving Negroes," the associate superintendent of education told the *Montgomery Advertiser.* "So far as I know, we are not empowered to coerce any teacher into taking unwanted assignments." The federal antipoverty agency disagreed. To remedy the situation, the oeo asked the school system to run an advertisement in the local newspapers seeking applications that would further the integration of the program. School officials claimed that this request arrived too late for a Sunday news release. In the end, relatively little was required to appease the oeo. In early August Heller backed off and left Burns a telephone message with the news. The antipoverty agency would allow the program to finish, but "no further educational program for the Mobile Schools [would be] sponsored by this Office of Economic Opportunity until there is a hearing which certifies that there will be a far better record of civil rights compliance in the future." Heller explained that the school system was off the hook for the sake of the children and in view of the superintendent's belated efforts to make changes, even though the oeo claimed that the Mobile Head Start Program was "one of the worst" in the country on civil rights compliance. Shriver later explained his agency decided to pay Mobile because nonpayment "would be unfair to hundreds of law-abiding people who bore no responsibility for the violation in the program, and who furnished goods and services . . . expecting in good faith to be paid."[38]

Superintendent Burns remained impenitent to the end, showing the distrust that had grown between the local school system and the federal government since the filing of the 1963 school-desegregation case. In a letter to Shriver complaining about Mobile's treatment by the oeo, Burns spoke clearly of his underlying suspicions. "Is the 'Head Start' program to be a real partnership, manned by people at all levels of government who respect each other and have faith in each other," he asked, "or will it be a political tool to help the Federal government gain control of education and administer same through uncoordinated [*sic*] bureaus who operate behind closed doors?" The progressive *Southern Courier,* however, pointed out that this old procedure would no longer work and warned Burns about his foot-dragging with the Head Start Program. Agreeing with the oeo's understanding that "poverty and segregation feed on each other," the paper found the actions of the Mobile school district out of step with the current reality. "There's an important lesson in all this for cities like Mobile, that have kept race relations calm so far, and have not had much federal intervention in their affairs," the weekly newspaper editorialized. "Racial peace in these cities no longer guarantees that the government will allow them to progress at their own pace, as they have in the past. Federal legislation in the last two years has created a civil rights program requiring major changes in the race relations of even the most progressive Southern cities."[39]

The OEO had struck out again in Mobile. As of yet, no CAA had been formulated for Alabama's second largest city, and the Project Head Start sponsored by the public school system resisted even the slightest form of integration, causing the board to refuse to participate in the child-development program in the future. The projects operated by the Catholic Church seemed to be the OEO's only hope of getting anything started in the region.

Catholic Charities of Mobile Joins the War on Poverty, 1965–1967

Fortunately for Mobile's poor, the antipoverty legislation permitted private organizations to operate projects when public institutions failed to do so. The OEO attorneys had also concluded that Head Start centers could be located in religious institutions. Steps had been taken prior to 1965 that made Mobile's Catholic Charities a prime candidate for this work.

The Catholic Church had been involved for several years in programs for children, including homes for dependent and neglected girls and boys of both races. The Church operated the only two facilities for black children in the state of Alabama. One, the Zimmer Memorial Home, was located in Mobile and was supported by Catholic Charities; and Father Caswell managed the other in Mt. Meigs, just outside of Montgomery. As the population of neglected black children living in Zimmer Memorial Home declined, discussions began about closing it and moving the residents into the all-white facilities of the Catholic Boys Home and St. Mary's Home for girls. Father Nunan, director of Catholic Charities for the diocese, remembered his discussions with Archbishop Toolen in making this decision: "I really believe we can do this," the thirty-five-year-old priest encouraged his superior. "I don't expect this is going to get an awful lot of attention, and I think we can make the thing fly." He remembered Toolen saying, "In the name of God, let's go ahead and do it." This action led to the archbishop's decision to integrate the diocese's parochial schools so that dependent black children could continue their education with the other residents of the children's homes. As a result, in April 1964 Toolen announced that the parochial schools across the diocese would be integrated beginning that fall.[40]

The initial steps to desegregate Mobile's parochial school system seemed to indicate that a small space had opened, creating room for new possibilities in the city. Nunan thought that the formation of the ABTAPC offered the chance to expand the Catholic Charities Office's traditional role: "Here, via the Economic Opportunity Act," he later said, "was a new way to be influential in the community vis-à-vis pointing to the needs of the poor and impoverished and getting something done about it." His work on behalf of the poor and working classes had been inspired by Pope Leo XIII's 1891 encyclical, *Rerum Novarum* (On Capital and Labor). The Second Vatican Council's call to reach out in an ecumenical way to help solve social problems reinforced Nunan's desire to make changes in Mobile. Nunan hoped that Vatican II would also bring a new Church attitude toward issues associated with its customary hierarchical rule and acknowledge what he called "the sense of the faithful" and their ability to make decisions about their faith and sense of morality.[41]

The young Irish priest quickly tried to develop ideas and obtain federal funds to support new attempts to assist the poor. His energy and vision propelled others into action. "He was so smart, he was so capable, and [he had] energy like no one," recalled Sara Kaffer, the first Head Start director for the ABTAPC. "You could catch him in his office at midnight, and he was there early the next morning at seven, . . . just completely focused." The Reverend Tom Weise, the assistant director of Catholic Charities, remembered early discussions about Project Head Start: "They're going to have a program that will get kids a head start in school," Nunan told the group. "So how many kids can we handle? . . . How many can we take?" Weise recollected that someone suggested, "Maybe we can take fifty," and Nunan said, "Go for a thousand." A handful of people soon began to take the necessary steps to operate Project Head Start through the ABTAPC. Commissioner Langan and the Director of Mobile County Pensions and Securities, Doris Bender, both Catholics and ABTAPC members, helped Kaffer draft the grant application. A Mobile native and a Presbyterian, Kaffer had heard about the program from a friend, who suggested that she apply for a position. She came to her new job with an education degree from Huntingdon College in Montgomery and several years of classroom experience. "I had taught long enough to have some really strong ideas about what I wanted to see in the school system, and this offered me the chance," she explained.[42]

Once the grant application had been written, Nunan hand delivered it to the OEO's southeastern regional office in Atlanta. He later recalled that the official he met there initially had doubts about the ABTAPC's plans. "We spent hours going over what we'd attempted to do and put together," Nunan said. At the end of the evening, the OEO administrator asked why Nunan should be trusted. The Mobile priest told him, "You've got to trust because you have no other choice in this community at this point in time, to my knowledge, and you have no one, no group that will even come close to the group that we've put together here." Nunan tried to reassure the official by saying, "We will do our best to see that it gets done right." After hearing that, the OEO executive telephoned his assistant and told him, in Nunan's hearing, to "complete the paperwork on this Archbishop Toolen Committee and move ahead with steps for funding." In late May the committee received notice that the grant had been approved.[43]

There is some question about why Governor Wallace did not veto this grant to the ABTAPC because it was clearly going to operate an integrated, public, child-development program. For one thing, the project appeared nonthreatening—it started out small, in only two centers, and as Kaffer put it, the archbishop "was not anybody's notion of a liberal at all." Rev. Weise speculated that the governor probably had an exalted view of Catholic power in Mobile. "If you ever knew Archbishop Toolen," he explained, "you wouldn't want to confront him." Commissioner Langan theorized along the same lines: "I just think [Wallace] thought it wasn't any real threat to his overall programs and that it might, by letting it go, win him some brownie points in the long run" with the Catholic vote. Finally, Nunan remembered that at this time "there was an awful lot of regard for Archbishop Toolen," and the longtime diocesan lawyer, Vince Kilborn, was a close friend of Wallace. The Catholic Charities director imagined that Kilborn told the governor, "You'll have more problems if you decide to do something about it," suggesting that the governor let the program go, "it's quiet enough."[44]

Although there is no written evidence to explain the governor's actions, it is possible to verify outsiders' images of the Catholic presence in Mobile, which could be seen every year at the annual celebration of Christ the King Sunday. For example, on October 30, 1966, an estimated ten thousand black and white Catholics walked through the streets of downtown in a solemn procession, with clergy in full regalia, children in brightly colored parochial school uniforms, and service clubs—the Knights of Columbus and the Knights of Peter Claver—represented. The group gathered at the City Auditorium for a public recitation of the Rosary, singing of hymns, a speech by Father Nunan, and a sermon by Archbishop Toolen. A makeshift altar had been erected inside the civic building, transforming it into a sacred space so that Mass could be held and those present could take Holy Communion. This annual event permitted Catholic Mobilians to claim the city as their own in an overt manner, with Archbishop Toolen standing out as their leader. With Wallace's political instincts, this phenomenon could explain why the governor did not oppose the Catholic-sponsored Project Head Start.[45]

Without a governor's veto, the OEO sent $59,550 to the ABTAPC, and the Catholic diocese contributed $8,216 for a summer Head Start Program operating in two centers. Because school was out of session, one of the programs sponsored 240 children in the parochial school of the Most Pure Heart of Mary on Davis Avenue. The Catholic Church established this parish for African Americans in 1899 in the middle of the black business district of downtown Mobile, and the priests for this parish came from the Society of Saint Joseph, whose mission was to serve the needs of black Catholics in the United States. Just as with the Head Start program operated by the Mobile County school commissioners, the OEO sent inspectors to see how well the ABTAPC operated its child-development venture, with a very different assessment. Joseph Rowland wrote a letter to Father John Harfmann of Most Pure Heart of Mary stating that he had an excellent program functioning at his school. "Few, if any others, in the state can equal yours and none can surpass yours in the quality of program you achieved," Rowland told the priest. "Your standards definitely meet those set up by OEO as I understand them and, frankly, they exceed the standards which I expected to find in any Alabama program."[46]

With the success of the small Head Start enterprise, Nunan decided in July 1965 to try to establish a CAA. "I guess we felt we had as good a claim to be a key part of that as anybody else and better probably than most because of the Head Start [program]," he later recalled. He joined forces with a combination of people from both City Commissioner Trimmier's old group and County Commissioner Stevens's former organization, both of which included traditional power brokers from the black community. The new United Citizens Committee (UCC) called a public meeting at the City Auditorium on July 12 and one week later completed a program-development grant for the OEO to support the committee's planning initiatives.[47]

By November, the original seven organizations that had hoped to form the area's CAA had dwindled to two, the UCC and the Mobile Committee for Economic Opportunity (MCEO). Each of these groups continued to act as if it would come out on top. The UCC filed its program-development grant with the OEO in late January 1966; the MCEO sent one as well. The federal antipoverty agency continued to insist that only one group could serve as the community's CAA, however, and in late March 1966 Nunan, Langan, and the OEO's southeast regional office mediated a compromise under which the UCC and the MCEO merged their operations, becoming the Mobile Area Community Action Committee (MACAC).[48]

Once the OEO approved the planning grant for the MACAC in June, Governor Wallace vetoed it, continuing his attempt to stall the federal antipoverty initiative in his state whenever it appeared to support autonomous forces out of his reach. Using his standard excuse, the governor told Shriver that the "Committee of the Mobile Area Community Action Committee here involved, in my judgement, is not as representative of the interests of Mobile County as the Committee of which I indicated I would sign a waiver letter." Wallace was being disingenuous, because by this point even Stevens wanted the governor to waive the thirty-day waiting period and let the grant through.[49]

Trying to interpret the governor's motivations, the OEO's southeast regional office deduced that he was unhappy with the temporary nature of the MACAC's board of officers, who had been elected on an ad hoc basis on June 17. It is just as likely, however, that he was acting in his own self-interest. Because Alabama law prevented Wallace from running for a second term in the November 1966 election, his wife, Lurleen, campaigned for governor as his replacement. About two weeks after Wallace struck down the MACAC planning grant, the OEO announced that it would fund antipoverty programs in Lowndes and Wilcox Counties under the title III (b) rural-poverty program, over which the governor did not have veto authority. In mid-July, Wallace spoke out against these grants, claiming that the OEO had circumvented the law to keep him powerless. He went on television on July 19 to lash out at these Black Belt antipoverty programs, insisting that they were led by "the founders and leaders of the 'Black Panther Party' " who "constitute the leadership of the 'Black Power' movement in this country." Although Mobile's CAA was not accused of such nefarious activity, the timing of the Wallace veto coincides with his grandstanding against the federal government to boost his wife's campaign for state office.[50]

Still without an approved CAA, Nunan continued his dual role as chair of the ABTAPC and of the MACAC. Throughout the winter and spring, plans for the 1966 Project Head Start progressed. Moving beyond the first summer's fledgling program, now the ABTAPC would supervise twelve centers across the city and in six neighboring counties in parochial schools as well as Protestant churches and public housing facilities. The central headquarters for the Head Start program was set up in St. Vincent's parochial school, which had been closed a few years earlier. Many of these centers were located in neighbor-hoods that were changing racially and had a ready population that wanted to participate in the program. Although the classes operated in parochial schools and Protestant Sunday school classrooms, Head Start administrators removed any evidence of Christian affiliation.[51]

That summer, the program served 1,095 children at a cost of $445,023. Nunan remembered when that he went to the state Economic Opportunity Office to seek approval for the second summer's Head Start program, Claude Kirk, the state director, asked if Nunan could help set up more Head Start pro-grams in the region around Mobile. This request seemed to be a bargain made between the state, which wanted to show some progress with the national an-tipoverty program, and the ABTAPC, which wanted to expand its operations in Mobile. The priest felt this assignment was tough. Through Kaffer's connec-tions, the ABTAPC moved out into the rural counties that surrounded Mobile, which ultimately led to Wallace leaving the archbishop's agency alone. "One of the things that made me best for this job," she explained, "was because I had grown up here and my father had worked all over the entire state." To bring Head Start programs to these rural counties, Kaffer had to get permission from the local probate judges: "Don't get me wrong, my dad supported George Wallace with all his heart and soul and hated what I was doing," she said, "but nonetheless he would say to me, 'Get out there and see so-and-so and tell him you're my daughter.'" Through her father's contacts, the Head Start director gained approval for the program and kept it from being more fuel for racist demagoguery. The leaders of the archbishop's antipoverty agency planned to operate these rural facilities for a short period and then spin them off to be run by locals so that Mobile County could remain the focus of the ABTAPC's efforts.[52]

While managing the summer Head Start Project, the ABTAPC also planned for a full-year program to begin in the fall to serve 865 children in fourteen centers located in three counties—Mobile, Washington, and Clark. The OEO would contribute $825,032, and Archbishop Toolen's committee would add $124,488, for a total of $949,520. By this time, the OEO wanted participants as well as teachers to be more integrated. Reviewing the proposal for the year-round program, federal officials noticed that twelve of the fourteen centers were located in black areas and were considered black facilities. "Recruitment for this project was aimed primarily at the Negro communities with little effort put forth by way of personal contact with poor white families," a member of the OEO's Inspection Division reported. To remedy this problem, the Atlanta

regional office contacted Nunan and asked him to document "efforts to secure proper sites which would facilitate involving the poor whites." Nunan
was skeptical about being able to meet the OEO's demands but agreed to try so
that federal funds would not be cut off. To insure that he would make every
effort to integrate the project, the grant had a special rider attached giving him
ten days before the start of the program to meet the requirements.[53]

Using all available resources, Nunan and Kaffer organized just over 100 volunteers to canvass poor white neighborhoods in the three counties to recruit
participants for the Head Start program. The volunteers were Spring Hill College ROTC students and members of the Christian Family Movement (a Catholic organization of married couples who came together to offer support to
each other). Kaffer's husband was an English professor at Spring Hill College, so she had access to the ROTC building there, which served as her headquarters. Equipped with maps dividing the three-county area into regions, the
volunteers worked from September 30 through October 2, contacting forty-
four white churches and 1,002 people. Kaffer had written a questionnaire and
handout, "Let's Go to Head Start," that explained the program so that white
families could make an informed decision about participating in the program.
As a result of the canvass, 113 additional white children registered for Head
Start, increasing the total white enrollment to 140. Even this tepid response received favorable recognition from OEO officials. "Although there was not complete acceptance and cooperation on the part of the white ministers," an OEO
inspector wrote, "neither was there complete rejection[;] thus an avenue for
continued discussions and negotiations has been opened in this three county
area which could result in a very decided improvement in future Head Start
programs in this area."[54]

The day after the survey had been completed, Nunan sent in the hard evidence of the volunteers' work. On October 4 the regional OEO office received
1,307 survey forms completed by the 104 workers from Mobile. "I trust that
this gigantic effort and—what I feel—reasonably good results will enable you
to get immediate approval for the Mobile Head Start Program," the Catholic
Charities director wrote to Al Krumlauf in Atlanta. The regional officials were
highly impressed with the work of the ABTAPC. "Father Nunan has proven, I
believe, beyond the shadow of a doubt," Krumlauf reported to his Washington
counterparts in the Inspection Division, "that if the community is properly
informed they will for the most part react favorably." Edgar May, the OEO inspector general, sent Nunan's report to the CAP director, boasting about the
antipoverty agency's success in pushing integration further in the South. "The

attached report indicates there is merit in being tough and that preconceived ideas about recruiting whites in the South in poverty programs may be just that—preconceived." The Inspection Division memo went all the way up the chain of command in the Washington OEO office. In addition to surprising the federal officials, the results amazed Nunan. The ABTAPC's work put the Mobile priest in a favorable light with the national and regional OEO offices. His intentions were no longer in question, and his willingness to accomplish difficult projects would serve him well in the future. The OEO approved the full-year Head Start grant in late October, and again the governor did not veto it.[55]

For the next four years the ABTAPC operated the only fully integrated public education program in the Mobile area. The project's administration rested in the hands of talented black and white personnel in the central office and in each center. The assistant director of Head Start oversaw the placement of all personnel. A college degree was not required, so Frankie Briggs looked for people who had "the ability to learn, the desire to work with children, and [the] need of a job." The majority of the staff came from the target communities, although people who had experience and were not poor also received positions. Yvonne King, Head Start's director of social services, remembered that white teachers worked in predominantly black centers and black teachers served in predominantly white centers. Titles of respect were used: "Everybody had to be [called] Mr., Mrs., or Miss." She thought the integrated faculty exposed everyone to the fact that "there were other people in the world who were different from them and they had to get along with them." Each Head Start center operated autonomously, with the directors determining for themselves, within the guidelines of good teaching, what was needed. Children were fed breakfast, a robust lunch, and a hearty snack before going home in the afternoon. In addition to providing the necessary food for healthy young girls and boys, the nutrition program inculcated good eating habits. Each child also received a physical examination, including urine and blood tests and immunizations. The children also visited a dentist, who cleaned their teeth, took X rays, and administered fluoride treatments. The ABTAPC contracted with local physicians and clinics to conduct these exams. For some students, this was their first opportunity to see a doctor.[56]

In addition to the educational and health aspects of Project Head Start, each center also supported a parent program that encouraged parents to adopt approaches and techniques taught in the Head Start Program in an effort to continue the improvement of their children's future. Each center held bimonthly meetings, and by July 1967 6,915 parents had volunteered in the program. To get parents interested, Zemula Woods, the director of the parents and volunteers program, hosted bingo parties at which turkeys, cases of Coca-Cola, and glassware were given away as prizes. Once parents understood the scope of what was being offered to their families, their involvement increased. Some parent committees advised the operations of their Head Start centers and assisted in hiring decisions. Parent groups also sold barbeque dinners to raise money so that children would have pocket change during field trips. After 1969 the ABTAPC began publishing "The Cultivator: A Newsletter Published for Head Start Parents" that passed on information about each center as well as health tips, ways to make free toys for children, ways to incorporate science into children's lives through everyday observations, and ways to encourage parents to volunteer. In May 1970 an evaluation team came to investigate the ABTAPC's ability to include parents. "Before leaving," a Head Start employee revealed, "the Evaluators reported that they were impressed and pleased with not only the interviews but with the amount of Parent Involvement in the program." King's social-services program worked in conjunction with the parent program, offering assistance to families who were in need of more help than the Head Start program provided. King developed a children's clothing bank and helped families learn about other federal benefits, such as Aid to Families with Dependent Children and food stamp and federal housing programs.[57]

The ABTAPC also improved the skills of its teaching staff. In-service training became a regular part of the experience of being a Head Start teacher or aide. Beginning in 1968, the ABTAPC offered post-secondary-school training for Head Start teachers, teacher's aides, counselors, and other staff personnel through the Human Relations Center of Spring Hill College, operated by sociology professor Father Albert S. Foley, S.J. The Head Start Supplementary Staff Training Program offered courses to obtain a child-development-associate credential. Students received credit for demonstrating teaching competencies in the seven major areas needed for managing a Head Start classroom. Spring Hill College personnel also supervised, coached, tutored, evaluated, and assessed services in the Head Start Centers where the candidates who sought the credentials worked. By the fall of 1970, Mobile Head Start staff members traveled across the state to train other people in managing the early-childhood-development program, and Woods became a Head Start training officer for the state, operating through the University of South Alabama.[58]

The Project Head Start sponsored by the ABTAPC did more than enhance the educational opportunities of the children who attended classes. It also connected parents to the program's teachers and other staff members. "I think a lot of children and families experienced a quality of life that they never would have had, had it not been for Head Start," Woods later said. The parents program reached out to thousands who had been isolated from available resources and connected them to a wider range of people and organizations. The ABTAPC took seriously the mandate to utilize the maximum feasible participation of the residents served by the program. The parent program was an example of that effort. Kaffer described it as "a totally parent-driven thing, to the degree possible." She remembered that many of the parents "displayed tremendous nobility" and were "willing to sacrifice for their children." In her contacts with parents whose children had enrolled in the program, Woods gained a renewed respect for the families and the circumstances in which some of them lived. Quite often, she was invited into their homes. After meeting with one woman in a shotgun house out in rural Washington County, she recalled that "this was one of the most poverty-stricken areas that I have ever seen in my life." Woods made the visit to obtain information on the family as well as to recruit the mother to volunteer in the Head Start program. "I don't know if I can really explain how I felt about being there," Woods later said. "There was compassion and then there was guilt, and I was just impressed with how kind she could be." Any time a job opened in a Head Start center, administrators considered people from the target communities for the position, recruiting teacher's aides and, when possible, teachers. "We certainly were able to give employment to a lot of young, black, well-educated people who couldn't get jobs anywhere else, other than menial labor," Kaffer explained. Opportunities for employment were also available on the maintenance and cooking staffs. Although the fringe benefits were limited, in many instances these were good, decent jobs, and the supplemental training program promised a future that had not been available to people living below the poverty line.[59]

This Head Start program also offered a concrete example of what was possible in a city that had not fully embraced the idea of racial equality. "It created another integrated element in the community," Weise thought, "and it involved a lot of people who might not have otherwise been involved, because there was tremendous publicity." Not only were the classrooms desegregated, but the faculty and office personnel were also made up of black and white people who held authority in making this a program that would meet the needs of the impoverished community on several levels. So, even though the ABTAPC Head Start program did not feed directly into the grassroots civil rights movement that began to form in Mobile after 1968, it did incorporate black and white children and their parents into programs into which they had never before been included on a day-to-day basis. This was rare in Mobile at the end of the 1960s, and it contributed to the atmosphere that the city was on the road to change.[60]

Seeking New Venues for Change, 1967–1970

The experience of the ABTAPC Head Start program prompted Rev. Nunan to look for ways to broaden his role in the community in an effort to extend the War on Poverty beyond the scope of the ABTAPC. The members of the Catholic Charities office associated with the antipoverty program (Nunan, Weise, and the Trinitarian sisters who administered the office), as well as the priests, nuns, and brothers who supported Head Start centers in parishes across the diocese, had established themselves as public allies in the struggle for equality, which eventually gave the Catholic Church greater credibility in the black community.

After Governor Wallace vetoed the MACAC grant application in June 1966, the organization continued to make plans to be the CAA for the area, officially incorporating in late July and voting for officers in early August. In a fourteen-to-seven vote, the board elected Rev. Nunan as its chair and gave him the duty of contacting the OEO regional office and the state's antipoverty officials to reinstate the original application for a planning grant. Unbeknown to him, he had an ally within the governor's office who tried to convince Wallace's aides to leave the Mobile CAA alone. The bureaucrat suggested that if Shriver overrode the veto, the state would "have no control over any of the Mobile projects." Trying to make the governor's office see the MACAC in a new light, he pointed out that "You must consider that with the addition of mayors, over 70% of the Mobile board will be white thereby guaranteeing some degree of control." He added, "No other CAP board in the state will approach this proportion." Remembering the boost Wallace received for vetoing the antipoverty programs in Lowndes and Wilcox Counties, the state official reminded the governor's assistants, "Politically you are gaining as a result of the Lowndes and Wilcox publicity, but is there any gain to be made here? I think not." After claiming that Wallace's support of the MACAC might "open the door for future cooperation which has not been available with OEO before," this administrator closed his memo by stating that if the governor rejected the second MACAC proposal, it would "be a complete and total mistake on your part." The governor's aides turned a deaf ear to these arguments because race was not the only issue in Mobile. There were white officials on the board of the antipoverty agency who were not the governor's allies, and even though his wife had made it past the primaries, the governor wanted to take every opportunity to make sure she won the general election. On September 13, 1966, Wallace for the second time disapproved the Mobile CAA's grant proposal. Shriver now had the capacity to override the governor's actions because Congress had altered the Economic Opportunity Act, in part because of Wallace's heavy-handed tactics. After the fall elections, Shriver overrode the Wallace veto. In late November, without fanfare or publicity, the MACAC planning grant finally received federal approval.[61]

Although Nunan had a good understanding of community action through his connections with the ABTAPC's successful Head Start program, the building-block approach the OEO had envisioned as a by-product of single-purpose agencies did not materialize in Mobile. The MACAC was not an outgrowth of the ABTAPC. The two groups were separate. Most of the people who served on the MACAC's racially integrated board came from public agencies, held elected office, or participated in existing community groups. Although members of the targeted communities sat on the MACAC board, officers and executive committee members made most of the decisions, and most of the representatives of the poor on the executive committee were ministers. As a result, most people involved in the MACAC did not have experience with the notion of participatory democracy that CAP had intended to foster. Greater participation could have been developed in the Mobile CAA if the executive director had made that a priority, but that did not happen.

The personnel committee received forty applications for the executive director position and chose Norman H. Davis for the job. A veteran of World War II, Davis returned to civilian life and worked as a county agent for the Agriculture Extension Service in Louisiana and then represented Cargill as a district marketing manager in the Mobile area. While the skills Davis brought to his new job made him a good bureaucrat, he did not inspire others or develop creative programs to fight poverty. The assistant program director and second assistant to the director were cut from similar cloth. Andrew J. Curtis had worked in the equal-opportunity program at Mobile's Brookley Field Air Force Base before it closed, and James McPherson came to his position after working on Senator John Sparkman's staff in Washington, D.C. All three men understood what it meant to work within large governmental agencies based on a top-down management style. Unfortunately, that was not what CAP was all about, and the MACAC would suffer as a result.[62]

Besides the shortcomings of the paid staff of the Mobile CAA, some of the black members of the board of directors had lost some credibility among the poorer sections of the African American community. With the passage of the Civil Rights Act and the Voting Rights Act, class conflicts that had been submerged in the African American community now surfaced. The traditional power brokers who had spoken on behalf of black Mobile now seemed out of step with the times. In February 1966 Mayor Langan appointed John L. LeFlore to the five-member Mobile Housing Board. The caseworker for the Non-Partisan Voters League became the first African American in recent history to serve at this level in city government. In tapping LeFlore for the position, Langan said, "Negroes now occupy some two-thirds of the units under the supervision of the Mobile Housing Board, and in the past they have found it difficult to communicate their problems with the board." LeFlore quickly found out that holding this position made it more difficult for him to speak as the leader of Mobile's black community. At a late February meeting of the Non-Partisan Voters League, he discouraged people from organizing public demonstrations against the board of school commissioners and the housing authority. One community activist, Dorothy Williams, disagreed. "We have gone to the school board and gone to the school board since 1954," she said, "and we've got only 39 or 40 children in the white schools." LeFlore, who had been instrumental in filing the *Birdie Mae Davis* case in 1963, argued that demonstrations against the school board would not solve the school problem. When the first demonstrators took to the streets in early April, protesting the cost of public housing and the slow progress of school integration, the housing commissioner said that as member of the housing authority, he could not participate in "any march or demonstration aimed at the housing board."[63]

LeFlore was not the only traditional black leader feeling the heat. C. H. Montgomery, a barber who had been the leader of the local NAACP branch when it reorganized in 1964, ran for one of the ten state representative positions from Mobile County, using "Remember It's Only One Out of Ten" as his campaign slogan. He knew he could not win without gaining white votes and thought his message conveyed the nonthreatening spirit he needed to get elected. Instead, his message signaled to the black community that he was not willing to stand out as a strong independent voice for his constituents. Unfortunately for him, this was the first election since the passage of the Voting Rights Act, and the shouts of "black power" had been rising across the state from the grassroots of the Black Belt. Montgomery's strategy cost him the respect of African American voters who saw this not as a time for compromise but as a time to embrace the political power for which they had worked so hard. During the demonstration against the school board and housing authority, Williams explained to the *Southern Courier* that "the march was aimed partly at these [black] leaders because they are, in her opinion, 'blocking progress here to some extent.' "[64]

In this atmosphere, the MACAC struggled for legitimacy. Its paid staff did not understand the nuances of community action, and some of its black board members could no longer claim the mantel of leadership they had maintained for so long. The ABTAPC had been doing a good job with its poverty programs, but it was not the MACAC. The original planning grant called for the Mobile CAA to use the OEO's building-block approach to develop new programs and attach the ABTAPC Head Start project to the MACAC as a delegate agency, giving Catholic Charities autonomy to continue running its own programs. Over time, MACAC staff scrambled to create poverty-fighting projects. The CAA proposed neighborhood referral centers as well as a legal services program, but neither project got started right away.

In May 1967 Davis suggested that the Neighborhood Youth Corps, sponsored by the ABTAPC and funded through the Department of Labor, should now be run by the MACAC. However, there was not enough time for the CAA to complete the paperwork to take over this program before the summer. In a board meeting, Mayor Langan suggested that he "would like to see MACAC develop several other programs—and get as many started as possible in this area" instead of absorbing those already in operation. This suggestion put Davis on the defensive. In the June MACAC board elections, Nunan's tenure as chairman ended; he was replaced by William B. Crane, although Nunan remained on the executive committee. By the fall, Davis initiated steps to expropriate the Head Start project, and a bitter power struggle ensued for the next two years between the MACAC and the ABTAPC. By November 1968 the issue was finally resolved, but not without damage to Mobile's CAA. Nunan was able to protect the Head Start program because it had earned the respect of OEO officials in Washington and Atlanta, and the MACAC seemed to be floundering in contrast. In a handwritten note, an MACAC official wrote, we "must turn Head Start over to the Toolen committee in order to save the Agency. . . . Atlanta has run out of excuses for MACAC—must now face facts. . . . Compliance with OEO (Washington) desires concerning [Head Start] will certainly be in our favor at this time." The fear of another organization replacing the MACAC as the county's CAA ultimately led the agency to loosen its grip on Head Start.[65]

That "other organization" referenced in the handwritten note was the Interfaith Committee for Human Concern organized by Nunan in the summer of 1968. After Martin Luther King Jr.'s assassination in April 1968, a grass-roots civil rights organization took hold in Mobile, especially in the city's poorer communities. The Neighborhood Organized Workers (NOW) spoke out against the city commissioners and demanded equal rights, better school integration, and job opportunities for black Mobilians. As it became clear to Nunan that the MACAC could not address the needs of the area's poor citizens, the director of Catholic Charities formulated the interfaith committee in hopes of developing programs that he thought were needed for the city's impoverished citizens. Working in three inner-city poor neighborhoods, the interfaith committee strove to create recreation, education, employment, and voter-registration projects. Although the organization was an ecumenical group with a board of directors that included Catholics, Protestants, and Jews, the funds for the group came exclusively from Archbishop Toolen and donations from Mobile's Catholic parishes. The interfaith committee's programs basically involved community organizing and operated with one director, Samuel Jackson, an African American and former juvenile officer for the Washington, D.C., Police Department, and forty field workers who were college students and seminarians.[66]

For the next year, the Interfaith Committee for Human Concern worked at the grassroots level, seeking ways to improve the lives of the people living in the Congress Street area, Mobile Terrace, and the Down the Bay area. At the same time, NOW held twice weekly mass meetings to bring changes in Mobile's schools, hiring practices, and election outcomes. The Josephite priests and Dominican sisters working at the Most Pure Heart of Mary Parish on Davis Avenue forged connections between the two groups. NOW held its Wednesday-night meetings there, and Sister Lorraine of the parish operated the tutorial program and study hall for the interfaith committee. The two groups also constructed more direct links. At an interracial forum sponsored by the University of South Alabama, Jackson spoke at the gathering as an alternate for NOW President Nobel Beasley. Jackson explained NOW's role in organizing groups to teach the poor what opportunities were available to them. Nunan was not a NOW leader, but he attended meetings and was aware of the organization's complaints. He was not alone. Many priests, nuns, and brothers allied with NOW and joined demonstrations, with some getting arrested in the process.[67]

By 1969 Mobile was in the throes of a direct-action civil rights campaign that caused great upheaval through the early 1970s. The MACAC stayed aloof from these issues until the board fired Davis in March 1969. The Mobile CAA stopped trying to take over the Head Start Program operated by the ABTAPC and developed its own poverty-fighting projects, such as distributing surplus commodities, sponsoring two hundred boys to attend Boy Scout camp, and operating neighborhood multiservice centers. While the CAA did not become the center of creative programs for the city's impoverished, by 1970 it did begin to work as an advocate for the poor. One MACAC community worker began organizing women on welfare after she assisted them in getting checks that had been stolen from a postal carrier's mail bag. The CAA's priorities for 1970 included developing "leadership abilities among Target Area residents so that these neighborhood groups can effectively solve community problems that are chosen by the neighborhood residents as being the highest priority."[68]

Early 1969 also brought a change in personnel at the Catholic Charities office. In late February Rev. Nunan announced his request for permission to leave the priesthood. In a prepared statement, he said his decision arose "fundamentally from my inability to fulfill what I consider to be my priestly duties within the existing framework of the priesthood." The dynamic priest left Mobile on April 1 after fifteen years of service. On later reflection, Nunan found that several things came together to prompt his decision to leave. First, Pope Paul VI issued *Humanea Vitae* in 1968, condemning the use of artificial birth control, including the birth control pill. Many people within the Church criticized the pope's actions as being out of step with the approach of the Second Vatican Council since he did not act collegially with the bishops in issuing his encyclical. This edict had stunned Nunan, who even wrote to the Vatican expressing this anger. He hoped that the Church would have put more stock in what he called "the sense of the faithful" instead of moving back to its more familiar hierarchal ways. He also resigned because even though the Catholic Church in Mobile "was the most active in the area of civil rights," he held "some disappointment . . . as to how far this Church of mine [was] able to go in all of those areas." Finally, he said that after working very hard for fifteen years, he was ready to "move on to some other environment." The Mobile Catholic Church was in for more change that year as the eighty-three-year-old Archbishop Toolen stepped down from his office, retiring in October.[69]

NOW also lost ground after the FBI arrested two of its leaders on extortion charges in the early 1970s. The organization's demonstrations had a lasting effect on the city, however, despite these leadership problems. NOW participated in a "no vote" campaign that led to Langan's defeat in the 1969 elections. His earlier actions as a racial moderate and later his support of traditional black leaders such as LeFlore and Montgomery had angered the leaders of the insurgent civil rights group. They targeted Langan's moderation as a roadblock to progress. The school protests NOW sponsored brought the problem of representation on the board of school commissioners to the attention of NAACP Legal Defense Fund attorneys who had been working on the *Birdie Mae Davis* case. In the late 1970s the NAACP filed a voting-rights case that went to the federal district court seeking to change the at-large elections of the city and county commission as well as the board of school commissioners.[70]

The Head Start program sponsored by the ABTAPC eventually became a part of the MACAC, and it operates in Mobile today. By 1970 President Johnson's War on Poverty clearly had not attacked all of the problems associated with poverty in Alabama's second-largest city. Nevertheless, Project Head Start did provide a concrete example of what was possible in a city unwilling to accept racial equality in the classroom. The antipoverty effort also led members of the Catholic Church to seek additional ways to assist Mobile's poor. "The stimulus was there," Nunan explained, "it did provide a new way to resolve continuing problems and actually even some problems that we hadn't addressed. . . . It just opened eyes. It sure as heck opened my eyes." When NOW formed, the public support of priests, nuns, and brothers also aided this insurgent movement.[71]

The original plans for community action put forth by the OEO could not overcome all of the problems associated with a city that was struggling to come to terms with its Jim Crow past. Instead of walking away from the quagmire, the OEO searched for a way to be involved, finding it in the ABTAPC. The federal antipoverty agency's commitment to fighting poverty and racial discrimination created a space for those people who were looking for ways to make changes in the social mores of Alabama's port city. The conflicts that followed in the wake of this federal support help us to understand how the South began to reconcile its racist past. In that regard, the War on Poverty in Mobile offered more than a head start to its citizens by playing a role in implementing landmark federal civil rights laws and creating new possibilities for many of its citizens.

Notes

1. Martha McKay to Haddad, April 15, 1965, CAP Office Records of the Director, State Files, 1965–69, box 1, record 381, Office of Economic Opportunity Papers, National Archives II, College Park, Md. (hereafter, OEO Papers). McKay reported that Mobile was 40 percent Baptist, 38 percent Catholic.

2. Peter Kihss, "Report on the South: The Integration Issue," *New York Times*, March 13, 1956; David R. Underhill, "Peacekeepers in Mobile," *Southern Courier*, October 3–4, 1965; "Education in Mobile Diocese: Marked Growth in Ten Years, Especially in the Number of Negro Schools," *Catholic Week*, December 13, 1946; Gretta Palmer, "Southern Catholics Fight Race Hatred: Three and a Half Million Dollars in Catholic Funds Have Been Spent in Alabama for the Negro," *Look*, March 29, 1950, 99–103; Charles V. Willie and Susan L. Greenblatt, *Community Politics and Educational Change: Ten School Systems under Court Order* (New York: Longman Press, 1981), 174–75; Joseph N. Langan, interview by author, Mobile, Ala., July 28, 1998; Patsy Busby Dow, "Joseph N. Langan: Mobile's Racial Diplomat" (master's thesis, University of South Alabama, 1993), 10, 13–15, 24, 26, 29, 31, 41–45.

3. Langan, interview; Dow, "Joseph N. Langan," 45; Willie and Greenblatt, *Community Politics*, 178–79, 183–85, 193–94, 203–4. The initial complaint in *Birdie Mae Davis et al. v. Board of School Commissioners of Mobile County* was filed on behalf of twenty students, including Birdie Mae Davis and Henry Hobdy, on March 27, 1963. In 1971 the case was consolidated with the *Swann v. Charlotte-Mecklenburg Board of Education* and the *McDaniel v. Barresi* cases in the U.S. Supreme Court. The last case associated with the original lawsuit was finally resolved in 1990 (*Davis v. Carl* 906 F. 2d 533 [11th Cir. 1990]). See also Forrest W. Harrison to C. H. Burns, with attachments, "Mobile Public Schools: Enrollment by Race, 1963–64, 1964–65, 1965–66, 1966–67," September 15, 1965, Governor's Legal Advisors' Files, School Files D–W (counties), box sg 20061, Alabama Department of Archives and History, Montgomery (hereafter, adah); David R. Underhill, "Joseph Langan Says and Does Whatever He Believes Is Right," *Southern Courier*, October 3–4, 1965. Evidence of the slow pace of integration in the city and the county of Mobile can be seen in the figures for black students attending formerly all-white schools: 1963–64: 2; 1964–65: 7; 1965–66: 40; 1966–67: 155.

4. Charles R. Morris, *American Catholic: The Saints and Sinners Who Built America's Most Powerful Church* (New York: Vintage Books, 1997), 323–24; Xavier Rynne, *Vatican Council II* (1968; Maryknoll, N.Y.: Orbis Books, 1999), 31; Michael J. Walsh, "The History of the Council," in *Modern Catholicism: Vatican II and After*, ed. Adrian Hastings (New York: Oxford University Press, 1991), 39–41; Austin Flannery, ed., *The Basic Sixteen Documents: Vatican Council II Constitutions, Decrees, Declarations* (Northport, N.Y.: Costello, 1996), 191–92, 194.

5. T. J. Toolen to "Dear Father," February 16, 1964, Archbishop Thomas J. Toolen Papers, Chancery Archives, the Archdiocese of Mobile, Mobile, Ala.; Toolen to "My Dearly Beloved Priest and People," November 22, 1966, Toolen Papers; Tom Stransky, "Paulist 'Ecumenism' (Unitatis Redintegratio)," and John McDade, "Catholic Theology in the Post-Conciliar Period," in *Modern Catholicism*, ed. Hastings, 113–17, 422; Thomas Nunan, interview by author, Alexandria, Va., September 24, 1998; James Hennesey, *American Catholics: A History of the Roman Catholic Community*

in the United States (New York: Oxford University Press, 1981), 314–15; Thomas Bokenkotter, *A Concise History of the Catholic Church* (New York: Image Books Doubleday, 1990), 368–70; "Diocese Plans a Priests' Senate," *Birmingham Post Herald*, February 10, 1968. The Constitution of the Sacred Liturgy became effective on February 16, 1964.

6. "Report of the Special Investigating Committee," [ca. 1968], reel 13, ser. 4, folder 63, "MACAC Progress 1968," Non-Partisan Voters League Papers, University of South Alabama Archives, Mobile (hereafter, NPVL Papers).

7. Nunan, interview; Toolen to "My Dearly Beloved Priests and People," April 22, 1964, Toolen Papers; "Archbishop's Letter on Integration of Schools," *Catholic Week*, April 24, 1964.

8. "Poverty and Urban Policy: Conference Transcript of 1973 Group Discussion of the Kennedy Administration Urban Poverty Programs and Policies," 231–32, 247–49, 254, 258, John F. Kennedy Library, Boston; William B. Cannon, interview, May 21, 1982, 24–25, Lyndon B. Johnson Library, Austin, Tex.; Bruce J. Schulman, *Lyndon B. Johnson and American Liberalism: A Brief Biography with Documents* (Boston: Bedford Books of St. Martin's Press, 1995), 183; Susan Youngblood Ashmore, "Carry It On: The War on Poverty and the Civil Rights Movement in Alabama, 1964–1970" (Ph.D. diss., Auburn University, 1999). Ashmore offers a more thorough discussion of the links between the Economic Opportunity Act and the South's racial politics.

9. Daniel Knapp and Kenneth Polk, *Scouting the War on Poverty: Social Reform Politics in the Kennedy Administration* (Lexington, Mass.: D. C. Heath, 1971), 138; Daniel Patrick Moynihan, *Maximum Feasible Misunderstanding: Community Action in the War on Poverty* (New York: Free Press, 1969), 86–87; OEO Reference Guide, [ca. late 1966 for FY 1967], box 6, Records Regarding the President's Task Force in the War against Poverty, OEO Papers; Administrative History—OEO, 2:297–98, box 106B, Records of the Office of Planning, Research, and Evaluation, OEO Papers (hereafter, OEO Admin. History); William F. Haddad, "Mr. Shriver and the Savage Politics of Poverty," *Harper's*, December 1965, 44.

10. *Congressional Record*, July 23, 1964, 16705.

11. Ibid., July 23, 1964, 16727, 16741, 16768, 16790; R. Sargent Shriver, interview, tape 2, 76–77, LBJ Library; *Congressional Record*, August 6, 1964, 18325. Congress removed the governor's veto from the Economic Opportunity Act in 1965, allowing the OEO director to override a governor's veto after thirty days, in part because of Wallace's actions.

12. U.S. Commission on Civil Rights, "Civil Rights under Federal Programs: The Civil Rights Act of 1964: An Analysis of Title VI," January 1965, Alabama Governors' Papers, 1963–79 (Wallace, Wallace, Brewer, Wallace), Administrative Files, box SG 22384, ADAH; OEO Admin. History, 1:57, 2:34, 141.

13. Pollack to Shriver, February 22, 1965, box 1, Inspection Reports Evaluating CAP,

OEO Papers. Dave Marlin was the Department of Justice official who sent Pollack this information.

14. William P. Kelly, interview, tape 2, April 11, 1969, 38–39, LBJ Library; Bertrand Harding, interview, tape 1, November 20, 1968, 15–16, LBJ Library; Michael L. Gillette, *Launching the War on Poverty: An Oral History* (New York: Twayne, 1996), 249–51; VISTA Press Conference, Sargent Shriver's remarks, September 27, 1965, box 1, Program Records of the Assistant Director for Civil Rights, OEO Papers; "The Quiet Revolution: 2nd Annual Report OEO," 1966, 124–25, box 210, White House Aides Files—Gaither, LBJ Library; "The Tide of Progress: 3rd Annual Report OEO," FY 1967, 113, box 239, White House Aides Files—Gaither, LBJ Library.

15. Edgar May, interview, 23–24, LBJ Library; Gillette, *Launching*, 189; "Poverty Bill Seeks to Coordinate Varied Programs," *Congressional Quarterly Fact Sheet on the Anti-Poverty Program*, August 7, 1964, box A 331, group 3, National Association for the Advancement of Colored People Papers, Manuscript Division, Library of Congress; Stephen J. Pollack, interview, tape 2, January 29, 1969, 12–13, LBJ Library; Haddad, "Mr. Shriver," 49; "Ladders of Opportunity," June 5, 1967, box 210, White House Aides Files—Gaither, LBJ Library.

16. John F. Collins to mayors and managers, March 16, 1964, Langan to John Sparkman, August 21, 1964, box RG7,S.3,B.10, Joseph Langan Papers, Mobile Municipal Archives, Mobile, Ala.; Jack Conway to "Dear Sir," August 12 1964, box RG7,S.3,B.13, Langan Papers; Langan to Robert F. Adams Sr., August 20, 1964, Langan, form letter, August 29, 1964, Langan to Shriver, September 4, 1964, RG7,S.3,B.10, Langan Papers; Langan, interview.

17. Underhill, "Joseph Langan"; Dow, "Joseph N. Langan," 4, 10, 13–15, 19–26, 29–32.

18. Mary Grice to Fred Hayes, March 17, 1965, box 1, Inspection Reports Evaluating CAP, OEO Papers.

19. Dow, "Joseph N. Langan," 19, 37–38; Clifton Dale Foster, Tracey J. Berezansky, and E. Frank Roberts, "Guide to the Mobile Municipal Archives," Mobile Municipal Archives, Mobile, Ala.; David E. Alsobrook, "Alabama's Port City: Mobile during the Progressive Era, 1896–1917" (Ph.D. diss., Auburn University, 1983); McKay to Haddad, "Report on Mobile, Alabama"; McKay to Haddad, "Preliminary Report on Mobile, Alabama," [ca. April 1965], box 1, CAP Office Records of the Director, State Files, 1965–68, OEO Papers.

20. Resolution 03-018, January 12, 1965, resolution 03-058, January 26, 1965, RG7.S.3, B.10, Langan Papers; Haddad to Berry, March 30, 1965, McKay to Haddad, "Members of Mayor Trimmier's Committee—Mobile, Al," April 19, 1965, box 1, CAP Office Records of the Director, State Files 1965–68, OEO Papers; Charles S. Trimmier, "Review of the Mobile Area Economic Opportunity Commission and Committee," [ca. July 1965], reel 15, ser. 4, folder 177A, NPVL Papers.

21. Claude Kirk to Wallace, December 21, 1964, February 17, 1965, Wallace to Rex Roach, December 22, 1964, Wallace to Shriver, April 9, 1965 Alabama Governors'

Papers, box SG 22390, ADAH; Frederick O'R. Hayes to Berry, March 31, 1965, box 1, CAP Office Records of the Director, State Files, 1965–68, OEO Papers.

22. "Assessment of the Anti-Poverty Situation in Alabama," April 6, 1965, box 1, CAP Office Records of the Director, State Files, 1965–68, OEO Papers; Marvin Watson to Bill Moyers, "Memo from Buford Ellington, Poverty Program in Alabama," June 7, 1965, box 56, White House Aides Files—Moyers, LBJ Library.

23. Nunan to Susie West, November 24, 1964, "Archbishop Hosts Poverty Meeting," October 22, 1964, Alabama Governors' Papers, box SG 22390, ADAH; Nunan, interview.

24. "Archbishop Hosts Poverty Meeting."

25. Toolen to Langan, October 27, 1964, David Sullivan to Langan, November 7, 1964, RG7.S.,B.10, Langan Papers; Nunan, interview. To understand Toolen's reticence, it is helpful to know the environment of Alabama when he arrived as bishop. In 1921, a Catholic priest had been shot on the porch of his rectory in Birmingham by a man who supported the Ku Klux Klan and the True Americans. The murderer was not convicted. Throughout his tenure as archbishop, Toolen built many facilities for African Americans that otherwise would not have been erected. Nevertheless, he was not one to support equality between the races and did not change his position as the civil rights movement roared through Alabama in the 1960s. See Paul M. Pruitt Jr., "The Killing of Father Coyle: Private Tragedy, Public Shame," *Alabama Heritage* 30 (fall 1993): 24–25; Glenn Feldman, *Politics, Society, and the Klan in Alabama, 1915–1949* (Tuscaloosa: University of Alabama Press, 1999). Feldman provides a thorough discussion of anti-Catholic violence in 1920s Alabama.

26. R. Sargent Shriver, interview, tape 4, 27–28, Theodore M. Berry, interview, tape 1, 24, Jule M. Sugarman, interview, tape 1, 24, Edgar S. and Jean Camper Cahn, interview, tape 1, 25, LBJ Library.

27. "A Nation Aroused," 1965, 31–32, box 14, White House Aides Files—McPherson, LBJ Library; Sugarman, interview, tape 1, 21; OEO Admin. History, 1:232, 236.

28. James T. Patterson, *Grand Expectations: The United States, 1945–1974* (New York: Oxford University Press, 1996), 570; Numan V. Bartley, *The New South, 1945–1980: The Story of the South's Modernization* (Baton Rouge: Louisiana State University Press, 1995), 369–70; Grady Poulard to Maurice Dawkins, May 13, 1967, box 7, Program Records of the Assistant Director for Civil Rights, OEO Papers; Shriver, interview, tape 4, 50–51.

29. "Project Head Start Supplemental Nondiscrimination Conditions," ser. 7, box A 370, Herman Talmadge Collection Senatorial Papers, Richard B. Russell Library for Political Research and Studies, University of Georgia Libraries, Athens; Gillette, *Launching*, 290; OEO Admin. History, 2:16, 23; Don Petit to Haddad, June 15, 1965, box 52, White House Aides Files—Moyers, LBJ Library.

30. Donald M. Baker, interview, tape 2, 12–13, LBJ Library; OEO Admin. History, 2:33, 38–39; Pollack, interview, tape 2, 27; Steven Lowenstein to the coordinators,

"Employment Discrimination in OEO Funded Programs," June 20, 1966, box 34B, Records of the Office of the Director, Records Relating to the Administration of the Civil Rights Program in the Regions, OEO Papers. Title VI of the Civil Rights Act of 1964 prohibits discrimination on the basis of race, color, or national origin in programs and activities receiving federal financial assistance. If discrimination is found and compliance is not achieved, the federal agency providing the assistance must begin the procedure to terminate the funds or refer the matter to the Department of Justice for further legal action ("Overview of Title VI of the Civil Rights Act of 1964," 42 U.S.C. sec. 2000d et seq.).

31. Baker, interview, tape 1, 15–16.

32. "Assessment of the Anti-Poverty Situation."

33. Sugarman, interview, tape 1, 16.

34. Jack C. Gallalee to Lister Hill, October 4, 1965, Lister Hill Papers, W. S. Hoole Special Collections, University of Alabama Libraries, Tuscaloosa.

35. Alabama Council on Human Relations, "A Special Report," July 13, 1965, Haddad to Shriver, August 20, 1965, box 87, Inspection Division Inspection Reports, OEO Papers.

36. Alabama Council on Human Relations, "A Special Report," July 13, 1965, Haddad to Shriver, August 20, 1965, box 87, Inspection Division Inspection Reports, OEO Papers; "OEO Insists on Mobile Integration," *Montgomery Advertiser,* July 30, 1965; John F. Hussey, "Head Start Funds Periled in Mobile," *Birmingham Post Herald,* July 30, 1965; "Negro Teachers in Middle: Reasons for OEO Holdup Told in Head Start Plan," *Mobile Press,* September 25, 1965. When the Hamilton School center closed, its nine white teachers refused to teach at other centers. See David R. Underhill, "Mobile Finally Gets Its Head Start Money," *Southern Courier,* November 13–14, 1965.

37. Heller to Burns, July 8, 1965, Burns to Heller, July 9, 1965, Governor's Legal Advisors' Files, School Files D–W (counties), box SG 20061, ADAH.

38. Heller to Burns, July 29, 1965, C. L. Scarborough to Heller, July 29, 1965, Scarborough to Burns, August 2, 1965, Governor's Legal Advisors' Files, School Files D–W (counties), box SG 20061, ADAH; Gallalee to Hill, October 4, 1965, Hill Papers; David R. Underhill, "Still No Payment for Mobile's Head Start," *Southern Courier,* October 3–4, 1965; David R. Underhill, "U.S. Pays Head Start," *Southern Courier,* October 9–10, 1965; David R. Underhill, "Mobile Gets U.S. Money," *Southern Courier,* October 23–24, 1965.

39. Burns to Shriver, September 23, 1965, Governor's Legal Advisors' Files, School Files D–W (counties), box SG 20061, ADAH; "Mobile's Lesson," *Southern Courier,* October 9–10, 1965.

40. Nunan, interview; Toolen to "My Dearly Beloved Priests and People," April 22, 1964, Toolen Papers; "Archbishop's Letter on Integration of Schools"; Francis J. Wade, "A Time to Love," *Catholic Week,* April 24, 1964.

41. Nunan, interview; Pope Leo XIII, *Rerum Novarum* (On Capital and Labor), May 15, 1891, available at http://www.ewtn.com/library/encyc/l13rerum.htm.

42. Sara Kaffer, interview by author, Mobile, Ala., May 20, 1998; Thomas Weise, interview by author, Phenix City, Ala., July 3, 1998; Langan, interview; Sara Kaffer, "Minutes of Archbishop Toolen's Anti-Poverty Committee," July 25, 1967, RG7,S.3, B.10, Langan Papers.

43. Nunan, interview; Hill to Associated Press bureau chief, May 27, 1965, box 378, Hill Papers.

44. Kaffer, interview; Weise, interview; Langan, interview; Nunan, interview.

45. George M. Cox, "Thousands of Area Catholics in Tribute to Christ the King," *Mobile Register,* October 31, 1966.

46. Hill to Associated Press bureau chief, May 27, 1965, box 378, Hill Papers; "Touring Josephite Missions: Sixth Stop: Mobile, Alabama," *Josephite Harvest* 77, no. 5 (September–October 1965): 16–17, Most Pure Heart of Mary Parish Files, Society of Saint Joseph Archives, Baltimore, Md.

47. Nunan, interview; J. Paul Keefe to "Dear Friend," July 12, 1965, "Program Development Grant . . . from the United Citizens Committee," July 19, 1965, RG7,S.3,B.10, Langan Papers; Frank Prial to Bob Clampitt, November 14, 1965, box 1, OEO Inspection Reports Evaluating CAP, OEO Papers; Nunan to Langan, January 25, 1966, RG7,S.3,B.10, Langan Papers.

48. Frank Sloan to Bernard Boutin, April 1, 1966, box 9, CAP Office Records of the Director, State Files 1965–68, OEO Papers; Langan to John Sparkman, February 18, 1966, Sloan to Langan, February 14, 1966, Nunan to Langan, March 1966, William Crane to Robert H. Moore, March 14, 1966, RG7,S.3,B.10, Langan Papers.

49. Ev Crawford to Berry, June 23, 1966, Wallace to Sloan, June 17, 1966, box 14, CAP Office Records of the Director, OEO Papers; Stevens to Wallace, June 17, 1966, box SG 19966, Alabama Governor—Administrative Assistants' Files, ADAH; Philip Sayre and Robert E. Smith, "Mobile Grant Is Stopped by Wallace," *Southern Courier,* June 25–26, 1966.

50. Wallace to Shriver, July 18, 1966, box SG 19970, Alabama Governor—Administrative Assistants' Files, ADAH; Report of the Alabama Legislative Commission to Preserve the Peace, July 14, 1966, box SG 21074, Papers of the Alabama Legislative Commission to Preserve the Peace, ADAH; George C. Wallace, press conference, July 19, 1966, box SG 22401, George Wallace Papers, Alabama Governors' Papers, ADAH.

51. Nunan, interview; Kaffer, interview.

52. Kaffer, "Minutes"; Nunan to Wallace, June 23, 1966, box SG 19966, Alabama Governor—Administrative Assistants' Files, ADAH; Nunan, interview; Kaffer, interview.

53. "Archbishop Toolen's Anti-Poverty Committee Head Start—Year Round Governing Body Members," [ca. 1966], RG7,S.3,B.10, Langan Papers; Kaffer, "Minutes"; A. C. Krumlauf to Edgar May, October 6, 1966, box 87, OEO Inspection Division Inspection Reports, OEO Papers.

54. Nunan, interview; Kaffer, interview; Nunan to Krumlauf, October 2, 1966; Krumlauf to May, October 6, 1966, box 87, OEO Inspection Division Inspection Reports, OEO Papers.

55. Krumlauf to May, October 6, 1966, Nunan to Krumlauf, October 2, 1966, May to Berry, November 7, 1966, box 87, OEO Inspection Division Inspection Reports, OEO Papers; Langan to Wallace, October 28, 1966, RG7,S.3,B.10, Langan Papers.

56. Kaffer, "Minutes." The full-year program for 1966–67 served 1,015 children in eighteen centers at a cost of $1,921,197 ("Recommendations for MACAC Staff," August 1968, reel 14, ser. 4, folder 75, NPVL Papers). For 1968, Head Start served 1,080 children at a cost of $1,518,962 (Andrew J. Curtis to MACAC Board of Directors, reel 13, ser. 4, folder 42, NPVL Papers). The 1969 full-year Head Start program served 960 children in thirteen centers and had 170 staff members (Yvonne King, interview by author, July 28, 1998, Mobile, Ala.; Kaffer, interview; Weise, interview; Zemula Woods Camphor Bjork, interview by author, July 27, 1998, Mobile, Ala.). The racial breakdown of the central staff was as follows: director, Kaffer, white; assistant director, Briggs, black; curriculum, Johnston, white; parents and volunteers, Woods, black; social services, King, black; nutrition, Booth, white; medical program, Jackson, black. When Kaffer resigned in 1969, Briggs became the director.

57. Kaffer, "Minutes"; Bjork, interview; *The Cultivator: A Newsletter Published for Head Start Parents,* October 20, 1969, reel 14, ser. 4, folder 73, NPVL Papers; "Head Start Activity Report for May 1970," Archbishop Toolen's Anti-Poverty Committee Delegate Agency, reel 13, ser. 4, folder 65, NPVL Papers; King, interview.

58. Bjork, interview; King, interview; "Head Start Activity Report for October 1969," Archbishop Toolen's Anti-Poverty Committee Delegate Agency, reel 13, ser. 4, folder 65, NPVL Papers; "Brief Description of Programs and Projects: 1974–1975 of the Human Relations Center Spring Hill College," Albert S. Foley, S.J., Papers, Spring Hill College, Mobile, Ala.; *Mobile Head Start News,* October 28, 1970, reel 13, ser. 4, folder 65, NPVL Papers; Voncille Hafler, "Mobile Head Start Report," November 1970, reel 13, ser. 4, folder 65, NPVL Papers.

59. Kaffer, interview; Bjork, interview.

60. Weise, interview.

61. MACAC meeting minutes, August 10, 1966, reel 13, ser. 4, folder 34, NPVL Papers; "Marty" to Cecil [Jackson] and Hugh [Maddox], [ca. August 1966], Wallace to Stevens, September 13, 1966, box SG 19966, Alabama Governor—Administrative Assistants' Files, ADAH; Wallace to Langan, September 13, 1966, Nunan to "All Members of MACAC," November 22, 1966, RG7,S.3,B.10, Langan Papers.

62. MACAC meeting minutes, March 14, 1967, reel 13, ser. 4, folder 34, NPVL Papers; Davis to Langan, with résumé attached, [ca. 1966], MACAC meeting minutes, April 17, 1967, RG7,S.3,B.10, Langan Papers; Nunan to John L. LeFlore, October 18, 1966, reel 13, ser. 4, folder 39, NPVL Papers.

63. David R. Underhill, "Mobile Mayor Names LeFlore," *Southern Courier,* February 12–13, 1966; "Mobile Rights Group Says No Demonstrations Now," *Southern Courier,* February 26–27, 1966; David R. Underhill, "In Mobile: Sparse Turnout," *Southern Courier,* April 9–10, 1966.

64. "Mobile Rights Group Says No Demonstrations Now"; David R. Underhill, "How Did Mobile Negroes Vote? Only Two Win Full Bloc," *Southern Courier,* May 14–15, 1966; Underhill, "In Mobile: Sparse Turnout."

65. Nunan to LeFlore, October 18, 1966, reel 13, ser. 4, folder 39, NPVL Papers; MACAC meeting minutes, March 14, 1967, reel 13, ser. 4, folder 34, NPVL Papers; MACAC meeting minutes, May 29, June 5, 27, 1967, MACAC membership list, [ca. 1967], MACAC Board of Directors meeting minutes, November 14, 27, 1967, MACAC Executive and Planning Committee meeting minutes, November 20, 1967, RG7,S.3,B.10, Langan Papers; MACAC Board of Directors meeting minutes, January 4, 1968, reel 27, box 10, folder 12, NPVL Papers; MACAC Executive Committee meeting minutes, February 15, 1968, reel 13, ser. 4, folder 36, NPVL Papers; MACAC Executive Committee meeting minutes, May 29, 1968, RG7,S.3,B.10, Langan Papers; Nunan to William W. Suttle, October 3, 1968, Suttle to C. A. Rettig, October 18, 1968, anonymous, handwritten note, November 11, 1968, reel 13, ser. 4, folder 67, NPVL Papers.

66. "5,000 Mobilians Attend King Services," *Mobile Press Register,* April 7, 1968; "Sidewalk March Held to Protest Hiring Policies," *Mobile Register,* May 16, 1968; Dow, "Joseph N. Langan," 51–55; Willie and Greenblatt, *Community Politics,* 185–87; Nunan, interview; Thomas M. Nunan, "Interfaith Committee for Human Concern, Inc.—A Program Report to July 31, 1968," Thomas M. Nunan, "Interfaith Committee for Human Concern, Inc.—A Program Report," December 9, 1968, reel 13, ser. 4, folder 22, NPVL Papers; Frye Gaillard, "Interfaith Group Struggling in Private, Anti-Poverty War," *Mobile Press Register,* November 24, 1968.

67. "Interracial Relations Head Forum," *Mobile Register,* July 25, 1968; Frye Gaillard, "Nunan Says Years in Mobile 'Good,' " *Mobile Register,* April 1, 1969; Beasley, Nathaniel Gibbs, and Ocie Wheat to Lambert C. Mims, August 23, 1968, box SG 22440, Alabama Governors' Papers ADAH; Frederick Douglas Richardson Jr., *The Genesis and Exodus of* NOW (New York: Vantage Press, 1978), 49; "At Pageant—Archbishop Raps Clergy in Protests," *Birmingham News,* May 12, 1969.

68. MACAC Executive Committee meeting minutes, May 29, 1968, RG7,S.3,B.10, Langan Papers; "Mobile Area Community Action Committee—Programs (Head Start, Operation Campout)," 1968, reel 14, ser. 4, folder 74, NPVL Papers; MACAC Board of Directors meeting minutes, April 1, 1969, reel 13, ser. 4, folder 42, NPVL Papers; "MACAC Report: Dialogue '69," August 26–27, 1969, reel 14, ser. 4, folder 76, NPVL Papers; D'Esther McGrue, MACAC monthly report, September 1970, reel 14, ser. 4, folder 79, NPVL Papers; "MACAC Plans and Priorities 1970," reel 13, ser. 4, folder 62, NPVL Papers.

69. Frye Gaillard, "With Deep Personal Regret--Monsignor Nunan Quits Priesthood," *Mobile Register,* February 21, 1969; Nunan, interview; Bokenkotter, *Concise History,* 370–71; Morris, *American Catholic,* 345–46; Wallace Henley, "Toolen Resigns," *Birmingham News,* October 8, 1969; "The Laborer Earned His Rest," *Birmingham News,* October 9, 1969.

70. Richardson, *Genesis and Exodus,* 135–45; Dow, "Joseph N. Langan," 55–57; Willie and Greenblatt, *Community Politics,* 204–5; *City of Mobile, Alabama, et al. v. Wiley L. Bolden et al.,* 446 U.S. 55, argued March 19, 1979, reargued October 29, 1979, decided April 22, 1980.

71. Nunan, interview.

Southern Feminism and Social Change

*Sallie Bingham and the
Kentucky Foundation for Women*

MARSHA S. ROSE

Authors of chapters in this volume have directed attention to two important government programs—the New Deal and the Great Society, with its War on Poverty. These programs used the federal government's vast resources to effect social and economic change. This final chapter diverges from the focus on government and instead explores the realm of private philanthropy. Federal spending on social programs exceeds that of private philanthropy. Even so, foundations such as the giant Ford Foundation or the more modest women's funds enjoy considerable flexibility in targeting specific problems or at least in targeting the problems identified by idiosyncratic donors. This chapter is about one philanthropist, Sallie Bingham, and the foundation she established, the Kentucky Foundation for Women (KFW). Since its beginning in 1985, the KFW has given hundreds of grants to female artists, writers, and playwrights whose work takes a feminist perspective. Although a case study of one woman and one foundation, this chapter draws attention to larger questions about the role of private philanthropy in regional change. In the process, I highlight the importance of feminism and women's movements in contemporary welfare policy.

In 1986, Barry Bingham Sr. sold his Kentucky media empire for $448 million.[1] His older daughter, Sallie, used $10 million of her $60 million share of the proceeds to fund the KFW, which represented a distinctive philanthropic organization. Up to that point, fewer than two dozen women's funds had been established nationwide, and none was located in the South. Equally important, the KFW was the only women's fund focused exclusively on women and the arts. The foundation was a device through which Sallie Bingham expressed her feminism, her interest in reform, and her identity as a southern woman. By 2001, the KFW had published a quarterly feminist literary magazine for fifteen years, delivered more than $5 million in grants to hundreds of women artists and writers, and maintained a retreat for feminist artists in residence. This chapter will explore the foundation while placing it in the larger context of feminist social reform.

"I Have Always Been a Feminist"

Sarah (Sallie) Bingham was born in 1937 to Kentucky media magnate Barry Bingham Sr. and his wife, Mary Clifford Caperton Bingham. The third of five children, Sallie's early years were those of a girl of privilege and intellectual promise. She attended private preparatory schools and in 1958 graduated magna cum laude from Radcliffe College. After graduation, Bingham moved to New York City and pursued a career as a writer, eventually publishing seven books, eleven plays, and more than two hundred short stories. Her most enduring legacy, however, will be the foundation she endowed as a vehicle for her philanthropy and feminism.

Sallie Bingham inherited part of a vast media fortune. In 1917, her grandfather purchased Kentucky's flagship newspaper, the *Louisville Courier-Journal.* By 1930, he had passed control of his media empire to his youngest son, Barry Bingham Sr. In 1966 Barry Sr. appointed his namesake and youngest son, Barry Jr., as the heir apparent to the family's businesses.[2] In 1975, amid rumors of hostile takeovers of Bingham companies, Barry Sr. appointed his daughters, Sallie and Eleanor, and daughter-in-law, Edith, to various family company boards of directors. The women's appointments, however, were titular. The male Binghams expected their women to attend meetings and do as Barry Jr.'s wife did—"needlepoint during board meetings."[3]

Sallie resented the privileges given to her brothers and denied to her and her younger sister.[4] In 1977, she returned home to Louisville, anticipating a more active role in the family business. Unfortunately, the cornerstone of the Bingham Enterprises, the *Louisville Courier-Journal,* had begun to slip in profitability and recognition. With their three hundred thousand dollar annual income from Bingham Enterprises dividends in jeopardy, the Bingham sisters started to question male hegemony and management practices. In 1984, frustrated by her lack of authority at the newspaper and by what she believed was her brother's ineptitude, Sallie decided to sell her interests in the family company.

When she refused a buyout at the price her brother offered, family members ostracized her. The saga of the breakup of the Bingham family business was intense, personal, and gendered.[5]

Sallie Bingham attributed the breakup of Bingham Enterprises to the differential treatment of the Bingham men and women. Journalists and others, however, blamed Sallie for the family problems. One writer portrayed her as "the black sheep" who had prompted the sale of Bingham Enterprises and destruction of a family empire.[6] Affirming her feminism, in 1986, Sallie took part of her assets from the sale and endowed the Kentucky Foundation for Women.

A Woman's Fund

Sallie Bingham's KFW was part of a larger effort to direct private philanthropy toward activities that benefited women and girls. The first foundations directed solely at improving the lives of women and girls developed during the early 1970s. Gloria Steinem, feminist and publisher of *Ms.* magazine, had created the Ms. Foundation, the largest of the nascent women's funds, in 1972, and over the next ten years a few other women's funds were established.

During the 1980s, a new generation of wealthy women created foundations aimed at fostering the welfare of women and girls. Where the Ms. Foundation was national in its programs, benefactors of the emerging women's funds directed their philanthropy and fund-raising at local communities. By 1985, more than twenty women's funds operated in the United States, including Bingham's KFW.[7]

Organizers of these women's funds brought a distinct agenda for social change. The feminist movement had heightened certain wealthy women's awareness of the paucity of grants directed at benefiting women and girls. (Less than 5 percent of grants from traditional foundations went toward programs that focused on females.)[8] In addition, by the 1980s, some women of inherited wealth wanted to use their resources to empower other, less fortunate women.[9] In these new organizations, women raised the money, and with women serving as executive officers and as most of the board members, women determined how that money would be spent.[10] In a women's fund, declared authors of an early brochure from the National Network of Women's Funds, "grants and allocations support programs that assist women and girls in overcoming racial, economic, political, sexual, and social discrimination."[11]

The Kentucky Foundation for Women

In 1986, Sallie Bingham endowed the Kentucky Foundation for Women with a contribution of ten million dollars. Bingham was in the vanguard of a philanthropic movement. Initially, her goals were the general goals of other women's funds' benefactors—improving the lives of women. Specifically, during several speeches delivered in 1985, Bingham stated that she wanted to "study, and make public, exactly what the status of women in [Kentucky] is" and that she planned to "show the many links between the personal and the political."[12] As a practical matter, Bingham connected the personal and political by sponsoring feminist work in arts and literature.

Bingham's goals for the KFW brought together the three issues of social reform, equal rights for southern women, and the importance of feminist perspectives in the arts. Social reform had been a theme in the Bingham household. During Sallie's childhood, her family had encouraged openness and tolerance, not hostility and bigotry. The *Courier-Journal* was, by all accounts, a liberal newspaper.[13] In the 1930s, her grandfather had lent his support to Franklin D. Roosevelt. In a conservative and heavily Catholic city, moreover, he openly favored birth control. During the 1960s and 1970s, the newspaper's editorials urged calm and an end to prejudice following school-desegregation orders.[14]

Sallie Bingham carried her family's tradition of tolerance and moderate social reform into the 1980s and 1990s. In her hands, those practices and outlooks took on a feminist tone and activist approach. For example, in 1987, Bingham was a keynote speaker at a prochoice rally in Cincinnati.[15] That same year, she spoke at a conference of American Women in Television and Radio, urging women to take leadership roles in the media.[16] Between 1988 and 1991, she served on the American Civil Liberties Union's National Advisory Board.[17] She lent strong support to Rev. Jesse Jackson's 1988 presidential campaign.[18] In 1990, she published an essay expressing concern over the misuse of "wild land."[19] In a 1997 letter to the president of Radcliffe, Bingham deplored the denial of tenure for a woman faculty member at Harvard.[20] And in 1998, she wrote a letter to the editor of the *New York Times* condemning the antigay murder of Matthew Shepard.[21]

Bingham reserved her most vocal reform message for changing the lives of southern women. In the gentility of Kentucky, she wrote, "gender roles are clear," and "women were meant to be ladies, 'dependable, passive, charming, and well-dressed.'"[22] In an unpublished 1990 essay, "Goodbye to All That: Another Southerner Quits the South," she described her disappointment in the South: "A friend of mine said recently that the only reason people stay in the south is family." Well, Bingham continued, "I found it comforting thirteen years ago, to return to the nest or cocoon of family. . . . But the comfort, in the end, is an illusion." Indeed, Bingham added, "The south has labeled me BAD, and when that happens, it's best to leave."[23]

Bingham went public with her feelings about the South in a 1991 review of four books for *Ms.* magazine. "Many women writers who were born in the South fled the region years ago," she wrote. Yet "most of us continue to write about a place where we can't live." Bingham urged women writers to escape the "baggage" of the South and not to allow others to enforce the label of southern woman writer. For Bingham, "The South neither respects nor repays the women writers who cling to her arid breast."[24]

Sallie Bingham and her KFW brought together the two issues of social reform and equal rights for southern women by directing their resources toward the third issue, that of feminist work in the arts. In this program, the KFW was unique. Most of the women's funds had provided grants to battered women's shelters, to centers for women's health and child care, or to organizations that fostered economic self-sufficiency for women. Bingham chose a different path for her foundation. In 1985, she summarized her goals in a speech at Midway College: "We are going to put together a group of writers and performers who can deal with such subjects as acid rain, discrimination on the job, juvenile delinquency, teenage pregnancies, and so on down the long, dramatic list of social issues which effect [*sic*] women particularly."[25] An early draft of a brochure describing the foundation stated the goals more broadly: "The Kentucky Foundation for Women . . . is organized for the purpose of illuminating the plight of women and serving as a catalyst for change on their behalf, primarily through *the Arts and Humanities.*"[26]

Bingham recognized that poverty, illiteracy, and unemployment imposed harsh burdens on women. She believed, however, that even her substantial fortune could not reduce such overwhelming problems among millions of women. Rather than attempt a small-scale effort at social and economic amelioration, Bingham chose a different approach. In an October 31, 1987, presentation to participants at the Conference on Socially Responsible Money Management, Bingham reported that she had "decided to work at the root of the prejudices against women, below the conscious level, where images and sounds can penetrate."[27] The road to a more fulsome life for Kentucky's women would wind slowly through feminist poetry, short stories, novels, and artwork.

In reality, Bingham's KFW represented her own political expression, an expression of her ideas about the South and about feminism. A contribution of ten million dollars would secure a growing constituency for that politics that her novels and short stories could not. The ultimate goal for Bingham and the KFW was to use the performing and visual arts as a vehicle for social change among women. To accomplish this lofty goal, Bingham, as the chief benefactor, established three program areas: (1) creation of a literary magazine, *The American Voice;* (2) grants to specific artists and artists' organizations that promoted women's interests; and (3) support of Hopscotch House, a farm that sponsored artists in residence.

In November 1985, *The American Voice* arrived in bookstores, the first issue of a publication that would appear three or four times annually until 1999. Bingham handpicked her coeditor, Fred Smock, a former editor of Kentucky arts and human-interest magazines. Like Bingham, Smock was committed to a magazine that included "feminism, liberalism and egalitarianism" as its political agenda.[28]

As Bingham envisioned it, *The American Voice* would be such a magazine, giving women writers a forum to present their craft to an international audience. "I believe that women writers are discriminated against when they try to publish by often subconscious attitudes on the part of male editors," wrote Bingham.[29] Bingham believed that women had disadvantages when it came to publishing their work.

Significantly, the magazine would carry pieces written "primarily by women." True, each entry would convey a feminist outlook, but men were invited to make submissions. Bingham was adamant that *The American Voice* would not limit itself to female writers. "Women writing for women," she asserted, would place women writers in a ghetto, a situation that was "to be avoided." Nor did she want to marginalize women writers and limit their audience.[30] In addition to the subjective quality of the piece, the major criterion for acceptance in the magazine was the author's commitment to feminist principles. Bingham wanted her magazine to be a catalyst for social change. In an interview for a Bloomington, Illinois, newspaper, Bingham asserted, "If the arts can begin to portray women as strong competent members of this society, then other changes will take place."[31]

The accomplishments of *The American Voice* were mixed. If Bingham's goal was to help disadvantaged writers, her success was limited. Few first-time authors published in the magazine. The largest group of authors held academic appointments, and many had had books published by leading presses. Editors Smock and Bingham also published works by several well-known, prolific, award-winning authors, such as Maya Angelou, Chaim Potok, and Joyce Carol Oates.[32] Contrary to the stated goal of publishing "the work of writers not generally acknowledged by the literary establishment,"[33] Bingham and Smock more than once succumbed to the allure of connecting *The American Voice* with already visible authors.

Conversely, as a straightforward vehicle for American women writers, *The American Voice* proved a success.[34] Hundreds of poets, essayists, and fiction and nonfiction writers published their work in the magazine. Many of the pieces received Pushcart awards, given for the best work in small press editions. Less visible, however, were the social, political, and intellectual changes that Bingham wanted her magazine to create. In the final issue of the magazine, Bingham wrote an afterword expressing her sentiments as she said "goodbye to an old friend." By 1999, the optimism for social change with which Bingham had launched *The American Voice* had receded, even disappeared: "I wish I could say that the plight of women writers is substantially improved over the sad situation I have encountered ever since I published my first novel in the early sixties. I don't think it has, although several distinguished women do publish regularly, and others infrequently. But in the main, women who take risks, who write about dangerous subjects or chose idiosyncratic points of view, are doomed to obscurity now as they were when we started the *Voice*. And this situation is not likely to change."[35]

Through the second program area, grants to artists, Bingham found a wider audience for her feminist ideals. In November 1986, one year after the inaugural issue of *The American Voice* appeared, the KFW announced its first round of grants. The two largest grants—one million dollars each—went to New York–based organizations with no direct links to Kentucky, the Women's Project and the Ms. Foundation. The Women's Project supports plays written and directed by women. Shortly before receiving the KFW grant, the largest in its history, the Women's Project had presented two of Bingham's plays, *Milk of Paradise* (1980) and *Paducah* (1985). Similarly, the grant to the Ms. Foundation was preceded by a cover story in *Ms.* magazine (the foundation's corporate sponsor) that pictured Sallie Bingham and the words, "The Woman Who Overturned an Empire."[36]

Not every grant brought such publicity. Bingham focused the remaining grants on smaller Louisville organizations such as the library and public television station, which received grants ranging from $250 to $5,000. Most grant recipients were located in Kentucky, and in 1996 the foundation directors approved a geographical limit on grantees: only persons or organizations that operated in Kentucky would be eligible. Exceptions would be made for "projects that would have great impact on residents of Kentucky."[37] The KFW thus would have a distinctly local cast.

When Bingham announced the creation of the KFW, newspapers throughout Kentucky hailed its arrival and the $2.2 million in contributions it distributed.[38] Bingham's $10 million endowment was the largest single gift to a woman's fund, a contribution that is especially impressive considering that in 2000, the ninety or so women's funds that belonged to the Women's Funding Network had combined assets of around $180 million.[39]

Since the foundation's creation, KFW directors have distributed more than $5 million in grants. Some groups, such as the Women Writers Conference at the University of Kentucky, Artswatch, and the Mary Anderson Center, have received money nearly every year. Most of the grantees, however, have been women writers and artists who have received between $1,000 an $5,000 to support their work. Naomi Wallace from Prospect, Kentucky, for example, received $4,050 "for a feminist adaptation of Hawthorne's *The Scarlet Letter* for the stage."[40] Kate Adamek of Louisville accepted $4,800 "to provide writing experiences to women in homeless shelters."[41] Nancy Safian conducted a "collaborative workshop exploring the lives of Jewish girls and women in Louisville."[42] Mary Anne Maier received $2,200 for a collection of writings on menstruation.[43] Hundreds of women received money from the foundation to encourage them in their work, whether writing fiction, poetry, or plays or making videos, sculpting, or painting.

Bingham wanted to use arts and literature to empower women. Positive images of women, she hoped, would lead to enhanced self-perceptions and greater independence. That revisions of *The Scarlet Letter* or articles on topics such as menstruation brought about reform was never a clear-cut matter. Bingham was aware of the disjuncture between ideas and social reform, especially on so vast a matter as women's inequality. In a 1986 article for *New York Newsday,* Bingham responded to the skeptics who could not envision the connection: "Through the actual experience of seeing functioning, talented women artists, some stereotypes are changing. Sure, this is abstract. And it will take a long time. But the alternative is subsistence aid that would show immediate results, but, in the long run, wouldn't have an effect on the structure of things."[44]

In 1995, as part of the celebration of the KFW's tenth anniversary, events showcasing women artists were held throughout Kentucky. The University of Louisville's Women's Center sponsored a series of events on "Feminist Art and Social Change." Northern Kentucky University exhibited works by KFW grantees. Lexington's Carnegie Center for Literacy and Learning hosted an evening of readings by KFW grantees. And in LaCenter, Kemba Webb performed as part of the African American Women's Literary Series. All in all, there were nine art exhibits, five concerts, two radio programs, seven readings/performances, and five panel discussions/lectures in addition to activities at Hopscotch House commemorating the foundation's anniversary. Ann Stewart summed up the excitement she felt after ten years of grant making: "As Executive Director, I have tried to attend most of the celebration events. . . . And, I am convinced that something significant is taking place. Women are finding empowerment. We speak self-confidently of work and interests and goals. We gain courage from one another and pass on energy to each other. I have heard dozens of stories of changed lives and have seen women actively and consciously laboring for the changes."[45]

Stewart's optimism evaporated the following summer. In her column for the KFW *Newsletter*, she reported on a finding from the Women's Funding Network that Kentucky was the state with the lowest voter turnout among women: "I am both ashamed and discouraged. Ashamed for our sisters across the country to read this statistic about us. Discouraged, because I had thought that we in Kentucky were becoming more active, were becoming, through the help of the Kentucky Foundation for Women and others, empowered, realizing the importance of our voices."[46]

It is easy to comprehend Stewart's anguish at the foundation's perceived failure. Yet Bingham was not interested in bringing about such reforms as increased voting among women. Instead, Bingham sought long-term change, the kind that comes about by changing attitudes over decades rather than individual performance over weeks or months. Throughout the KFW's early development, Bingham continually acknowledged the circumspect way in which she wanted to help women. In a speech for a 1987 conference sponsored by the Boston Women's Fund, Bingham told her audience, "I decided to work at the root of the prejudices against women, below the conscious level, where images and sounds can penetrate. . . . I think change in attitudes only comes through an increase of empathy—when the men who are at the top of the society begin to imagine the lives of women." Each time she spoke about the KFW, Bingham reiterated the importance of enabling women artists, in small ways, so that they could grow professionally and deliver their message of feminist empowerment. She spoke about financing a program to train high school teachers in Kentucky in ways to incorporate women's studies materials in their classrooms, about buying a piano "for a music teacher in a remote part of Appalachia," and about sending "a young woman to architectural school in Cincinnati."[47] In July 1985, she defended her goals to the River City Businesswomen: "I think poetry can lift the limits on our lives, give us a sense of breadth and hope, a new perspective. So we will begin by offering small grants to individual women in the arts, money for babysitting, maybe, so a project can be completed, money for a typewriter, for a writing course, for travel. And because there are not many professional artists here, or in any state, we will be attempting to redefine that illusive term, amateur—which, after all, comes from the same root as to love."[48]

Bingham herself may not have appreciated the often invisible consequences of her many grants. Hundreds of women writers and artists whose work might have remained unfinished or whose work would not have begun were able to start and finish projects important to them. Each foundation newsletter, moreover, announced the public presentation of one or more of the grantees' works in a theater, gallery, or published volume. In the past sixteen years, KFW grants have helped nourish the infrastructure of feminist books, plays, and poems. As early as September 1988, the lifestyles editor for the *Bowling Green (Kentucky) Daily News* wrote privately to Bingham, "You have made Kentucky a state of feminine renaissance."[49] Whatever the precise quality of its work, the foundation enabled and legitimated the voice of energetic and talented women in Kentucky who worked in less visible surroundings and whose audiences were composed of women (and some men) like themselves.

The third foundation program involved Hopscotch House, a retreat for women writers and artists. Starting in 1986, groups of women and a few men have been able to reserve space at the well-appointed farmhouse for readings or workshops or to provide group members with an opportunity for reflection. Guests at Hopscotch House routinely take nature walks through the wooded surroundings, learning about environmental sensitivities and plant systematics. For example, in November 1992, a dozen women engaged in food sampling led by Hopscotch House naturalist Wren Smith. A "Seed and Stalk Discovery Walk" of winter plants took place on January 24, 1993. From 1985 through 1995, on the second Tuesday of each month, Hopscotch House hosted a "Women's Enchantment": guests were asked to bring their "favorite percussion instrument or sound-maker to this participatory rhythmic experience."[50] In July 1993, Hopscotch House hosted its first "Ecofeminist Writers' Residency."[51] Like other programs that Bingham and the KFW supported, Hopscotch House would bring social change over the long term.

Feminism and Social Change

Feminism—whether as politics, a social movement, or a theoretical paradigm—is well discussed in both academic and popular literature. Liberal, radical, Marxist, socialist, and psychoanalytic feminists vary in their interpretations of gender difference. Nevertheless, feminism at its very least represents a focus on inequality based on gender. Feminists have sought to lessen this inequality.

In a September 1988 interview, Sallie Bingham asserted, "I have always been a feminist."[52] Bingham's feminism has been apparent throughout her adult life. In numerous speeches, interviews, and articles, Bingham announced her dissatisfaction with the gender inequality within her family and within American society.[53] Both her critics and her supporters cite Bingham's feminism as a key element in the public breakup of the Bingham companies. Sallie Bingham, too, identified gender inequality as a critical part of her separation from the family business. In an interview published in the June 1986 *Ms.*, Bingham said, "It seemed to me that those are the choices women have here—the choice of marriage-dependency-poverty, or the choice of being an accessory to a powerful man, through being his secretary, his wife, his mistress, or by collaborating with him. When I decided to sell out and realized the amount of money involved, I began to think about what I could do to effect some change."[54]

Bingham translated her feminism into social action through the KFW. During the 1980s and 1990s, advocates of feminist principles and philanthropy shared a common goal of social reform.[55] Feminists sought to alter the power balance in public and private relationships and structures based on issues of gender. Similarly, philanthropists hoped to change the circumstances of individuals and groups that often lacked the social, political, or economic agency for self-reform. Such organizers of women's funds as Bingham merged feminism and philanthropy. These women of wealth rejected traditional philanthropy, believing that their new funds would serve as instruments through which philanthropy would become more democratic, more diverse, and more willing to help some of the most underserved groups, especially women and girls.[56]

Bingham created the KFW, *The American Voice*, and Hopscotch House as agents of social change. Her goal, she reported, was "to try to create new images, new words, new sounds, which would both encourage women to persist, to solve their problems, and create greater receptivity to women's strength on the part of the rest of the world."[57] She tirelessly promoted the foundation, delivering several speeches a week. Her talks about the KFW most often centered on three themes: first, with her limited resources, Bingham could not reduce the level of poverty among Kentucky's women; second, the best way to upgrade women's status was to change attitudes toward and images of women; thus, the third and larger goal of eliminating poverty would start with the smaller goal of enhancing women's sense of self-worth through creative expression. By creating the KFW, Bingham was supporting women artists and writers whose work conformed to the foundation's feminist goals. Bingham used her "money for women in arts, interpreting the arts as a vehicle for social change."[58]

Accepting the Lexington, Kentucky, YWCA Women of Achievement Award on October 3, 1986, Bingham told her audience, "The Foundation will be an example of the way the personal, in life, is the political."[59] This assertion has been a mantra of feminist thought.[60] For Bingham, the personal is found in her flight from the South, from her family, and from the constraints of patriarchy. In a 1991 book review essay for *Ms.*, Bingham asserted, "We alone who have escaped [the South] must resist the categorization implying that women, already condescended to because of gender, can be further manipulated and marginalized as regionalists."[61] In fact, one writer described Bingham as a "quintessential Southern lady notorious for being so gentle, so feminine, so charming, and as sharp and as tough as nails."[62] The creation of the KFW coalesced the personal into the political.

Women's funds and other private philanthropy, however, cannot and should not replace government largesse. The few thousand dollars available to grantees from women's funds are dwarfed by the money that was available from immense government programs and agencies such as the Farm Security Administration or the War on Poverty. Nevertheless, social-welfare reform occurs at different levels. For example, the federal government does not make grants of two thousand dollars to the Lexington, Kentucky, YMCA for an exchange program for women writers in rural communities. But Bingham's KFW makes precisely this type of award.

Bingham left Kentucky in 1991 and moved to Santa Fe, New Mexico, where she continues to support the arts. Just before moving, she placed the editorship of *The American Voice* in Smock's hands. In September 1994, she resigned from the KFW's board of directors. Bingham currently holds the status of "Founder, Permanent Member, Emerita" on the board. The KFW continues to thrive, allocating two hundred thousand dollars in 2001 to women in Kentucky under two programs, Artist Enrichment and Art Meets Activism.

The Kentucky Foundation for Women has matured and grown since Sallie Bingham endowed it in 1986. The foundation's cornerstone—sponsoring feminist work in the arts—continues to influence Kentucky's cultural landscape. While Bingham no longer has an active part in the foundation's work, her legacy of supporting feminist projects endures.

Notes

The author thanks the staff at the Duke University Special Collections Library, particularly Elizabeth Dunn and Cristina Favretto, for their assistance during my two visits. I am grateful for helpful and insightful comments from Elna Green, Ellen D. Goldlust-Gingrich, and the anonymous reviewers. Finally, my gratitude to my husband, whose historian's editorial pen has, I hope, improved this sociologist's prose. I gathered most of the research for this chapter during two visits to the Sallie Bingham Papers, housed at the Rare Book, Manuscript, and Special Collections Library at Duke University, Durham, N.C. During my first visit, in May 1998, the materials were unprocessed, and many items were restricted. I received permission from Sallie Bingham to examine the documents concerning the KFW. During my next visit to the archives, in May 2000, many documents had been processed and an inventory made available. Restricted materials remained unavailable, however, including several documents related to the foundation. The material from my first visit will be cited as "unprocessed May 1998."

1. Most of the money came from selling the two newspapers to the Gannett Corporation for more than three hundred million dollars. See Susan E. Tifft and Alex S. Jones, *The Patriarch: The Rise and Fall of the Bingham Dynasty* (New York: Summit, 1991), 489.

2. Appointing the youngest rather than the oldest son to carry the family mantel was an unusual inheritance practice. In the case of Barry Sr., his older siblings were not considered viable leaders: his older brother was an alcoholic, and his sister, Henrietta, flaunted her lesbianism and sought refuge among the Bloomsbury writers in London (David Leon Chandler with Mary Voelz Chandler, *The Binghams of*

Louisville: The Dark History behind One of the Country's Great Fortunes [New York: Crown, 1987], 220; Tifft and Jones, *Patriarch*, 81–82, 87–89). Barry Jr. received his position through tragedy and disinterest. His older brothers died prematurely in separate, freakish accidents. Sallie, the older daughter, showed little interest in the business, and Eleanor, the youngest child, was caught up in the social movements of the 1960s.

3. Sallie Bingham, *Passion and Prejudice: A Family Memoir* (New York: Applause Books, 1989), 399.

4. Michael Kirkhorn, "The Bingham Black Sheep," *Louisville Today,* 1979: 36–41, Subject Files Series, box 2, "Newspaper Clippings, 1952–80" folder, Sallie Bingham Papers, Rare Book, Manuscript, and Special Collections Library, Duke University; Alanna Nash, "The Woman Who Overturned an Empire," *Ms.,* June 1986, 44; Sallie Bingham, "The Truth about Growing up Rich," *Ms.,* June 1986, 48; Sallie Bingham, "Biting the Hand: The Break-up of the Bingham Family Empire," *Radcliffe Quarterly,* June 1986, 32; Sallie Bingham, "Women and the Creative Process: A Widening Vision," speech delivered at Oberlin College, December 5, 1987, Speeches Series, box 1, 1987 folder, Bingham Papers; Bingham, *Passion and Prejudice,* 433–34; Sallie Bingham, "The Garden of Eden," speech for a conference on women in media, January 24, 1989, Speeches Series, box 1, 1989 folder, Bingham Papers; Sallie Bingham, "Developing New Perspectives: Women Who Live near Power," n.d., Writings Series, box 5, Bingham Papers.

5. Histories of the Bingham family include Bingham, *Passion and Prejudice;* Marie Brenner, *House of Dreams: The Bingham Family of Louisville* (New York: Knopf, 1988); Chandler and Chandler, *Binghams;* Robert I. Curtis, "The Bingham School and Classical Education in North Carolina, 1793–1873," *North Carolina Historical Review* 73 (July 1996): 328–77; William E. Ellis, *Robert Worth Bingham and the Southern Mystique: From the Old South to the New South and Beyond* (Kent, Ohio: Kent State University Press, 1997); George E. Marcus with Peter Dobkin Hall, *Lives in Trust: The Fortunes of Dynastic Families in Late Twentieth-Century America* (Boulder, Colo.: Westview Press, 1992), 207–19; Tifft and Jones, *Patriarch;* Joe Ward, "The Binghams: Twilight of a Tradition," *Louisville (Kentucky) Courier-Journal Magazine,* April 20, 1986, 16–38.

6. Kirkhorn, "Bingham Black Sheep"; John Nielsen, "After a Woman Is Scorned, a Publishing Family Cashes Out," *Fortune,* January 5, 1987, 93; obituaries of Barry Bingham Sr., August 15–16, 1988, Subject Files Series, box 1, Bingham Papers. In 1991, Alex S. Jones, one of the authors of *The Patriarch,* told a reporter for the *Lexington Herald-Leader* that "Sallie had her role [in bringing down the empire], but it was only one of several leading roles. And at the end, Sallie was really not an important player" (cited in Kevin Nance, "Villainess Image Beginning to Fade," *Lexington Herald-Leader,* April 14, 1991, K1, Subject Files Series, box 1, "Articles about and Interviews with Bingham, 1958–97" folder, Bingham Papers).

7. To coordinate the work of these foundations, the National Network of Women's Funds (NNWF) was established in April 1985 (National Committee for Responsive Philanthropy, "Two Dozen Women's Funds Launch National Network," *Responsive Philanthropy* [spring 1986]: 14; Christina H. Joh, "Diversity in Feminist Organizations: A Case Study of the Women's Funding Network's Community" [unpublished paper, University of Minnesota, 1997), 15]). The NNWF, later renamed the Women's Funding Network (WFN), currently has sixty-nine partner members and thirty-three nonvoting associate members. In addition to hosting an annual meeting, the WFN provides technical support for new women's funds and is a clearinghouse for survey data about women's funds.

8. Teresa Odendahl, *Charity Begins at Home: Generosity and Self-Interest among the Philanthropic Elite* (New York: Basic Books, 1998), 188.

9. Combining wealth with social action is often anomalous (Susan Ostrander, "Charitable Foundations, Social Movements, and Social Justice Funding," *Research in Social Policy* 5 [1997]: 174–75). However, using money to change the system that delivered a privileged position was precisely the goal of the alternative fund movement that began in the early 1970s.

10. Marsha Shapiro Rose, "Philanthropy in a Different Voice: The Women's Funds," *Nonprofit and Voluntary Sector Quarterly* 23 (fall 1994): 229–31.

11. National Network of Women's Funds, *Imagine* (St. Paul, Minn.: NNWF, n.d.).

12. Sallie Bingham, "Goals for My Foundation," speech delivered to River City Businesswomen, Hurstbourne, Ky., July 8, 1985; and Sallie Bingham, "The Personal Is the Political," speech delivered to YMCA, Lexington, Ky., October 3, 1985, Speeches Series, box 1, 1985 folder, Bingham Papers.

13. Bingham, "Biting the Hand," 32; Sallie Bingham, "Censorship and Books," speech delivered to New York Civil Liberties Union Meeting, Syracuse, May 20, 1988, Speeches Series, box 1, 1988 folder, Bingham Papers; Brenner, *House of Dreams*, 24–25; Chandler and Chandler, *Binghams*, 221–22; Tifft and Jones, *Patriarch*, 161–63.

14. Chandler and Chandler, *Binghams*, 221–22; Tifft and Jones, *Patriarch*, 162.

15. Photos and flyers, rally sponsored by the Cincinnati NOW, 1987, unprocessed May 1998, Bingham Papers.

16. Joe Ward, "Sallie Bingham Attacks Electronic Media," *Louisville (Kentucky) Courier-Journal*, October 9, 1987, Subject Files Series, box 1, "Articles about and Interviews with Bingham, 1958–97" folder, Bingham Papers.

17. ACLU *of Kentucky Newsletter*, January 1988, Subject Files Series, box 1, "Articles about and Interviews with Bingham, 1958–97" folder, Bingham Papers.

18. Lawrence Muhammad and William Keesler, "Jackson Pins Hopes on His Reputation," and Yvonne D. Coleman, "Kentucky Women Join in Support of '88 Presidential Campaign," *Louisville (Kentucky) Courier-Journal*, February 26, 1988, Subject Files Series, box 1, "Jesse Jackson Campaign, 1987" folder, Bingham Papers.

19. Sallie Bingham, "A Woman's Land," *Amicus Journal* 12 (fall 1990): 36–38, Writings Series, box 20, Bingham Papers. Sallie Bingham linked her feminism with her ecological interests in a 1991 lecture, "The Green Goddess." "Ecofeminism," Bingham contended, "applies the basic insights of feminism to ecology. As women are exploited, the earth is exploited; as women are raped, the earth is raped" (Bingham, "The Green Goddess," speech delivered to the Women's Studies Program and Women's Studies Council at Indiana University Southeast, April 6, 1991, Speeches Series, box 1, 1991 folder, Bingham Papers).

20. Martha Ann Fuller to Bingham, May 22, 1997, Bingham to Fuller, June 2, 1997, Linda Wilson to Bingham, June 21, August 20, 1997, Bingham to Wilson, August 4, 1997, Subject Files Series, box 1, "Hiring, Tenure of Women at Harvard/Radcliffe" folder, Bingham Papers.

21. Bingham to the editors, October 14, 1998, Subject Files Series, box 1, "Matthew Sheperd [*sic*] Death, 1998" folder, Bingham Papers.

22. Sallie Bingham, "Goodbye to All That: Another Southerner Quits the South," 1990, Writings Series, box 6, Bingham Papers; Susan Lawrence, "Women, Money, and Social Responsibility: Saying No to Male Dominance," *Second Century Radcliffe News,* April 1988, 10, Subject Files Series, box 1, "Articles about and Interviews with Bingham, 1958–97" folder, Bingham Papers; see also Bingham, *Passion and Prejudice;* Sallie Bingham, "(Southern?) Women Writers," *Ms.* May–June 1991, 68; Sallie Bingham, speech before the Kentucky Business Leader of the Year Awards Banquet, December 11, 1985, Speeches Series, box 1, 1985 folder, Bingham Papers.

Bingham's fiction also expressed her intolerance of southern prejudices about women. With few exceptions, the characters in Bingham's fiction were strong women. In her writings, Bingham lamented the constraints of the South while acknowledging its tenacious pull on its residents. See, for example, Sallie Bingham, *Matron of Honor* (Cambridge, Mass.: Zoland Books, 1994); Amy Wolfford, "Bingham's 'Hopscotch' Shows Women Are Strong," *Danville (Kentucky) Advocate-Messenger,* April 1, 1988, Writings Series, box 6, "Hopscotch (Reviews)/1988" folder, Bingham Papers; Sallie Bingham, "A Handmade Life," Writings Series, box 6, Bingham Papers.

23. Bingham, "Goodbye to All That."

24. Bingham, "(Southern?) Women Writers," 69, 70. Bingham's niece, (Barry Jr.'s daughter), confirmed her aunt's dilemma about the South. In a letter to Sallie, Emily Simms Bingham wrote, "I suppose the label has so much meaning because it allows a great many women to feel that sense of rebelliousness without the sting of rejecting one's own past. . . . Region sticks in a troublesome way. . . . As long as I label myself Southern, my sphere is somehow restricted" (July 5, 1991, Subject Files Series, box 2, "Mind Torn . . . Spirit Broken" folder, Bingham Papers).

25. Sallie Bingham, "The Future for Women in Kentucky: What Does It Hold," speech delivered at Midway College, Midway, Ky., October 11, 1985, Speeches Series, box 1, 1985 folder, Bingham Papers.

26. Kentucky Foundation for Women, "Preserving the Past, Altering the Present, Influencing the Future of Women," [ca. 1985], unprocessed May 1998, Bingham Papers. This document appears to be a copy of the original brochure announcing the foundation.

27. Sallie Bingham, "Haymarket Speech," Cambridge, Mass., October 31, 1987, Speeches Series, box 1, 1987 folder, Bingham Papers. See also Sallie Bingham, interview with Bonnie Cox, 1988, Subject Files Series, box 1, Bingham papers.

28. "Ms. Bingham's New Voice," *Louisville (Kentucky) Observer,* [ca. 1985], unprocessed May 1998, Bingham Papers.

29. Sallie Bingham, *Harmonious Notes* (KFW newsletter), November 1985, unprocessed May 1998, Bingham Papers.

30. Ibid.

31. Elaine Graybill, "High-Profile Style Allows Heiress to Shine Light on Creative Women," *Bloomington-Normal (Illinois) Pantagraph,* October 17, 1986, C3, unprocessed May 1998, Bingham Papers.

32. Maya Angelou, "Dreams May Be Deep Talk," *American Voice* 31 (1993): 89–93; Chaim Potok, "B.B.," *American Voice* 46 (1998): 56–71; Joyce Carol Oates, "Pinch," *American Voice* 50 (1999): 110–12.

33. Kentucky Foundation for Women, "Preserving the Past."

34. Some writers, however, questioned Bingham's motives. Tifft and Jones viewed her philanthropy in self-serving terms: "The bulk of her new riches [following the breakup of Bingham Enterprises] was devoted to gaining an audience for her writing" (*Patriarch,* 500). Tifft and Jones were not, however, objective observers of the Bingham family. They wrote their book, *The Patriarch: The Rise and Fall of the Bingham Dynasty,* with the cooperation of Sallie Bingham's parents and brother, with whom she had combative relationships. In part, the book was a counterthrust to Chandler and Chandler's earlier book, *The Binghams of Louisville,* which presented a negative portrait of the Binghams and had been published despite the vehement objections of Sallie's family but with her cooperation. Another self-described Bingham biographer, Marie Brenner, presented a sarcastic, contemptuous portrait of Sallie. Brenner reported, without citation, that Bingham told a friend that *The American Voice* would be printed in a nonunion shop because it was so much cheaper than a union shop (*House of Dreams,* 360). This assertion reportedly occurred after Sallie criticized her brother for using nonunion labor in one of his endeavors.

It is true that many of Sallie Bingham's works were published in *The American Voice.* Specifically, from 1991 through 1999, she had at least ten articles in the magazine, far more than any other author. However, it is a stretch to impugn Bingham's sincerity in creating the magazine. In both press releases and speeches announcing the magazine's publication, Bingham reaffirmed her belief that the journal could be a voice for those affected by the "law of silence" (Bingham, "Working with Quotas," [ca. 1986], Speeches Series, box 1, "Misc. n.d." folder, Bingham Papers). She told the *Washington Post,* "We're prepared to lose money *forever*" on the magazine ("American Voices," *Washington Post,* [ca. 1986], unprocessed May 1998, Bingham Papers). Moreover, Bingham reiterated the importance of paying a respectable wage to the authors in her magazine and of making certain the magazine was polished in its presentation—"no Xerox copies, no staples, no amateurish graphics" (Bingham, "The Kentucky Foundation for Women: A Model for Change," [ca. 1986], Speeches Series, box 1, "Misc. n.d." folder, Bingham Papers). The dozens of grants to women writers, poets, playwrights, and artists confirms Sallie Bingham's sincerity. In Bingham's mind, *The American Voice* was a vehicle for social change.

35. Sallie Bingham, "Afterword," *American Voice* 50 (1999): n.p. With publication ceasing of *The American Voice,* the KFW began a new journal, *The Hopscotch Annual.* The new journal is limited to emerging Kentucky writers, particularly those who participate in "the workshops, seminars and residencies" held at Hopscotch House ("Notice to Subscribers," *American Voice* 50 [1999]: n.p.).

36. See Sallie Bingham résumé, unprocessed May 1998, Bingham Papers; and *Ms.,* June 1986. Bingham's critics noticed these potential conflicts of interest. Brenner contended that Bingham's one million dollar grant to the Ms. Foundation "saved the magazine from collapse" (*House of Dreams,* 385; see also Tifft and Jones, *Patriarch,* 500). In fact, the grant was used to finance the woman-of-the-year issue and to allow the publisher to distribute the magazine to women's studies programs at no cost to the them (unidentified clipping from Kentucky Newsclip; dispensation of the Bingham grant quoted from Joanne Edgar, a senior editor of *Ms.,* unprocessed May 1998, Bingham Papers). Tifft and Jones accused Bingham of using her "new riches" to gain "an audience for her writing." Citing the grant to the Women's Project, Tifft and Jones reminded their readers that "soon after [Bingham] gave a $1 million gift to The Women's Project, . . . it staged a rehearsed reading of two of her plays-in-progress" (*Patriarch,* 500). In a particularly nasty remark to the *Lexington Herald-Leader,* Jones is quoted as saying, "What we noted was that the Kentucky woman who seems to have benefited most from the Kentucky Foundation is Sallie" (Kevin Nance, "The Faces of Sallie Bingham," *Lexington [Kentucky] Herald-Leader,* April 14, 1991, K2, Subject Files Series, box 1, "Articles about and Interviews with Bingham, 1958–97" folder, Bingham Papers). The authors fail to mention, however, that the Women's Project staged two of Bingham's plays prior to receiving any money from her (Charlene Baldridge, "Sallie Bingham: Patron Saint of Santa Fe," *American Theatre* 12 [October 1995]: 78). Moreover, according to an article in the *Wall Street Journal,* the Women's Project is "one of the most notable" theater groups directed at female playwrights. "The project . . . has read thousands of scripts by women and produced more than 200 staged readings and studio productions," and the income from the one million dollar grant will "keep its work going for some years to come" (Edwin Wilson, "Theater: Separate and 'Subversive,' " *Wall Street Journal,* eastern edition, September 23, 1987).

37. Ann Stewart Anderson, "Dear Friends," *Kentucky Foundation for Women Newsletter*, March 1996, unprocessed May 1998, Bingham Papers.

38. Five clippings from Kentucky Newsclip, November 16–December 1, 1986, unprocessed May 1998, Bingham Papers.

39. Women's Funding Network, 2000 Annual Report (available at WFNet.org).

40. *Kentucky Foundation for Women Newsletter*, January 1993, unprocessed May 1998, Bingham Papers.

41. *Kentucky Foundation for Women Newsletter*, January 1996, unprocessed May 1998, Bingham Papers.

42. *Kentucky Foundation for Women Newsletter*, January 1994, unprocessed May 1998, Bingham Papers.

43. *Kentucky Foundation for Women Newsletter*, January 1993, unprocessed May 1998, Bingham Papers.

44. Michele Ingrassia, "The Weight of Her Wealth," *New York Newsday*, August 7, 1986, 4, Subject Files Series, box 1, "Articles about and Interviews with Bingham, 1958–97" folder, Bingham Papers.

45. *Kentucky Foundation for Women Newsletter*, December 1995, unprocessed May 1998, Bingham Papers. See also *Kentucky Foundation for Women Newsletter*, April 1995, September 1995, and October 1995, unprocessed May 1998, Bingham Papers.

46. *Kentucky Foundation for Women Newsletter*, summer 1996, unprocessed May 1998, Bingham Papers.

47. Bingham, "Haymarket Speech." See also Bingham, "Goals for My Foundation"; Bingham, "The Future for Women in Kentucky: What Does It Hold"; Bingham, "Why a Foundation for Women in Kentucky?" Speeches Series, box 1, "Speeches, Misc., n.d." folder, Bingham Papers; Bingham, "Women in the Boardroom: 1980's Fashion," Speeches Series, box 1, 1986 folder, Bingham Papers; Bingham, "The Kentucky Foundation for Women: A Model for Change."

48. Bingham, "Goals for My Foundation," 4.

49. Katrina Larsen to Bingham, [ca. August–September 1988], Subject Files Series, box 1, "Barry Bingham Sr.'s Death, 1988" folder, Bingham Papers.

50. *Kentucky Foundation for Women Newsletter*, October 1992, unprocessed May 1998, Bingham Papers.

51. *Kentucky Foundation for Women Newsletter*, December 1992, January 1993, summer 1993, unprocessed May 1998, Bingham Papers.

52. Bingham, interview with Cox.

53. See, for example, Bingham, "Truth," 48–50, 82–83; Beth Campbell, "Slowly but Surely," *Louisville*, February 1986, 24, Subject Files Series, box 1, "Articles about and Interviews with Bingham, 1958–97" folder, Bingham Papers; Sallie Bingham, "Rich Women Lose When They Play by the Rules," *Cosmopolitan*, 1986, Writings Series, box 17, Bingham Papers; Sallie Bingham cited in Chandler and Chandler, *Binghams*, 231; Bingham, "Biting the Hand," 32–33; Nielsen, "After a Woman Is

Scorned," 93; Sallie Bingham, "Women and Autobiography: Writing Our Version," October 16, 1991, Speeches Series, box 1, 1991 folder, Bingham Papers; Sallie Bingham, "Politics," [ca. 1988], Writings Series, box 15, Bingham Papers; Bingham, "Women and the Creative Process"; Sallie Bingham, "Doing without Them," n.d., Writings Series, box 5, Bingham Papers; Sallie Bingham, speech delivered to the Rotary Club, April 1986, Speeches Series, box 1, 1986 folder, Bingham Papers; Bingham to "Joan," March 5, 1991, Subject Files Series, box 1, "Indiana University Information" folder, Bingham Papers; Sallie Bingham, "On Being a Feminist Mother," *American Voice* 23 (summer 1991): 91–99; Sallie Bingham, "The Prison of Subjectivity," 1997, Speeches Series, box 1, 1993–98 folder, Bingham Papers.

54. Nash, "Woman," 81.

55. Feminist principles and philanthropy, however, are not always compatible. Issues of classism can interfere with benevolence. The hyperagency of the wealthy—that is, the ability to fix society's norms and cultural capital—can lead to an imperialist doctrine of appropriate behavior (Paul G. Schervish, "The Moral Biographies of the Wealthy and the Cultural Scripture of Wealth," in *Wealth in Western Thought: The Case for and against Riches*, ed. Schervish [Westport, Conn.: Praeger, 1994], 202). Similarly, wealthy feminists, through their philanthropy, can impose their standards on the women they claim to benefit. (Amanda Porterfield, "Philanthropy and Feminism: Tensions and Congruences," paper presented at the Association for Research on Nonprofit Organizations and Voluntary Action Conference, Indianapolis, December 1997, 9). The paradox of wealth and gender is a theme in Bingham's writings and speeches. She regularly bemoaned the plight of wealthy women and the grip of patriarchy. See, for example, Bingham, "Truth"; Campbell, "Slowly but Surely," 24; Bingham, "Rich Women Lose"; Bingham, "Women and the Creative Process."

56. Marcy Murninghan, "Women and Philanthropy: New Voices, New Visions," *New England Journal of Public Policy* 6 (spring–summer 1990): 260. See also Teresa Odendahl, "Women's Power, Nonprofits, and the Future," in *Women and Power in the Nonprofit Sector*, ed. Odendahl and Michael O'Neill (San Francisco: Jossey-Bass, 1994), 304–8; Rose, "Philanthropy in a Different Voice."

57. Bingham, "The Kentucky Foundation for Women: A Model for Change," 4.

58. Bingham, "Women in the Boardroom," 5.

59. Bingham, "Personal Is the Political," 3.

60. Susan Ostrander, "Feminism, Voluntarism, and the Welfare State: Toward a Feminist Sociological Theory of Social Welfare," *American Sociologist* 20 (spring 1989): 32–33; Porterfield, "Philanthropy and Feminism," 7.

61. Bingham, "(Southern?) Women Writers," 70.

62. Lenny Golay, "Sallie Bingham: Challenging the Status Quo," *Carnegie Hill News*, fall 1996, 8, Subject Files Series, box 1, "Articles about and Interviews with Bingham, 1958–97" folder, Bingham Papers.

Selected Bibliography

Abrams, Douglas Carl. *Conservative Constraints: North Carolina and the New Deal.* Jackson: University Press of Mississippi, 1992.

Aiken, Charles S. *The Cotton Plantation South since the Civil War.* Baltimore: Johns Hopkins University Press, 1998.

Alston, Lee J., and Joseph P. Ferrie. *Southern Paternalism and the American Welfare State: Economics, Politics, and Institutions in the South, 1865–1965.* Cambridge: Cambridge University Press, 1999.

Anderson, Robert E., Jr. "Welfare in Mississippi: Tradition vs. Title VI." *New South* 22, no. 2 (1967): 64–72.

Ashmore, Susan Youngblood, "Carry It On: The War on Poverty and the Civil Rights Movement in Alabama, 1964–1970." Ph.D. diss., Auburn University, 1999.

Beito, David T. "Black Fraternal Hospitals in the Mississippi Delta, 1942–1967." *Journal of Southern History* 65, no. 1 (1999): 109–40.

Biles, Roger. *The South and the New Deal.* Lexington: University Press of Kentucky, 1994.

———. "The Urban South in the Great Depression." *Journal of Southern History* 56, no. 1 (1990): 71–100.

Byerly, Victoria. *Hard Times Cotton Mill Girls: Personal Histories of Womanhood and Poverty in the South.* Ithaca, N.Y.: ILR, 1987.

Campbell, Margaret M., ed. *Making a Difference, 1914–1989: Tulane School of Social Work.* New Orleans: Tulane University, 1990.

Carlton, David L., and Peter A. Coclanis, eds. *Confronting Southern Poverty in the Great Depression.* New York: St. Martin's, 1996.

Carlton-LaNey, Iris B., ed. *African American Leadership: An Empowerment Tradition in Social Welfare History.* Washington, D.C.: NASW Press, 2001.

Cash, Floris Barnett. *African American Women and Social Action: The Clubwomen and Volunteerism from Jim Crow to the New Deal, 1896–1936.* Westport, Conn.: Greenwood Press, 2001.

Cobb, James C. " 'Somebody Done Nailed Us on the Cross': Federal Farm and Welfare Policy and the Civil Rights Movement in the Mississippi Delta." *Journal of American History* 77, no. 3 (1990): 912–36.

Cole, Olen. *The African-American Experience in the Civilian Conservation Corps.* Gainesville: University Press of Florida, 1999.

Cowden, Jonathan A. "Southernization of the Nation and Nationalization of the South: Racial Conservatism, Social Welfare, and White Partisans in the United States, 1956–92." *British Journal of Political Science* 31 (2001): 277–301.

Davidson, John, and Robert Fisher. "Social Planning in Houston: The Council of Social Agencies, 1928–1976." *Houston Review* 18, no. 1 (1996): 1–28.

Donohue, John J. *Social Action, Private Choice, and Philanthropy: Understanding the Sources of Improvements in Black Schooling in Georgia, 1911–1960.* Cambridge, Mass.: National Bureau of Economic Research, 1998.

Fatout, Marian. *Teaching Welfare: Fifty Years of Social Work Education at* LSU. Baton Rouge: School of Social Work, Louisiana State University, 1987.

Fishback, Price V., Michael R. Haines, and Shawn Kantor. "The Impact of the New Deal on Black and White Infant Mortality in the South." *Explorations in Economic History* 38, no. 1 (2001): 93–122.

Flores, Carol A. "U.S. Public Housing in the 1930s: The First Projects in Atlanta, Georgia." *Planning Perspectives* 9, no. 4 (1994): 405–30.

Funigiello, Philip J. "The New Deal in the Urban South." *Journal of Urban History* 16, no. 11 (1989): 99–103.

George, Paul S., and Thomas K. Petersen. "Liberty Square: 1933–1987: The Origins and Evolution of a Public Housing Project." *Tequesta* 48 (1988): 53–68.

Glen, John M. "The War on Poverty in Appalachia: Oral History from the 'Top Down' and the 'Bottom Up.'" *Oral History Review* 22, no. 1 (1995): 67–93.

Gooden, Susan T. "Local Discretion and Welfare Policy: The Case of Virginia (1911–1970)." *Southern Studies* 6, no. 4 (1995): 79–110.

Grey, Michael R. *New Deal Medicine: The Rural Health Programs of the Farm Security Administration.* Baltimore: Johns Hopkins University Press, 1999.

Grubbs, Donald H. *Cry from the Cotton: The Southern Tenant Farmers' Union and the New Deal.* 1971; Fayetteville: University of Arkansas Press, 2000.

Haber, Carole, and Brian Gratton. "Old Age, Public Welfare and Race: The Case of Charleston, South Carolina, 1800–1949." *Journal of Social History* 21, no. 2 (1987): 263–79.

Hamilton, Dona Cooper, and Charles V. Hamilton. *The Dual Agenda: Race and Social Welfare Policies of Civil Rights Organizations.* New York: Columbia University Press, 1997.

Heinemann, Ronald L. *Depression and New Deal in Virginia: The Enduring Dominion.* Charlottesville: University Press of Virginia, 1983.

Henry, Annie Belle. "Philanthropic Foundations and Their Impact on Public Education for Blacks in Florida, 1920–1947." Ph.D. diss., Florida State University, 1988.

Hester, Albert C. "Landscapes of Reform: The Material Culture of the New Deal in Manchester, South Carolina, 1934–1945." *Proceedings of the South Carolina Historical Association* (1998): 91–105.

Jones, Jacqueline. *The Dispossessed: America's Underclasses from the Civil War to the Present.* New York: Basic Books, 1992.

Kelly, Thomas. "Free Enterprise, Costly Relief: Charity in Houston, Texas, 1915–1937." *Houston Review* 18, no. 1 (1996): 29–62.

Kiffmeyer, Thomas J. "From Self-Help to Sedition: The Appalachian Volunteers in Eastern Kentucky, 1964–1970." *Journal of Southern History* 64, no. 1 (1998): 65–94.

————. "From Self-Help to Sedition: The Appalachian Volunteers and the War on Poverty in Eastern Kentucky, 1964–1970." Ph.D. diss., University of Kentucky, 1998.

LaMonte, Edward Shannon. *Politics and Welfare in Birmingham, 1900–1975.* Tuscaloosa: University of Alabama Press, 1995.

Lee, Joseph Edward. "Through the Safety Net: A South Carolina Community Action Program Copes with the First Year of the Reagan Revolution." *Proceedings of the South Carolina Historical Association* (1995): 77–84.

Levinson, Marc. "Aid to Families with Dependent Children in Georgia." *Crisis* 87, no. 1 (1980): 31–33.

Lieberman, Robert Charles. "Race and the Development of the American Welfare State from the New Deal to the Great Society." Ph.D. diss., Harvard University, 1994.

Lofton, Paul. "The Columbia Black Community in the 1930's." *Proceedings of the South Carolina Historical Association* (1984): 86–95.

Marcello, Ronald E. "The Politics of Relief: North Carolina's WPA." *North Carolina Historical Review* 68, no. 1 (1991): 17–37.

Marshall, Ray, and Lamond Godwin. *Cooperatives and Rural Poverty in the South.* Baltimore: Johns Hopkins University Press, 1971.

Mertz, Paul E. *New Deal Policy and Southern Rural Poverty.* Baton Rouge: Louisiana State University Press, 1978.

Moran, Robert Earl, Sr. *One Hundred Years of Child Welfare in Louisiana, 1860–1960.* Lafayette: Center for Louisiana Studies, University of Southwestern Louisiana, 1980.

————. "Public Relief in Louisiana from 1928 to 1960." *Louisiana History* 14, no. 4 (1973): 369–85.

Morgan, Thomas S., Jr. "A Step toward Altruism: Relief and Welfare in North Carolina, 1930–1938." Ph.D. diss., University of North Carolina at Chapel Hill, 1969.

Mulcahy, Richard P. *A Social Contract for the Coal Fields: The Rise and Fall of the United Mine Workers of America Welfare and Retirement Fund.* Knoxville: University of Tennessee Press, 2000.

Nelson, Lawrence J. "Welfare Capitalism on a Mississippi Plantation in the Great Depression." *Journal of Southern History* 50, no. 2 (1984): 225–50.

Noll, Steven. "Care and Control of the Feeble-Minded: Florida Farm Colony, 1920–1945." *Florida Historical Quarterly* 69, no. 1 (1990): 57–80.

Pollard, William L. *A Study of Black Self Help.* San Francisco: R & E Research Associates, 1978.

Quadagno, Jill. *The Color of Welfare: How Racism Undermined the War on Poverty.* New York: Oxford University Press, 1994.

————. "From Old-Age Assistance to Supplemental Security Income: The Political Economy of Relief in the South, 1935–1972." In *The Politics of Social Policy in the United States,* edited by Margaret Weir, Ann Shola Orloff, and Theda Skocpol. Princeton: Princeton University Press, 1988.

———. "Promoting Civil Rights through the Welfare State: How Medicare Integrated Southern Hospitals." *Social Problems* 47 (2000): 68–89.

———. *The Transformation of Old Age Security.* Chicago: University of Chicago Press, 1988.

Rikard, Marlene Hunt. "An Experiment in Welfare Capitalism: The Health Care Services of the Tennessee Coal, Iron, and Railroad Company." Ph.D. diss., University of Alabama, 1983.

Ruechel, Frank. "New Deal Public Housing, Urban Poverty, and Jim Crow: Techwood and University Homes in Atlanta." *Georgia Historical Quarterly* 81, no. 4 (1997): 915–37.

Rungeling, Brian. *Employment, Income, and Welfare in the Rural South.* New York: Praeger, 1977.

Salmond, John. *A Southern Rebel: The Life and Times of Aubrey Willis Williams, 1890–1965.* Chapel Hill: University of North Carolina Press, 1983.

Salvaggio, John E. *New Orleans' Charity Hospital: A Story of Physicians, Politics, and Poverty.* Baton Rouge: Louisiana State University Press, 1992.

Schulman, Bruce J. *From Cotton Belt to Sunbelt: Federal Policy, Economic Development, and the Transformation of the South, 1938–1980.* New York: Oxford University Press, 1991.

Scribner, Christopher MacGregor. "Federal Funding, Urban Renewal, and Race Relations: Birmingham in Transition, 1945–1955." *Alabama Review* 48, no. 4 (1995): 269–95.

Shores, Elizabeth F. "The Arkansas Children's Colony at Conway: A Springboard for Federal Policy on Special Education." *Arkansas Historical Quarterly* 57, no. 4 (1998): 408–34.

Smith, C. Calvin. "Serving the Poorest of the Poor: Black Medical Practitioners in the Arkansas Delta, 1880–1960." *Arkansas Historical Quarterly* 57, no. 3 (1998): 287–308.

Sparks, Randy J. " 'Heavenly Houston' or 'Hellish Houston?' Black Unemployment and Relief Efforts, 1929–1936." *Southern Studies* 25, no. 4 (1986): 353–66.

Storrs, Landon R. Y. "Gender and the Development of the Regulatory State: The Controversy over Restricting Women's Night Work in the Depression-Era South." *Journal of Policy History* 10, no. 2 (1998): 179–206.

Tate, Roger D., Jr. "George B. Power and New Deal Work Relief in Mississippi, 1933–1934." *Journal of Mississippi History* 46, no. 1 (1984): 1–16.

Taylor, Brenda Jeanette. "The New Deal and Health: Meeting Farmers' Needs in Ropesville, Texas, 1933–1943." *Journal of the West* 36 (January 1997): 38–46.

Tullos, Allen. "Win This One for the Reaper: Southern Hunger in the Eighties." *Southern Changes* 6, no. 6 (1984): 6–16.

Valentine, Patrick M. "Steel, Cotton, and Tobacco: Philanthropy and Public Libraries in North Carolina, 1900–1940." *Libraries and Culture* 31, no. 2 (1996): 272–98.

Watson, Denton L. "Miracle in Mississippi: NAACP Relief Fund." *Crisis* 79, no. 4 (1972): 115–20.

Weisenberger, Carol A. *Dollars and Dreams: The National Youth Administration in Texas.* New York: P. Lang, 1994.

Williams, Thomas E. "The Dependent Child in Mississippi: A Social History, 1900–1972." Ph.D. diss., Ohio State University, 1976.

Contributors

Susan Youngblood Ashmore received her Ph.D. from Auburn University and is currently assistant professor of history at Oxford College of Emory University.

Ann Short Chirhart, currently assistant professor of history at Indiana State University, received her doctoral degree from Emory University. She is the author of the forthcoming book, *Torches of Light: African American and White Women Teachers in the Georgia Upcountry.*

Jeffrey S. Cole received his Ph.D. from Bowling Green State University. He is currently assistant professor of history and chair of the American studies program at King College in Bristol, Tennessee.

Kent B. Germany received his Ph.D. from Tulane University. He is currently assistant professor at the Miller Center of Public Affairs at the University of Virginia.

Elna C. Green holds a Ph.D. from Tulane University and is the Allen Morris Associate Professor of History at Florida State University. She is the author of the forthcoming monograph *This Business of Relief: Richmond, Virginia, and Welfare Policy in the Urban South.*

Georgina Hickey is an assistant professor of history at the University of Michigan at Dearborn. She received her Ph.D. from the University of Michigan and is the author of *Hope and Danger in the New South City: Working-Class Women and Urban Development in Atlanta, 1890–1940* (2002).

Robert R. Korstad holds a doctoral degree from the University of North Carolina at Chapel Hill. He is associate professor of policy studies and history at the Terry Sanford School of Public Policy at Duke University. He is the author of the forthcoming study, *Democracy Denied: The Rise and Fall of Civil Rights Unionism.*

James L. Leloudis holds a Ph.D. from the University of North Carolina at Chapel Hill, where he now serves as associate professor of history. He is the author of *Schooling the New South: Pedagogy, Self, and Society in North Carolina, 1880–1920* (1996).

Steve McDonald is a Ph.D. candidate in sociology at Florida State University. He works as a research analyst for the Claude Pepper Institute on Aging and Public Policy and FSU's Survey Research Laboratory.

Ted Olson holds a Ph.D. in English from the University of Mississippi. He is currently assistant professor of English and director of the Appalachian, Scottish, and Irish Studies Program at East Tennessee State University.

Jill Quadagno received a Ph.D. from the University of Kansas. She is professor of sociology at Florida State University, where she holds the Mildred and Claude Pepper Eminent Scholar Chair in Social Gerontology. She is the author of *The Color of Welfare: How Racism Undermined the War on Poverty* (1994).

Marsha S. Rose has a Ph.D. from Ohio State University and is associate professor of sociology at Florida Atlantic University. She is the coauthor of *Technology and American Life* (2001).

Brenda J. Taylor holds a doctorate from Texas Christian University. She is associate professor of history at Texas Wesleyan University.

Index

5538